Barcode in Back

JOURNALISM AND THE NOVEL

Journalistic fiction is a rich field for study that has played an important role in the creation of the English and American literary canons. In this original and engaging study, Doug Underwood focuses on the many notable journalists-turned-novelists found at the margins of fact and fiction since the early eighteenth century, when the novel and the commercial periodical began to emerge as powerful cultural forces. Writers from both sides of the Atlantic are discussed, from Daniel Defoe to Charles Dickens, and from Mark Twain to Joan Didion. Underwood shows how many literary reputations are built on journalistic foundations of research and reporting, and how this impacts on questions of realism and authenticity throughout the work of many canonical authors. This book will be of great interest to researchers and students of British and American literature.

DOUG UNDERWOOD is Professor of Communication at the University of Washington.

JOURNALISM AND THE NOVEL: TRUTH AND FICTION, 1700–2000

DOUG UNDERWOOD

 CAMBRIDGE
UNIVERSITY PRESS

CAMBRIDGE UNIVERSITY PRESS
Cambridge, New York, Melbourne, Madrid, Cape Town, Singapore,
São Paulo, Delhi, Dubai, Tokyo

Cambridge University Press
The Edinburgh Building, Cambridge CB2 8RU, UK

Published in the United States of America by Cambridge University Press, New York

www.cambridge.org
Information on this title: www.cambridge.org/9780521899529

First published 2008

A catalogue record for this publication is available from the British Library

ISBN 978-0-521-89952-9 Hardback

Transferred to digital printing 2010

To my mother, Mary E. Underwood
Whose love of literature and whose loving support have inspired
me always

Contents

Acknowledgements

I have a lot of people to thank for their help and support in the research, shaping, and writing of this undertaking. My wife, Susanne Kromberg, and our two girls, Marika and Alida, were a priceless source of love, inspiration, and affection throughout (as manifested in the delight of seven-year-old Alida, who loves *Charlotte's Web*, in discovering that E. B. White is both an author in this study and someone who shares with her Daddy a one-time employer, *The Seattle Times*). My department chair, Jerry Baldasty, gave invaluable advice in the development of the manuscript and encouragement throughout the process. Other University of Washington colleagues, including David Domke, Patricia Moy, Phil Howard, Matt McGarrity, Cindy Simmons, Crispin Thurlow, Tony Giffard, W. Lance Bennett, Keith Stamm, Roger Simpson, Tony Chan, Richard Kielbowicz, David Sherman, and Diana Smith, also were supportive in various ways. Dana Bagwell, my graduate student collaborator in our study of contemporary journalists' literary ambitions, and my undergraduate researchers (Carly Avery, Bill Hayes, Ollie McMillan, Roop Randhawa, and Molly Talbert) provided great assistance. I am particularly grateful to Ray Ryan for seeing the possibilities in the manuscript and helping to make its publication a reality.

Introduction

The editor believes the thing to be a just history of fact; neither is there any appearance of fiction in it.
— From the preface of Daniel Defoe's *Robinson Crusoe*

There is … scarcely any species of writing of which we can tell what is its essence, and what are its constituents; every new genius produces some innovation, which, when invented and approved, subverts the rules which the practice of foregoing authors had established.
— Samuel Johnson

Though as we have good authority for all our characters, no less indeed than the vast authentic book of nature … our labors have sufficient title to the name history. Certainly they deserve some distinction from those works, which one of the wittiest of men regarded only as proceeding from … a looseness of the brain.
— Henry Fielding in defending *Tom Jones* against charges that it was a mere "novel"

The two most engaging powers of an author are to make new things familiar, and familiar things new.
— Samuel Johnson

In the middle of the contemporary novel, *Long John Silver*, a fanciful account of what happened to Robert Louis Stevenson's treacherous and enigmatic pirate hero, there appears a character based upon a real-life literary figure who has long intrigued journalism and literary historians: Daniel Defoe, the eighteenth-century novelist and journalist who – in Bjorn Larsson's fictional memoir – meets Long John Silver while putting together a book about pirates.

Sitting in a London tavern that looks out upon the town gallows, Defoe describes himself to Silver as "slinking around like a criminal, condemned for my opinions … no more than a shadow, a word on everybody's lips except my own, a supposition, a murmur in society." Of his writing philosophy, he scoffs at how easily English readers are deceived and how badly they want to believe that Defoe's characters, including his pirate heroes, were real. "I have been laughing up my sleeve," he says. "It was all invented from beginning to end ... Ordinary people and even the educated have such a desire to believe that everything that is written is true."[1]

In our post-modern world, where things aren't what they seem and where deception, false identity, and the concealments behind words and language fascinate us, it is perhaps fitting to find a new historical hero in Defoe, the spy, the man of many disguises and professional intrigues, and the "hack," "hustler," and professional wordsmith who had no idea that his efforts to make a buck out of imaginative writing would lead him to be hailed as one of the originators of the English novel. Perhaps it also is fitting that Defoe has emerged as a figure of fascination in an age when critics debate whether non-fiction has surpassed fiction as the preferred literary form, when scholars ponder whether "deconstruction" of texts and a post-modern worldview mean that truth is always relative and subjective, and when writers and scholars alike debate whether the categories that traditionally have kept up a barrier between the practice of journalism and the art of novel-writing should come down. Interestingly, there is no one better prepared than Defoe was to understand the ironic manner in which traditional terms (the facts of fiction, the fables of fact, the non-fiction novel) have been newly juxtaposed by contemporary literary analysts.[2]

As an innovator in the development of both the commercial newspaper and the modern novel, Defoe is the personification of the ground-breaking prose stylist and one of the earliest prototypes of the journalist-literary figure that is at the beginnings of both the journalistic and the fiction-writing tradition in the English language. The literary forms that have come to be viewed as separate ones – fiction, journalism, the novel, popular literature, biography, narrative or interpretive history, the topical essay, the short story, humor-writing, the advice column, literary criticism, journal-keeping, travel-writing – were blended together in Defoe's era in ways that were only beginning to be distinguished in the minds of his contemporaries. Since all these kinds of writing tended to be on display in the pamphlets, the periodicals, and the emerging commercial newspapers of the time, journalism historians see them as integral elements of the written record out of which modern journalism grew. However, since literary scholars also lay claim to much of the same material, the world of what today we call "literature" and "fiction-writing" also has an ownership interest in Defoe and a number of his fellow early experimenters in written forms.

It is an intriguing twist of history that the investigation of the connections between journalism and fiction in our contemporary context should begin in a time when the practitioners of the literary and journalistic forms recognized little distinction between the two. Our words "journalism" and "the novel," in fact, bear little resemblance to what Defoe and his fellow scribblers thought they were doing or what they named their writing activity. The etymology of the word "journalism" probably better applies to what someone such as Defoe's near contemporary, James Boswell, the great biographer and author of *The Life of Johnson*, accomplished in his major writings (not only did he write in his journal in the evening as the basis for his biography of Samuel Johnson, he wrote a column for a London periodical, in which he had an ownership interest for a time, published news accounts of hangings, wrote travel literature, and mined quotes from "sources" with whom he socialized) than it does to the activities of contemporary journalists. Simultaneously, the contemporary meaning of the term "the novel" did not come into widespread use until the late eighteenth century, and Defoe's and Boswell's contemporaries struggled to find a term for the act of fiction-writing. The subject of Boswell's great work, the lexicographer, essayist, and critic Johnson, called works such as Defoe's *Moll Flanders* and Henry Fielding's *Tom Jones* "familiar history," and he valued them to the degree that he did because he felt they presented a more authentic and truthful picture of the world than did the romance books (so popular in his time and ours) which he greatly disliked.[3]

It is perhaps unsurprising that many "journalistic" novels – literary non-fiction or semi-fictional prose works that are built around real people and real life events – have been written in the years since Boswell and Johnson by a group of journalists or ex-journalists who have constructed a literary legacy out of the values that they learned in journalism. From the beginnings of the novel in English, writers who had experience in the world of journalism have been at the center of a movement that has repeatedly returned to journalistic methodology as the basis for developing realistic plots and journalistic research to provide the material for the construction of literature that draws upon actual events as the inspiration for dramatic narrative.

What has been called the "documentary" or "pseudo-factual" novel has played an important role since the emergence of the narrative-driven, book-length, imaginative story-telling form in the eighteenth century.[4] Novels such as Defoe's *Robinson Crusoe*, William Thackeray's *The History of Henry Esmond*, Theodore Dreiser's *An American Tragedy*, and Richard Wright's *Native Son* present their picture of the world through the traditional conventions of fiction, but they graft onto their fictional schemes some claim to empirical validity. The attraction of this form of writing has been strong throughout history. For example, eighteenth-century writers such as Defoe and Fielding were laying claim to a broadly realistic version of "truth" that gave their pseudo-factual novels a degree of credibility that both romance and other periodical writings of their time lacked. Today, "new journalists," such as Tom Wolfe, have made a variation of this claim by arguing that the methodologies of journalistic research, combined with the narrative techniques of the novel, are producing more vibrant and compelling forms of literature than those written by conventional contemporary novelists who have become fixated upon rarified stylistic techniques. This contemporary genre, as promoted by Wolfe and others, has created a great deal of excitement among both journalists and scholars of journalism and – even though few anymore accept the notion that there is much that is "new" about "new journalism" – the study of today's practitioners of this form of writing has received growing attention within scholarly circles.[5]

However, what has been less documented is the impressive range and depth of the reporting and the research that have served as the basis of other novels that don't meet the test of empirical validity outlined by Wolfe and Truman Capote in their conceptions of what qualifies as "new journalism" or non-fiction literature. The amount of journalistic preparation by the journalist-literary figures throughout literary history who operated on the margins of "fact and fiction" has been of only peripheral interest to the mainstream of literary scholars who tend to be most concerned with matters of writing style, textual interpretation, and aesthetic theories and techniques, or to scholars of literary journalism, who have tended to focus on writings, both contemporary and historical, that meet the definition of journalism by the journalism profession's contemporary factual standards and/or Capote's definition of what he called the "nonfiction novel" (for example, it is essentially "factual" in basis and the author has limited the "liberties" taken with the material to the incorporation of literary stylistic techniques into the narrative). And yet, the preponderance of the novels and short stories by the most prominent of the journalist-literary figures would not meet Capote's definition or the standards of scholars of literary journalism, even though they could be called "pseudo-factual" in basis. Many of the most important of these works must be seen as the products of journalistic research and reporting and owe much of their realistic texture and their sense of authenticity to what these authors learned during their experiences as journalists.

This study hopes to fill in some of these gaps by examining the ongoing and continuous historical connection between the journalistic and the literary traditions – and the fiction- and novel-writing tradition, in particular. It focuses upon a group of novelists, poets, playwrights, and other literary figures that I have identified as having been strongly connected to the world of journalism and traces their contributions to the literary canon from the early eighteenth century when the novel and the commercial periodical were emerging as powerful cultural forces. These writers were influenced by their involvement in journalism in the development of their literary philosophy, and journalism and the world of fiction were reciprocally influenced by their literary contributions.

In my discussion, I hope to make clear the connections between the experiences of these journalist-literary figures and the predicament of journalism today. Contemporary news organizations are undergoing great upheavals, and there is an intense dialogue taking place about what the newspaper of the future should look like in a media world being reshaped by the internet and the emergence of other electronic forms of information exchange, economic and ownership pressures upon journalistic organizations, and a population that increasingly is forsaking the traditional newspaper in print for other news and entertainment choices. I would suggest that today's environment is reminiscent of the era of eighteenth-century journalism, where newspapers – such as Joseph Addison and Richard Steele's *Tatler* and *Spectator* – had to compete as literary and entertainment vehicles to gain audience attention. Already "literary" and "narrative" journalism techniques are being adopted at newspapers which are moving away from delivering news in the traditional formulas (the inverted pyramid, the who-what-when-where-why-how model) and encouraging journalists to produce in-depth, literary, and stylized stories in place of news as a formulaic and impersonal regurgitation of events. I conclude the book with the hope that by studying these journalist-literary figures in the context of both their journalistic and their fiction-writing careers, it will lead to a greater understanding of the role that journalism has played throughout the breadth of literary history and to a better recognition of the creative devices that have enabled journalistically oriented writers to transcend the traditional limitations of commercial journalism and to transform journalism-based writing into important literature.

One of the reasons that journalism does not get the credit due for its contribution to the field of literature, I will be contending, is that the profession's contributions have not necessarily always been positive ones in the eyes of either the scholarly community or many of the journalist-literary figures themselves. A primary aspect of my examination will be the frustration that many of these writers felt in trying honestly to portray the way they saw the world within the restricting formulas of conventional journalism and how they often decided they needed to take up fiction-writing to convey authentically what they saw as genuine and "real" about life and the people in it. It may seem curious to be advancing the argument that, in driving many of the journalist-literary figures out of jobs in journalism, as has been commonly the case, the field of journalism should get some kind of inverse credit for helping to launch the careers in fiction of some of its most celebrated alumni. And yet, the involvement of the journalist-literary figures in newspaper and periodical work has made for a rich and complex dynamic, and most have harbored love-hate feelings about the profession of journalism in which they gained their early writing experiences. This situation – in which the field of fiction-writing has proved to be a more congenial place than that of journalism, with its pretensions to a "tell-it-like-it-is" view of the world, for the journalist-turned-fiction-writer to express his or her "truths" about life – is a central theme of this study.

At the same time, one cannot minimize the impact of journalism on the imaginative development of these literary-journalist figures simply because the environment of deadlines, editorial oversight, and predictable news formulas ultimately did not prove to be a hospitable place for them to fully develop as writers. A case can be made with Thackeray, for example, that his journalistic background and material were seminal to the writing of *Vanity Fair*, but that he had to step outside journalism in order to create the imaginative distance to produce the novel. Ernest Hemingway also argued for the value to a young writer in learning to pare down one's writing to compelling essentials and to use simple language to convey strong feeling as long as that person left journalism before coming to rely too much on its stock characterizations and easy-writing formulas.[6]

That journalism sometimes turned out to be a place where ambition was frustrated and where the journalist-literary figures were kept from fulfilling their writing potential does not mean that the values and ideals of journalism did not impress themselves deeply upon them. As a foil for their satire, as a place to test their idealism about life and literature, as an introduction to the realities of the world, as a field where they were encouraged to indulge their intellectual curiosity and explore the possibilities of self-expression, as a place to learn the discipline of clear and appealing writing – in all these ways and more, journalism served the best known of the journalist-literary figures quite well, even if they often had to move beyond the journalistic workplace in order to write in ways that they felt were fully authentic. In this respect, one must view the situation with a considerable sense of irony. Quite often, without encountering the limitations of the journalistic professional world-view, a journalist-literary figure would never have recognized the narrowness of pursuing the "facts" as defined in commercial journalism nor come to the conclusion that fiction-writing was a better place to convey a more expansive sense of what the world was really like.

Although the appendix enumerates the professional history and major literary works of more than 300 writers that I have identified as important journalist-literary figures, this volume focuses upon a core group of these writers who worked for newspapers and periodicals, who strongly identified themselves as journalists, and who continued to be influenced by their exposure to journalism (positively or negatively) even after they attained literary success. In compiling the appendix, I looked for writing figures whose experiences in journalism left a strong impression upon them and had an impact on the development of their literary imagination and philosophy. Some of the best known of these emerged as major figures in this study because of their role in demonstrating and articulating the central importance of journalism in the development of the British and American literary tradition. All worked for newspapers or periodicals as the modern concept of the journalistic professional and the modern news organization was emerging; all imbibed deeply the professional atmosphere of journalism and thought of themselves as journalists; all acknowledged that their journalism experience shaped their attitudes toward literature; and most continued to practice journalism in some form in intervals between their fiction-writing activities.

The selection of writers to be included in the appendix provides an important feature in my argument that journalism has had a significant impact upon the literary and fictional tradition. Even though not all the writers in the appendix are discussed in detail in this volume, the compilation of the names of more than 300 important literary figures connected to the world of journalism speaks for itself, I believe, in making the case for journalism's influence upon the development of literary and fictional writing in the US and the British Isles. I hope this list will be helpful to future scholars and will lead to greater scholarly scrutiny of the important connections between the journalistic and the literary heritage within English prose.

As a critical element in the foundation of this study, I owe a debt to the scholars who have begun to rectify the neglected place of journalism's literary contributions within the world of literary scholarship. In recent years, there have been a number of works that examine the historical ties between the journalistic and the fiction-writing tradition, and such scholars as Ian Watt, Diana Spearman, and Grahame Smith have written valuable examinations that touch upon the connections between journalism and fiction in the "cradle" years of the novel. Lennard Davis and Richard Cook have probed the duplicitous nature of eighteenth-century journalism and linked its artful falsehoods with the development of fictional techniques that were pioneered in the early novels of Defoe, Fielding, Jonathan Swift, and other novelists of the period. Shelley Fisher Fishkin has produced ground-breaking work in this area by analyzing the journalistic influences in the literature of Dreiser, Mark Twain (Samuel Clemens), John Dos Passos, Ernest Hemingway, and Walt Whitman. Michael Robertson has examined the work of Stephen Crane and other nineteenth-century journalist-literary figures whose journalism he links to their literary values and their mixing of the conventions of journalism and fiction. Jean Marie Lutes has explored the role of newspaperwomen in American literary culture at the turn of the twentieth century. Barbara Foley, Phyllis Frus, and William Dow have provided perspective for this discussion, Foley by analyzing the "documentary" novel within the context of various contemporary literary theories of interpretation, Frus by exploring the role of journalistic narrative in the writings of Crane, Hemingway, and others, and Dow by calling for documentary fiction to be seen as an essential force in the development of American literature. Brian McCrea and Thomas Strychacz have studied the bias against the plain-spoken tradition of the journalist-literary figures within the literary academy and literary scholars' preferences for literary texts that are complex, difficult, and amenable to specialist analysis.[7]

In addition, important scholarly analyses have been done on the journalistic origins of the literary visions of some of the major journalist-literary figures. These include: Michael Allen's study of the impact of Edgar Allan Poe's journalistic experience upon his literature; Richard Pearson's, Virgil Grillo's, and John M. L. Drew's examinations of the role of journalism in the artistic development of Thackeray and Charles Dickens; Louis L. Cornell's work in probing the role of journalism in Rudyard Kipling's early artistic production; Charles Fenton's and M. Catherine Downs' studies of the journalistic influences in the literature of Hemingway and Willa Cather respectively; Karen Roggenkamp's critique of the blended forms of newspaper and literary writing in the works of Poe, Richard Harding Davis, and other journalist-literary figures of the nineteenth century; and Christopher P. Wilson's examination of the manner in which progressive journalistic values influenced a number of the major American novelists and journalist-literary figures who brought literary professionalism into vogue in the nineteenth and early twentieth centuries. Howard Good, Thomas Berry, and Loren Ghiglione also have produced studies that connect the fiction and literature of a number of the major journalist-literary figures with their journalistic output, journalistic values, and/or the portrayal of journalists in their work.[8]

Perhaps not surprisingly, the major period that has caught the eye of scholars interested in the relationship between journalism and fiction is our own. What has come to be called "literary journalism" – and particularly the so-called "new journalism" movement that began in the 1960s and 1970s – has received increasing attention from a host of critics and scholars, including John Hartsock, Barbara Lounsberry, Norman Sims, Mark Kramer, Thomas Connery, Ionia Italia, Richard Keeble, Sharon Wheeler, Robert Boynton, and others.[9] A number of these studies focus upon the American novelists and journalists who have been associated with the rise of "new journalism" – Capote, Wolfe, Norman Mailer, Joan Didion, Gay Talese, John McPhee, Hunter Thompson, Tracy Kidder, and others. And yet, it is a sign of our self-absorbed times that journalists today are considered great innovators by turning back to the literary traditions of old (it can be argued, for example, that Defoe's *A Journal of the Plague Year* did in 1722 exactly what the "new journalists" have done in combining journalistic fact-gathering with literary stylistic techniques). Although scholars have noted the ahistorical nature of the claims of the "new journalists" (and the fact that there have been a number of periods when what was called "new journalism" has been practiced), they have sometimes demonstrated their own tendencies to let contemporary preoccupations dominate the analysis of the influences of journalism upon the development of the literary tradition. This is partly because of the concerns of literary journalism scholars (many ex-journalists) to maintain the distinction between truth and fiction that is embraced within contemporary journalism organizations and by scholars in literature departments who operate by standards of "high" and "popular" art and who sometimes are reluctant to take journalism seriously as literature and/or show only passing interest in studying journalistic influences within the body of the works considered to be part of the literary canon.

The insights of Davis, Fishkin, Robertson, Wilson, Foley, Frus, Lounsberry, and Hartsock have been particularly important in my thinking in this volume. Davis' analysis of what he terms the "news-novels discourse" in the writings of Defoe and Fielding in the early part of the eighteenth century has encouraged me to examine similar connections in later eras. Robertson's extension of this discussion into the late nineteenth-century world of commercialized journalism and fiction-writing has helped me to better understand the influence of industrialization in the publishing world and the possibilities for succeeding as a writer who straddles the border between fact and fiction. Fishkin's textual examinations of the writings of Twain, Dreiser, and others demonstrated that journalism's influence in important fictional works can be identified in very specific ways and should not be discounted in any literary analysis of their imaginative writings.

Although I value the ground-breaking aspects of Davis', Fishkin's, and Robertson's scholarship, my interest has been a different one from scholars who have engaged in in-depth investigations of particular texts or focused upon a group of journalists who were influential in particular periods when journalism had an especially powerful effect upon literature. My aim is to explore the larger sweep and scope of the relationship between the journalistic and fiction-writing traditions and to identify the major journalist-literary figures who have made their mark throughout the eras of modern literary history. I hope to do this by demonstrating their influence upon each others' careers and showing that they shared similar views on the role of journalistic-style writing in literature. Where meaningful, I will quote from the writings of specific journalist-literary figures and draw upon the critical literature that analyzes their work, even though I don't claim to have a specialist's knowledge of any particular writer. However, I will apply judgments about the importance of a piece of writing to the study of journalistic literature, and I will draw attention to the works that demonstrate the role of journalism or journalistic values in their creation.

In her book, *From Fact to Fiction*, Fishkin noted the great number of novelists who began their careers in journalism, and she asked why the phenomenon has received so little attention among scholars. Hartsock tried to answer that question in his history of American literary journalism by enumerating the reasons why the study of fiction is held in the highest esteem by scholars and critics and why the study of literary non-fiction (and journalism) has been marginalized in the world of literary scholarship. Included in his explanations are: the traditional hostility of the literary establishment to the world of the commercial press with its view of journalism as a low-brow and inferior literary activity, the linkage of fiction to neo-classical forms aimed at the educationally privileged, the historical aim of commercial newspapers to appeal to less educated readers with crime and other sensationalized news, the emergence after the American Civil War of the modern study of letters focusing upon aesthetic style and self-consciously artistic themes that meet the tastes of the intellectual elite, and the transition of journalism studies in universities to social-science departments, with their bias against the study of journalism in a non-empirical or liberal arts context.[10]

In her explanation of why journalistic writing seldom qualifies as literature in the view of many contemporary scholars, Frus said journalistic writing "is tied to everyday life and is thus hampered by its pragmatic function, which is to provide information," and, in contrast to "fiction's imaginative freedom and creativity, journalism is discursive and mundane" and doesn't deal in the "higher truths" that fiction does. In this sense, she added, journalistic writing with its popular appeal is considered "inferior to an elitist" notion of literature, and with some exceptions (largely from the eighteenth- and nineteenth-century journalism of Johnson, Swift, Twain, and William Hazlitt) seldom meets the aesthetic standards that scholars use to judge which literature should endure.[11]

To Hartsock's and Frus' observations, I would add a few others – many of them coming from the journalist-literary figures themselves. The newsroom is regularly portrayed in fiction by journalists as a graveyard of talent, a living burial in a deadline-harried environment of hack work and hackneyed writing, prostituted values, formulaic thinking, and miserable employee morale. "I tell you I have been in the editorial business going on fourteen years, and it is the first time I ever heard of a man's having to know anything in order to edit a newspaper," declared Twain at one point. "Journalism is not a career," added the muckraker journalist, David Graham Phillips, who wrote novels under the pseudonym John Graham. "It is either a school or a cemetery. A man may use it as a stepping stone to something else. But if he sticks to it, he finds himself an old man, dead and done for to all intents and purposes years before he's buried." And yet, journalism's position as an activity that even its most honored practitioners have lambasted as compromised and second-rate sometimes blinds literary critics and scholars to the many interesting and complex ways that the journalist-literary figures' involvement with the press spurred their imaginative growth and influenced their vision of what literature could be (as well as to the fact that, when they were not creating stock journalistic characters or engaging in typically cynical and self-deprecating humor about their former profession, they often expressed a deep pride in and respect for the journalistic mission in a democracy).[12]

Frus contends that the contemporary blending of the traditional categories of fiction and non-fiction have made this division "problematic," and it may be time to reconsider the view that journalism is inherently an inferior category to fiction – and I would tend to agree up to a point.[13] From my perspective, critics have a sound basis for concluding – with some notable exceptions – that the fictional works of the journalist-literary figures tend to be artistically superior to their journalism produced on demand, and that their aspirations to become fiction writers reflected an apt recognition of the novel as a medium where more creatively expansive opportunities to portray the deeper truths of life were open to them. However, I also believe that contemporary scholars tend to come to their judgments without paying sufficient attention to the high quality journalism produced by some of the journalist-literary figures and, even more importantly, to the influence of their journalistic training and writing upon their fictional creations – and thus miss important connections between journalism and fiction in their assessment of the development of the literary tradition.

I cannot stress enough how the professionalization of the study of literature has shaped the nature of the literary canon, or the way competing scholarly methodologies have tended to frame the study of "literary journalism" and "journalistic literature" (or other terms attached to the field). Journalistically oriented scholars claim that a factual work can be distinguished from a fictional one, and this often sets them in opposition to the scholarly literary establishment that tends to be skeptical that this division can be made (these scholars – heavily influenced by post-modern literary theories – tend to see all writing as enmeshed in subjectivities, cultural biases, and subject in a meaningful manner only to specialist textual interpretations). Even more to the point, those who assert that journalism (even "literary" or highly creative journalism) should be considered "art" have faced a daunting prospect in convincing many scholars in English and literary departments, with their taste for more recondite and highly literary forms of writing. One reason that the term "literary journalism" has come into fashion is that, by using it, its advocates hope to root in a scholarly category their argument that certain forms of journalism can and should be classified as literature. However, in order to make this case, they have generally wanted to narrow the discussion to writing that is deemed to be non-fictional, yet literary in quality and to exclude a body of material such as novels, short stories, and other fictional writing that contains journalistic reporting as its basis but where the authors have shaped the material beyond any definition of what could be called fully "factual."

Hartsock's history of literary journalism has been particularly influential among the journalists and scholars who have been part of a movement to bring more creative narrative techniques to the field of journalism. Like most other scholars and teachers of literary journalism, he opposes the idea of letting the definition of literary journalism slip into the realm of fiction-writing. However, while Hartsock claims "the need to insist ... that an account is factual" before it can be classified as literary journalism, he also acknowledges "just how permeable" the boundaries can be between fiction and non-fiction and wrestles with whether or not there should be separate categories for what he calls narrative and discursive literary journalism and the challenging nature of trying to draw those distinctions for some writers. Other scholars don't fully agree with Hartsock. For example, Frus and Lounsberry – who come from the field of literary scholarship – have questioned the need to apply traditional or defined categories to the blended forms of writing found in much journalistically influenced literature. Meanwhile, the literary journalist and critic Kramer finds a place for semi-fictional writing and works that "straddle the line" between fiction and non-fiction within his definition of the "breakable rules" for literary journalism, although he implies that it is best applied to literary works that were written before the modern understanding of what literary journalism is.[14]

What this study suggests is the potential for a hybrid form of scholarship that mirrors the hybrid nature of much journalistically influenced literature. I attempt to draw from the competing camps of the literary scholars and the scholars of literary journalism by focusing broadly upon the cross-pollinating effect of journalism on the fictional world as well as the field of what has been classified as non-fictional literature. In probing the influence of journalism upon the professional values and the literary writings of the major journalist-literary figures, I pay close attention to patterns that are discernible in their personal and professional lives and can be seen as connecting their literary and artistic views to their experiences in journalism. In essence, what this study hopes to do is to recognize what writers' experiences in journalism and with journalistic research methodologies have contributed to the literary and fiction-writing tradition as much as what the importation of literary narrative methods has meant to the journalism tradition.

In order to avoid definitional disputes, the term "journalist-literary figure" will be used here rather than the term "literary journalist" and the term "journalistic literature" rather than such terms as "literary journalism" or "narrative journalism" or "literary reportage" that scholars have commonly used to define the genre of journalistically based writing that has been influenced by fictional techniques. I have done this, in part, because of the debate about what makes a writer a "literary journalist" – and because I wanted to respect the work of someone such as Hartsock who has expended so much energy trying to determine which writings of the past would fall into the category of literary journalism.[15] However, since I wanted to include in this study journalistically influenced writers who produced fiction and/or non-fiction, I settled upon terms that would include writers whose literary vision was influenced by their experiences in journalism and journalistically oriented writing that encompassed fictional novels, fictional short stories, poetry, drama, or forms that blended fictional writing techniques with non-fiction-writing.[16]

In my analysis, I will be advancing three major conclusions from my reading of the journalist-literary figures that I have identified as having crucially influenced the literary heritage in the US and the British Isles.

First, I will be contending that journalists and journalistic values have played critically important roles in the creation of the British and American literary canon, and I will describe the values and the experiences these writers gained from journalism and show that they played a vital part in the development of their literary visions. Second, I will be arguing that the field of journalism deserves more recognition for its contribution to the literary tradition in the broadest of contexts. Third, I will be examining why journalism's influence upon the fictional and literary writing tradition is not better understood, and why it is that many of these well-known journalist-literary figures themselves didn't always acknowledge their debt to the profession that helped to shape their writing so powerfully.

With this background in mind, it should be noted that I have put more emphasis upon the biographical details of the journalist-literary figures than have many other scholars of literary or narrative journalism or narrative literature. There is growing recognition in some scholarly circles of the value of using biography as a way of illuminating important cultural and sociological patterns that tie the lives of well-known figures to broader historical currents of their time.[17] In what American studies historian David Reynolds calls his "cultural biography" of Whitman, for example, Reynolds shows how Whitman's poetry absorbs and affirms nineteenth-century American slang, dialect, sermons, therapeutic thought, humor, reform rhetoric, spiritualist language, popular music, and dramatic acting styles (Reynolds calls Whitman a "cultural ventriloquist" who fused into his poetry various "mass" interests of his time).[18] I have found biography to be particularly illuminating when it comes to better understanding the influence that journalism has had upon these writers' lives – in finding similarities in their careers and their works of art, in examining how the experiences they shared in journalism influenced their views of literary and journalistic developments, and in noting the connections between their literary viewpoints and the cultural currents of their age.

Throughout this discussion, my focus will be on the epochs in which the major journalist-literary figures played a particularly meaningful role in shaping the literary canon in the US and the British Isles. These periods include:

– The period of the rise of the early commercial newspapers and the era of the "birth of the novel" throughout the eighteenth century. This period was the launching point for the careers of the journalist-novelists Defoe, Fielding, Swift, Tobias Smollett, Oliver Goldsmith, Delariviére Manley, and Eliza Haywood, as well as such literary journalists as Boswell, Johnson, Addison, Steele, Benjamin Franklin, and Thomas

Paine. Characterized by the brief period where the novel didn't have an as yet agreed upon definition but was a hit with the public, this was an age of experimentation and innovation in prose, and the journalist-literary figures were some of its key pioneering figures. Major developments in this period included Defoe importing artful dissembling from his journalism into his prose works; Fielding struggling against critics who saw his novels as "low works" and explaining the kind of writing that he was doing in *Tom Jones* (an explanation that scholars now largely accept as the definition of the modern novel); Boswell trying to develop an empirical basis for his biographical portrait of Johnson that post-modern scholars now scoff at in the same way that contemporary media critics scoff at journalists' claim to be "objective" chroniclers of the world; and Manley and Haywood cross-fertilizing the Grub Street journalistic and the romance-novel-writing traditions in their respective *Female Tatler* and *Female Spectator* periodicals and in their scandal chronicles and spirited historical fantasies.

– What has been called the "Age of Periodicals," in which the advent of the steam-powered printing press and new publishing technologies led to an explosion of publications in the US and British Isles. There was a six-fold growth of American periodicals between 1825 and 1850, many of them modeled upon the great British literary magazines that rose to prominence in this period. This was the age when Dickens, Thackeray, Poe, and George Eliot (Mary Ann Evans) made their mark upon the magazine, the newspaper, and the fiction-writing world, and where Hazlitt, Samuel Taylor Coleridge, Charles Lamb, William Godwin, Thomas DeQuincey, Leigh Hunt, Washington Irving, Thomas Carlyle, Lord Macaulay (Thomas Babington), Harriet Martineau, Margaret Fuller, Fanny Fern (Sara Payson Parton), Henry Adams, John Ruskin, William Morris, and George Meredith made important contributions to journalism and other literary fields. This period established the intellectual backdrop – with the tension between English and American Romanticism and the rise of literary realism, the reshaping of the "American Dream" (and its British equivalent) by the forces of commercialism and industrialization, and the replacement of the partisan press system with the urbanized "Penny Press" newspapers with their mass-market appeal – that played such an important role in the careers of Twain, Whitman, William Dean Howells, William Cullen Bryant, John Greenleaf Whittier, Bret Harte, Ambrose Bierce, Hamlin Garland, and other writers who were influenced by their experiences in commercial journalism. It was in this period that the journalist as a recognizable type began to appear in the fiction of Thackeray, Dickens, and Howells, who set a number of their novels within a periodical world that was commercializing in ways that were disturbing to all three authors but provided a rich foil for their fictional plots and their satiric typecasting of journalists as figures of ridicule and often disdain. This was also the period when the novel, as serialized in periodicals by Dickens and Thackeray, became both popular in the marketplace and embraced by the literary establishment and where the critical writings of Coleridge, Lamb, Hazlitt, De Quincey, Carlyle, Bryant, Poe, and other journalist-literary figures influenced by the romantic movement helped to elevate fictional prose to the same artistic status as poetry and drama.

- The hey-day of the literary realism movement and its phasing into the era of literary naturalism with both movements dominated by literary figures with extensive experiences in journalism. This period – which spanned the mid-to-late nineteenth and the early twentieth centuries and saw the coming of the telegraph and telephone and instantly communicated news – produced figures such as Twain, who worked on both the provincial newspapers of the partisan era and the big city Penny Press newspapers, and Howells, who spent the latter half of the nineteenth century promoting realistic literature and recruiting other writers who came out of journalism. A number of the writers who have been labeled as naturalists, including Dreiser, Crane, Frank Norris, and Jack London, became known for blending dark and bleak messages drawn from Darwinian theory and European continental philosophy into the basics of realistic writing that helped set the stage for twentieth-century existentialism and other pessimistic philosophies that have influenced contemporary journalism. By this time, both the popular and the artistic view of what was considered "literature" and "journalism" was set in place. The image of a journalist as a broadly literate writer editing or writing for a small publication of wit and erudition, as was the case with Addison and Steele, Johnson, and Franklin, was fading away. It was replaced by the stereotype of the functionary within a large commercial organization that processed news, packaged information within marketing formulas, and sought mass audiences as a result of the transformation of the news business that came with the Industrial Revolution.

- The "Age of Newspapers" (dubbed as such because they were at the peak of their circulation and influence). This period – from the later decades of the nineteenth century through World War I – encompassed important historical developments that had a major influence upon the journalist-literary figures, including the emergence of the foreign correspondent as a celebrity figure in covering the imperial aspirations of the US and the

UK; the era of "Yellow Journalism" when the Hearst and Pulitzer newspapers developed sensationalistic formulas and championed American jingoism; the period of the "empire" journalism of Kipling; and the emergence of the professionalized and bureaucratized newsroom. The superstar journalists of this period, such as Crane, Norris, and Davis, as well as the muckrakers Lincoln Steffens, Upton Sinclair, Ida Tarbell and others, both drew upon and helped to burnish the romantic role of the journalist as war correspondent and intrepid investigator of corruption in a time (called the "Gilded Age" by Twain) of industrial consolidation, vast accumulations of industrial wealth, and military adventures abroad. The magazines that made muckraking popular – including *McClure's* and *Collier's* – also had a great influence upon the American scene, and the ethos of investigative journalism became infused within the journalistic value system as a reflection of a news business that embraced the reform ideals of the progressive period while growing more cynical about the opportunism and fortune seeking that was prevalent throughout the business and political worlds.

– The era of the 1920s, 1930s, and 1940s when journalist-literary figures working at the *New Yorker* magazine and other publications gathered at the famed Algonquin Round Table to cultivate their roles as media celebrities or lived as expatriate writers overseas and helped to foster a romantic ethos that surrounded the writer-journalist hoping to escape narrow and provincial attitudes at home. The cosmopolitan romanticism of humor and despair, of domestic alienation and international adventure, was cultivated by the likes of Hemingway, Dos Passos, George Orwell (Eric Blair), Graham Greene, Evelyn Waugh, Sherwood Anderson, Sinclair Lewis, Erskine Caldwell, John Steinbeck, James Thurber, Dorothy Parker, Robert Benchley, Ring Lardner, Katherine Anne Porter, and others who were influenced by the philosophical, political, and economic turmoil of the period and the impact of the Great Depression and the two world wars. Hemingway, in particular, stands out as the most influential journalist-literary figure of this period, with his bravado Hemingway "code" (drawn heavily from Crane and Kipling and other journalistic figures before him) of what makes up the mix of stoicism, epicureanism, and adventurism in the ideal journalist and his notions that a greater and deeper truth can be expressed in fiction-writing than through a commercial journalism bound up in formulaic writing conventions and lifeless newsroom routines. Hemingway, like Greene and other journalist-literary figures of this period, also followed the naturalist tradition by cultivating the role of the "anti-hero" in literature, and Hemingway's Jake Barnes in

The Sun Also Rises and Greene's Thomas Fowler in *The Quiet American* became the prototypes for the image of the contemporary journalist as detached, disillusioned, emotionally scarred, vaguely corrupted, self-indulgent, and indifferent to the fate of the world. This period trails into the 1950s and beyond, when many of these writer-journalists were still influential but when the inward-looking political trends of the post-World War II years led younger artists to increasingly see themselves as challengers of the cultural status quo.

– The period of the 1960s and 1970s, when the so-called "new journalism" movement appeared on the scene as a reaction to the "daily-ness" of mainstream journalism and the increasingly esoteric trends in contemporary fiction-writing and academic literary criticism. As a challenge to the traditional media and literary establishment, this movement both reflected and drew upon the socially disruptive forces of the times – including the US Civil Rights movement, the anti-Vietnam War protest years, the challenges to traditional sexual and social mores – that made this period one of rich literary experimentation. This era saw the rise to celebrity of a group of ex-journalists who have become identified as "beat" or "rebel" writers, including Thompson, Jack Kerouac, Henry Miller, Charles Bukowski, Kurt Vonnegut, Jr., and Tom Robbins, whose countercultural values greatly influenced other late twentieth-century writers. It was also the period when Capote, Wolfe, and Mailer became the self-promoting proselytizers for a new form of radical journalism that would allow journalists to express themselves in highly personalized, stylized, and textured forms of writing that broke from conventional journalistic traditions but reflected the solipsism of the artistic vision that characterized much of twentieth-century creative life.

Underlying this discussion is the thorny question of how one defines journalism, the novel, and the term "literature" – and, to complicate the matter even more, how those activities, and the definitions applied to them, have changed over the years. The definition of journalism in this study is a broad and liberal one, and it reflects the fact that the commonly held usage of the term "journalist" was applied until the early nineteenth century to someone who simply kept a private journal or engaged in supplying excerpts of his or her journal for occasional publication. (The original definition was typically like the one used by Addison in 1712 when he wrote in the *Spectator*: "My following correspondent … is such a Journalist as I require … Her Journal … is only the picture of a Life filled with a fashionable kind of Gaity and Laziness." In that same year, Swift referred to "what the French call a journalier," and in 1726 he had Gulliver mention those who carry a "Journal

Book.") Since the content of what might be in a public journal or periodical wasn't delineated into categories, a journalist before this time period could be someone (such as Johnson was) who produced historical and biographical material, book and theater reviews, critical essays, travelogues, advice columns, political tracts, short narratives, verse, and imaginative writing. In his first dictionary in 1755, considered the first comprehensive one in the English language, Johnson includes no definition for "journalism." (The closest terms to apply would be "Grub Street," which Johnson defined as a place "inhabited by writers of small histories, dictionaries, and temporary poems" and "journalist," which he calls simply "a writer of journals.")[19]

It also is important to remember that the newspapers of this cradle period of the English novel were only loosely connected to what we call newspapers today. The typical publication circulated on a much smaller scale than do contemporary newspapers, and they were aimed at a relatively elite audience of intellectuals, artists, government and religious officials, politicians, lawyers and other professionals, aristocrats and gentry, and the emerging commercial classes, many of whom spent their time in the coffee houses and cafes of London of that day, where the newspapers (relatively expensive by today's standards) circulated and were talked about. The guiding principle of the eighteenth-century newspaper was to entertain its readers and to make a political point in the most telling yet disguised fashion possible, and it used a full range of literary devices to do so. Newspapers – such as Addison and Steele's highly popular *Tatler* and *Spectator* – contained a mix of essays and social commentary, satire and caricature, brief narratives, invective and propaganda, poetry, gossip and letters to the editor (many editorially inspired), virtually all written with a thinly veiled anonymity that made guessing authorship one of the favorite activities of newspaper readers. This mixture of what we today would call literature and journalism was usually seen as an extension of the personalities of these editors, many of them now famous for their contributions to literary, political, and other fields. In their periodicals, they would write much of the material, solicit contributions from friends or political allies, and include only a smattering of what today we might call news (such as, perhaps, a bit of information about military campaigns and battles, executions, ship sailings, and some trade and commercial information).

As recently as the early nineteenth century, the term "journalist" still meant someone who shared material from a personal journal, although increasingly the term began to be applied to a writer for newspapers and magazines. The *Oxford English Dictionary* quotes Hunt in an 1812 London *Examiner* as first employing the term "journalist" for someone who earns his or her living by editing a public journal ("The congratulations of friends and brother-journalists"). The first formal definition of "journalism" as an occupation or a profession that involved writing for periodicals appears in 1833 in the *Westminster Review* ("The power of journalism is acknowledged ... to be enormous in France"), and in 1837 the historian-journalist Carlyle wrote: "Great is journalism. Is not every able Editor a Ruler of the World, being a persuader of it?" However, even then, the meaning of the term was still in a fluid state, and the 1828 *Webster's Dictionary* was still defining a "journalist" as a writer of a journal or a diary.[20]

Today the term "journalist" carries with it the expectation of professionalism – something that wasn't necessarily connoted in the early nineteenth century and before. In contemporary times what was once lumped together has become segmented into specialties – fiction, essay writing, reviews, biography, narrative history, travel writing, news accounts, humor, and so forth – with writers, often trained in one specialty area, aiming with a high degree of self-consciousness to produce one written form or the other, and critics and scholars jealously guarding the specialty categories and the critical terms that have grown up to dissect and distinguish the various forms of writing. This situation would have been unknown to the pioneers of journalistic literature, and any and all of these forms could show up in the newspapers or periodicals of the eighteenth and early nineteenth centuries. The techniques used by those who wrote for those early periodicals – Boswell and Johnson, for example – have become viewed as ground-breaking examples of contemporary specialty areas, such as the biography (which, in Boswell's case, was nonetheless a very different product from the contemporary biography) or as awe-inspiring demonstrations of writing versatility (it has been suggested that Johnson, the early "journalist," also worked in areas of the oration, sermon, Horatian ode, elegy, Anacreontic lyric, epigram, and advertisement, to name just a few).[21]

The novel, in turn, is a term that is derived from various Latinate forms (meaning "new" or "unusual") that found their way into English usage largely through the French romance *nouvelles* that became popular in England. Interestingly, in its more archaic definition (dating back to the late fifteenth century), the "novel" was a synonym for "news" or "tidings" and the "novelist" for a "newsmonger" or "news carrier." By the sixteenth and seventeenth centuries, the term was being used for a tale or a short story (the poet and playwright John Dryden refers to "trifling novels" in 1697). It wasn't until the mid-seventeenth century that the term began to be applied to a fictitious prose narrative or a tale written at length, although the term still tended to be a slightly derogatory one. (In 1643, the poet John Milton referred to the "mere amatorious novel" and in 1711 Steele wrote: "I am afraid thy Brains are a little disordered with Romances and novels.") By the late eighteenth century, the modern definition of the novel – as a lengthy book of fictional writing – was largely established. However, for many years, fiction-writing wasn't fully distinguished from non-fiction-writing, and in the earliest novels it was their verisimilitude to life that was valued and that distinguished those works from romances.[22] In this sense, the contemporary distinction between the novel and the term "journalism" came most forcefully into place during the mid-to-late nineteenth century as daily journalism took on the aspiration of presenting news and information in a balanced and even-handed fashion – including, as science came into ascendancy, in terms that laid claim to a certain form of empirical objectivity.

In contemporary times, the term "literature" has proven to be a useful umbrella term for those who have struggled to decide whether journalism – and if so, what form of journalism – should be considered to be on the same level as the acknowledged great works of written art. The term "literature" has evolved from the period (the late fourteenth century to the early eighteenth century) where it referred generally to the written production of persons of letters who were dealing with matters of polite and refined learning into a category of writing established through the application of judgment among people with a claim to critical authority. In 1759, Goldsmith referred to a man of "literary merit" and Johnson in 1773 talked of someone with a "literary reputation." (In 1779, Johnson described an author whose "pregnancy of imagination and elegance of language have deservedly set him high in the ranks of literature.")[23] Today, literature is largely determined by what the members of the literary establishment – most notably the critics who write for literary publications and those who teach and practice literary scholarship in university departments – decide will be read, studied, and critiqued as part of their reviewing, publishing, teaching, and scholarly research. These judgments invariably are affected by the subjective individual views of the critics and scholars, as well as the collective assumptions, unspoken and spoken, within the outlooks of various literary disciplines and specialty areas, and they reflect a myriad of complex issues – what does one mean by "high" art versus "popular" art, does one see the novel as the highest form of artistic achievement in prose or would journalistic writing qualify, is fiction inherently more aesthetically and artistically accomplished than non-fiction, and what does one make of the artists and journalists who have tried to blend the two into hybrid art forms?

Thus it was a challenging task to determine when to include a writing figure under the spreading umbrella of the terms "journalism," "literature," and "the novel." I can't pretend that my research was exhaustive – the subject is simply too vast to know for sure what one may be missing – nor do I expect that there won't be those who disagree with the conclusions that I have reached. The more than 300 writers that I selected for this study and its appendix include a wide variety of writers – from those who are highly familiar to scholars of literature and journalism to those who may be surprising choices as literary figures or journalists.

In choosing when to classify a writer as an important journalist-literary figure from the standpoint of whether he or she could be called a journalist, I used the following criteria that I felt could be applied to both historical and contemporary circumstances, including whether a writer fits one or more of the following criteria:

– writing with a popular audience in mind for some kind of publication or periodical
– writing on general topics, as well as trying to make narrow or specialized issues understandable to regular readers
– writing on deadline
– dealing with the need for compression, clear communication, and building audience rapport
– editing or owning a publication, or working under editors as a reporter, essayist, columnist or periodical contributor, generally at close hand
– identifying professionally with journalism and thinking of oneself as a journalist or participant in the periodical world
– experiencing the life of a journalist, working in journalists' company, and imbibing the profession's values and attitudes
– identifying with the mission of journalism, including the mission of the journalist as a watchdog of institutions, and the role that journalism plays in a democratic society
– wrestling with the writing formulas and/or the demands that journalism in a commercial marketplace imposes on writers
– working within a network of journalists and journalist-literary figures who influence each other's work, support and/or feud with each other, share friendships and/or enmities, and share similar values when it comes to writing and their approach to journalism and artistry.

Although newspapers were my principal focus, I included people who wrote principally for magazines in recent times – including Parker, Thurber, Benchley, E. B. White, and James Agee – and this made for some complicated judgments, given the ready market for today's established writers to serve as reviewers for and contributors to magazines, reviews, and literary journals. Some had newspaper experience, others didn't, although some spent significant periods as employees or members of a staff of paid writers for magazines or worked as freelance contributors for extensive periods. The key factor was that their periodical work, whether performed as staffers or independent writers, involved nitty-gritty participation in editorial tasks and exposed them in vivid ways to the culture of journalism. I included a number of figures who wrote only short stories and humor pieces and never successfully tackled the serious novel (Poe, Bierce, Lardner, Benchley, Parker, Thurber). A few writers (London, Anderson, Steinbeck, Mailer) took on the identity of journalists after earlier fiction-writing achievements, and they tended to produce mostly journalism or become involved in journalistic ventures late in their careers. However, all had important experiences in the field of journalism, and all produced some journalistic writings and/or essays that could be deemed to fall into the category of literary non-fiction.

In my analysis and in the compilation of the appendix, I took an expansive view of the literary world and included former journalists who made their principal mark in areas other than fully serious adult literature and/or prose writing, including in the areas of poetry (Coleridge, Philip Freneau, Robert Frost, Carl Sandburg, Conrad Aiken, John Masefield, Hart Crane, Wallace Stevens, Archibald MacLeish, Dylan Thomas, Hugh MacDiarmid [C. M. Grieve], James Fenton, Craig Raine), stage drama (George Bernard Shaw, Richard Brinsley Sheridan, Eugene O'Neill, George S. Kaufman, Brendan Behan, Tom Stoppard), children's literature (White, Edith Nesbit, Arthur Ransome, James M. Barrie, L. Frank Baum, Laura Ingalls Wilder), and science fiction (H. G. Wells, Aldous Huxley). I did this because I felt that it was important to illustrate the full impact of journalists and ex-journalists upon the literary tradition and because, with the lines often blurred between fiction, journalism, and other literary forms, many writers made their marks in other genres that still allowed them to demonstrate journalistic influences upon their literature. While critics and scholars have focused upon such writers as Stevens and Hart Crane almost exclusively as poetic stylists, my focus was upon their experiences in journalism and how those experiences may have influenced their writing and artistic outlook. As one-time journalists, it is almost certainly no coincidence that many of the modern poets (Sandburg, Frost, Aiken, Hart Crane) are viewed in the tradition of the "plain speech" poetic tradition that dates back to Whitman and Bryant, who had careers in journalism, too. In a similar vein, while Stevens and O'Neill wrote complicated, highly-crafted artistic works (Stevens) and psychologically complex dramas (O'Neill), their experiences as journalists played an important role in their life history and influenced their literary outlook (for example, O'Neill developed some of his drinking habits while a young journalist;

Stevens' insecure view of himself as an artist can be measured against his envy of Stephen Crane and Hemingway as heroic journalist models he didn't feel he could measure up to).[24]

The determination of which writing to include in the "literary" part of the definition of a journalist-literary figure proved to be an even more challenging task. The decision to elevate a piece of writing or a body of writing to the category of literature invariably involves both personal judgment as well as the collective assessment of the literary establishment (and, to some degree, the popular marketplace). In most cases, I acceded to the consensus of the critical community in evaluating what made a writer's work memorable and qualified it to be seen as a lasting contribution to the culture's literary heritage. However, if this involved a close call, I was generous in my viewpoint even if a writer would not receive the favorable judgment of the bulk of the literary establishment. In particular, I included some artists whose writings are treated in some scholarly quarters as too "slight" or "popular" if those writers have had a strong influence upon other journalists who had ambitions to write literature and/or if they have emerged as important figures among scholars who have attempted to bring more gender and racial diversity to the literary canon. I also included a few critically recognized crime and detective novelists (Raymond Chandler, James M. Cain, Horace McCoy, Ian Fleming, Dick Francis, Tony Hillerman, Edna Buchanan), although I had to draw the line here in relatively tight terms, given the prolific contributions that journalists have made to the adventure novel tradition. Although essay writing today is now seen as a distinct genre from either routine journalism or fiction-writing, "popular" essayists, such as H. L. Mencken and A. J. Liebling, made it into the study, largely by dint of their backgrounds on newspapers and periodicals, the widely praised quality of their essay writing, and their importance as cultural commentators and figures of influence within the journalism community.

Humor writing, with roots in the earliest days of mass market journalism and the beginnings of fiction, is the most continuous connecting cord to the journalist-literary figures of today, and I have included a sizable number of figures in this field. Some of the best known journalist-literary figures worked in this vein, including Twain, Harte, Bierce, Benchley, Thurber, White, Parker, Waugh, P. G. Wodehouse, and S. J. Perelman, but they were heavily influenced by a host of less remembered writers who as newspaper and regional humorists were models for the ongoing tradition of journalistic humor-writing, including Finley Peter Dunne, Artemus Ward (Charles Farrar Browne), George Ade, Eugene Field, Don Marquis, and Franklin Pierce Adams, with his influential "Conning Tower" column in the *New York World*. In some instances (such as in the case of Ward and Adams) these newspaper humorists helped promote the careers of their now more famous proteges. Much of the writing of these pioneers in newspaper humor is lost to us, or if it is known, it is only through the interests of specialists and out-of-print collections of columns and essays, despite their great influence upon the journalistic humor-writing tradition and the popular humor writers of today.

At the other end of the spectrum, reform and radical writing has played a major part in the role of journalists within the development of the literary tradition. I included many of the great "muckraking" journalists – Phillips, Sinclair, Steffens, Tarbell, Frank Stannard Baker, Will Irwin, William Allen White – in part because they wrote novels (although not always good ones), and in part because their social reform message was influential in writing developments of the late nineteenth and early twentieth centuries. Reform themes also were prominent in the writings of a number of the journalist-literary figures of the eighteenth, nineteenth, and early twentieth centuries (Defoe, Paine, Godwin, Hunt, Martineau, Shaw, Wells, Fuller, Frederick Douglass, Lydia Maria Child, Henry Mayhew, Jacob Riis, Hutchins Hapgood, Charlotte Perkins Gilman, Edward Bellamy, George R. Sims, Ruth McKenney, Josephine Herbst, Elizabeth Jordan). In the nineteenth and twentieth centuries, a host of radical authors – including Ruskin, Morris, Howells, Garland, London, Sinclair, Gilman, Shaw, Wells, Sandburg, Nesbit, Lewis, Orwell, Theresa Malkiel, Katharine Glasier, Dorothy Day, Susan Glaspell, Rebecca West (Cicely Isabel Fairfield), J. B. Priestley, Floyd Dell, James T. Farrell, and Mary Heaton Vorse – publicly called themselves socialists, joined the socialist party, were associated with socialist organizations, wrote for socialist publications, or voted for socialist candidates at some point during their literary career. Wright, Caldwell, Parker, Orwell, Dreiser, Hemingway, MacDiarmid, Agee, Greene, Dos Passos, Steffens, Anderson, W. E. B. DuBois, John Reed, Anna Louise Strong, Charlotte Haldane, Meridel Le Sueur, Agnes Smedley, Edmund Wilson, Mary McCarthy, Langston Hughes, Malcolm Muggeridge, and Myra Page (Dorothy Markey) openly supported communist candidates, aided communist military or political campaigns, wrote for communist publications, and/or joined the communist party.[25] Often they used narrative literary techniques to dramatize their social message and touch readers emotionally with the plight of their subjects of economic injustice. Although political conservatives also showed up in the ranks of the journalist-literary figures, a number of them – including Mencken, Kipling, and Evelyn and Auberon Waugh, as well as Muggeridge, Dos Passos, and Hilaire Belloc, who switched from the left to the right during their lifetimes – also were quite vociferous in their politics and might be considered radical conservatives rather than passive supporters of the status quo.

In looking for the contributions in terms of ethnicity, gender, and sexual orientation, I had an easier time of it than do scholars in other fields in finding diversity in the ranks of many professions. Although "dead white men," as they say, dominated the field in the early eras, women moved into journalism relatively early compared to other professions. Thanks to recent scholarship by Lutes, Paula Rabinowitz, Charlotte Nekola, and others, it has become clear how much the journalistic and literary tradition owes to women writers whose journalistic and literary work often has been overlooked by the overseers of the literary canon. These contributions come from such well-known as well as lesser-known female journalist-literary figures, ranging from Manley, Haywood, and Susanna Haswell Rowson in the eighteenth century, Child, Martineau, Fuller, Fern, Eliot, Violet Hunt, Nellie Bly (Elizabeth Cochran), and Rebecca Harding Davis in the nineteenth century, Cather, Parker, Jordan, Glaspell, Smedley, Le Sueur, Porter, Virginia Woolf, McCarthy, Margaret Mitchell, Edna Ferber, Djuna Barnes, Miriam Michelson, Zona Gale, Martha Gellhorn, Sophie Treadwell, Josephine Lawrence, Eudora Welty, Mary Lee Settle, Angela Carter, Angela Lambert, and Gloria Emerson in the twentieth century, to a plethora of women writers today (including Buchanan, Lillian Ross, Gloria Steinem, Gail Godwin, Doris Betts, E. Annie Proulx, Jane Kramer, Frances Fitzgerald, Nora Ephron, Sara Davidson, Susan Cheever, Bobbie Ann Mason, Anita Shreve, Annie Dillard, Anne Lamott, Barbara Kingsolver, Anna Quindlen, Susan Orlean, Muriel Gray, and Julie Burchill). Even though their numbers don't equal the men in this study in total (they make up over 25 percent of those listed in the appendix), their accomplishments reflect on the gains for women in a work world where women's entry into any profession has not always been a welcoming one and an academic world where women scholars have gone about rectifying the imbalance in the attention paid to women writers of earlier periods. Many of these same issues apply to the sixteen African-American writers I discuss and/or include in the appendix – Douglass, Du Bois, Wright, Hughes, Charles W. Chesnutt, Pauline Hopkins, Ida Wells-Barnett, Victoria Earle Matthews, James Weldon Johnson, Paul Laurence Dunbar, Alice Dunbar-Nelson, George Samuel Schuyler, Zora Neale Hurston, Maya Angelou, Benilde Little, and Colson Whitehead. All had or have had interesting and significant involvement in journalism as part of their literary and artistic careers, and all have been important figures in the world of African-American arts, journalism, cultural studies, and politics, and in the broader literary and political world as well. Two Asian-American women writers are included, Sui Sin Far (Edith Maude Easton), who is recognized as the first writer of Asian descent to have her works published in North America, and the contemporary writer, Andrea Louie, as well as the Hispanic writers Richard Vasquez, Richard Rodriguez, and Cristina Garcia. The gay and bi-sexual journalist-literary figures were an interesting group (there has been some scholarly speculation, for example, as to whom that group should include). While there were a number of figures who were openly or almost certainly gay (including Whitman, Capote, Hart Crane, E. M. Forster, and Edmund White) or bi-sexual (Kerouac, Djuna Barnes, Dorothy Thompson), there are others (such as Cather) who never revealed their sexual orientation – and, given the eras they lived in, their literature seldom deals openly with issues of sexual orientation.[26]

The practice of literary criticism made for some particularly tough decisions. Most well-known writers have many opportunities to become involved with book reviewing, and many of the journalist-literary figures (including Poe, Benchley, Parker, Wodehouse, Orwell, Greene, Woolf, and V. S. Pritchett) were prodigious contributors to arts reviews and literary periodicals. However, in none of their cases was their literary reputation based solely on their arts reviewing. In the appendix, I have included a number of figures who were best known in their time as critics and cultural commentators – including Hazlitt, Carlyle, Macaulay, and Fuller – and who are admired for the literary quality of their prose even though they never wrote conventional fictional novels. I also included a number of important twentieth-century critics – including Dell, Wilson, and McCarthy – largely because they also wrote novels (which, interestingly, did not always meet with critical approval) or because (as in the case of George Jean Nathan) they are such central figures in the publishing life of many other journalist-literary figures.

I have included a number of contemporary writers in my analysis whose place in the literary canon is far from a settled issue. It is difficult to assess who of those writing today will achieve durability of literary reputation, and I decided to try to apply some empirical measures to the discussion. For many of the recent authors in the study, the judgments were my own, based upon criteria that I have outlined here. However, I also included in the appendix the contemporary journalist-literary figures who were identified as influential by at least five (or 1 percent) of 658 respondents in a survey I administered in 2004 to 2005 to big-city American daily-newspaper journalists who said that they had written and/or planned to write literature.[27] With such a plethora of writers today who could be called literary journalists or journalist-literary figures, I felt that this method insured that today's writers who are held in high regard by their generational colleagues were noted in the study.

Finally, I should explain that I decided to limit this study to British and American journalist-literary figures largely because the line had to be drawn somewhere, and because these two traditions are so intertwined and have so greatly influenced each other. However, this close historical relationship between journalism and fiction-writing does not mean the phenomenon is a unique one to the UK and the US. In fact, it is clear that the connection between the journalistic and the literary tradition can be found in cultures throughout the world.[28]

In today's specialized scholarly environment, it may prove impossible to gain anything like consensus upon how the relationship between journalism and literature should be studied – nor is it possible to imagine scholars analyzing these questions without viewing them through the lenses of their own disciplines. But I hope that a book that sits on the boundaries of scholarly specialties will serve a useful purpose in bringing this discussion to people – journalists, writers, teachers and practitioners of literary journalism, scholars, and readers – who have enjoyed the writings of many of the journalist-literary figures and are comfortable analyzing the phenomenon in the kind of language and writing terminology that the journalist-literary figures themselves generally used. As an ex-journalist with a strong commitment to scholarship's need to communicate to a broader public, I have seen my task as that of a synthesizer and interpreter – of scholarly terms into general language, of specialized studies into interpretive overviews, of biographical material that when expanded and connected to other biographical material can throw light upon important themes that connect the journalistic to the literary world.

In the first chapter, I examine the historical circumstances that accounted for the parallel rise of the commercial periodical industry and the emergence of the novel in English and how those developments were intertwined in ways that powerfully connect the journalistic tradition with the literary tradition in the US and the British Isles. In this chapter, I discuss the eighteenth-century period, when the novel in English was brought into the marketplace by Defoe, Swift, Fielding, and others, most of them journalists and ex-journalists, as well as by the multi-talented writers, such as Boswell and Johnson, who struggled to define what it meant to write across the contemporary genres of what today would be called journalism, fiction, semi-fiction and a plethora of other literary categories. This era was followed by the developments of the early nineteenth century – known as the "Age of Periodicals" – when Dickens, Thackeray, Eliot, and other journalist-literary figures emerged out of journalism to use the expanding periodical marketplace to firmly fix the notion of the novel at the center of literary culture.

Chapter two examines the rise of literary realism in the mid-to-late nineteenth century, a movement which was championed by Twain and Howells, in the context of the growing commercialization of the journalism industry, the migration of the population from villages and small towns to the industrialized urban centers, and the fixation of the "realistic" writers upon the traumatic changes brought about by the Industrial Revolution. Literary realism phased into what has been called the "naturalist" tradition, the next major literary movement of the period, and one which was strongly connected to literary realism. The journalist-literary figures that are identified as naturalists, including Stephen Crane, Norris, Dreiser, and London, are key figures in ushering in contemporary literary attitudes with their focus upon the gritty details of urban life, the brutality of warfare, and the bleak worldviews that rose out of Darwinism, industrialization, and the coming of modern imperialism.

The tradition of the documentary novel and the use of journalistic reporting and research methods in the creation of the fictional and semi-fictional novels of the journalist-literary figures are the subjects of chapter three. In this chapter, I suggest that there may be advantages to expanding the study of journalism's influence upon the fiction, as well as the non-fiction, writing tradition as a way to gauge the profession's and its practitioners' full influence upon literary history.

Chapter four traces the impact of journalistic activities upon the late-life careers of the journalist-literary figures, their frustrations with and continued attraction to the practice of journalism throughout their writing lives, as well as critics' tendency to dismiss them when they turned from novel-writing to journalism. Finally, I close with some thoughts about the future of journalistic literature – including why it may be threatened by both the best-seller book market available to contemporary journalists and the control of the literary canon by scholars and critics who often have only a marginal interest in the "plain-speaking" tradition in which most of the journalist-literary figures have written.

There are many factors that have led to public and scholarly discussions about the relationship between "news" and "fiction" within contemporary media – the wide-open environment of the internet that has allowed for the abandonment of factual standards of traditional news organizations, scandals surrounding journalists (Janet Cooke, Stephen Glass, Jason Blair, and others) who have fabricated material in stories, journalists and teachers of narrative journalism in universities who are pushing for greater use of literary journalistic techniques in newspapers as a way to grab the attention of readers, and a post-modern climate among literary and media scholars who tend to look with suspicion upon journalistic claims of "objectivity" and who feel that the distinctions between fact and fiction are largely illusory. A "narrative evangelism" has taken hold in newsrooms, one narrative journalism teacher recently told a gathering of journalism educators, and newspapers today are becoming the "storypaper" where "slow journalism" is replacing the stories that race to compete with the immediacy of broadcast and internet media.[29] And yet, things have become so topsy-turvy in the writing world that it also has led *Newsweek* columnist and novelist Anna Quindlen to declare, "People just don't seem to believe in fiction anymore. It's very disorienting – after 'One True Thing' came out, I kept having people come up and say, 'I just loved that book about your mother.' I'd always respond, 'It's a novel.' But reality now is so strange – people assume that journalism is made up."[30]

Interestingly, since the time that Addison and Steele arrived on the English periodical scene with their witty mix of what we today would call literature and journalism, the journalist-literary figures have been ruminating about these questions. The discussion, for example, is reminiscent of Twain's concerns in the nineteenth century about his brother Orion's newspaper that Twain felt was foundering through its use of dry news reports and standardized journalistic accounts, and Twain's view that the newspaper needed more humor and entertainment material (including pranks and made-up stories, if need be, which Twain provided when he filled in for his brother as editor) to connect with its audience. However, Twain himself never favored abandoning the standards of balance and fairness that had emerged by his time as an ethic for the news pages (there is evidence that he enforced them with diligent professionalism while serving as the managing editor of the *Buffalo Express*).[31] No one – least of all this author – is suggesting that the press should jettison its standards of truth-telling and simply allow fictionalized material to be included in standard journalistic accounts on the news pages. Still, the "package" that makes up the newspaper has been in a constant state of evolution, and who knows if a literarily enhanced journalism or the inclusion of carefully labeled journalistic literature may not add to the editorial mix in ways that other strategies have not. In expanding the understanding of the contribution of journalism to the literary tradition, I hope that this study may help to put the dilemmas of today's media organizations into a broader historical context and might prove useful to those who want to see the possibilities for creative solutions to journalism's troubles.

Writers who have been connected to journalism, I believe, deserve greater attention for their role in the development of the literary canon. The great literary works that have been created upon a journalistic foundation make up an impressive part of the literary legacy in the US and the British Isles.

Hopefully, this study will help lead to a deeper and fuller recognition of the accomplishments of these journalist-writers who have demonstrated the highest levels of literary artistry and will encourage other journalists, critics, and scholars – as well as the reading public – to better appreciate journalism's important part in advancing the literary-writing tradition in English prose.

CHAPTER I

Journalism and the rise of the novel, 1700–1875: Daniel Defoe to George Eliot

> I declare upon my honour, that I have neither added nor diminished; nay so scrupulous have I been, that I would not make the smallest variation even when my friends thought it would be an improvement. I know with how much pleasure we read what is perfectly authentick.
>
> – James Boswell on his biographical methods.

> I am … joined with eleven others in reporting the debates in Parliament for a Morning Newspaper. Night after night, I record predictions that never come to pass, professions that are never fulfilled, explanations that are only meant to mystify. I wallow in words.
>
> – Charles Dickens from *David Copperfield*

> Oh, for shorthand, to take this down.
>
> – Another comment by Boswell on his biographical methods.

> All poets are humbugs, all literary men are humbugs; directly a man begins to sell his feelings for money he's a humbug.
>
> – William Thackeray

One night, when James Boswell was socializing with Samuel Johnson, the eighteenth-century Englishman of letters and the subject of Boswell's biography that turned both men into literary legends, Johnson rose up in annoyance at the barrage of questions Boswell was aiming at him. Boswell and Johnson had a warm friendship, and, even though Johnson was flattered, knowing Boswell's intention of memorializing him for the ages, he couldn't contain his irritation. "Don't you consider, Sir, that these are not the manners of a gentleman? What man of elegant manners teases one with questions so? I will not be baited with *what*: what is this? What is that? Why is a cow's tail long? Why is a fox's tail bushy?"[1]

Boswell was doing what he did incessantly in the coffee houses, taverns, and at the dinner tables of eighteenth-century London: he was exasperating his friends and making them nervous by keeping a record of their private conversations which he often went home and recorded late into the night.

Boswell was forever trying to coax biographical material from Johnson (and other friends) by playing the devil's advocate, the gadfly provocateur, and the straight man for their wit and repartee. While Boswell is best known for the intimate portrait of Johnson that he bequeathed to posterity, he was perpetually gathering material for the articles he wrote for the newspapers of his era. In the process, Boswell alienated some of his friends by revealing personal confidences, by attacking the political high-and-mighty, and by promoting himself and his pet political causes in the periodicals circulating throughout London. Once, perplexed by the cooling of his once-fond relationship with Sir Edmund Burke, the famed parliamentarian, a friend explained to Boswell that the cause of Burke's "coldness" was "your habit of recording" that throws a restraint on "convivial ease." Added Johnson in a letter to Boswell: "Your love of publication is offensive and disgusting, and will end, if it be not reformed, in a general distrust among all your friends."[2]

But Boswell was undaunted. Like the generations of journalist-literary figures who came after him, Boswell's creative and literary life and his impulse to publish what he saw fit were not easily thwarted. While today we might shun the notion of Boswell as a journalist (he was widely seen in his time as a sycophant who hung on Johnson's every word in the hope of preserving it for the ages), his rich picture of the coffee house society of eighteenth-century London and his portrait of Johnson as a supercilious sage and dyspeptic philosopher of the Age of Reason can hardly be called anything but journalism at its earliest, and perhaps its best. This was the case even though Boswell, a lawyer by training and a Scottish aristocrat by birth, conducted his research and comported himself in ways that were considered dubious in his time, would be considered "unprofessional" by journalists or biographers today, and are still the subject of heated debate among scholars.

To begin any discussion of the pioneers of journalism and literature, one must start with the people who were pioneering new literary techniques at a time when there weren't the distinctions among literary categories that we draw today. Boswell's work – where he mixed insider journalism, celebrity interviewing, and character sketching, all the while feeling for the right line between what could be discussed in the newspapers of his day and what should be held back for later literary publication – was ground-breaking in the development of the fields that we have come to call journalism, biography, confessional literature, and journal-writing. Johnson, the great scholar, essayist, and commentator upon his age, worked in so many different literary forms and was an innovator in so many areas that many scholars see it as ironic that he is now best known for his conversational skills as chronicled in Boswell's biography of him. Another irony is that Johnson and Boswell struggled with defining the emerging literary activity of fiction-writing and how to fit it into the literary categories of the time, while never recognizing that some future literary scholars would come to the conclusion that Boswell (with Johnson's encouragement) was engaging in fiction-writing himself. Boswell thought of himself as a biographer (the genre was a new but recognized one in his time), but there are a number of scholars who have come to see his biography of Johnson as more inspired in Boswell's imagination than as an example of the empirical methods of contemporary biography.

In looking back to the eighteenth century as the birthplace of both the modern novel and modern journalism, one has to imagine a time when the line between the real and the imagined was very much blurred and when notions of "objectivity" and "factuality" were in a fluid and largely undefined state. Today it has become important for writers to delineate between fact and fiction, between truth and falsehood, between news and propaganda. But for Boswell, Johnson, Daniel Defoe, Jonathan Swift, Henry Fielding, Tobias Smollett, Oliver Goldsmith, and other writers of the eighteenth century, the distinction was less clear. The explosive growth of periodicals in the early eighteenth century that contained news, essays, criticism, political commentary, gossip, polemics, humor, satire, burlesque, parody, poetry, invented and imagined tales – often appearing in mixed and varied formats – was the "primordial soup" from which today's fiction and literary journalism emerged, as Jenny Uglow has put it. The elements of what today we call the newspaper also were just becoming apparent in the publications that circulated through the coffee houses and small shops of London and were read by a growing range of the population whose lives were being transformed by better and cheaper printing techniques, greater availability of education, new scientific discoveries, and a world pushing outward into trade, commerce, and exploration. Goldsmith, for example, is best remembered for his play, *She Stoops to Conquer*, and his novel, *The Vicar of Wakefield*, but he also was a prominent journalist who worked on a publication of Smollett's, edited his own newspaper, and was a coffee-house companion of Johnson and Boswell who was repeatedly derided by Johnson for his social ineptitude in Boswell's biographical account (Boswell apparently didn't think highly of Goldsmith's social skills either). But Johnson nonetheless captured the breadth of Goldsmith's talent (as well as the literary spirit of his age) when he wrote for Goldsmith's memorial tablet in Westminster Abbey: "Poet, Naturalist, Historian, who left scarcely any kind of writing untouched."[3]

Goldsmith was only following in the footsteps of Defoe and the other multi-faceted literary talents who gave birth to novel-writing in the English language (Goldsmith was born in 1730, the year before Defoe died, and only a few years after the period in Defoe's late life in which he penned his pioneering novels). Defoe, Swift, Fielding, Smollett, Goldsmith (and, to a lesser degree, Samuel Richardson) all produced their ground-breaking fictional works using writing techniques that they also used in their notable careers as journalists of that era (Richardson was a commercial printer but engaged in very little journalism as such). The now recognized fictional "classics" that these five eighteenth-century journalist-literary figures produced – Defoe's *Robinson Crusoe, Moll Flanders, A Journal of the Plague Year,* and *Roxana*; Swift's *Gulliver's Travels*; Fielding's *Joseph Andrews, Tom Jones,* and *Amelia*; Smollett's *Roderick Random, Peregrine Pickle,* and *Humphry Clinker,* and Goldsmith's *The Vicar of Wakefield* – are intimately connected to the world of eighteenth-century journalism, and the writing style, authorial voice, and literary viewpoint manifested in those early novels reflect the practices of a time when journalism often looked like what we call fiction today and fiction could look like journalism.

Even though they never wrote novels, perhaps the most influential figures upon the other major journalist-literary figures of the eighteenth century were Joseph Addison and Richard Steele. Their masterful periodical-writing in the *Tatler* and the *Spectator* was a model for their fellow writers and is studied today as both journalism and literature – replete as it was with wit, whimsy, satire, biting personal and social commentary, political advocacy, philosophical speculation, advice on manners, and serious moralizing. In their publications, which were praised in their time by competitors such as Defoe and later emulated in both the United Kingdom (Johnson's *Rambler* and *Idler* had many of the same aims and some of the characteristics of the *Tatler* and the *Spectator*, as did Fielding's *Champion*) and America (Benjamin Franklin used Addison and Steele's writings as a model for his early journalism), Addison and Steele were able to capture the imagination of their marketplace in the days before the telegraph and the wire services and the television screen, when it was literary creativity that sold the newspaper, not the day's breaking news. Their success in satisfying a popular audience created a demand for a new kind of writer-artist – a person whose imagination was on ready display, whose success depended on pleasing both popular and elite tastes, whose livelihood was based upon reflecting prevailing social values but carefully and gently ridiculing them, whose mastery of the art of subterfuge and hidden meanings helped to circumvent detection by the authorities, and whose reputation depended upon the continuous production of material that skirted the boundaries between fact and fiction and pushed the limits of good taste without offending respectable readers.

That the writers who were up for this task often came from the margins of class and aristocratic culture is probably no surprise. Fielding's parents had social connections but fell on hard times and had no inherited wealth; Boswell was a titled member of the gentry with a large estate in Scotland, but he largely abandoned it for the life of a London socializer and bon vivant; Johnson sometimes put on aristocratic airs, but he grew up in modest circumstances in Lichfield and was unable to complete his studies at Oxford University for lack of funds. Addison and Steele were from semi-privileged backgrounds and Oxford-educated (Addison received a degree while Steele didn't), but they made their way on the edges of genteel life as coffee-house habitues and hangers-on in London social and political life; Delariviére Manley and Eliza Haywood, who suffered drops in social status after the failure of troubled, early marriages and took up Grub Street writers' existences before launching the *Female Tatler* and *Female Examiner* respectively, dealt with rumors about their personal lives that were as scandalous as their gossipy periodicals and the novels of amorous adventures that they wrote for a fascinated public. In this way, these early commercial writers set the stage for other aspiring journalist-literary figures from less than privileged backgrounds who would follow their example on to literary success, and they helped to ready a popular audience for the kind of literary experimentation from which the modern novel would emerge.

The model of Addison and Steele continued to exercise a hold over British periodical journalism throughout the late eighteenth and early nineteenth centuries, even as the economics of periodical publishing began to intensify with the coming of the Industrial Age. The period of the early to mid-nineteenth century has been called the "Age of Periodicals" or the "Age of Magazines" – 800 publications were launched in London alone in the 1840s – and it was one of the earliest mass consumer markets to develop. The industrial forces that were transforming the rest of British and American industry were also operating in the field of newspapers and periodicals, and investment that hoped to capitalize on a growing mass marketplace for reading material was flowing into the publishing business. The widespread use of the steam-powered printing press in the first part of the nineteenth century greatly accelerated the trend toward the control of journalism and novel-publishing in the hands of business interests. When Charles Dickens and William Thackeray entered the journalism business (Dickens in 1831 as a parliamentary reporter for the *Mirror of Parliament*; Thackeray as a part-owner, editor, and writer for the *National Standard* periodical in 1833), magazines and newspapers had become a big business in comparison to the days of Boswell, Johnson, and Addison and Steele.[4]

Throughout the UK and in places in the US, there came onto the scene a new kind of literary aspirant – semi-gentlemen and adventuresome women writers who straddled the still somewhat genteel world of British arts and letters and the offices of the rowdy scribblers who were making their names on the new breed of commercial publications. Often dabblers in the other literary arts who wrote arts criticism and across different literary genres, they continued to work to integrate the artistic tradition with the increasingly intrusive commercial goals of periodical journalism. William Godwin, Leigh Hunt, William Hazlitt, Charles Lamb, Thomas De Quincey, Henry Lewes, and Harriet Martineau worked on commercial newspapers and/or contributed to the growing number of magazines that were becoming prominent on the British literary scene, and they came to constitute a bridge in the tradition of journalistic literature from the days of Defoe's, Swift's, and Fielding's early experiments in novel-writing to the full flowering of the novel as a popular artistic form in the hands of Dickens, Thackeray, and George Eliot. These transitional writers were a notch up in prestige and education from the likes of the freelancers, poorly paid hack workers and literary hangers-on who inhabited Grub Street in Johnson's time, and many thought of themselves as professionals in aspiration and status. In this environment, with the opportunities it still offered for mixing the conventions of journalism with other artistic genres, there remained powerful vestiges of an honored literary tradition, particularly in England, and all these writers were seen as moving knowledgeably throughout the world of arts, history, politics, biography, and cultural commentary. This class of intellectual popularizers and commentators who operated in the Johnsonian tradition of wit, critical insight, and largeness in learning included Thomas Carlyle and Lord Macaulay (Thomas Babington) who, as periodical essayists before they made their marks as historians, were figures of the popular journalistic marketplace as well as being accorded high social status by the elite reaches of the critical establishment.

In the period of the late eighteenth and early nineteenth centuries, the American fiction-writing tradition was still relatively rough-hewn and undeveloped, and American journalist-literary figures had not yet begun to have much impact upon the field of novel-writing. (James Fenimore Cooper is the only American novelist born in the eighteenth century who has been included in *The Harper American Literature*; Nathaniel Hawthorne and Herman Melville, both born in the early nineteenth century, would not become influential until the publication of their major fictional works around and after 1850.) The major American contribution to the literary world in this period was by the non-fiction writers of the American transcendentalist movement, such as Ralph Waldo Emerson, Henry David Thoreau, and Margaret Fuller, as well as in poetry where a number of journalist-literary figures – including Philip Freneau, William Cullen Bryant, John Greenleaf Whittier, and Walt Whitman – had backgrounds in journalism while they also made their names as verse writers. However, the British influence upon the handful of American journalist-literary figures of this period was important, and Washington Irving and Edgar Allan Poe both strongly believed in the need to elevate the tone of American letters (while re-packaging American folk tales and creating local color sketches, Irving traveled widely in Europe, meeting famous literary figures and writing travel literature; the short-story writer Poe was highly envious of the UK's literary magazines and lived much of his professional life hoping to import their savagely witty and irreverent spirit to the American periodical journalism field).[5]

In a milieu where public discussion of literature was still of great importance and literary celebrities were among those with great name recognition, it was only natural that the tension between private artistic vision and the demands of the marketplace would become a preoccupation of artists, critics, and even the public itself. Dickens' gift in combining critical with commercial success was seen as the height of artistic accomplishment in an era where the capacity to maximize one's talents and integrate them into the growing reach of the mass communication industry was becoming the key to literary success. Dickens' career took off soon after the invention of the steam-powered printing press had made it possible for printers and publishers to produce cheap, mass-market publications designed to appeal to large audiences and to make their profits based on economies of scale. Along with the appearance of mass-market magazines and specialty periodicals, these new ventures in publishing ushered in a period of steady industrialization of the media marketplace where commercial imperatives, artistic innovation, and a growing public appetite for information and entertainment combined into a new formula that gave the word "best-seller" its earliest modern meaning.

This was also the period in which the contemporary distinctions that are drawn between the practice of journalism and the production of written art and literature began to take clear shape, and increasingly people saw literature as something distinct from what was produced in the news columns of the newspapers of the day. When Dickens and Thackeray were working for them, the typical early Victorian newspaper was a fairly hum-drum product, written in haste through the use of repetitive news formulas by reporters who saw themselves as little more than journeyman wordsmiths imparting information to a mass public. Although the British literary magazines of this era attempted to meld popular writing forms and commercial goals with elements of high art, the term "journalism" became increasingly associated with the industrialized newspapers, which had become relentlessly factual, with little analysis or interpretation, where graceful writing had been replaced by utilitarian recitations of official information and statistics.[6] Dickens' and Thackeray's serialized novels – many of which ran in magazines that they had founded and edited – provided a brief historical platform when high-quality novel-writing flourished as a product of mass periodical production. However, the growing place of the "serious" novel as an extension of the "high" artistic world and the role of newspapers, periodicals, and popular romance and adventure books in meeting the "low-" and "middle-brow" tastes of a commercialized marketplace was becoming a fixed idea in the mindset of critics, scholars, and even many of the journalist-literary figures themselves.

What came to be seen as the distinctive journalism of this period was often showcased in a plethora of clever, high-quality literary periodicals – the *Edinburgh Review*, *Blackwood's*, *Fraser's*, *London Magazine*, *Punch*, *Westminster Review*, London *Examiner* – that were widely read and wielded influence not only over the world of British letters, but of those of politics, commerce, and cultural life. Across the Atlantic, Poe was an avid reader of these British magazines while working for a series of less discriminating American ones. Poe hankered to bring the tradition of the British literary periodical – with its saucy and acerbic prose, its intelligent but often stinging reviews, and its carefully calculated marketplace strategies – to the American scene. But as Poe learned through a series of ill-fated publishing ventures (as well as the considerable hostility generated by his slashing, take-no-prisoners reviewing style), the American audience was not particularly receptive to the high-toned and sword-clashing cultural and literary discussion of the British magazines. It is worth noting that Poe – who is acclaimed today as a master of the short-story mystery/macabre-thriller genre and a ground-breaker in the development of the detective story – was seen in his time largely as a literary critic (and a vituperative one at that), and that his greatest ambition and his deepest disappointment revolved around a magazine (the "Stylus", as he wanted to call it) which he never got off the ground. Poe's longing to fuse his literary ideals with commercial and artistic success was shared by poet-journalist Samuel Taylor Coleridge (like Poe, he also pined to make a success of a literary magazine) who proclaimed the literary magazine of his day "an unprecedented phenomenon in the world of letters (that) forms the golden – alas! the only – remaining link between the Periodical Press and the enduring literature of Great Britain."[7]

It is an important commentary upon the evolution of journalism and
fiction-writing in the UK and the US to recognize how Dickens and
Thackeray used periodical journalism to straddle the divide between art
and commerce and became beloved celebrity figures across all social and
economic lines. Both writers shrewdly recognized how in this new publishing
environment, the movement between journalism and fiction-writing was a
ticket to celebrity and riches. In fact, the management of one's career as an
author could be a business in itself – and, as revered public figures, Dickens
and Thackeray occupied the superstar status that we today confer upon
high-salaried rock musicians, athletes, and movie stars. While they were
at the height of their literary fame, Dickens and Thackeray founded magazines (*Household Words* and *All Year Round* by Dickens, the *Cornhill* by
Thackeray), expended considerable energy editing them while also producing serialized fiction for their pages, and reaped major financial rewards in the
process. In exploiting the role of fame in the new mass marketplace to make
themselves enormously important public figures in Victorian England,
Dickens and Thackeray established the standard for career promotion in a
commercialized mass media marketplace, and their practices were imitated
by Mark Twain, Bret Harte, Stephen Crane, Jack London, and others.

The link between the periodical-writing tradition and the emergence of
the novel as an artistic force can be seen at the British humor magazine,
Punch, whose hard-edged political satire and reform sympathies set the tone
for British political comic journalism up to contemporary times. Founded in
1841, the magazine was run by a trio of British journalist-literary figures,
Mark Lemon, Douglas Jerrold, and Henry Mayhew, who are not widely
known in their own right but who played important roles in the careers of
Dickens and Thackeray. Lemon was a close personal friend of Dickens;
Jerrold, as did Lemon, worked for a time on the newspaper, the London
Daily News, that Dickens founded and briefly ran from 1845 to 1846.
Thackeray found at *Punch* a working environment that allowed him to
ascend from his role as a peripatetic, journeyman journalist to a major figure
on the British literary scene. Thackeray's satirical journalism – most notably
The Book of Snobs, which grew out of a series of contributions to *Punch*, "The
Snobs of England" – is considered foundational in the development of
his serialized novels, particularly *Vanity Fair*, with its accounts of the tattered
gentry operating upon the margins of British high society, and *Pendennis*,
The Newcomes, and *The Adventures of Philip*, which parody the world of
London periodical writers.

In the highly commercialized publishing environment of the early to mid-
nineteenth century, journalism not only played a key role in the training of

the journalist-literary figures as writers, but it also provided the backdrop for their fiction. With the genre of the novel coming to full flower in the Victorian era, fiction-writing was also being shaped by many of the forces – artistic, commercial, and technological – that were transforming public attitudes about literature and altering the role that journalism played in the production of high art. Critics, for example, have argued that Dickens' serial production of many of his novels had a major impact on the structure and execution of his work and helped to shape public expectations about fiction, as well as writers' views of how to appeal to the public. Thackeray was the first novelist in English to make the world of mass publication a setting for his fiction. Thackeray filled his novels with characters who worked for, or were associated with, newspapers, magazines, or arts journals, and he was acutely conscious of what the expansion of the media industry and the commercialization of literature meant for the artist and the journalist.[8] Dickens also caricatured journalists and the press in his novel, *Martin Chuzzlewit*, and he complained vociferously about the intrusive and sensationalistic habits of newspapers – and American newspapers, in particular – in his account of his first visit to the US, *American Notes for General Circulation*. Poe (who had a fascination with Dickens and tried to ape Dickens' path to marketplace success) borrowed from newspaper stories for plots and story-lines in his short stories, and his detective-protagonists prided themselves on solving crimes that the newspapers and the police couldn't. William Dean Howells picked up Thackeray's strategy and also set a series of his novels, including *A Modern Instance, A Hazard of New Fortunes*, and *The Quality of Mercy*, inside the commercial publishing world that Howells (like Thackeray) watched with growing concern as it subsumed many aspects of artistic culture into the mass marketplace.

Inevitably, this state of affairs had a class dimension in a time of enormous economic and cultural dislocations and new patterns of social mobility. As happened with the transition of the party press to the Penny Press system of publishing in the US, the coming of the steam-powered printing press in England led to the phasing out of the partisan-subsidized model for publishing in Defoe's, Swift's, and Fielding's era and the replacement with a commercial model. A socially connected poet, such as William Wordsworth or Lord Byron in England, or a New England literary "Brahmin," such as an Emerson and Henry Wadsworth Longfellow, still stood aloof from the increasingly commercial taint of the industrializing publishing industry. But many of the successful journalist-literary figures of this era lacked the genteel background that had traditionally been associated with the literature of high learning and high social status. Thackeray found himself sometimes pleased and sometimes vexed to be associated with the sidewalk intellectuals and precocious commoners – expatriate Irishmen, cockney upstarts, and university drop-outs – who filled periodical staffs in the UK of that era. These native wits and self-schooled scholars moved freely back and forth between jobs on the more conventional journalistic publications and the literary periodicals that based their market success upon framing the controversies of arts and letters in a manner that intrigued and entertained both a popular and an elite audience. As a gentleman who had lost his family legacy and was forced to mingle with some distinctly non-gentleman types in his periodical jobs, Thackeray was acutely aware of the melding of the social divisions. Most of Thackeray's early works are credited to aliases, and it was not until the early 1840s that he felt confident enough to emerge from the shadows of the faintly disreputable environment of periodical writing and to publish a serialized book under his own name.[9]

Dickens and Thackeray, too, continued in their rivalry a cultural dynamic that was reshaping the face of English society and the world of literature. Like Defoe, a dissenting Protestant who was born into the newly emergent small business and trading classes, Dickens' struggling, middle- to lower-middle-class background put him on the side of the forces in English life that were emphasizing capitalist opportunity, an up-by-the-bootstraps view of life, and democratic values at the expense of aristocratic tradition and the settled ways of the ruling establishment. Dickens was the first major celebrity figure to be created out of the merging of art and journalism that came to alter the public consciousness in the early Victorian period. Dickens' feat – he was a hugely popular best-selling author, a veritable literary phenomenon whose exalted public image put him on a pedestal nearly equivalent to the Queen's but who also was embraced by most of the critical community of his time – was largely the product of the new organs of mass communication that were transforming society. Dickens was a literary ground-breaker in a number of ways – he was the first highly successful serialized novelist, the first novelist to probe the injustices of the Industrial Age and to use reform themes as the overt basis of his plots, and the first novelist to build a reputation of great respectability and social status from his popular literary success. Although the model of the novel was there before him in the writings of Defoe, Fielding, and Smollett, Dickens fixed it in the popular consciousness in a manner that had never been done before. Dickens waded into social and political controversy with the full belief that the themes in novels could change people's hearts and alter political circumstances. His plots involving poverty, economic deprivation, and class brutality were packaged within dramatic devices to manipulate emotion and draw upon traditional views of good and evil that were the mainstay of newspaper journalism. This made Dickens' works acceptable in Victorian drawing rooms despite their frequently critical (and often highly caricatured) view of established authority, and his popularity in upper-class households ultimately left Dickens himself so concerned about his public stature that he began to back away from the more radical elements of his political philosophy.

Of the many parallel features to their careers, Dickens and Thackeray shared one that added to their bank accounts but came at a high personal cost: they both continued to slog away in the periodical trenches even at the height of their fictional success. In particular, Dickens felt the demands of journalistic deadlines and editorial tasks pressing upon him throughout his prolific writing career and compounding the burden upon a fragile nervous system. Dickens dealt with the pressures – the editorship of two magazines, the production of much of the journalism in the publications, all the while writing many of his novels as magazine serials on deadline – with enthusiasm and energy until he died of heart disease, complicated by anxiety, depression, and other ailments, at the relatively young age of fifty-eight. Dickens' driving ambition, his need for money, and his sense of his role as the towering figure of Victorian literature gave him a prodigious capacity for work. When Thackeray embarked on his own magazine venture in 1860 with the founding of the *Cornhill*, he clearly hoped to emulate Dickens' success, although as a forty-nine-year-old established author, with a much less driven temperament and having spent many years removed from the nitty-gritty responsibility for editorial tasks, it was to be expected that his role would be as something of a figurehead editor whose worn-out body never allowed him to recapture the journalistic zest of an earlier day.[10]

The specter of Dickens' workaholic life and Thackeray's vain efforts to rediscover his journalistic youth was not a spur to all their journalist-literary figure colleagues, and a number spurned the easy money that was available in writing for the periodical industry. Few other artists openly criticized Dickens or Thackeray for capitalizing upon their marketability in the periodical world, and their magazines were largely admired as graceful products with thoughtful and at times provocative journalism packaged around their serial literature. But there was an undercurrent of disdain, particularly from fellow authors whose pretensions still leaned toward the image of literature as lofty and above the masses. When Eliot demurred from producing her novels for serial publication – despite strong inducements from Dickens and others to do so – she wrote:

Do you see how the publishing world is going mad on periodicals? If I could be seduced by such offers, I might have written three poor novels and made my fortune in one year. Happily I have no need to exert myself when I say, "Avoid thee, Satan!" Satan, in the form of bad writing and good pay is not seductive to me.[11]

Others, such as Poe, were forever torn – and Poe's literature, half high-brow in intent, half imitative of hackneyed conventions, reflected his dual-mindedness and was redeemed only by his brilliance in raising popular art forms to masterful levels. The issue of what today would be called "popular-izing" obsessed him throughout his career. Poe clearly adapted his short story style and content to make it more palatable to editors and attractive to popular audiences. To do this, he drew on the Gothic traditions of tradi-tional sentimental and romance writing; he recognized the appealing fea-tures of clichéd magazine formulas and shaped them to his talents; and he knew the attraction that horror and mystery stories held in the folk tale tradition. As a critic, however, he was stinging in his treatment of those he viewed as producing a compromised form of literature that appealed to the great, untutored public. He felt, for example, that it was a "grievous wrong" for Dickens to cater to popular judgment. However, Poe's jealousness of artists who had attained financial success was palpable in much of his criticism, and his ambivalence about his own efforts to do the same thing can make much of his criticism seem less than dispassionate today. Poe preferred to maintain the idea of himself as a "conspiratorial" mass-journalist. "What can I care for the judgment of a multitude, every individual of which I despise," Poe once said. But he was deeply conflicted on the question of popularity and success and also wrote: "I love fame – I dote on it – I idolize it – I would drink to the very dregs of the glorious intoxication ... No man lives, unless he is famous! How bitterly I belied my nature, and my aspirations, when I said I did not desire fame, and that I despised it."[12]

This theme – the brilliant artist bruised by the forces of commercialism and wasting away amid compromised circumstances and philistine public tastes – fed the preoccupations of the emerging romantic movement of the period and became something of an archetype within romanticism itself. Coleridge, for example, was both mocked and pitied for the way that he projected his romantic broodings into his quest for journalistic success. Like Poe, Coleridge lived much of his life as a struggling artist, debt-ridden and harried by the needs of a large family; like Poe he saw himself as a voice for a cultured elite trying to win a place in the organs of popular journalism; like Poe he was ridiculed for his elitist views of the literary arts while failing to find popularity in a journalistic medium; like Poe he was emotionally unstable and addicted (Poe to alcohol, Coleridge to opium). And like Poe he hankered after journalistic and financial success throughout his life, even as his artist's idiosyncrasies and an obscurantist prose style made him largely unfit for the journalist's profession. In typically romantic fashion, Coleridge invested his experiences in journalism with a glow of hopefulness and imagined possibilities, and he thought of periodical success as confirmation of his self-worth as a communicator of great, literary ideas. (When his first journalistic venture, the *Watchman*, folded after only six months of life, he wrote: "O Watchman! Thou hast watched in vain, said the prophet Ezekiel, when I suppose, he was taking a prophetic glimpse of my sorrow-sallowed cheeks." One reader – almost certainly unaware of the historical irony – wrote to the *Watchman*: "Sir, I detest your principles, your prose I think very so-so. But your poetry is so exquisitely beautiful, so gorgeously sublime, that I take your *Watchman* solely on account of it.")[13]

DEFOE, SWIFT, AND FICTION AS "FACTS"

Although Defoe and his cohorts have come to be seen by many as the founders of the novel-writing tradition in English, they weren't the first persons to market artful and invented tales to an audience with a growing appetite for being entertained by the new products of the printing press. Romance novels (mostly translated from French), accounts of voyagers and adventurers, and crude biographies and journals abounded in the England of Defoe's time, and he borrowed from those forms in the creation of his novels. And yet, the ingredients that Defoe built his imaginative writing upon were the prose techniques that he had practiced and perfected while working as a journalist. The elements in Defoe's fiction that are admired today – the flowing, readable prose, the real-life circumstances of his characters and their pragmatic approach to meeting life's challenges, his understanding of how things (such as machinery, crops, navigation) work, the gritty circumstances of his characters' backgrounds and his focus upon the challenges that average people face in their struggle to survive – can be found in the material of journalism he practiced in an age when the boundaries between journalism and fiction, fact and fancy, were less distinguishable than they are today.[14]

For example, Defoe's *A Journal of the Plague Year*, which was narrated by a fictionalized "survivor" of the bubonic plague year of 1665 that wiped out 70,000 people in England, was based on a piece of book-length journalism, *Due Preparations for the Plague*, that Defoe wrote in 1722 to warn contemporary England of a possible reoccurrence of the plague. Defoe dug into the records of the 1665 plague – or the "bills of mortality," as they were known – that had been put together by witnesses and were kept in the municipal archives. Although he clearly saw the dramatic benefits of fictionalizing his account, much of the book was filled with practical advice about how to survive a plague (the cause of which was still then unknown), such as the way to disinfect a house, the food needed if one's house was quarantined, and material about how the plague affected foreign and domestic trade. (Defoe's warnings, it turned out, were needless – the plague was dying out on the continent and in England – and only an occasional flare-up occurred after the early eighteenth century.)[15]

It is fascinating to realize how in the eighteenth century, many people wanted more "truth" in the novel, and that Defoe and his fellow "novelists" felt bound to defend their imaginative writing as something more than mere fiction. Many eighteenth-century English people were fed up with romances and looked to the novel to inject actuality into reading material. Defoe, Fielding, and Smollett all advertised themselves as "realists" who used nature as their guide in the sense that they built their books around recognizable personality types, authentic events, and real places. Fielding, for example, called himself a periodical essayist rather than a journalist. In fact, the *Champion*, the periodical where Fielding first worked, looked more like a launching pad for his fiction – with its use of irony, drama, narrative, parody, invective, literary discussion, and classical allusion – than the spare, facts-oriented, information-based newspaper of today. Johnson, who had a special loathing for works of romance (as well as a deeply skeptical view of the popularly-oriented periodicals of his day), also recognized the capacity for fiction-writing to convey a greater truthfulness about life than other forms of writing in his time, and his own didactic *The History of Rasselas* has some elements of the novel in it. (As a critic, however, Johnson's favorite among this new breed of fiction writer was Richardson; Johnson recognized the importance of Richardson's subtle development of psychological character in his heroines and their verisimilitude with real life human complexity.)[16]

In blending the factual with the imagined to give the text a "you are there" feeling that transcends a simple journalistic account, Defoe let his instincts guide him in the creation of a new art form. He commonly followed the practice of the "new journalists" of today: he researched his material so it was based (at least, loosely) in fact, he used characterizations of real-life people, places, and events as models for his literature, and he imaginatively embellished the material for dramatic effect and audience appeal. The success of Defoe's "novels" was built upon the same techniques that led to marketplace success in the journalism of his day, including:

– writing simply
– appealing to a wide audience of a variety of levels of literacy and education
– developing a strong narrative

– using average people and their life circumstances as the setting for the story
– cultivating a personal bond between writer and reader
– not letting ornate style or rhetorical flourishes divert the story line or blur communication with the audience
– not worrying about crossing the line into fiction, but using as much realistic material as possible to keep the story vivid and engrossing
– producing characters and tales of such believability that the audience can't tell, or won't worry about, whether the author is disguising or inventing or obscuring facts and details in order to advance the story
– hoping to make money by selling and marketing the literary product to as wide a base of customers as possible
– using one's reputation and celebrity status as a promotional device.

When Defoe was writing, he didn't really think he was inventing a new art form. Effectively barred from politics and business because of his financial misdealings and questionable political alliances and looked down on by many of his contemporaries, it was perhaps the obvious next step for Defoe to find refuge in writing so-called "autobiographical" accounts of shipwrecked mariners, criminals, and vagabond characters.[17] In Defoe's literature, his irreverence mixed with deep religious belief, his tolerant (and even sympathetic) portrayal of immorality, his support of women and their push for independence, his progressivism and reform instincts, and his admiration for the underdog with the personal courage to buck the system set the tone not only for future novelists, but particularly those future novelists who, like Defoe, would come out of a journalistic background.

Both as a novelist and during his more than thirty years as a journalist, Defoe was staggeringly prolific. As the editor of the *Review*, one of the best-read of the early London newspapers in the decades immediately following the removal of censorship from the British press, Defoe produced over 5,000 pages of the newspaper, most of which he penned himself. The *Review* was written in easy-to-grasp, straightforward language that appealed to a non-elite, non-classically educated audience, and its support of the "getting and spending" of trade and commerce led it to be held in suspicion by the aristocratic and gentry classes. In fact, Defoe always believed it was faintly disgraceful to be engaged in fictional story-telling – at least, when compared to what he felt was the more honorable profession of journalism. In a milieu of partisan rhetoric masquerading as fact, it was commonplace in the eighteenth century for political benefactors to support major political newspapers, even though the editors of those publications rarely publicly advertised the fact. Although a Whig,

Defoe offered himself and his newspaper in service to the ministry of parliamentary leader Robert Harley (Lord Oxford), a one-time Whig who had become a Tory, during the early decades of the eighteenth century. Harley employed Defoe in a number of clandestine tasks, including traveling as a spy throughout Scotland to help defuse resistance to the merger of Scotland and England and using the *Review* to defend Tory policies to a largely Whig audience (Defoe, for example, publicly lied about receiving money from Harley).[18]

In his novels, Defoe was well prepared to mix fact with fancy because his journalism had been so filled with deceit pretending to be truth. English law on libel and off-and-on government moves to restore censorship left Defoe and his contemporaries hoping to avoid detection by cloaking their polemics in the form of satire, allegory, or circumlocution. Few citizens of eighteenth-century England looked to newspapers for a balanced perspective or dispassionate discussion of the issues. Newspaper accounts of Defoe's period were usually written anonymously, the subjects of articles were often given made-up names or invented characteristics, and elements of articles could be editorially inspired. However, the astute reader often had little trouble recognizing who and what an article was about and who had written it, and the authorities were seldom diverted by these techniques from incarcerating writers or prosecuting lawsuits for libel or slander. As a result, Defoe and his fellow journalists would protest, often in pro forma fashion, that their journalism was true and yet still find themselves jailed for their written improprieties (as both Defoe and Smollett were). In this environment, it was only one small step further for writers to make the same claim for their novels (which, in a sense, were often truer than their journalism, in that they didn't rest upon outright falsehoods). For a journalist such as Defoe, the novel – with its imagined characters based upon real people and its settings that closely resembled real places – was simply another form for disguising slightly the otherwise fully recognizable characteristics of the real world.[19]

In different ways, Defoe signaled to his readers that the lives of Crusoe, the shipwrecked slave trader who discovered a new, fortified inner self while marooned on an uninhabited island for thirty-five years, or Moll Flanders, the opportunistic heroine who dallied her way through the landscape of eighteenth-century life, or Roxana, the jilted housewife who abandoned all moral scruple to rise in the world, were meant to be believed as if they were real stories about real people. The big city, in particular, aroused great curiosity, and people were fascinated by the vast spectacle of humankind to be found there – including those who lived by principles that weren't advocated in the pew or acknowledged in the drawing room. Accounts of criminal tales – whether editorially inspired confessions, fabricated autobiographies, or other dramatizations – in the publications of the eighteenth century help to explain how the rogue, the thief, and the outsider became such grist for the early fiction of Defoe and Fielding and others. For example, Defoe's time in Newgate prison has led to speculation that he based Moll Flanders and Roxana on characters that he met there. The fact that both Defoe and Fielding wrote "lives" of Jonathan Wild, the notorious "scourge" of the London gangs, who was made into a Robin Hood-style legend in the sensationalized newspaper accounts of the time, is interesting for the claims made by the two authors – Defoe insisted that his account was "true" and verifiable, while Fielding made no effort to present the material as anything other than imaginatively inspired and invented.[20]

Robinson Crusoe is the best example of how Defoe blended a story based loosely on a real event and then expanded it into a ground-breaking piece of literature. Historians have speculated that Defoe got the idea for the novel from accounts of a Scottish sailor named Alexander Selkirk who was marooned for five years on a deserted island, and whose story was recounted in the press of Defoe's time. As he did in so many of his fictional works, Defoe claimed *Robinson Crusoe* was an authentic account. But even in his day, Defoe's assertion as to the factuality of *Robinson Crusoe* was roundly challenged (one critic chastised Defoe for claiming that his "telling a lie will make it truth"), and Defoe soon altered his story: he argued that *Robinson Crusoe* was really an allegory and that the "truth" was a moral and spiritual one. This contention fit with the medieval view that spiritual truths took precedent over empirical ones. But it didn't go over well in his era, when Enlightenment values had already begun to elevate scientific empiricism above religious justifications. In the end, Defoe altered his explanation once more: his characters, he claimed, were always based on some kind of actuality and his fiction was a form of truth, if not absolutely faithful to reality.[21]

There are other links between Defoe's fiction and the journalistic milieu from which it emerged. Many eighteenth-century English newspapers contained short stories or narrative accounts in serialized form (thus *Robinson Crusoe* was reprinted in a number of regular periodicals). The early novel, like the early newspaper, encouraged a rapid, inattentive, almost unconscious kind of reading habit, and speed and copiousness in writing were rewarded in the production of reading material for the expanding numbers of average people beginning to enjoy the benefits of literacy. As both a merchant and journalist (he was involved in trade ventures, owned a brick factory that went broke, and engaged in other entrepreneurial activities), Defoe preferred a clear tongue and the speech of artisans and trades people over scholarly language, and his Puritan plain speech sensibilities made him suspicious of ornate prose. Verbal sophistication, complication of structure, rhetorical methods of argument and exposition all took time and revision, and Defoe generally wasn't interested. Evidence suggests that Defoe didn't plan his novels but worked piece-meal, very rapidly, with an eye toward a large output. (There are indications that Defoe would revise only if extra remuneration was involved.) He once said, "I shall be caviled at about my mean style, rough verse, and incorrect language, things I indeed might have taken more care in." Defoe's prose contains a higher proportion of short, descriptive Anglo-Saxon words and many fewer of Latin origin than most of his writing contemporaries. In this, Defoe's novels mimicked his journalism, where in the *Review* he told readers he had "chosen a down-right plainness" because it was "more generally instructing and clear to the understanding of the people I am speaking to."[22]

The literary rivalry of Defoe and Swift during their journalism careers illustrates the social transformations that were both reflected in and catalyzed by the commercial press – and the cutting-edge role that the journalist-literary figures have played in advancing controversy and change. At every level, Defoe and Swift, despite their dislike of each other, were pioneering thinkers, rabble-rousers, and controversialists. Politically, Defoe was a liberal and a progressive for his era – and his treatises on institutional reform (advocating for proposals that can be seen as precursors to such modern concepts as the inheritance tax, universal health care and education, and government support for the poor and the elderly) and his attacks upon legal provisions that limited the political rights of Protestants who dissented from the Church of England were major advances in eighteenth-century political thinking. In cultural terms, Defoe also was a pioneer. His open-minded and tolerant attitudes toward human transgression and his sympathy for the struggles of common people modified his fundamentally Puritan moral outlook and modernized and humanized it to fit with the fast-paced changes brought about by commercial expansion and democratic challenges to the aristocratic order.

Swift, on the other hand, was a cynic, a determined careerist, and an Anglican clergyman who defended the privileges of the high church, the prerogatives of the landed gentry, and the policies of the party that most effectively flattered him and made him feel socially important. However, Swift also advocated for his political principles in ways that were innovative in their use of satire and avant-garde literary techniques. His *Tale of a Tub* and *Gulliver's Travels* are viewed as sophisticated political parody, sly cultural innuendo, and risk-taking literary experimentation for a period still emerging from medieval attitudes about art and writing. Swift was an envelope pusher, too, in his use of ribald and imaginative devices for working his stories at multiple levels – such as in *Gulliver's Travels*, which can be read as a children's story, spiritual allegory, political satire, or a simple adventure story. Even today, the rivalry between Defoe and Swift is reflected in the two branches of literature that can be identified with each. Defoe is often hailed as the storytelling father figure of popular literature – a writer who incorporated the fluent and plain-speaking elements of journalism with narrative techniques he borrowed from other popular writing sources to forge a new fictional literary genre that captured popular attention. Swift, the allusionist, the mocker of things sacred, and the lover of layered meanings, is a favorite of the academic and the scholarly world, where his writings can be parsed, deconstructed, and scoured for hidden messages.

When compared to his rival, Swift, Defoe was only a moderately kept man. When Swift went to work in service to Harley in 1711 and took over the editing of the Tory propagandizing *Examiner*, he joined Defoe on Harley's payroll. Harley's craftiness in luring these two antagonistic personalities to work in the same cause is a credit to how well he understood the wellsprings of human personality, and how much he had come to recognize the importance of newspaper support in winning over public opinion in the liberalized political environment of early eighteenth-century England. In editing the *Examiner*, Swift's technique was to proclaim himself an unbiased observer free of party affiliation and obligations, but his purpose was always to advance Tory causes. The vehemence of Swift's propagandizing and his willingness to use slander, while privately admitting that he didn't believe everything he wrote, reveals a cynicism that is rivaled – interestingly – in the cynical outlook that he expresses toward human behavior in *Gulliver's Travels*. At the same time, Swift's willingness in the *Examiner* to use character assassination and innuendo in advancing his case set the tone for the often scurrilous party polemics that came to dominate elements of early English and American journalism. For example, when Swift set out to discredit the Duke of Marlborough (John Churchill), the leader of the British forces in France, as part of the Tory's campaign to end the War of the Spanish Succession, he did it with a rhetorical dagger, attacking Marlborough as avaricious, cowardly, and without personal character. But after belittling Marlborough's military record in print and accusing him of prolonging the war to enrich himself, Swift wrote to his close woman friend (Stella) in private correspondence:

"I think our friends press a little too hard on the duke of Marlborough …
I question whether ever any wise state laid aside a general who had been
successful nine years together." Later he said to Stella about a pamphlet he
had written about Thomas Wharton, the lord lieutenant of Ireland: "Here's a
damned libelous pamphlet come out against lord Wharton, giving the
character first, and then telling some of his actions: the character is very
well, but the facts indifferent."[23]

In their different ways, Defoe and Swift found the gray area between fact
and fiction a useful place to make their points and to accomplish their
purposes, even if Defoe wasn't as accomplished as Swift in the practice of
it. It might be going too far to call the development of the literary techniques
that Swift pioneered in *Gulliver's Travels* a direct result of the dangerous
circumstances in which he wrote, but one can certainly find in his journalism
and his fiction the use of anonymity, parody, invented narratives, cloaked
meanings, hidden digs, and code words directed at those in the know that
were commonplace techniques among the newspaper editors of the era. Swift
was clearly a master at avoiding facing the repercussions of his vinegar wit. It
has been noted, for example, that Defoe's clumsy use of irony contributed to
the first of his two jailings. In a pamphlet, "The Shortest Way with
Dissenters," Defoe parodied a bill pending in Parliament that attempted to
abolish the use of "occasional conformity" (a practice which permitted
dissenters to hold office if they were willing to take communion in the
Church of England) by arguing that dissenters should be banished and
their preachers hanged. Once he was identified as the author, and the
pamphlet to be a hoax, Defoe's enemies chose to interpret his words literally,
and he was jailed in Newgate prison and sentenced to stand in the pillory.
Swift, on the other hand, succeeded in deflecting repercussions for his
subversive tract, "A Modest Proposal for preventing the Children of poor
People in Ireland from being a burden to their parents or country," by
signaling in the title and other places that this was satire, and that one should
not take literally his call for fattening up the children to be eaten.[24]

It is perhaps no surprise that the two men expressed a loathing for each
other in print. Power was passing from Swift's aristocratic and conservative
class into the middle-class trading ranks that Defoe represented. In the
Examiner, Swift called Defoe a "stupid, illiterate scribbler" and a "fanatick
by profession" and referred to his "dirty hands" and his "being of a level with
great numbers among the lowest part of mankind." Defoe thundered back in
the *Review* by saying, "nothing can render a Gentleman so Contemptible …
as to lose his Breeding" and labeling Swift a "Cynick in Behaviour, a Fury in
Temper, Unpolite in Conversation, Abusive and Scurrilous in Language, and

Ungovernable in Passion." (There is no evidence that the exchange of insults was the result of a personal feud or quarrel – most scholars believe the two never met – and both men almost certainly understood the eighteenth-century art of name-calling and would have recognized that what they wrote about each other was hardly excessive for the age.)[25]

However, their journalistic exchange was only a prelude to the way Defoe and Swift have been twinned in the annals of literary critical history. Critics have noted that despite the vast differences in their political outlooks they share many characteristics, and their two major books, *Robinson Crusoe* and *Gulliver's Travels*, have come down from the eighteenth century as linked companions. Defoe is remembered for a realism in his fiction that came easily to a journalist used to dealing in facts and figures; Swift for his satire which he honed in his arch commentary about his political enemies in the *Examiner* and then turned into allegorical accounts that were used to pantomine and satirize his opponents. *Robinson Crusoe*, as well as *Moll Flanders* and *Roxana* (earthy, real-life variations upon the Puritan journals and the popular romance novels of the time), had aspects of the travelogue (many of which Defoe had read), the pirate tale (in which Defoe also made his mark), the personal journal (Crusoe's introspections and his religious musings), the news account (for example, in the instances when Crusoe fights off the invaders of his island), and the character sketch (his descriptions of his man, Friday), all built around suspense (will Crusoe be rescued? Will Moll and Roxana survive the ups and downs of their vagabond lives?) and recurrent adventures and plot twists. Swift moved farther away from traditional journalism in *Gulliver's Travels* by letting his imagination roam even more wildly, and he can be seen as one of the pioneering figures of fanciful serious literature (or what some might call "experimental" or "absurdist" writing). However, the journalistic elements of Swift's fiction were still evident – in his clear, discursive writing style, in his use of indirect techniques for jabbing his political enemies, and in his employment of the devices of parody and prose parrying so popular in the newspapers of the day.[26]

FIELDING, SMOLLETT, GOLDSMITH AND THE DEFINITION OF THE NOVEL

Of all the eighteenth-century journalist-novelists, it was Fielding who was most conscious of what he was doing in developing the novel and who most acutely understood the coming dichotomy between journalism as an organ of "truth" (which could produce great falseness) and fiction as a medium of fancy (which could tell important truths that journalism did not). Fielding had tenuous claims to social status – his father was a socially connected soldier who became a chronic debtor, his mother was from a wealthy family but with no right of inheritance; he himself attended Eton but dropped out of the University of Leyden when his funds ran out, and he soon was forced to rely on his wits to make his way in the world. Working as a playwright in London until the government censored his bawdy performances that aimed their parody at those in political power, Fielding took his satirical tools into journalism and wrote for a series of partisan newspapers – most notably the *Champion*, which he edited from 1739 to 1740 – that launched scathing and sometimes scurrilous attacks upon a myriad of political figures that Fielding viewed as corrupt (or, more to the point, that opposed the politicians who were paying Fielding and supporting his publications). Although a version of a "reform" Whig (or a broad-bottom, as his faction was known), Fielding had a vacillating career in the volatile world of partisan eighteenth-century publications, bitterly attacking Whig Prime Minister Robert Walpole, then defending Walpole's allies and successors, and then shifting again when different patrons put him on their payroll. Fielding's work as a loyal partisan journalist was ultimately rewarded with an appointment to the bench, and he spent his last years as a well-regarded magistrate hearing court cases and dispensing remarkably even-handed justice for the time.[27]

In 1741, Fielding began penning novels, beginning with his first serious ventures – *Joseph Andrews* and *Tom Jones* – that specialized in the creation of comic rogues whose adventures sprawled across the English countryside. Fielding had a conscious sense that he was doing something new in the world of arts (in *Tom Jones*, he calls his narrative a "new province of writing" and delineates in explicit fashion what he felt distinguished his form of story telling from the "indecent" and "nastily derived" novels and romances of his time; in *Joseph Andrews* he called what he was doing "a species of writing … hitherto unattempted in our language"). Unlike Defoe, Fielding did not pretend that his stories were true or factual, and he did little factual research for his novels. Fielding often presented himself as the voice of the author in the role of an observer and commentator and openly remarked upon the fictional material in his prose. Fielding appeared to be carefully distinguishing his fictional work from both the journalism of his day and the kind of novels that Defoe had written. Fielding complained that "novels of plain matter of fact must overpower every reader" and that they amounted to little more than a "newspaper of many volumes."[28]

To see Fielding's fiction as connected to, and even an outgrowth of, his political journalism would not be going too far, and the years he spent perfecting his style as an essayist, polemicist, and moral critic helped pave the way for the authorial voice of his novels. In his journalism, Fielding's inconsistencies – heaping abuse upon Walpole and then siding with Walpole and his successors – have often been blamed on the patronage system that led first the anti-Walpole faction, then the successors of Walpole, to support Fielding's publications. But his newspaper work played a clear role in the development of Fielding's literary vision, and he saw his novels, his plays, and his anonymously written political journalism as seamlessly linked. While Defoe's novels contain little direct political material, Fielding's do. Fielding's Jacobite characters always appear to be foolish and his anti-Jacobite characters admirable (as a "reform" Whig, Fielding reserved his greatest loathing for those who hoped to return the Catholic-sympathizing Stuart dynasty to the English throne). *Tom Jones* is not primarily a political novel – but the anti-Jacobite bias in the creation of characters (particularly the unflattering portrait of the Jacobite Squire Western) are clear throughout its pages. Critics have focused upon the "striking" resemblances between the political material in the novel and the mocking satire in two of Fielding's newspapers, the *True Patriot* and the *Jacobite's Journal*, which were founded in 1745 and 1747 respectively. They have even speculated that Fielding included topical accounts of the Jacobite Rebellion of 1745 and portrayed the events in the way that he did in his novels in order to correct the record of the time. Given Fielding's complaint about novels of "plain fact," it is ironic that Richardson, for example, criticized Fielding's novels for being too "verisimilitudinous" to life (Fielding, in turn, wrote his own tongue-in-cheek knock-off of Richardson's novel, *Pamela*, called *Shamela*).[29]

Fielding's novels, like Defoe's, were often considered to be "low" works, lacking in necessary moral lessons and presenting themselves as little more than scandalous endorsements of a libertine morality. Johnson, for example, once wrote to a lady friend that he was "shocked to hear you quote from so vicious a book" as *Tom Jones*. "I am sorry to hear you have read it; a confession which no modest lady should ever make." It was this kind of criticism that led Fielding to pause in the middle of *Tom Jones* to both define and defend his work as a "proper" form of literature. (In distinguishing what is "true" and "genuine in this kind of historic writing" from what is "false and counterfeit," Fielding suggested a list of criteria, including creative invention, moral judgment, a competent knowledge of history and letters, a keen capacity for observing the world, an ear for conversation among both the high and low born, a sympathy for one's characters that grows out of the author's own experience, and "a quick and sagacious penetration into the true essence" of things – all of which would distinguish it from the "swarm" of "monstrous" romances that were spreading "scandal" and "calumny" and "depravation of morals" among readers. This definition of the novel, as critics have noted, holds up well today.)[30]

Some critics have seen the style of his novels – where he alternately flatters and then abuses his audience – as reflecting Fielding's experience in the rough-and-tumble, give-and-take of combative eighteenth-century partisan journalism. Like other journalist-literary figures to come, Fielding (often because of a desperate need of cash) continued to pour out political pamphlets and engage in political journalism even after his novels appeared. But he believed his comic writing to be erudite and polished, and he saw it as moral commentary on the sorry state of contemporary culture.[31] Interestingly, Fielding shared the disgust of many of his high-brow contemporaries at the democratization of the world of writing, and he felt that moral and aesthetic values were threatened by the outpouring of material that catered to popular taste.

In the final phase of his life, after being appointed a court magistrate, Fielding brought the linking of his life activities full circle. (In a sense, his life imitated his journalism, too; in the *Jacobite's Journal* and the *Covent-Garden Journal*, as well as in the earlier *Champion*, Fielding used a device where he set up a court in the newspaper and gave his journalistic alter ego the right to try cases on literary or topical issues that caught his eye. At one point, Fielding even used the court motif to defend *Amelia* from the attacks of his critics and enemies.) *Amelia*, his last novel, is didactic and reads almost like a reformist tract of the period and, in fact, runs in parallel with the reform themes in the *Covent-Garden Journal*, Fielding's last journalistic venture, which was founded in 1752. One of the most vehement critics of Fielding during that period was Smollett, who wrote a pamphlet accusing Fielding of everything from scandal mongering to literary theft to smuttiness to drunkenness – thus helping to solidify Fielding's reputation for profligacy for posterity.[32]

Like Swift, and unlike Fielding and Defoe, Smollett was a died-in-the-wool conservative and a partisan Tory. Also like Fielding and Boswell (both trained attorneys), he had professional training outside journalism (he was a doctor by background and served as a naval physician). All three of Smollett's Grub Street publications – the *Critical Review*, the *Briton*, and *British Magazine* – were high quality journalistic productions that were filled with foreign news and analysis, reviews, sections about painting and engraving, and conservative commentary upon a wide range of intellectual fields. However, Smollett's journalistic work didn't win him the patronage he sought from parliamentary leaders, and he turned to other writing ventures – including the production of his best-known satiric novels, *Roderick Random*, *Peregrine Pickle*, and *Humphry Clinker*. Smollett's characters, like Dickens' (who was inspired by Smollett), are often eccentric to the extreme. Smollett – who as a journalist was quite willing to feed the eighteenth-century appetite for scandal with his attacks upon Fielding and a wide range of prominent figures – continued that tradition in his novels by parodying the many types of persons he found odious in life. However, critics also credit the practice of journalism, which Smollett continued in sporadic fashion through his novel-writing period, with improving his art and encouraging him to abandon the purely picaresque for themes of greater sensibility. Those who complain of Smollett's use of exaggeration sometimes forget just how extreme life could be in his time. His descriptions of the deplorable conditions on the naval ships of the era, for example, actually may have understated the reality of the situation. Smollett's quasi-fictional accounts have been credited with helping both to pave the way for reforms that followed and to lay the foundation for the use of literature as a tool of reform that was perfected by Dickens.[33]

Goldsmith owed a good deal to the experiences that he gained working as a journalist on Smollett's *Critical Review*, particularly in terms of the confidence it gave Goldsmith to overcome his own checkered professional history. Goldsmith's experiences as a failed professional (he also was a doctor), chronic debtor, and vagabond job hopper (there is speculation that he earned his living for a time working in Richardson's print shop), combined with his reputation as a social buffoon, made him an unlikely figure to emerge as one of the era's most multi-talented literary personalities. (Johnson said of Goldsmith, "No man was more foolish when he had not a pen in his hand, or more wise when he had.") Goldsmith's journalistic touch – he wrote in a relaxed, fluent, and easy-to-read manner – helped to make *The Vicar of Wakefield* an endearing work of art with its humorous tone and gently engaging style (despite the many digressions that have been blamed upon Goldsmith's expository training in the sometimes meandering journalism of his day). Goldsmith's affability – which never translated into the kind of attack journalism favored by Defoe, Swift, Fielding, and Smollett – is also evident in his potpourri of fictional essays, *The Citizen of the World*, his popular poetry, and his classic piece of light drama, *She Stoops to Conquer*.[34]

BOSWELL, JOHNSON, AND THE "ANGLE" AS TRUTH

The controversies surrounding the fidelity of Boswell's biography provide a classic example of the clash of post-modern scholarship with the optimism of eighteenth-century empiricism, and they mirror the debate among contemporary scholars over whether it is possible for journalism (or biography) to portray an "objective" version of reality. In today's world, entire professional structures and institutions have grown up around different epistemological definitions of "truth." Journalists tend to defend the Enlightenment notion that it is important to seek a discernible notion of "objective" truth, and that one should give great credence to writers who try to do this. Post-modern literary scholars, on the other hand, are prone to dismiss distinctions that are made between factual and fictional writing as illusory and to assert that all aesthetic categories have blurred edges when it comes to formulating a real picture of the world. Much of today's scholarship about Boswell – as well as Defoe, Fielding, and Smollett, who also made claims about the broader "truths" of their novels – can be seen as disputations about post-modernism applied retroactively to the works of writers who were only beginning to grapple with the distinctions that are now made between journalism, biography, non-fiction, and the novel. This has happened, at least in part, because – as pioneers in the development of new genres of literary writing – they were caught up in the evolving notions of where the line should be drawn between fact and fiction.

Until recent years, Boswell was widely thought of as the first great modern biographer, a writer whose skill in getting people to talk and whose facility for remembering details aided him in penning *The Life of Samuel Johnson*, which is still greatly admired for its stylish writing, its witty and absorbing method for presenting Johnson's droll and pithy sayings, and its vivid and intimate insights into Johnson's personality. If one chooses to call Boswell a "journalist" for contributing to the periodicals of his day, one should also recognize the ways in which he operated as contemporary journalists do. Boswell's use of techniques that we associate today with the profession of journalism – in the skills of interviewing, the application of quotations, the use and manipulation of sources, the decisions he made about what was "off the record," the employment of research and fact-checking – makes him a fascinating study for anyone who is trying to identify the roots of contemporary journalistic methodology. The most famous product of his literary ventures – his *Life of Johnson* – is thought of as biography. But the devices he used to fill out his portrait of Johnson have as much in common with the techniques used by the contemporary journalistic interviewer or profile writer as they do with the methods of contemporary biographers who only rarely have the opportunity, as Boswell did, for close-up, personal, contemporaneous interaction and inspection of the subject of their work.

As a fully-fledged contributor to the hybrid literary culture of this period, Boswell wrote hundreds of articles for the newspapers of his time, penning pieces about freezing bodies for later resuscitation, bankruptcies in Scotland, the rebellion of the Corsicans, patronage in the Church of Scotland, the brutality of England's penal laws, the chief of the Mohawk Indians, the

Shakespearean actor David Garrick, and theater performances. One of his favorite topics was famous murder trials, and he wrote often about executions, which he loved to attend. Sometimes his journalism was painfully self-revealing, other times disastrously impetuous. He often was willing to put his own personal life on display, as he did in a long-running column in *London Magazine* about, among other topics, the effects of depression or what he called "hypochondria" (the column – written anonymously and called "The Hypochondriack" – was penned with the hope of fending off the serious bouts of melancholia and depression that plagued him all his life). Much of Boswell's journalism can be admired today for its forth-rightness, though other parts of it cannot. Boswell was willing to sacrifice his own political prospects (he long harbored a vain hope to win a seat in Parliament) by taking on important political figures when he felt they deserved criticism. On the other hand, he used the newspapers and period-icals to lobby for personal and idiosyncratic political causes and, more problematically, penned articles (though technically anonymous, people knew it was him) that supported his legal cases and praised his own books and publications.[35]

Boswell never wrote what today we call "novels," and his literary produc-tion, while deemed "literature" by the standards of many literary historians, does not bring into play the same issues surrounding the blending of fact and fiction that apply to Defoe, Swift, Fielding, and others. However, Boswell's approach to biography – and the questions that have been raised about his methods for distinguishing "truth" from subjective interpretation – have led certain critics to criticize his biography of Johnson for the liberties Boswell takes with the facts. They claim that Boswell shaped his portrait of Johnson more in Boswell's image of himself than in the way Johnson really was. "As a novel, as admitted fiction, it is an honest book," wrote Donald Greene, a prominent Boswell critic. "If presented to us as biography, as alleged truth, we should feel that the author was being dishonest with us."[36]

In this respect, Boswell was like an artful journalistic feature writer. He picked a "frame" or an "angle" that allowed him to show his readers the deeper humanity of Johnson below his haughty and often off-putting person-ality. Boswell steered their conversations in directions that would get Johnson to speak to issues that mattered to Boswell, and he often seemed most interested in the bon mot, the crushing comeback, the "good quote."[37] As generations of journalists have in fact learned, Boswell knew that he could engineer his readers' impression of Johnson with carefully chosen questions and by guilefully making a point without doing it too bluntly. This manip-ulation is cited by contemporary scholars who contend that Boswell's goal was not an objective portrait of Johnson but a craftily manufactured portrait of a man whose reputation Boswell hoped to burnish for posterity.

In calling Boswell's literary work "journalism," at least in the formative sense, one only has to look at the professional questions he wrestled with that would be highly familiar to today's journalists (and particularly political journalists), and the bold (and still controversial) solutions he arrived at to deal with them:

- How much of his social conversations should he record publicly? Boswell struggled with this on a regular basis. Was he violating informal understandings and bonds of trust in the circles where he socialized? When should private revelations be matters of public discussion, and when was it fair to use them to shape public reputations? Boswell sometimes delayed these decisions by recording material in his nightly journals, but eventually he had to decide when, and if, his private journals should become matters of public record.

- How accurate were Boswell's quotes from Johnson and the details that Boswell used about Johnson's life, and how reliable were Boswell's sources? Boswell prided himself on the time and effort he took to research the background of Johnson's life and to expand his sources beyond events he had personally witnessed. However, posterity's fascination with his *Life of Johnson* rests largely upon the force of Johnson's quotations and Boswell's chronicling of the details of their many conversations during twenty-one years of socializing. Boswell has been credited (and he credited himself) with a great memory, a talent for accurately reconstructing dialogue, and a gift for getting others to reveal themselves in conversation. However, in recent years critics have raised questions about the faithfulness of Boswell's portrait of Johnson by looking closely at the amount of editorial shaping and reconstruction that went into his *Life* and by comparing Boswell's version with the accounts of contemporaries who were also collecting material about Johnson.

- What did Johnson – as well as Boswell's other friends and social acquaintances – think of Boswell, knowing that he was writing down everything that they said? How self-conscious were they – and thus how "real" was the picture they presented of themselves to him? What Boswell had to face was the "mirror effect" that contemporary journalists deal with every day – for example, the knowledge that the people they are interviewing know that everything they say has the potential to see public light and often utter every word with this knowledge in mind. Boswell's critics have accused him of not being sufficiently aware of this potential for a "constructed" reality in his accounts of Johnson's sayings and of underestimating the potential for Johnson to manipulate the situation for the sake of dramatic effect or the shaping of his image for posterity.

– How much did the pressure Boswell felt about violating his friends' privacy influence the way he portrayed matters and how much was this affected by his own self-interests? Boswell could be stubborn in his determination to publish, and there were times when he refused to back down, despite pressure from his friends. However, there were other instances where he altered material – including changing things from one edition of the *Life* to the next – in response to complaints.

– The ridicule Boswell faced for revealing his personal life was reinforced by his "Hypochrondiack" column in the *London Magazine* from 1777 to 1783. Boswell wrote so honestly about his personal issues that he became a laughing stock in the eyes of many of his contemporaries (as well as some historians). Boswell wrote to help process his inner conflicts and to deal with his feeling that life didn't have meaning unless he chronicled it. His insights and self-revelations, particularly in regard to the consequences of depression and anxiety, were courageous in his willingness to offer up his own pain for public inspection, and they prefigure our contemporary era when psychological interpretation, medical advice, self-help material, and the revelation of private lives have come to be regular features of the newspaper world.

– Boswell's fixation with executions, and his writing about them for the periodicals of his day, put him at the beginning of a long historical line of journalists and journalistic publications that have made voyeurism into the criminal world and the criminal mind a key appeal of newspapers. Boswell's fascination with the abnormal personality and the aberrational in life put him in good company with the journalists of the future who would stalk the police stations, the court houses, and the jails looking for stories of crime, violence, and punishment as a marketing tool for news organizations eager to satisfy the public's craving for glimpses into the "dark side" of society.

– Boswell's touting of the accuracy of his material and the thoroughness of his methodology – and the sometimes dubiousness of his claims – is reminiscent of today's news organizations that maintain they operate by strict standards of "objectivity" despite the doubts of media critics and scholars. It is a commentary upon the empirical optimism of the eras that followed Boswell that his pretensions to objectively portraying Johnson went uncontested for so long. The limitations of Boswell's chronicling abilities, the flaws in his research methods, his superficial understanding of Johnson's critical work, and his eagerness to confirm his own beliefs in

Johnson's – all have been held up as evidence that Boswell does not meet the rigorous standards of verisimilitude required by contemporary biography.

– Boswell's ethics and his professional standards – as is the case with the news business today – are a mix of the admirable and the venal, the public-spirited and the self-serving, the principled and the opportunistic. Boswell has been praised for the thoroughness of his interviewing and note taking, the care in his research and his fact-checking, and his determination to tell the whole story despite the consequences – even if he didn't fully achieve the professional requirements of today. Ethical standards for a writer were only beginning to emerge in Boswell's time, and he stood head and shoulders above the biographers of his day in the depth of his characterization and the clarity of his insights. Yet in other ways, Boswell can be seen as failing the test of journalistic and biographical integrity – even if he was only following the shabby practices of the fellow scribblers of his time.

Unquestionably, Boswell believed he was operating in the realm of the empirical, and his methodological limitations have to be seen in the context of the contemporary challenges to the optimistic epistemology of the eighteenth century, where Newtonian and Lockean concepts of a discernable and ordered universe were interwoven into the popular consciousness and where few questioned the idea that the human mind (and thus the human writer) could create an accurate picture of reality. However, the early twentieth-century discovery of Boswell's more detailed journals could not have come at a better time for today's scholars, who tend to look askance at any claim for a truth that exists beyond subjective perceptions. Scholars have leaped upon the factual errors discovered in Boswell's work to challenge those who maintain that the "truth" of Boswell's portrait of Johnson survives, even if one must grant Boswell some artistic latitude.[38]

Although the discovery of Boswell's journals, diaries and papers in the 1920s, 1930s, and 1940s (large portions of them published as Boswell's *London Journal*) has led to a steady erosion of Boswell's image as a fact-gatherer and recorder, the controversies surrounding his research methods can prove interesting to contemporary journalists curious about how historical figures dealt with many of the same professional challenges faced by reporters today. Although he argued that he had pictured Johnson "warts and all," Boswell's was a carefully manufactured image of Johnson with a modified presentation of his oddities. Meanwhile, the journals revealed elements of Boswell's own out-of-control personal behavior that threw doubt on his credibility, including his compulsive whoring and chasing after servants, his myriad affairs and the strains they put on his marriage, his multiple bouts of gonorrhea, his heavy drinking and gambling, and his sometimes bizarre social behavior.[39]

Boswell's defenders have argued that the purpose of history and biography is still met in the *Life of Johnson*, even with the compromises of literal truth. But they have had to resort, as journalist-literary figures and journalist-novelists from Defoe forward have done, to the defense that Boswell was revealing a "greater truth" than a purely empirical one. Boswell, they say, must be appreciated for using interpretation, supposition, and assumption to fill in the gaps of his knowledge of Johnson. However, even Boswell's supporters will concede that his most questionable act was not in using fictional techniques but in disguising the extent to which he did. Boswell did not habitually take notes (this was unacceptable in company); usually he hastened to his room to recount the material from memory. It was discovered, for example, that his diary entries were sometimes as little as thirty words, from which he constructed much longer excerpts, and the changes he made to his journal records in the *Life* were often major. In some instances in the *Life*, he was reconstructing material from many years earlier, and thus relied upon mere "snippets" of Johnson's talk. In places, Boswell acknowledged that he failed to record material or didn't do so for many days but claimed that he always had the "Johnsonian aether" to fall back on. Yet Boswell continued to insist that what he wrote was trustworthy. "Authenticity is my chief boast," he said.[40]

To think of Johnson as primarily a journalist also stretches the definition of the contemporary term, but it is more than applicable given Johnson's involvement with a profusion of writing techniques that have come to encompass contemporary journalism and much more. The fact that Johnson is studied today as a moral philosopher, an essayist, a lexicographer, a wisdom teacher, a psychologist, a writer of literature, and a social and political theorist is a testimony to the astonishing range of his talents, but it doesn't obviate the fact that he was performing many of the tasks that in his day were identified with journalism. Johnson's facilities can be seen as a commentary upon the extraordinary range of eighteenth-century English journalism – and the subsequent narrowing of what we have come to expect from contemporary journalism. Among his many contributions to the journalistic tradition, Johnson can be seen as journalism's first official theorist and philosopher of the profession and one of the first to outline its professional and ethical responsibilities. "To write news in its perfection requires such a combination of qualities that a man completely fitted for the task is not always to be found," Johnson said. Johnson was responsible for writing manifestos about editorial policy (what we might call mission statements today) for a number of periodicals. In one, he said that the journalist's duty is to "disentangle confusion and illustrate obscurity … and honestly lay before people what inquiry can gather of the past, and conjecture can estimate of the future." For Johnson, journalism should always be in service, as he put it, to the "stability" of truth.[41]

Johnson's most memorable journalism was the prose that he composed for his *Rambler* newspaper from March, 1750 to March, 1752 – often penned in great haste and without being looked over after it was written. He sometimes just handed batches of sheets to a copy boy for transportation to the printer as he was finishing others. (Johnson acknowledged that the periodical writer who produces twice a week on deadline "will often bring to his task an attention dissipated, a memory embarrassed … a mind distracted with anxieties, a body languishing with disease.") Johnson's *Rambler* (along with his later newspaper, the *Idler*) had a small, but loyal following (the *Rambler* had about 500 subscribers, compared to the *Spectator*'s 10,000 at its height), and Johnson took pride in not stooping to appeal to popular opinion. In fact, Johnson did the reverse of what would be called for by the savvy marketing of today's newspaper, often dropping obscure words and Latinate polysyllables into his articles as a way of improving the vocabulary of his readers. Somehow, his use of words such as "adscititious" and "equiponderant" and "papilonaceous" and his refusal to pander proved to have a charm for his audience. Readers who asked for more variety or criticized his circumlocutory prose were ignored. However, he also managed to demonstrate a shrewd promotional sense when it suited him. His biography of Richard Savage, for example, was a popular hit because it drew upon the emerging tradition of realistic fiction, the popularity of the criminal biography, and the moral sentiments of one who looked askance at the tawdry material that he was exploiting at the same time for its commercial appeal.[42]

The majority of Johnson's essays in the *Rambler* were about "morality" in eighteenth-century terms, but psychology or psychiatry or even "self-help" would be the better contemporary term. Johnson was trying to help his readers (often using himself and his own psychological state of mind as a case in point) to negotiate the changing social and economic landscape of a fast-changing eighteenth-century world. A key ingredient in all that he wrote was to recommend psychological techniques in which contentment can be found. He often talked of the torment of self-consciousness, the desire to be liked, the anxiety of irresolution, and the embarrassment of social awkwardness. His essays were written for the ordinary person "in need of instruction." The newspapers of his period did much to create Johnson as one of the early celebrity figures of the dawning media age and the most celebrated person of letters of his day. ("Hardly a day goes by when I am not in the papers," he once told Boswell.) And yet, Johnson was irked by the commercialization of literature, which he thought thwarted genuine learning, and he criticized many of his competitors for contributing to the erosion of public taste. "The compilation of news-papers is often committed to narrow and mercenary minds, not qualified for the task of delighting or instructing," he said.[43]

Johnson's critical views of fiction are interesting, too, for the light they shed upon posterity's continued debate about the relationship of fact and fancy. For Johnson, fiction was any departure from literal truth. Before the spread of novel reading, many readers looked to periodical essays for what Johnson called "the living world" or "life in its true state, diversified only by accidents that daily happen in the world." Johnson's own fiction (*Rasselas*) is didactic and hardly qualifies as what contemporary critics would call a novel. Johnson also shared the contempt of many for the scribblers and starving artists of Grub Street (in whose camp he would have put Fielding), and the *Rambler* mocked periodical writers who stooped to whatever the public would have and composed flattering anonymous letters about themselves for publication (as Boswell, interestingly, often did).[44]

DICKENS, THACKERAY AND THE FORGING OF LITERARY CELEBRITY

With a sense of financial insecurity both similar to and different from his rival, Thackeray, Dickens saw himself as the fulfillment of the rags-to-riches story that was so popular during the Victorian era. With a civil servant father who was imprisoned for indebtedness and forced to work as a youth in a shoe blacking factory, Dickens began his meteoric rise in the literary world after an uncle secured him a job as a parliamentary and political reporter for the *Mirror of Parliament* in 1831. Dickens was not only a talented writer, he was an impressive entrepreneur who recognized the new opportunities in the democratized and commercialized media marketplace. Dickens produced sketches of interesting urban personalities for the London *Morning Chronicle*, where he began working in 1834, and other periodicals while still in his early twenties. When they were collected into a book, *Sketches by Boz* (the pseudonym under which he wrote them), his reputation began its ascent. Dickens soon was producing novels in serial form in weekly and monthly periodicals as a way to maximize the financial rewards. After the success of his early ventures (*The Pickwick Papers, Oliver Twist*), everything Dickens did – founding two magazines which he himself edited, building his celebrity on the lecture circuit, and carefully cultivating his reputation as a public favorite and the preeminent Victorian literary figure – was designed to advance his literary reputation and to do it in a way that insured maximum economic benefits to himself. Dickens' psychological motivations were somewhat different than Thackeray's. He was driven by the insecurity of his family's indebtedness and his educational deficiencies rather than by Thackeray's sense of himself as a pedigreed gentleman whose financial entitlement had been denied him. However, their similar life experiences left them filled with ambivalent feelings about each other throughout their careers, during which they were wary friends at times, competitors at others, filled with a dueling mixture of envy, peevishness, and large-spirited admiration for each others' work.

Critics have discovered in the Boz sketches the seeds of Dickens' novels – particularly in the idiosyncratic characters he focused upon in his journalistic feature stories. The sketches are built around people that Dickens encountered in his wanderings throughout London, and they were his first hit when published in book form in 1836 and 1837. Dickens' love of the slightly cracked, extreme personalities who came to populate his novels shows up first in the Boz sketches. The sketches, which purported to show real people in action without any plot, were collected from his work for a number of different periodicals. Dickens was one of many sketch-writers grinding these things out, but he did them with an aplomb that established his reputation before he had ever penned a novel. Virgil Grillo has found in the Boz stories the outline of such characters as Turveydrop and Miss Flite in *Bleak House*, Oliver in *Oliver Twist*, Nicholas in *Nicholas Nickleby*, and Little Nell in *The Old Curiosity Shop*, and Grillo notes that the rhetorical effect of the early chapters of *The Pickwick Papers* is similar to the early Boz tales.[45]

Dickens' precociousness is legendary, and his astonishing range and productivity were evident in his journalistic years. On the *London Morning Chronicle*, he demonstrated a driving ambitiousness and began to stretch himself artistically, but he soon became overcommitted and overextended. In May 1836, at age twenty-four, he agreed to write for one publisher a three-volume novel; he then signed a contract with another publisher to edit a monthly publication as well as furnish original articles of his own. At this point, he resigned from the *Morning Chronicle*, where the publisher claimed he owed articles for which he had already been paid. With all this, he worked himself into sickness and fatigue (he also had an infant and a depressed wife at home). This situation – which grew out of Dickens' combination of insecurity, arrogance, and intemperateness – became a life pattern, but his furious artistic production also came to serve him as a way to stay steady through the vicissitudes of his life.[46]

Serial plotting had a profound impact on the structure and style of Dickens' novels, as did his trafficking in the stereotypes familiar to reporters of the Victorian daily newspaper. His fifteen novels, written over thirty-four years, were all produced serially for weekly and monthly periodicals. Dickens seldom completed a monthly number more than ten days before it was printed; four weeks ahead was the customary advance time for his weekly serials. He had little opportunity to revise his work, and he tended to plan chapter by chapter and not beyond. Dickens' deadlines denied him the opportunity to provide a unifying, organic vision that could be polished by rewriting, and he was often only able to give his novels the crudest structure. To one friend, he wrote drolly, "The contents of one number usually require a day's thought at the very least."[47]

As the once peripatetic political writer, Dickens liked to visit the places he intended to write about. Much like his *Tale of Two Cities*, for which he traveled to France to witness the results of the French Revolution, Dickens' novel about labor unrest in Victorian England, *Hard Times*, was built around the reporting he did in the town of Preston, which was experiencing a labor strike in 1854. The theme of the novel – which criticized "dry-as-dust" utilitarian economists who had no feeling for the workers' hardships – grew out of his visit to Preston in January, 1854, after he had read about the strikes and the threat of violence in the newspapers. John M. L. Drew, for example, has noted that the strike leader was the model for the novel's Gruffshaw. In the novel, and in material he wrote for his magazine, *Household Words*, Dickens attacked "an abstract political economy that broke human beings on the wheel of iron theory." However, Dickens was no radical, and – refusing to believe that the interests of the workers and owners were that divergent – he decided that his role should be as a compromiser. In the end, he capitulated to friends who worried that he might decide to endorse the strike as a solution to the problem. Still, the circumstances of labor unrest became a fixation with him and, in hurriedly writing the novel to meet its magazine installment deadlines, he described himself as "three parts mad and the fourth delirious, with perpetual rushing."[48]

The conflict between journalism and the pursuit of literature at the most practical level can be seen in the tension surrounding Dickens' decision, at the very height of his career, to take up an offer to edit a new London daily newspaper – to be known as the *Daily News* – in 1845. A glutton for detail and control, his talents didn't include delegating authority. However, within a few months, he came to realize that the job was a "daily noose."

By the time of the trial edition on January 19, 1846, Dickens (who was also under contract to produce a novel in twenty monthly parts) was exhausted and wasn't sleeping well at night. Although Dickens felt everything looked well for the start, most people felt the first edition was thin with little in it (thus greatly relieving the competition). His friends were glad when Dickens decided the load was too much and in February, 1846, walked away from the publication and turned the reins over to his close friend and advisor, John Forster (who privately conceded that the newspaper under Dickens was intellectually vapid and that "no one could be a worse editor than Dickens.")[49]

The last of Dickens' workaholic ventures into journalism made its debut on March 30, 1850 – the initial edition of *Household Words*, the first of two magazines he launched in the mature phase of his career. Dickens had a co-editor for the publication, but he made all the decisions while acting as general editor, acquiring editor, copy-editor, business agent, and writer. By its second issue, the magazine was a clear success; over nine years, it maintained an average weekly sale of 40,000 copies and the addition to Dickens' income was substantial. Although Dickens always had assistants, he was a hands-on editor of his magazines, wooing contributors, reading every submission, editing prose, marking-up page proofs. (He once commented on his page proofs as a "dreadful spectacle ... which look like an inky fishing-net.") He even did investigative reporting, and the magazines' pages gave him a forum to push the many social causes that preoccupied him. Throughout his writing life, Dickens enjoyed the company of journalists, and at different points employed both his father and one of his sons as journalists on his staff. It was inevitable that he would start contributing fiction to the magazine, which he did in *Household Words* from 1850 to 1858 (he wrote *Hard Times* as a serial contribution), as well as in his second magazine, *All the Year Round*, which was published from 1859 to the end of his life in 1870. (*All the Year Round* contained the serial publications of *A Tale of Two Cities* and *Great Expectations*.)[50]

It is interesting that the success-seeking Thackeray was critical of writers (most notably Dickens) who Thackeray believed wrote to the fashions of the day. Dickens clearly always had his eye on the bottom line (he was willing to change a book based on audience response, for example; at one point in the serialization of the novel *Martin Chuzzlewit*, he announced that his character was going to America, as a way to boost poor sales). Thackeray disapproved of the sentimentality and the comic grotesquery of certain of Dickens' plots and characters and went so far as to suggest that the "twopenny newspaper" of the day contained more about real life than did Dickens' novels.[51]

Thackeray, too, typified in his early life the lot of the talented nineteenth-century journalist with greater ambitions, struggling to make ends meet, overwhelmed with journalism work, and wondering if he had the talent – or the self-discipline – to rise to the challenge of writing memorable literature. Thackeray's literary apprenticeship in the hot house of early Victorian periodical publishing began with his work as a newspaper correspondent and editor on a variety of publications before he came upon the ideal publication for his talent: the satiric organ of wit and parry, *Punch* magazine.

Raised in modestly upper-class circumstances in India by a privileged mother and stepfather, Thackeray lost his modest fortune when the Indian banks failed in 1833, and he always felt great tension in the circumstances that forced him to make his living among the journeyman writers who populated the London publishing world. However, his genteel background – including his brief time as a student at Cambridge University – served him well in his literary endeavors. Thackeray combined a nose for highbrow follies with an amused disdain at the pretensions of the upper class in forging the satirical journalism that appeared in *Punch* and later his portraits of the shabby gentility in his best-known novel, *Vanity Fair*. Like Poe, Thackeray could never decide if he was a journalist and a man of the people (he never ceased enjoying hobnobbing with the journalistic ne'er-do-wells at *Punch*) or a person of privilege (he relished success, delighted in being the toast of the town as a literary celebrity, and generally ate and drank himself into corpulence in his last years). And yet his wry and mocking eye on the English class system – honed through years of pungent commentary at *Punch* and in other periodicals – served as the bedrock of his fiction, particularly in the creation of Becky Sharp in *Vanity Fair*, whose sharp-tongued and clever scheming amid a cast of tattered characters who hustle along the margins of British society made her an attractive figure, despite her fundamentally devious nature.

Despite his criticisms of Dickens as too market-oriented, the tug of financial need – and the accommodations he had to make to the growing power of the marketplace – plagued and distressed Thackeray. For many years as a journalist, Thackeray had refined his understanding of public taste, particularly in the areas of humor and satire, and he had emerged as one of the cleverest and shrewdest performers in the London periodical scene. Thackeray followed the model of Dickens in using the serial form of novel-publishing to catapult himself into the ranks of the great Victorian literary figures. However, when he undertook *Vanity Fair*, Thackeray was a much different person than the precociously successful Dickens – a middle-aged journalist who had produced highly intelligent and artful journalism but who was facing a literary world that had been transformed by the possibilities of the novel and had come to disdain even the best journalism as something that, almost by definition, fell short of the standards of great art. Thackeray early on had made it clear he felt he was "slumming" it when he wrote to a friend that leaving art (he had dabbled briefly in art studies) and taking up newspaper work was "like quitting a beautiful wife … to take up with a tawdry brazen whore." But he went on to add, "I am sorry to say that I like the newspaper work very much, it is a continual excitement, and I fancy I do it well, that is very sarcastically." Thackeray's knowledge of the newspaper and periodical world was an intimate one – and this knowledge informed both his journalism and his fiction. His first sustained attachment was to *Fraser's* magazine beginning in 1837, where he was sympathetic to its ethos of Tory journalism, even though he was a liberal, not a Tory, in his politics. Still, Thackeray managed the situation masterfully – and, with the culmination of the writing of his masterpiece, *Vanity Fair*, which was issued in monthly parts from 1847 to 1848, he emerged triumphant over his checkered past. But the precariousness of his financial and professional life penetrated deeply into his sinews, and his vision of literature was permanently shaped by it.[52]

It didn't escape Thackeray that the press was prone to its own corruptions and compromises, and he developed a keen understanding of the nature of journalistic hack work and the people who performed it. In his work for *Fraser's*, he created two pseudonymous characters, "Yellowplush" and "Titmarsh," who represented two sides of his critique of the moral ambiguities of the periodical press. The working-class Yellowplush spoke of having been "fool enough to write in magazines" and alluded to such employment as sinking below his footman's status. Titmarsh was a painter, an amateur journalist, and a caricature of the "puffing and fishing" self-promoting journalist who believed in his own pompous superiority. In *Punch*, his "Bashi-Bozouk" character (or "Mick") "reported" on the Crimean War and said of his work: "What the nation wants is TRUTH. Truth pure, Truth unadulterated. Truth gushing from the original tap, such as perhaps no other man in Europe but myself is in a condition to supply." By the time he had established his literary reputation, Thackeray had become the perfect commentator on the journalism of his era; he knew all the tricks because he had used them. In fact, the newspaper world was simply too perfect a vehicle for Thackeray's preoccupations – newspapers were read by the wealthy, but their writers were marginalized and considered outside the bounds of comfortable gentility – and newspapers influenced the lives of many of the characters in his novels. For example, in *The Adventures of Philip*, which was serialized in the *Cornhill* in 1861 and 1862, Philip, like Thackeray, had lost his fortune and found himself working for a variety of newspapers in different countries. At the fictional *Pall Mall Gazette*, Philip is told (ironically) that there is "no puffing, or jobbing, or false praise, or funfair censure now. Every critic knows what he is writing about, and writes with no aim but to tell truth." Still, despite criticizing the press' failings, Thackeray, as the hard-working journalist, often defended the press – which he called the producers of "fleeting literature" – and professional writers, particularly when it came to being paid for their work and the difficulties they faced working within a world of commerce.[53]

Thackeray's use of personas was legion, and their names memorable. In addition to Yellowplush and Titmarsh, there were: Mr. Snob, the Fat Contributor, Mr. Spec, Fitz-Boodle, Doctor Solomon Pacifico, Molony (an Irish reporter) and Hadjee Aboo Bosh (an Arab journalist). Thackeray's use of clever personas was a recognition of the smoke and mirrors aspect of Victorian journalism and the need for a gentleman engaged in a dubious profession to mask his identity. Compared to the world of Swift, Johnson, and Fielding, Thackeray felt the periodical world of his day was decidedly un-genteel and was dominated by profits and commerce. When Thackeray's first *Punch* piece appeared, he described the magazine to his father-in-law as a "very low paper" that offered good pay and "a great opportunity for unrestrained laughing sneering kicking and gambadoing." But Thackeray also described *Punch* as "the father and protector of the press," and its satire was often built around newspapers' curious priorities and melodramatic comment (making *Punch*, in essence, the first journalism review). However, Thackeray ultimately came to a reluctant acceptance that art must survive in a commercial environment. His character, Pendennis, who in the novel turned his autobiography into a best-seller, reflected Thackeray's wistful but pragmatic view of the changing circumstances for writers of his time. ("Rags are not a proof of genius," a key journalistic figure, George Warrington, says in *Pendennis* – which is probably something close to Thackeray's view of the matter. "Whereas capital is absolute, as times go, and is perforce the bargain-master. It has a right to deal with the literary inventor as with any other.")[54]

Thackeray was not a natural novelist, and his creation of *Vanity Fair* was deeply rooted in the habits, insights, and patterns of periodical journalism that had helped him to refine his sharp eye for the foibles and pretensions of the upper classes. The development of the novel was almost startlingly ad hoc. By February 1845, when Thackeray was hard at work on the early chapters, he had little idea what to do with it – whether it would be a magazine serial, a work sold in monthly parts, or a multi-part novel. A sharp operator with an eye toward what magazine editors and readers wanted to buy, the opening chapters were accepted by Bradbury and Evans, the owners of *Punch* magazine, where Thackeray was at work on his *Punch* series, "The Snobs of England." Both works reflected Thackeray's fascination with Regency high life, and both were built around sketches that gave Thackeray's fiction and his journalism their bite. To print the novel serially, Thackeray had to meet a rigorous publishing schedule, but he seemed to find it invigorating, and much of the historical research that went into the novel was done at great speed. For example, in the "Snobs" series, Thackeray described a visit to the country "Snobs" – the Ponto – which is told acidly and with the same attention to detail and recognizable locales that gave *Vanity Fair* a documentary feel for the contemporary reader. Many of the same characters and character types are transferred directly from his periodical work into his fiction, as Richard Pearson has noted, including the foppish "Squinny" in Thackeray's 1843 story, "The Ravening," in *Fraser's Magazine* who becomes "Tapeworm" in *Vanity Fair* and the character "Peter Brock" in the 1839 to 1840 series, "Catherine," in *Fraser's* and "Deuceace" in *The Yellow Plush Papers*, who transform into the many characters in *Vanity Fair* (most notably Becky Sharp) who live by their wits and the practice of "agreeable vice" as their fortunes rise and fall.[55]

In founding his magazine, the *Cornhill*, in 1860, Thackeray, determined to rise above the hack work fate of Pendennis and his other periodical-worker protagonists, became the director of a culturally respected journal where he sought high-quality content and popular material with a sophisticated tone. Less ambitious in many ways than Dickens, Thackeray was nonetheless as practically minded in his goals for his magazine. "We mustn't say a word against filthy lucre, for I see the use and comfort of it every day more and more," he wrote. It is fair to say that unlike Dickens, whose manic efforts at writing while editing a periodical helped to end his life prematurely, Thackeray couldn't claim overwork as a contributing factor in his death at a relatively young age (fifty-two). He was already overweight, indulged in great bouts of eating and drinking, and was always busier with his social schedule than anything else. Still, Thackeray's connection to journalism – so dubious to him in his slow-developing early career – was highly profitable in his later years and helped solidify his standing with the literary establishment that had become more receptive to commercially oriented literary writing. Lord Macaulay's brother indicated that "the last book my brother read was the first number of 'The Cornhill Magazine.' It was open at Thackeray's story, on the table by the side of the chair" in which Macaulay died.[56]

POE AND HIS ENVY OF THE 'GREAT' BRITISH
JOURNALISTIC LITERATURE

A copy of a review written by Poe once came in a letter to Dickens, a writer whom Poe once greatly admired but came to despise. The review was about Dickens' novel, *Barnaby Rudge*, which Dickens was publishing serially in the magazine, *Clock*. In the review, Dickens was informed how the mystery of the plot would unravel and, correctly, "who done it." In recounting this incident, as well as others where Poe tried to meet and curry influence with his then writing hero, literary critics and biographers have noted the ways that the literary canon was becoming shaped by journalist-literary figures on both sides of the Atlantic. "Between them, Poe and Dickens, both journalists, may be said to have brought short fiction and the English novel to maturity," wrote Calhoun Winton.[57]

Dickens may have been one of Poe's major literary fixations (Poe ultimately turned on Dickens after Poe concluded that he was the anonymous author of unfavorable material written about Poe – which Dickens almost certainly wasn't). But it was Thackeray who shared many of Poe's grievances against the social order and the periodical world, fixated as both were upon their perhaps dubious but nonetheless absorbing claims to genteel status and their misgivings about a journalism profession from which they couldn't engineer their escape. Poe, like Thackeray, illustrated how authors could be pulled in two directions by the growing rift between literature as a focus of an educated elite and the popular literary marketplace. Poe's struggle to appeal to the "few" and the "many," as one critic put it, was a central issue in his life and was one of the many tensions that helped to undo his fragile and unstable personality. Poe worked fervently to reconcile the commercial expectations of the periodical world where he eked out a marginal living with his view of himself as a representative of the life of Virginia squiredom and his identification with southern aristocratic literary pretensions. Poe saw himself as a divided figure, addicted to the quest for popularity (as he was addicted to alcohol and other things) while at the same time despising literature that didn't aspire to lofty and elitist stature. Tortured by the mundane nature of much of his periodical work, and resentful of those with a serious and well-compensated literary career, he vented his frustration with savage critical campaigns against a number of the major voices of American literature (most notably the poets Bryant and Longfellow).[58] In Poe's mind, the device to span the gap between the rarified world of artistic letters and the realities of marketplace success was the popular literary magazine modeled upon British publications that he worked for years to found in America – but which ultimately eluded him.

Throughout his career, Poe insisted that there was little distinction between his fictional and non-fiction magazine articles, and he often claimed for his fictional detective stories a scientific purpose that he saw as a medium for important truths. For example, his "Mystery of Marie Roget" is built around the rebutting of speculation in the New York City newspapers covering the case. In this way, Poe claimed he was entering into a rigorous analysis of the New York tragedy by examining the clues raised in the press with the purpose of uncovering the "true principles which should direct enquiry in similar cases." Poe saw his analytical murder mysteries or "tales of ratiocination" – including "The Murders in the Rue Morgue," "The Man in the Crowd," "The Gold-Bug," and "The Purloined Letter" – as case studies to aid scientific criminal probes, and he used newspaper articles as guides and places to pick up hints and story lines. In this manner, Poe mixed the commonplace practices of the Penny Press with his rich imagination to inaugurate what today is called the "detective" story, and many of Poe's stories were printed in the newspapers and popular magazines of the time among other Poe writings on cryptography and other forms of mental puzzle solving.[59]

There are many ironies to Poe's role as a magazine journalist and a master writer of tales of the macabre. Poe eventually was acclaimed by a mass audience who made him one of the most popular story writers of all time. And yet, in his day, he argued vehemently for the importance of writing for a sophisticated elite, scorned popular taste, and bitterly criticized those he felt had sold out their literary ideals for commercial success. Poe resented the routines and the hack work of periodical journalism, and yet throughout his life he pined to own and operate his own magazine. As an artist, Poe was satisfied to toss off his tales of suspense, which he carefully tailored to appeal to the marketplace – practices which he regularly scorned in others. Poe saw himself as an assiduous critic of literary failings and a learned judge of artistic accomplishment. At the same time he was a sloppy researcher who borrowed regularly from other writers and recycled his own work. He gained much of his learning by moving quickly and often superficially over sources (anthologies, encyclopedias, magazines), frequently with an incomplete understanding. Poe believed himself to be high-minded, scrupulous, and exacting in his literary standards, but others saw him as envy-ridden, mean-spirited, and faulty in his judgments. Poe was quick to turn on those he admired, and his sense of being slighted was colossal. "I intend to put up with nothing that I can put down," he once said.[60]

Poe saw himself as a brilliant but misunderstood victim of the money-making milieu of nineteenth-century journalism who toiled away, underappreciated for his path-breaking fiction and despised for his too-honest approach to literary criticism. Despite his elitist attitudes, his ambition forced him to alter his techniques and make his fiction more accessible. Over and over again, he organized his stories around a protagonist isolated in some strange, horrific situation – knowing full well how much that met the formula needs of editors. This may have been what led Poe to say that "genius of the highest order lives in a state of perpetual vacillation between ambition and the scorn of it." Ironically, while Poe's criticism is little read today, he succeeded through a soaring reputation after his lifetime in becoming what he had so scorned – the epitome of the popular writer, a favorite story spinner of teenagers and fans of tales of mystery, horror, and the bizarre, his stories cherished by adolescents fascinated with abnormal psychology, his poems quoted in advertisements and on tee-shirts, his stories of the beleaguered victim and the mentally unstrung criminal providing a model for the stock dramas of television and movies. Throughout his life, Poe was stretched on a tightrope of financial desperation and a hunger for popular triumph, and yet he was forever yearning to express the aesthete's side of his artistic personality. "To coin one's brain into silver, at the nod of a master, is to my thinking, the hardest task in the world," he wrote.[61]

This tug-of-war in Poe's aesthetic imagination played out against the backdrop of his emotional instability, his tragic upbringing, his drunkenness, his strange marriage, and his quarrels with many of the artistic figures of his day. Like Thackeray, Poe was the product of the "marginal" gentility – his father, who came from landholding Virginia gentry, ran off, never to be heard from again, his mother, an actress, died while he was a toddler and left him to be raised by a wealthy merchant foster father with whom Poe quarreled and from whom he grew estranged. In his first magazine job – a post with the *Southern Literary Messenger* that he obtained in 1835 after dropping out of the University of Virginia – Poe, already an alcoholic with suicidal fantasies, behaved in self-destructive ways that eventually led to his being let go at the magazine, brought back, and then let go again. He advised the editor, Thomas Willis White, that the public wanted sensational subjects treated in a charged style, "the ludicrous heightened into the grotesque: the fearful coloured into the horrible: the witty exaggerated into the burlesque: the singular wrought out into the strange and mystical," and he set out to meet that standard. In his "Murders in the Rue Morgue," which appeared six years after his beginnings in journalism, Poe drew from Penny paper accounts of bloody crimes and trial material that he blended with the popular gothic formulas of the day. Few works can claim to have given rise to a popular genre, but "Murders in the Rue Morgue" has become the prototype of the modern detective story (the word "detective" didn't exist in English at the time Poe wrote). Many of his fixations – premature burial, portraits come to life, physical decay, garishly lit mansions and castles, heroes in isolation, lunacy and extreme sensibility, madness – came from this mixed tradition of Gothic romance and newspaper crime reporting. Poe particularly liked tales – popular in the periodicals of his time – of solitary victims in life-threatening situations in which their reactions would be described with heightened awareness of the minutest changes around them.[62]

Poe's love of the great literary magazines of early Victorian England – *Blackwood's, Fraser's, London Magazine, New Monthly* – convinced him that only in a "quality popularity" journal could journalism aspire to art, and that he could bring both the British magazines' sophistication and their venom to the American literary scene. Magazines such as these offered scurrilous and attacking reviews, literary gossip, and semi-learned fiction modes – all aimed at maximizing circulation. A number of American magazines of the period were modeled after these publications – although not to Poe's satisfaction. "The finest minds of Europe are beginning to lend their spirit to Magazines," he wrote. "In this country, unhappily, we have no journal of the class." At the same time, Poe also penned an article, "How to write a Blackwood Article", where he implied that the magazine required fiction written to formula and faked-up learning mixed with sensationalism. (Be sure, Poe said, that an article has:

an air of erudition … By casting your eye down almost any page of any book in the world, you will be able to perceive at once a host of little scraps of either learning or *bel-espirit-ism* … You may make a great deal of that little fact. You see, it is not generally known, and looks *recherche*. You must be careful and give the thing with a downright improviso air!)[63]

Poe's faults were many – not least his hypocrisy and willingness to bend his principles to advance his career. He slammed others for pilfering from other writers and serving as their own best public relations agent, while he did it himself. Writing anonymously in *Alexander's* magazine, for example, he commended his simultaneous work in *Burton's*. Poe liked to quote another author's garbled sentence in his reviews and then rewrite it with greater grace, conciseness, and clarity. However, one New York newspaper pointed out that Poe was responsible for "blunders quite as gross as those on which it was his pleasure to descant." He was particularly critical of the press for over-praising bad novels – although he tended to let his own personal piques and running feuds influence his critical judgment. Of one inflated review in the New York *Mirror*, Poe wrote: "Well! – here we have it! This is *the* book – the book *par excellence* – the book bepuffed, beplastered, and be-*Mirrored.*" And yet, he was known to write to authors he had slammed and beg for endorsements of his own work.[64]

The *Broadway Journal* was the only magazine Poe ever controlled – briefly and unsuccessfully. Poe had always believed his idea of an elite magazine could rescue himself and other writers from servitude. "To be controlled is to be ruined," he said. The owners of the *Journal* were willing to make the drunkard Poe part-owner and editor in October, 1945 only because the magazine was on the brink of failure. The job was one of Poe's most taxing. Of his fifteen-hour days, he said: "I never knew what it was to be a slave before." During this period, Poe zestfully defended magazines, saying the magazine's power was "illimitable ... The whole tendency of the age is Magazine-ward." But in the end, his bad habits and the deadline pressures led him to reprint old stories, curtail art and drama criticism, review books that he had not had time to read, and make numerous proofreading and editing errors. "I really believe that I have been mad," he said of the strain. After one month in charge, he had to sign back his half interest and then took off on one of his fits of drunkenness as the magazine headed into oblivion.[65]

Even so, to his last, dying days, Poe was obsessed with his "Dream Magazine", which he planned to call the "Stylus." At one point, he found a financer and printed a prospectus, but his backer bailed out. What little money Poe made in his last years was the result of his publishing stories – sometimes recycled versions of his most popular ones – and writing fillers and slight pieces with an idiosyncratic twist for anybody who would print them. Toward the end of his career, he was working as a New York correspondent for a couple of small Pennsylvania newspapers, and writing for the New York *Mirror* and other popular publications. In April, 1849, he still had hopes for the launching of the "Stylus," which he continued to promote right up to the days of his final collapse and death.[66]

ELIOT, LEWES, AND THE SECRET LIFE OF FICTION

Eliot demonstrated both how journalism aided women in their strides toward professionalism and artistic achievement during the Victorian period, and the considerable constraints women professionals still operated under. That Eliot took a male nom de plumbe is symptomatic of the fact that at this stage journalism offered openings to accomplished women writers but not an unobstructed path to success. The daughter of a prosperous country farm manager, Eliot got her start in journalism with the *Coventry Herald*, where she wrote political and news articles which brought her to the attention of John Chapman, the editor of the prominent London-based *Westminster Review*. Eliot's involvement with the *Review* introduced her to many of the people who would ultimately help to make her career, but at the price of humiliating personal experiences. While working as an editorial assistant, Eliot became Chapman's lover while living in his London home with his wife and his other lover, the family governess. Although working anonymously and without a formal title, Eliot served as the de facto editor of the *Review*. In this role, she was forced to endure blows to her pride both professionally and personally. Chapman implied to Eliot that he couldn't love her because of her homeliness (as later did the philosopher, Herbert Spencer), and she ultimately left his household. As an editor and journalist, she helped to maintain the high quality of the literary reviews, but she had to do it behind the scenes and without credit. When she needed to negotiate with high-profile figures, she was forced, due to the dubious nature of her position, to ask the editorially inexperienced Chapman to play the public role of editor, as happened, for example, when Eliot was left to pace the sidewalk outside the home of Carlyle while Chapman negotiated with the Scots historian and essayist for editorial contributions.[67]

Eliot met Henry Lewes, who was to prove to be her journalistic ally, life-long companion, and the inspirer of her art (the man behind the great woman or Mr. George Eliot, as one biographer called him) through Chapman and her journalistic activities at the *Review*. Lewes was a prominent periodical writer and a popularizer of science, philosophy, and history who had a large following among the British reading public. As their intimacy deepened, she became his staunchest supporter and even (in somewhat problematic fashion) tried to fend off critical commentary on Lewes' work by keeping allegations of inaccuracies out of the *Review*. Meanwhile, she was spending more and more time correcting proofs and writing articles for the London *Leader*, which Lewes co-owned. In early 1859, she faced the difficult task of explaining to Chapman why she could no longer write for the *Review*, and, after some acrimony between them, their friendship and their professional relationship were sundered.[68]

Interestingly, the final dispute between Eliot and Chapman centered around her emerging role as one of the great Victorian novelists and the camouflaging of her identity behind her authorial pseudonym. Lewes and Eliot were the target of scorn from much of Victorian society for their free-thinkers' views and their decision to co-habit outside of marriage (Lewes' estranged wife had borne a number of children by Thornton Hunt, Lewes' co-editor at the *Leader*, but nonetheless wouldn't let Lewes out of the marriage). As a way of dealing with her isolation, Lewes urged Eliot to consider trying her hand at fiction-writing. In order to shield her from the opprobrium she faced for her private life, she chose to write her novels under the name George Eliot – which was kept a tightly held secret with only herself, Lewes, Spencer, and her publisher in the know. However, after Chapman, who had his suspicions about the true identity of the author of *Adam Bede*, her second novel, pressed the matter, Lewes felt it necessary to send Chapman a prevaricating denial in Eliot's behalf. "As you seem so very slow in appreciating her feelings on this point, she authorizes me to state, as distinctly as language can do so, that she is not the author" of *Adam Bede*, he wrote. However, eventually Eliot's identity as the author became widely known.[69]

After Eliot made her mark as a novelist, she had little to do with the world of British journalism – except, of course, through her connection with Lewes. As a literary editor, Lewes was a talent spotter, and some have sensed a mercenary motive in his advice to Eliot. The popularity of novel-writing had reached a peak, and novels were making writers such as Dickens and Thackeray rich – and they did Eliot, too. And yet, the stature of journalism versus novel-writing is demonstrated by the multitude of studies and biographies of Eliot today, while Lewes the journalist is a figure who is largely neglected. In their time, though, Lewes was a prolific commentator in a wide variety of publications, and his non-fiction books were as widely read as Eliot's fiction. In fact, Lewes displayed a wry pragmatism in his acceptance of marketplace dictates. Of those who complained that always writing for the market degraded public taste, he responded, "Perhaps so; and perhaps not. But in granting a want of due preparation in the public, we only grant that the author has missed his aim."[70]

COLERIDGE, LAMB, DE QUINCEY, AND JOURNALISM AS ADDICTION

Coleridge, troubled emotionally and addicted to opium as he was, always felt that writing for periodicals was good for his creative health. However, he shared Poe's distress at trying to make a living in the world of newspaper and commercial journalism. Coleridge's nearly ten years as a contributor and political reporter for the London *Morning Chronicle* and the London *Morning Post* gave him a taste of journalistic writing but also led him to say, "never pursue literature to a trade." Coleridge tended to segregate newspaper journalism in his mind from more elevated pursuits, saying the press promises neither "fame to myself or permanent good to society – but only to gain the bread which might empower me to do both the one and the other on my vacant days." He described himself in that period as "a pure Scribbler," and said, "We Newspaper scribes are true Galley-Slaves." But Coleridge also talked of the satisfaction he gained from the knowledge that his essays contributed to placing the events of the day within a moral point of view. Perhaps not surprisingly for a drug addict, he spoke of his journalistic work as highly stimulating and difficult to withdraw from. (Journalism, he said, tends to "narrow the Understanding and ... acidulate the Heart," which he compared to a "disease" that "I know not how to get rid of it. Life were so flat a thing without Enthusiasm – that if for a moment it leaves, I have a sort of stomach-sensation attached to all my thoughts, like those which succeed to the pleasurable operation of a dose of Opium.") In fact, Coleridge never shook either his opium addiction or his desire to make his mark as a journalist and as an editor of an intelligent and cultured periodical.[71]

And yet, his two forays into founding periodical publications were unqualified disasters, both from a financial and critical standpoint. His first publication, the *Watchman*, was an idealistic venture to provide an independent newspaper in Bristol, England, that would counter a corrupt, government-controlled press in the city. But the paper lasted only six weeks, folding in 1796. Coleridge had little journalistic experience, his copy was dull, despite sometimes being indiscreet, and he was overwhelmed in trying to write most of the copy for the paper while performing other editorial and financial tasks. His second venture, the *Friend*, which he published from 1809 to 1810, was an even greater public failure because it happened after he had achieved his reputation as one of England's great romantic poets. His friends saw it as an impending disaster; Coleridge's personality was unstable, his ambitions too large, and the magazine was written above the head of the average reader. Even Coleridge described the publication as "dull, paradoxical, abstruse, dry, obscure and Heaven knows what else!" Hazlitt called the *Friend* "an enormous title-page ... an endless preface to an imaginary work." He added that Coleridge should "live in a world of enchantment ... Let him talk on for ever in this world and the next; and both worlds will be the better for it. But let him not write, or pretend to write nonsense. Nobody is the better for it."[72]

Lamb was a member of a remarkable circle of early and pre-Victorian journalists (which included De Quincey and Hazlitt) who managed to achieve literary fame and influence as essayists and critics without producing particularly memorable poetry, drama, or fiction themselves. Like his good friends, Coleridge and De Quincey, Lamb moved in and out of the robust journalistic life of hard-drinking and intense good fellowship, all the while cultivating the reputation of a warm-spirited dilettante who was more interested in children's literature than in producing great art or settling journalistic scores. A good friend of what one critic has called a roll call of the major figures of the Romantic Age, Lamb tried his hand at poetry and imaginative writing – but most of his efforts at high literature demonstrated a lack of genius that he good-naturedly accepted as fair judgment (he "gave up" writing poetry many times, as he put it, as he did smoking).[73]

In the end, Lamb's forte proved to be the periodical essay, written in a "quaint" and "archaic" style filled with Latinates that had a mellifluous appeal to certain readers of his day. Lamb's accomplishment in the essay form was exemplified by his conversational form of expression and his method for building his discussion around an interesting character or character-type that he had known. Although largely apolitical and disinterested in politics, he wrote for liberal, reformist periodicals, such as the *Albion*, the *Morning Post*, the *Examiner*, and the *Champion*. (Lamb once said of his work at the *Albion*, which attacked the government regularly, that "our occupation … was to write treason.") Lamb hated to hear it said of him, but he was "gentle-hearted" in print. (Lamb suggested to Coleridge, who kept describing Lamb this way, that he substitute: "drunken dog, ragged-head, self-shaven, odd-eyed, stuttering, or any other epithet which truly and properly belongs to the gentleman in question.")[74]

Lamb put in his time in the vineyards of newspaper journalism – but his figure was (like Sinclair Lewis, E. B. White, and John Steinbeck) one of the first of the prototype of failed daily journalists who did better (at least marginally) at producing elevated literature. Lamb was no good at deadline writing ("I can't do a thing against time," he lamented), nor did he take his journalism terribly seriously (of his work for the *Albion*, he wrote, "the seal of my well known hand-writing was enough to drive any nonsense current.") Lamb's humor, his modesty, and his "moral sense," in the words of Thackeray (who celebrated Lamb as a model), led Coleridge to write of Lamb that "he is not great, yet eminent; not profound, yet penetrating; not passionate, yet gentle, tender, and sympathizing."[75]

Like Coleridge and Lamb, De Quincey also accepted writing as a trade, just as he accepted his opium use as an addiction. However, he made little distinction between journalistic and more literarily elegant forms of writing and suffered less than Coleridge from the sense that journalism stifled his originality. De Quincey could write about anything, and he often found himself discoursing about topics that he knew very little about. He worked a good deal for *Blackwood's* magazine, but he had a stormy relationship with the publication, whose Tory biases he never accepted. He also wrote political essays and analysis – much of it for the *Edinburgh Saturday Post*, another conservative publication – where he keyed off the news of the day and spun his own reflections (which, despite his misgivings, had to hew to the publication's political line).[76]

Once a great admirer of Coleridge, De Quincey was responsible for tarnishing Coleridge's posthumous memory with a series of articles in 1834 for *Tait's* magazine that praised Coleridge's genius but mingled it with references to his addiction to opium. At one point in their friendship, De Quincey became aware of Coleridge's troubles with opium – although he apparently did not acknowledge his own addiction to his friend. Interestingly, the work that made De Quincey's name – *The Confessions of an English Opium-Eater* – was never published in *Blackwood's*, to which it had been contracted. The magazine's editor, John Wilson, had worked hard to lure De Quincey into the magazine's stable of Tory wits. However, De Quincey was forever dallying in his production. Owing the magazine money for advances on work not completed, De Quincey wrote a long letter to Wilson and mentioned an article on opium: "Opium has reduced me for the last six years to one general discourtesy of utter silence. But this I shall think of with not so much pain, if this same opium enables me (as I think it will) to send you an article." However, when the piece finally arrived, it led to a tiff with Wilson over whether it had arrived too late for the magazine's January, 1821 edition. The fight led to an exchange of insults that eventually resulted in the publication of De Quincey's masterpiece in *Blackwood's* rival, the *London Magazine*. (The dust-up – along with allegations that *Blackwood's* was mocking Coleridge by baiting him into writing problematic contributions to the magazine – was also one of the factors in a feud that led to a duel between *London Magazine* editor, John Scott, and *Blackwood's* agent, Jonathan Henry Christie, costing Scott his life.)[77]

Even though commercialism and industrialization were fast changing the periodical world, the hard lines of modern specialization hadn't yet set in during the eighteenth and early-to-mid-nineteenth centuries when Defoe, Swift, Fielding, Dickens, Thackeray, and Lamb wrote, and they could engage in a wide range of literary pursuits that still constituted the practice of journalism in the eyes of their contemporaries. The lively relationship between the literary and the journalistic worlds during this period is, in many respects, a testimony to how impoverished the discourse of both the arts and of journalism has become in our more professionally narrow time. One must be wary of romanticizing "The Age of Periodicals," as it has come to be known, just as much as the "Age of Johnson," as some of his admirers have done in treating with great nostalgia the coffee-house culture of

Johnson's time. Partisanship, polemics, mean-spiritedness, score settling, and problematic ethical and professional journalistic practices were still major features of the era. However, the practice of a literarily enriched and politically influential journalism was enhanced by a periodical environment that made it possible to market provocative and creative ideas to both an intellectual elite and a mass audience. The stream of literary and journalistic history would soon separate in the specialized days ahead. But one must pay homage to this 150-year-period as an important stage in the development of a journalism that lays claim to a higher artistic purpose and a literature that draws upon the strength, directness, and honesty of the journalistic endeavor.

CHAPTER 2

Literary realism and the fictions of the industrialized press, 1850–1915: Mark Twain to Theodore Dreiser

(Your literature is) all such truth – truth to life; everywhere your pen falls it leaves a photograph. I did imagine that everything had been said about life at sea that could be said – but no matter, it was all a failure and lies, nothing but lies with a thin varnish of fact – only you have stated it as it absolutely is.

— Mark Twain to William Dean Howells

I have known ... men as truthful, but not so promptly, so absolutely, so positively, so almost aggressively truthful. He could lie, of course, and did to save others from grief or harm; he was not stupidly truthful; but his first impulse was to say out the thing and everything that was in him.

— William Dean Howells on Mark Twain

I was never more confounded than by the discrepancy existing between my own observations and those displayed here, the beauty and peace and charm to be found in everything ... Perhaps, as I now thought, life as I saw it, the darker phases, was never to be written about ... I read and read, but all I could gather was that I had no such tales to tell, and however much I tried, I could not think of any.

— Theodore Dreiser in his memoirs, describing the magazines
he read in the days when he was trying to establish
himself as a serious writer

The art of depicting nature as seen by toads.
— Ambrose Bierce's definition of Realism in the *Devil's Dictionary*

While he scanned the snarled banks and the turbulent waters as a young pilot-in-training on a Mississippi River paddle-wheeler in the late 1850s, Mark Twain had no idea he was receiving the perfect training for a future writer and pioneer in the school of American literary realism. Twain (who was still called Sam Clemens, and hadn't yet taken the famous pen name that came from the cry of Mississippi River pilots signaling water depth) had just been told that his job would require him to memorize every detail along the river in order to safely pilot the boat downriver – at night, if necessary.

"Now if my ears hear aright, I have not only to get the names of all the towns and islands and bends, and so on, by heart, but I must even get up a warm personal acquaintanceship with every old snag and one-limbed cottonwood and obscure wood pile that ornaments the banks of this river for twelve hundred miles," he complained in his memoir-travelogue, *Life on the Mississippi*. " … I wish the piloting business was in Jericho and I had never thought of it."[1]

In the intervening years between Twain's cub-pilot days and his emergence as a master of American humor and one of the most popular literary figures of his time and ours, Twain honed his descriptive skills as a newspaper reporter and editor, first on the *Territorial Enterprise* in Virginia City, Nevada, where he developed the art of writing half-truthful articles to entertain his audience of miners and roughnecks, then as a reporter on the *San Francisco Daily Morning Call*, where he learned that straight news reporting was not for him, and finally as the managing editor of the *Buffalo Express*, where he demonstrated his talent as a conventional journalistic editor but also learned how little he enjoyed the job and how much he had come to scorn the business. "That awful power, the public opinion of a nation, is created in America by a horde of ignorant, self-complacent simpletons who failed at ditching and shoemaking and fetched up in journalism on their way to the poorhouse," Twain once opined.[2]

And yet, throughout Twain's literary career, he never strayed far from journalism – perhaps to the detriment of the ultimate body of his literary production, some critics have claimed. For example, Twain took a break from the writing of his classic novel, *The Adventures of Huckleberry Finn*, to produce a journalistic account of his visits to his boyhood home in Missouri and other Mississippi River valley towns which had been transformed by the Industrial Revolution from the idyllic place where Twain remembered growing up. That non-fictional account, later expanded and published as *Life on the Mississippi*, contains Twain's memories of his cub-piloting experience, as well as his fulminations at the impact of the Gilded Age, as Twain dubbed the period of great nineteenth-century American industrial fortune making, on the urban and rural communities of inland America.

Like many other American journalist-literary figures, who often were deeply influenced by Twain, Twain's literary philosophy was shaped by his experiences growing up in small-town America – in his case, the Mississippi River Valley town of Hannibal, Missouri – and then as a journalist in both the American hamlet and the large city. This was a period when, as Twain's own career attests, American newspapers were being transformed from the desultory products of print shops that contained low art and folksy humor, haphazard news items, and florid, sentiment-laden writing into the large-scale, bureaucratized, mass-produced products of commercial and industrial efficiency of today. Twain, whose working life spanned both sides of this development, came to feel that the small-town newspapers where he had learned his trade as a printer and reporter could not provide the needed scope for his creative talent. But he also decided that he could not fit himself and his vision of honest self-expression into the strict writing and reporting formulas of the newly emergent big-city newspaper. Twain – like his contemporaries William Dean Howells and Ambrose Bierce, as well as later journalistic figures who emulated him, including Sherwood Anderson, Theodore Dreiser, Erskine Caldwell, Richard Wright, Sinclair Lewis, Ernest Hemingway, and John Steinbeck – believed in an uncompromising presentation of life's circumstances as they were experienced by average people. And newspapers – whether they were in small towns or big cities, as Twain learned through experience – were not fulfilling this mission in their lack of candor, intelligence, and deeper social perspective in which they presented the events of the world. "Mentality," Twain once said of his work at the *San Francisco Daily Morning Call*, "was not required or needed in a *Morning Call* reporter."[3]

To a striking degree, themes revolving around the movement of the population between provincial settings and the urban centers make up a large body of the work of the journalist-literary figures. Even among the realists who turned their backs on their rural and small-town upbringings (or what has been termed the "revolt from the village"), the themes and plots and characters of their novels are often focused upon, one might even say obsessed with, the social and economic cleavages that the movement from the countryside to the large cities was creating in industrialized society. Some of their novels sentimentalized country and small-town life; sometimes they painted a picture of the hollowness of small-town booster life and the claustrophobic world of provincial people who all know each others' business. Some of their novels presented a glittering picture of the urban world discovered by those who had fled the hinterlands; others presented urban life as harsh and forbidding and offered a grim picture of the rural immigrants who foundered there. But in virtually all the works there is the message that something about the shift of the population brought about by industrialization and the commercialization of the culture had left a psychological mark on the lives of their contemporaries. As real-life adventurers who personally experienced the transformation from small-town innocents to cosmopolitan urbanites, the literary realists were fascinated by the way that the Industrial Revolution, and the cultural changes that flowed from it, were reshaping the fabric of society and leaving many people torn between a simpler past they sometimes romanticized but were happy to abandon and a cosmopolitan future that often promised more than it could deliver.

The period between the 1830s and the 1890s, when the steam-powered printing press was widely introduced into the newspaper business and the model of the "Penny Press" newspaper grew to dominate the journalistic scene, can be seen as a demarcation line in the journalist-literary figures' recognition of the small town as a distinct culture from the big city. Before that period, the life of the small town was incorporated into a seamless national vision in the literature of the journalists who are now studied as serious artists. Writers such as Daniel Defoe, Jonathan Swift, Henry Fielding, Benjamin Franklin, Oliver Goldsmith, and Washington Irving wrote about the small town as part of a fabric of a national culture that saw many people (and particularly the gentry) living in both cities and the country. After the 1830s (and certainly by the American Civil War) there is a split in the portrayal of characters associated with small towns and the rural countryside from those living in the big city. The small town as the focus of a form of literary sociological analysis becomes ever more prominent in the writing of the journalist-literary figures who make up what has become known as the literary realism movement – and in that of the American ones, in particular. In their work, it is often city dwellers looking back (or down) upon the small town or rural life that they have left that constitutes many of the plots and the tensions between the characters in their literature. The portraits of provincial life in this turbulent period became dominant elements in the literature of Twain, Howells, and Bret Harte as they experienced the Industrial Revolution transforming both urban and rural life. Even as they moved their literary attention to urban life (and as they permanently settled there), their literature and their autobiographical writings tended to look upon the small town with nostalgia and an affectionately satirical eye. By the late nineteenth century and into the early twentieth century, the focus of the writers who are considered to be the inheritors of literary realism (many of them ex-journalists) became ever more centered upon the activities of urban society – and particularly the mass culture of the industrialized cities. The writers who continued to focus on rural and small-town life tended to do it from the perspective of social parodists or literary sociologists. Interestingly, virtually all the journalist-literary figures in this camp – including Twain, Howells, Harte, and Bierce, as well as Dreiser, Wright, Lewis, Caldwell, Steinbeck, Joel Chandler Harris, Hamlin Garland, O. Henry (William Sydney Porter), Willa Cather, Ring Lardner, James Thurber, E. B. White, James Agee, and Katharine Anne

Porter – wrote from the perspective of small-town or small-city natives who had migrated to the urban centers and had no intention of returning.

A number of these small-town transplants – including Garland and Cather, for example – are sometimes also classified as "naturalists" and a bridge generation to the group of grim and fatalistic writers who (almost all journalists by background) have become known for ushering in the bleak artistic vision that characterized much twentieth-century literature. Literary historians tend to characterize naturalism as an extension of literary realism and the naturalists as a depressive next generation of advocates of the same experience-based writing philosophy that was aligned against false sentimentality, pious rhetoric, and upbeat orthodoxies of life. Unlike Twain and Howells, whose disillusionment was uplifted by strong strains of idealism and cultural confidence, the naturalists reflected a worldview imbued with grim messages about the bleakness of life and the tragic fate that awaited all creatures.[4] The application of Darwinian biological notions to social and economic circumstances was embraced by a number of the naturalists, who put to literary use the concept of "survival of the fittest" (a phrase of the economist Herbert Spencer) in their portrayals of the ruthless business practices and harsh social and economic conditions of late nineteenth- and early twentieth-century life. Books such as Stephen Crane's *Maggie: A Girl of the Streets*, Frank Norris' *McTeague*, Jack London's *People of the Abyss*, and Dreiser's *Sister Carrie* and *The Titan* are seen as the American equivalents of the literature of Emile Zola, the French naturalist who argued that a writer should treat one's characters as if they were the subjects of a scientific experiment and examine their actions with the clinical detachment of a researcher tracking the movement of laboratory animals. This form of behavioralism – while endorsed only up to a point by most of the American literary naturalists – is often seen as the decisive characteristic of the naturalist's philosophy, and its elements play out to a greater or lesser degree in many of their novels. In this view, the naturalists can be seen as the embodiment within literature of the completion of the transition of the US to an industrialized economy – and of a press culture whose locus had shifted from the village print shop operation to the large industrialized newspapers that needed urban economies and stories of the "concrete jungle" to prosper.

The connection between the emergence of literary realism and the convulsions of American social and economic life during the mid-to-late nineteenth century has been commented upon extensively. When one examines the backgrounds of the lives of the majority of the writers in this movement, certain shared patterns help to explain why they put such a premium upon forthright and even brutally honest expression, and why the journalism of the period played such a significant role in spawning a literature that attacked excess sentimentality, false piety, economic inequity, racial prejudice, aristocratic notions of class, and oppressive religion. Industrialization was transforming American life, often in dual fashion – undermining village production of goods and services and rural farming practices while providing new opportunities for displaced workers in factories and urban industries, creating boom-and-bust cycles where wrenching recessions followed expansionary periods, and reshaping traditional businesses (such as newspapers and periodicals) through the coming of new technological inventions (for example, the steam-powered printing press, which came to big-city American newspapers in the 1830s, and the updated and more efficient spindle-screw press, which was a boon to village and small-city publications). Genteel cultural patterns were replaced with a rawer populist atmosphere where money, mass markets, and dreams of riches fueled business life, and the democratic optimism of Walt Whitman, the transcendentalism of Ralph Waldo Emerson and Henry David Thoreau, and the domination of letters by the New England literary Brahmins gave way to a rowdier and more commercialized literary environment. The opportunities that Twain and the other small-town or small-city transplants found in journalism were critical to the growth of their confidence that they had something to say to the world and contributed greatly to their finding a literary platform that allowed them to confirm in their early lives a vision of truth that did not shirk from showing how real people lived in a world that was being transformed in sometimes breathtaking ways.

Realism's commitment to regionalism can be seen as a reflection of the localism and provinciality that still percolated within the early nineteenth-century American press and the lessons that the realists learned from working on small newspapers located on the western frontier. The importance that Twain, Harte, and Bierce (and, in a more refined fashion, Howells) put upon satire and irony reflects the important role of humor-writing as a distinctive product of American regional journalism. Harte is sometimes denigrated as little more than a regional writer who never rose above stock devices in his celebration of the Californian gold rush country. In contrast, Twain – who, with his work on the *Territorial Enterprise* and his early imitations of Artemus Ward and other newspaper humorists (as in "The Celebrated Jumping Frog of Calaveras County") – is often credited with both transcending the regionalism of his literary beginnings and relying upon it in the creation of many of his most celebrated works. In reality,

Twain would never have ascended to the status of literary celebrity without the tone of regional writing that he drew upon, and he might never have developed the confidence to stretch his creative talents if he hadn't found his early efforts in journalism so enthusiastically greeted by his small-town newspaper audiences. One of the ironies of this period is that Twain, who came to evince such hostility to his one-time mentor, benefited so greatly from Harte's early editing at the *Overland Monthly* and encouragement to move beyond the role of regional humorist. Harte suffered much abuse from Twain in later years, not least because Twain argued that Harte never managed to transcend a regional vision in his writing. This judgment – fair as it may be in many respects – neglects the achievement of Harte in defining the western myth that has continued to shape America's (and Hollywood's) image of the frontier. If Harte sentimentalized his caricature gamblers, saloon gals, and prospectors, his contribution to the realistic tradition reflected many of the same stereotypical patterns as Twain's use of American types in the creation of the footloose, small-town prankster boy, the noble, big-hearted escaped slave, and the freedom-loving, truth-telling hillbilly urchin.[5]

The emphasis that the literary realists put upon personal experience, the need to continuously test notions of truth, and the practical benefits of any theory or hypothesis were imported directly from a pragmatic and empirically oriented newsroom ethic that had come to permeate journalism by the latter half of the nineteenth century. Journalists of this period were coming to side with science in the great debates of the age – science versus the Bible, Darwin and his supporters versus biblical literalists in explaining the origins of the cosmos and of humankind – and the press as an institution liked to believe that its methodologies were the product of science and the scientific method. In similar fashion, the literary realists' rejection of dogmatic principles or fixed philosophical formulas reflected the spirit of a news business that saw itself dealing in the flux and flow of world events and in day-to-day truths that of necessity must be modified by changing circumstances. The "relative" morality of the literary realists – with their spurning of absolutist, moralistic, or rigidly judgmental value systems – reflected a tolerant, live-and-let-live view of ethics and morals that could be seen in the typical newsroom of the day, such as Dreiser describes in his memoirs about his early newspaper days.[6]

Although the realist literary movement is considered to have touched British literature (George Eliot, for example, is often categorized as a realist), British journalist-literary figures of this period did not, for the most part, come from the same backgrounds or follow the same career paths as their

American counterparts. Charles Dickens and William Thackeray, as well as Eliot, demonstrated a strong interest in the nitty-gritty details of real life, and their various life deprivations played an important role in how they viewed the world as writers. However, none seemed as committed to a form of literary populism as were their American counterparts, and none promoted it as a literary philosophy with the proselytizing zeal of a Howells or a Twain. Of the other British journalists-turned-novelists born in the nineteenth century, George Meredith, Rudyard Kipling, and E. M. Forster also can be seen as manifesting elements of literary realism and naturalism in their writing, but again the principles that guided those two movements in America could not be considered as foundational to their writing or as important as a literary philosophy as they were to Twain, Howells, and later to the American naturalists whose writing principles grew out of literary realism.

The US Civil War is often seen as the defining event that brought disillusionment with nineteenth-century views about inevitable progress, and the war's impact reverberated intensely through the lives and careers of the literary realists. Coverage of the Civil War brought to the forefront the large American newspaper, with its advanced technology and reporters at the front of the action to satisfy a nation demanding up-to-date accounts of the war. The war helped to breed notions of the press as an organ for bad news, as a voice that could be an adversary to the government, and as an institution that could exacerbate divisions within a nation whose sense of unity and destiny in the world had been torn apart by the conflict. The war had little direct impact upon Twain, Howells, or Harte personally (Twain was briefly a member of the Confederate-sympathizing Missouri State Guard but never saw any battlefield action; Howells used health issues to avoid service in the Northern Army; Harte spoke at pro-Union rallies in California but didn't feel the need to join up as a soldier).[7] However, the war (with its carnage, its opportunity for people to buy their way out of the service by paying substitutes, and the crushed pride of the South) was one of many factors that contributed to a growing air of cynicism and defeat in many quarters of the country. Twain and Howells both shared their generation's disillusionment that grew out of the war's colossal loss of life, and they became acerbic critics of America's growing militarism and aggressiveness in asserting its national self-interest overseas. A major thrust of American literary realism was to expose the divide between American platitudes of commerce and religion and the realities of life in the US as an emergent industrial and imperial power. Twain and Howells, as well as Garland, another important ground-breaker in documentary fiction, with his stark exposés of the troubles of farmers and rural communities, did this with dedication. Perhaps the most intense of these debunkers was Bierce, who in some respects had the strongest claim to being a realist – at least, based on his personal experience as a soldier in the Civil War, where he survived a near-fatal wound while an officer in the Union Army. Many critics have seen Bierce's melancholy and his alienation from what he saw as the sham elements of American political and literary life as rooted in the trauma of his war experiences.

The literary realists were fixated upon issues of wealth and economics, and both Twain and Howells were deeply troubled by what today we would call the "structural" inequities of money and power in American society. Howells ultimately came to call himself a Christian socialist; Twain coined the phrase the "Gilded Age" to describe the vast fortunes accumulated by the industrial capitalists of the day (including, he would add, the capitalist-journalists who industrialized the American press). The transformation of newspapers from the print shop ownership and partisan publications of Twain's and Howells' early lives into the powerful industrial bureaucracies that made fortunes for their owners was completed within the lifespan of the two. Twain disliked from the *San Francisco Daily Morning Call* to a large extent because he saw the paper as identified with the political and economic powers-that-be in the city, and he didn't believe that minorities and groups low on the economic ladder got a fair shake in news coverage. Howells became something of a radical in his economic philosophy – particularly in his later years when, deeply influenced by the Christian socialism of Russian writer Leo Tolstoy, he protested plans to execute the Haymarket rioters. Garland's best writing was acutely realistic in nature, and it was carried out as a protest against urban slum conditions and the plight of Midwest farmers struggling against economic and political odds. Like Twain and Howells, Garland was highly political in outlook (interestingly, he considered Howells and Twain frivolous and superficial in their choice of themes and felt they missed the essential economic tragedy of American life). Bierce, too, was a consistent protester of economic injustices in American society – although one would have to term his a "conservative populism" compared to the more liberal Twain, Howells, and Garland. For example, while working for William Randolph Hearst and his chain of newspapers, Bierce made headlines with his one-man crusade to block the Southern Pacific railroad from garnering a major federal subsidy from Congress. Bierce's detestation of Hearst but his willingness to work for him throughout his career typified the way Bierce's cynicism about the self-serving nature of human motives – whether his or others – always came first for him, and his reform instincts second.

The mixed tendency of the realists to draw upon romantic images (of the West, of the American small-town, of the frontier) and to debunk them oscillates throughout Twain's and Howells' fiction. Twain, for example, romanticized small-town life (in *The Adventures of Tom Sawyer*) but grew contemptuous of small-town culture (in *Huckleberry Finn* and *Pudd'nhead Wilson*). And yet, in many places Twain can be accused of engaging in something of the same ruse that was practiced by the big-city journalism of his time – namely, utilizing typecasting while claiming it to be a "realistic" picture of life – and many of his characters draw upon stereotypes that were familiar to readers of nineteenth-century newspapers and popular literature. Later literary realists who came to write in this tradition (such as Lewis, Anderson, and Caldwell) were much more thoroughly devoted to puncturing the myth of the American small town as a healthy and whole-some place, and they went far beyond Twain in lambasting the compla-cency, narrow-mindedness, and collective meanness found there.[8]

Twain's and Howells' views of the benefits of a small-town upbringing, in fact, were highly ambivalent. Both retained a deep love of the memories of growing up in small towns, both lamented the changes that had been visited upon rural and village America by the Industrial Revolution – but both (and Twain, in particular) came to resent the provincial attitudes and racist views that could be found among small-town residents. In the end, both found the lure of the metropolis irresistible in their own lives. As soon as they had established their reputations, they capitalized upon the possi-bilities brought about by journalism in an age of industrialization and mass markets and settled in the East. Both recognized the benefits of celebrity in a mass media age at the same time they shared the Jeffersonian vision of a democratic American fabric of yeoman farmers and small-town residents drawing their civic sustenance from their rural roots. In their own ways, Harte and Garland, too, celebrated the small town and rural world – Harte with his sentimentalized portraits of life in California mining country towns, Garland with his realistic but sympathetic portraits of farmers in the heartland heroically rising above their bitter circumstances. Interestingly, Harte and Garland, too, carried out their careers in big cities, as did Bierce, who grew up in small towns in Indiana but worked in major urban centers throughout his journalistic life. Harte's well-publicized pilgrimage across the country, where he and his family traveled by train to the east coast to "cash in" on his fame as a Californian story writer, had the elements of a morality play with the west coast writer who had sentimentalized frontier life symbolically abandoning the provinces for the opportunities of the great urban centers of the East.

In this respect, the literary realists were fascinated with the rise of the role of cities in an Industrial Age, but they were repelled by it, too. Howells, in particular, thrilled to the teeming scenes of urban life in his many realistic novels placed in big-city settings, and he enjoyed the privileged life he lived in Boston and New York City after becoming a successful editor and author. On many occasions, Howells, like Twain, contrasted the cold impersonality of the city to the simplicity of the small town, and he seldom neglected mentioning the alienating potential of urban life in his city novels. In their own careers, though, Twain and Howells embraced the big city as a place of professional challenge, economic opportunity, intellectual stimulation, and individual excitement.[9] One only has to visit the Twain mansion in Hartford, Connecticut (with its quasi rural setting on the edge of a burgeoning city) to recognize how much the literary realists, like so many American citizens of their time and ours, wanted it both ways, promoting the Jeffersonian faith in the health and integrity of provincial life as they themselves migrated from the farm or small town to find their opportunities in the big city.

The interest of the literary realists in character development (as opposed to plot) and the inner psychology of the individual can be seen as both a product of, and a reaction against, the developments in the increasingly larger and more industrialized newspapers of the nineteenth century. The growing importance of the feature story in the Penny Press newspapers pushed journalists to explore the inner emotional life of the individual; at the same time, the requirement that those emotions be expressed within marketable and socially acceptable formulas worked against authentic explorations of the human psyche. The growing importance of psychology in crime coverage, the use of women feature reporters (sometimes known as "sob sisters") in writing dramatically about the human angle to tragedy, the emphasis put upon "color" stories about city life – all tended to balance the growing tendency of the news to be presented in dry, fact-based conventions (such as the inverted pyramid story structure, leads built around the formula of who-what-when-where-why-how, the use of a spare, wire-service style of writing). However, the emphasis upon writing efficiency and practical forms of communication slowly won out over long, discursive narratives and journalism written with rhetorical flourishes. This transformation of the nineteenth-century newspaper from a forum that incorporated elements of literary expression to a nuts-and-bolts vehicle for the practical conveyance of information helped to set the stage for the twentieth century's view of journalism and literature as two distinct writing categories. Twain, by all accounts, was a conventionally successful editor during his stint as managing editor of the *Buffalo Express*, but he chafed under the routine and exited as soon as he could convince his wife (his father-in-law had helped Twain purchase an interest in the newspaper) that his prospects were greater in an independent writing and public-speaking career.[10]

The literary realists' embrace of simple, colloquial language that spurned romantic sentimentalism and the excesses of romantic expression were reflective of the stylistic and philosophical changes occurring within a press that increasingly operated by the credo of showing life as it was and the facts as they were. The technological and commercial pressures that were transforming newspaper writing – the coming of the telegraph, the creation of the wire services, the development of a neutral, "objective" presentation of the news – filtered into the forms of literature championed by Howells and Twain. However, style was always subordinate with Twain to the realistic portrayal of the world, and even his greatest exaggerations are designed always to make a point that he feels tells an important truth. While Twain sometimes utilized the rhetorical flourishes that can be identified with the era of print-shop newspapers, he also came under the influence of the short, staccato, concise prose style that came to characterize the news columns of late nineteenth-century newspapers. Although Twain liked spinning fantasies and telling tall tales, he put a high premium upon the importance of facts, and he believed in honest writing as a method to cut through cant, double-talk, and false pieties (or "soul, butter, and hogwash," as Huck Finn put it).[11]

Literary realism's rejection of sentimental stereotypes and excessive emo-tionality (such as that reflected in the propagandistic themes and emotion-ally manipulative personalities of Harriet Beecher Stowe's *Uncle Tom's Cabin* or the romance literature of Sir Walter Scott) led to the movement's embrace of an unadorned picture of "real" life and a portrayal of "human feelings in their true proportion," as Howells put it. The growing grittiness of the urban newspapers and their focus upon the underside of urban life (sex, crime, scandal, etc.) cultivated an appetite in the reading public for the painful and even violent truths of life and a fascination with the rule-breaker and the aberrational personality. Although Twain and Howells exploited the notion of the "rogue" and the "risk-taker" in their literature, both were too much products of a genteel age to do more than deal gingerly (if at all) with issues of sex, extreme violence, and human perversion. It would be left to the heirs of the realists – the naturalists – and the no-holds-barred artists of the twentieth century to move realism into more graphic portrayals of human sexuality and cruelty.[12]

At the same time, literary realism's commitment to life in its complex and ambiguous forms is clearly a turning away from the sentimental and sensationalistic formulas that had begun to define the approach of the nineteenth-century big-city newspapers in marketing the news. Even though Twain, in particular, engaged in his own form of stereotyping in the creation of his characters, his and Howells' disgust with the cardboard-cut-out portrayal of life in the daily press can be seen, at the literary level, in their rejection of sensationalized scenarios and improbable plot twists and their commitment to recognizable settings, characters fraught with human flaws, and real life events. Howells was accused of belonging to the "reporting" school of literary art, but he wasn't afraid to employ the tedium of detail when he felt it was needed to convey a picture of life as it really was. However, the literary realists' recognition of what appealed to the popular imagination encouraged them, in the marketing of their literature and their journalism, to rely sometimes upon the low arts (parody, farce, burlesque, tall tales, in the case of Twain's literature and his journalism; bombast, extravagance, and vituperation, in the case of Bierce's journalism, and the use of the bizarre, the mysterious, and the grotesque in his fiction, for example). Twain's willingness to build his literary career out of low-brow humor and satire led the somewhat stuffy Howells to opine of Twain that "it would be limiting him unjustly to describe him as a satirist; and it is hardly practicable to establish him in people's minds as a moralist; he has made them laugh too long; they will not believe him serious; they think some joke is always intended."[13]

The political progressivism and personal humanism of the literary realists was a parallel development to the emergence of the progressive editorial page of the nineteenth-century newspaper that, in the tradition of James Gordon Bennett, Horace Greeley, Joseph Pulitzer, Charles Dana, and E. W. Scripps, touted reform, egalitarianism, and open government. While Twain and Howells spurned romantic sentiment and were suspicious of avowals of piety, they were fully idealists in their political values. Despite Twain's growing cynicism about the possibility for human beings to over-come their sinful nature, he and Howells sided strongly with the progressive reformers who were protesting economic and political abuses in American life. Literary realism as an extension of political reform in the late nineteenth- and early twentieth-century follows in the tradition of American journalism as "objective" but reform oriented when need be.[14] To say Twain and Howells gained their reform notions from their experience in journalism would be a simplification. But journalism as a calling (and their contribution to the shaping of the journalistic ethic in America) owes much to the identification that they and other like-minded journalistic reformers made between the unearthing of "facts" and the use of those facts to challenge social and economic inequities.

Their orientation toward the practical and the down-to-earth might be expected to contribute to a hostility by the literary realists toward the utopian thinking and romantic idealism that was prevalent in the early nineteenth-century (such as that touted by the widely admired Greeley, a transcendentalist, social reformer, and supporter of the Brook Farm experiment). But this wasn't the case at all. With his Quaker and Swedenborgian ancestry, Howells, who had always shown an interest in utopian communities and their relationship to a "wicked world," grew more sympathetic in his later years toward those who had withdrawn from the world to pursue a more perfect way of living. This sympathy was demonstrated in *The Undiscovered Country*, which painted a sympathetic picture of the Shaker religious community, as well as in his *A Traveler from Altruria* and *Through the Eye of the Needle*, both of which documented a visit to America by an imaginary alter ego from an idealized country that had corrected the economic and political conditions that so distressed Howells. Twain, too, was drawn to discuss notions of utopian and romantic perfectionism, which were so popular in nineteenth-century fiction (much of it inspired by their fellow journalist-literary figure Edward Bellamy's *Looking Backward*) but in Twain's usual divided and ambivalent fashion. In his most complex literary exploration of the subject, *A Connecticut Yankee in King Arthur's Court*, Twain holds up two nineteenth-century ideals in America – the romantic fascination with the legends of King Arthur's court as expressed in Sir Thomas Malory's *Le Morte d'Arthur* and the nineteenth-century belief in the superiority of technology, democracy, and constitutional government – and finds both wanting. In his satire of a nineteenth-century Connecticut tradesman who finds himself in the medieval "hell" of King Arthur's England, Twain sought to burst both the romantic myth of the glories of a long-lost chivalric age and the optimistic nineteenth-century assumption that "modern" life was superior to the ways of the past. Twain clearly was parodying the romantic and utopian fantasies of his age, but he was equally debunking the view that modern democratic ideals had produced a better world.[15]

While Twain is revered as one of the founders of the realistic movement in American literature (his writing, to a great degree, encompasses the very definition of the term), his literary vision was expressed in oscillation between two extremes on the scale of human feelings. He was a powerful romantic at heart, but his sentimental accounts of growing up in early nineteenth-century small-town America were equaled by his bitter screeds against the bathos and false piety of American culture and the greed of the American economic system. Even today, there is no more trenchant and widely quoted commentator on the light and the dark side of the American dream, and Twain continues to fascinate scholars and literary critics as much as readers of popular fiction who have never ceased to enjoy the product of his idyllic view of growing up as a scuffling boy in Hannibal, Missouri as much as his wit-laden polemics against the hypocrisies and narrowness of American culture. Twain's reputation as both a literary realist and a scathing critic of the self-delusions of American society – who all the while marketed his own brand of romance and sentimentalism – is mirrored in the works of his friends, erstwhile friends, and fellow "realists," Howells, Harte, and Bierce, who also saw themselves as chiding a naïve American idealism and mocking provincial American attitudes at the same time they were romanticizing and typecasting them (in Harte's case), excoriating them (in Bierce's case), and dissecting them through satirical critiques of the self-satisfaction of American manners and social values (in Howell's case).

TWAIN, HOWELLS, AND THE PRINT SHOP
AS THE "POOR BOY'S COLLEGE"

Twain's fiction was earthy, hard scramble – a lot like his life – and Twain profited mightily from his experiences in the democratic traditions of American journalism. For Twain, the addition of humor and levity was what he believed the public wanted and what made the journalism business fun for him. Twain's humor – cultivated in the low-brow commentary, the telling of tall tales, and hoaxes perpetuated to amuse the mining camp audience of the *Territorial Enterprise* – was considered crude, but was widely effective in building a popular following. Twain's characters were usually lower-middle-class to poor in economic origins and almost always people who learned life's lessons from the direct experience of it. From his early work on his older brother, Orion's, newspapers in Hannibal (the Hannibal *Journal*) and Muscatine, Iowa (the *Muscatine Journal*), Twain concluded that standard American journalism was too bland and serious in tone (he blamed his brother's too-earnest approach to journalism for his lack of economic success in the business). Twain learned many of his early lessons by trying to add zest to his brother's paper, which carried mostly telegraph and big-city news, polite literature, and windy editorial analysis. Twain's opportunity came in September, 1852, when his brother was out of town and left the paper in charge of the teenage Twain (still known as Sam Clemens). Twain soon graced the pages of the paper with a satiric discussion of a fabricated proposal to kill all dogs in town as a way of countering dog bites, and he "exposed" a hoax from a so-called account of a Hannibal pioneer who had charged admission to see a broken bone laid over a bacon rind (called "Bonaparte Crossing the Rhine"). Upset when he got back, Orion soon softened when he saw the new accounts and subscribers, and gave his brother a local affairs column. (However, Twain chafed under his brother's iron rule and finally left his employment, nursing the first of many grudges against people who attempted to tell him what to do.)[16]

In his first reporting job with the *Territorial Enterprise*, Twain experienced an increasingly rare aspect of nineteenth-century journalism that still connected it to the days of Addison and Steele, when entertaining the audience with an array of literary devices took precedence over "accuracy" or "objective" news standards. Twain caught on with the *Territorial Enterprise* after traveling west in 1861 with Orion, who had been appointed the territorial secretary of Nevada. Twain as a reporter could be accurate, but he found it to be tiresome. When news was slow, he loved to embellish the details in order to fill both space and time. This delighted his editor, Joseph Goodman, who gave Twain almost unlimited freedom to amuse his audience of miners and roughnecks by producing copy that included burlesques, the baiting of rival editors, lampoons, and scientific spoofs. While working on the *Enterprise*, Twain said he learned to hate "solid facts" and "to revel in the blood-curdling particulars and be happy ... I reasoned within myself that news, and stirring news too, was what a paper needed, and I felt that I was peculiarly endowed with the ability to furnish it."[17]

It was inevitable that the demands of sticking to the "hard facts" would prove to be too restrictive for Twain. His move to fiction-writing was pushed along by his brief experience in 1864 on the *San Francisco Daily Morning Call*, the first large newspaper he worked for – and one which typified the evolution of the big-city urban newspapers that were turning into the "respectable" publications of today. Twain, however, found the newspaper anything but respectable – nor did the constraints it put on its reporters meet Twain's idea of truth-telling. Twain famously recalled his reaction to the job at the *Morning Call*: "It was godawful drudgery for a lazy man." However, behind the quips, Twain felt that the news formulas at the *Call* whitewashed the truth and didn't allow for coverage of what was happening in the city. He was particularly disturbed when the *Morning Call* wouldn't print his account of hoodlums stoning a Chinese man for fear that

it would offend the newspaper's Irish readers. In this and other ways, he felt
the newspaper was neglecting its public responsibility. ("I have told them
that Christmas is coming, and people go strangely about, buying things," he
wrote of his *Morning Call* reporting. " … I glorified a fearful conflagration
that came so near burning something, that I shudder even now to think
of it … I printed some other extraordinary occurrences – runaway horse –
28 lines; dog fight – 20 lines; Chinaman captured by officer Rose for stealing
chickens – 90 lines; unknown Chinaman dead on Sacramento steamer –
5 lines … . Much other Wisdom I disseminated, and for these things let my
reward come hereafter.") When the newspaper dismissed him, editor
George Barnes softened the blow by telling Twain that he was out of his
element in routine reporting. "You are capable of better things in literature," he said.[18]

Twain's mixing of his journalistic and his fictional projects were legion
throughout his career. Twain (and his collaborator, Charles Dudley Warner)
used up-to-date political material – including a scandal that broke within
the Grant Administration in 1873 involving an alleged bribery and vote-
buying scheme by a Republican US senator – to fashion the dramatic
situation for *The Gilded Age*, Twain's first foray into full-scale fiction-
writing. Twain (who had already described an earlier visit to Washington,
DC as "a perfect gold mine" that had provided him with "enough material
for a whole book") used the outline of the scandal as a plot and drew
characters from the political news of the day (changing names in the merest
bow to the conventions of fiction, as one biographer put it), even though
critics have complained that the novel collapses under a welter of melodramatic conventions, mislaid characters and contemporary allusion, over-
complicated plot-lines, and improbabilities.[19]

However, those who believe that Twain's fiction suffered from his
continuous forays into journalism often ignore the fact that his journalism
also served at times to re-ignite his creative imagination and to catalyze his
fictional endeavors. For example, his 1875 reminiscences about his youth
as a cub riverboat pilot learning the Mississippi River, first published as a
series of articles he wrote for Howells and the *Atlantic*, have been linked to
the germination and development of *Tom Sawyer*. Similarly, during a
break in his labors while writing *Huckleberry Finn*, he traveled in 1882 to
Hannibal and its environs to gather material for *Life on the Mississippi*, the
expanded account that grew out of the earlier series and a work that has
often been deemed by critics to be his highest quality book-length journalism. However, in undertaking the project, Twain almost gave up on the
possibility that he would ever finish *Huckleberry Finn* and, under pressure

to meet the deadline of a book contract he had signed, went so far as to borrow and adapt a chapter from the partially completed novel to help wrap up the non-fictional project. In turn, he describes in *Life on the Mississippi* a household much like the feuding Grangerford family in *Huckleberry Finn* and, as Shelley Fisher Fishkin has noted, borrowed a number of other scenes from his journalism about the Mississippi River Valley to complete the novel. Interestingly, Twain's foray into reporting apparently convinced him that the theme of *Huckleberry Finn* was topical (realistic books about the South had become popular) and provided him with the incentive to get the planned sequel to *Tom Sawyer* back on track.[20]

Even so, it has been said that Twain's writing never abandoned the elements of the newspaper sketch or the correspondent's letter, and that he had little skill or patience with the organizational structure and plotting of a novel or with fully and roundly developing a character. In this respect, Twain never escaped his journalistic origins, and his most memorable characters – most notably Huck and Jim – can be seen as stereotypes raised to a literary level. While the friendship of Huck and Jim reflects a depth of humanity that has given *Huckleberry Finn* its iconic stature within American literary culture, theirs is still an idealized nobility that draws upon the good-versus-evil scenarios that could be found within the columns of nineteenth-century popular periodicals. In fact, Twain's notions of "realism" lined up with the most confused of newsroom cynics (they still can be found everywhere within journalism) whose fundamentally optimistic view of human nature is rivaled by their scoffing at those who believe that idealistic solutions can be found to overcome the unrelieved depravity of humankind. Twain's ambivalence on this question can be seen throughout *Huckleberry Finn*, for example, where he contrasts the good-hearted Huck and Jim to the malevolent characters on the shore who have been irredeemably corrupted by civilization's ways. Twain's view of the "damned human race" that embittered him in his old age put him in good company with the many disgruntled idealists in the newsroom who have decided to sit on the sidelines while carping against any and all schemes to set right the hopeless human condition.[21]

In many respects, Twain's position as a cultural icon overshadows the place that his literature occupies in the pantheon of great American writing. Twain is revered for the democratic impact of his art – its use of the authentic American voice, its celebration of America's small-town roots, its combination of provincialism and cynicism in viewing life beyond the Mississippi River valley where Twain grew up, its affection toward the

down-and-outers and iconoclasts within American society, and its irreverent view of American public pieties. However, much of what Twain wrote is
frivolous in nature and, with the exception of *Huckleberry Finn*, is not
viewed as serious art by major segments of the critical establishment. Twain's
approach – learned early on in his work for his brother's newspaper – was
always to entertain first, whether through humor, parody, or the telling of a
good story. For someone who jeered at the sentimental elements in the
American literary tradition, Twain was obsessed with ideal worlds and
imagined historical epochs in his own fiction, and his art contains vast
elements of the romanticism it was protesting. His targets – Camelot and
King Arthur's Round Table (*Connecticut Yankee*), the courtly life of the
English monarchy (*The Prince and the Pauper*), schoolboy games of pirates
or outlaws or Aladdin's lamp (*Tom Sawyer* and *Huckleberry Finn*), southern
chivalrous values and the romances of Sir Walter Scott (*Life on the
Mississippi*) – were the very things that had fed his own boyhood imagination. Twain can be called a realist only in a limited sense, if by a realist
one means a person with a bluff, clear-eyed, and unruffled outlook and a
willingness to look unblinkingly at the mortal truths of life. However, the
fact that Twain wrote so often for children is a sign of how much the
romantic imagination of childhood still operated in his adult life, and how
much it contributed to his disappointment and bitterness when life's harsh
realities were visited on him and his family in his later years.

   Despite Twain's popular success, the formal public face of the literary
realist movement was Howells, Twain's life-long friend and mentor, who
from his position as editor of the *Atlantic* magazine, campaigned for a
literature forged out of real-life experience and promoted the careers of
writers who shared his philosophy. From the moment they first met in 1869,
Twain and Howells recognized their remarkable kinship. The list of the
shared experiences of the two "brothers" in realistic literature is a long one
and connects both of them to journalism throughout. Both had limited
formal education and gained much of their learning from the "poor boy's
college" (as Benjamin Franklin once dubbed print-shop employment),
Howells as a youthful type-setter for his father on a series of partisan,
small-town Ohio newspapers, Twain as a type-setter in Hannibal for his
brother and others before also taking on his small-town writing jobs. Both
tasted newsroom life in the big-city newspapers that were being transformed
by the steam-powered printing press and the coming of modern industrialization to the newspaper business – Twain in San Francisco and Buffalo,
Howells in Columbus and Cincinnati. Both made their names as "real-
thing" Midwesterners, whose authentic writing and genuine personalities

won over the east coast literary establishment. Even in their personal lives, the impious and fun-loving Twain, with his tangle of white hair, his trademark cigar, and his white suits, and the paunchy Howells, with his Victorian sense of propriety and his self-conscious cultivation of the role of the "dean" of nineteenth-century letters, were far from the odd couple that they appeared to be. Both became populists who grew angry at the injustices of the American economic system, yet held deeply ambivalent personal views about their own financial success; both moved to the East and established themselves in upscale, literary society; both suffered from depression, anxiety and other emotional troubles throughout their lives; and both were married to intelligent, cultured women who helped "civilize" them (in Twain's case) and gave them the encouragement to move in refined society (in Howells' case).[22]

Howells, like Twain, had his struggles with the constraints imposed upon the journalist by journalistic formulas, but journalism was also in his blood. By the time Howells was twelve, he was working six days a week from five in the morning until eleven at night carrying out his print-shop duties, then was up delivering papers to subscribers at four o'clock in the morning. The printing and publishing business provided Howells' family with a precarious and peripatetic existence, but it also offered Howells crucial training in the skills of composition and editing. Howells' father sometimes let him leave the printing office early to read and study, and Howells felt that he led a double life, with his literary dreams hovering over the grinding existence of print-shop demands. Like Twain, Howells was always slipping sketches, stories, poems, and serial romances into the family paper. As a teenager in 1854, he launched his first fully-fledged novel, *The Independent Candidate*, which was serialized in his father's *Ashtabula (Ohio) Sentinel*. Free-flowing and bold at the start, the novel proved to be over-plotted and over-populated with eccentric Dickensian characters. Caught in the embarrassing position of presenting installments before he knew where the book was going, he finally just killed off some characters and drove the whole enterprise to a hasty conclusion.[23]

Howells spent parts of his early years in journalism shunting between posts at the hometown family newspaper and the *Ohio State Journal* in Columbus, where his father also served as editor and recorder of legislative debate. It was during this period that the realist-to-be discovered that "real" journalistic life was too much for him. In 1857, Howells was offered a staff position involving coverage of police and city government at the *Cincinnati Gazette*, for whom he had served as a legislative correspondent in Columbus. Howells gave up the job after a brief tenure, due to nervous afflictions exacerbated by the difficulties he found in dealing with the seamy side of big-city life. Declaring that "my longing was for the cleanly responsibilities," he came to see little chance for a literary career in dealing with the sordid wife beatings, assaults, robberies, confidence schemes, murders, and attempted suicides that filled the *Gazette.* (Howells described, for example, how his psychic turmoil grew so great that he could not even bear the "impossible stress" of reading the scare headlines and the sensationalized content of the Sunday newspapers.) After returning briefly to Ashtabula to recover his emotional health, he went back to the *State Journal* where he found the work as a political analyst – looking through newspapers, writing commentary and humorous items, translating foreign papers, producing reviews and literary critiques – more compatible with his temperament.[24]

During his Columbus years, Howells felt himself to be outwardly a young journalist but inwardly an aspiring poet. He complained that he hated to put his literary work into the "predatory press ... tossed upon a newspaper sea, a helmless boat, with no clearance papers aboard." Writing home, Howells described his work at the *State Journal* in unflattering comparisons to the poems he was submitting to the *Atlantic* and other national publications: "I am working very hard – reading, studying, and scribbling constantly – aside from the drudgery I perform on the Journal." In 1860, at the age of twenty-three, he traveled to Boston to propose himself for an assistant editor's job at the *Atlantic* and to meet with Dr. Oliver Wendell Holmes, James Russell Lowell, James T. Fields, and other figures of New England literature. It proved to be one of the most celebrated odysseys of self-promotion in American literary history. Howells so greatly impressed the literary Brahmins with his untutored talent that Lowell described him as a "singular fruit ... of our shaggy democracy." As the "uncombed youth" whose "vigor surpassed that of the hereditary scholars," Howells reportedly provoked Holmes to say to Lowell: "Well, James, this is something like the apostolic succession, this is the laying on of hands."[25]

Although he didn't immediately gain the post at the *Atlantic* he had hoped for, Howells' rise in the literary world followed the arc of the Horatio Alger novels of the period. After securing a stint as the American consul in Venice by writing an authorized campaign biography of Abraham Lincoln, Howells came to New York in 1865 to work for the *Nation.* The next year, he moved to Boston to become an assistant editor at the *Atlantic* before rising to the editor's job in 1871. When he became editor, Howells struggled greatly with the wearisome burdens of editing – which he came to call "gilded slavery" – while he was developing his novel-writing career at the same time. His good friend and fellow novelist, Henry James, called

Howells' years with the *Atlantic* "a life of bondage," although Howells makes only passing reference to the exhausting routine of proofreading, editing of manuscripts, and corresponding with contributors in his auto-biographical writings. Described as a person of ease, geniality, and sweet humor, he demonstrated in the job very real capacities of intelligence, critical acumen, and editorial insight (although, like his friend Twain, he believed he didn't have the "discipline" necessary to be a real journalist).[26]

Borrowing from techniques of both journalism and fiction, Howells' first novel, *Their Wedding Journey*, weaves the narrative of a recently wed couple around the structure of a journalistic travel sketch. With this as its beginning, Howells' fiction-writing career skirted the world of journalism at every turn, and he often drew upon journalistic techniques and research methods to forge the "realistic" fictional atmosphere that he so prized. When Howells decided to make a newspaper person the focus of *A Modern Instance* in 1881, he wrote: "I'm making the hero of my divorce story a newspaper man. Why has no one struck journalism before?" Howells then traveled to Indiana to observe a divorce case proceed through a county court and to gather details that would add to the novel's verisimilitude. Howells' knowledge of the magazine-publishing industry was instrumental in his creation of *A Hazard of New Fortunes* with its plot revolving around the creation of a new magazine in New York City. "The modern novel and the newspaper are beginning to assimilate," Howells wrote, "and are becoming very much alike ... The progress of fiction-writing has brought the novelist down to the affairs of everyday life."[27]

As the *Atlantic*'s editor, Howells was himself responsible for luring Twain away from his literary projects for journalistic tasks. In 1874, he commissioned Twain to do a retrospective about growing up in the Mississippi River Valley that was eventually expanded into book form as *Life on the Mississippi*. While editing the first draft of the series (then called "Old Times on the Mississippi"), Howells advised Twain: "Stick to actual fact and character in the thing, and give things in detail. All that belongs with old river life is novel and is now mostly historical. Don't write at any supposed *Atlantic* audience, but yarn it off as if into my sympathetic ear." Howells was not only responsible for coaxing Twain away from the novelist's table at times, but he also served as a lifelong editor of Twain's manuscripts. For example, Howells convinced Twain to clean up the language (sprinkled with hells and damns) in the manuscript of *Tom Sawyer*, as he would with *Huckleberry Finn* and other later works. Twain had complete faith in Howells' editing ("Cut it, scarify it, reject it – handle it with entire freedom," he once told Howells in dealing with a manuscript). Twain knew he was encroaching on a busy man's time, but Howells would faithfully read the material, mark it up, and (improved as it was by Howells' editing) enthusiastically tell Twain that his effort was bound to be popular.[28]

HARTE AND BIERCE – TWO "FRIENDS" OF THE REALISTS (IF NOT NECESSARILY OF REALISM)

As another member of this famous cohort (all of whose writing lives were in a state of continual interaction), Harte was once called the "first American realist," although few would grant him that distinction today. Contemporary critics have moved Harte to the camp of the "romanticists," even though it can be argued that the romantic tendencies in his literature are no greater than Twain's. Harte was seen in his time as a firm member of the realists' school – perhaps because among his contemporaries the romantic elements of his literary vision weren't as apparent as they are today. As with Twain, Harte's emphasis on regionalism and the vivid portrayal of his characters as place-bound products of the wild American West dazzled the readers of his time by their apparent verisimilitude (even though few were able to judge just how real his portrait of Californian frontier life was). At first, his stories were as enchanting to his eastern readers (who saw them as quaint and authentic) as they were upsetting to his Californian readers (who objected to the portrait of westerners as crude bumpkins whose foibles should be grist for the amusement of eastern audiences). In time, critics began to question Harte's literary picture of western life, while Californians came to embrace his romantic portrayals as the lore of "Bret Harte" country and something to be capitalized upon for the sake of tourism and regional pride.[29]

To what extent were Harte's characters and stories drawn from real life? "To a greater or lesser extent," Harte answered. Realism had become the predominant taste among the literati of his time (romance was seen as something false and inferior), and there was, and continues to be, intense discussion about the historical accuracy of Harte's portrayal of Californian life. While today we might appreciate the imaginative portrait of his characters, regardless of discrepancies about geographical details or personal characteristics, Victorian readers took seriously the view that a writer had a moral obligation to tell the truth and to authenticate a fictional portrayal on the basis of personal experience. In the early days of his career, Harte's stories were acclaimed by some critics as mirrors of the West. Others, however, complained that his "pathos very often runs into sentimentality" and that he needed to work hard to keep from lapsing into "falseness and mawkishness." Harte defended himself by saying:

I may say with perfect truth, that there were never any natural phenomena made use of in my novels of which I had not been personally cognizant … My stories are true not only in phenomena, but in characters. I believe there is not one of them who did not have a real human being as a suggesting and starting point.

Like Defoe, Harte tended to claim an authenticity for his stories, even though this sometimes subjected him to entanglements in half-truths and evasions.[30]

One thing is incontestable, though – Harte's experiences in journalism were as formative to his literary career as were Twain's, and every bit as problematic in their contribution to his ultimate literary accomplishments. Harte has described how his work as a youthful compositor on the *Northern Californian* forged both his views about the substance and the style of writing. ("I was very young when I first began to write for the press," he recalled. "I learned to combine the composition of the editorial with the setting of its type," adding that "to save my fingers mechanical drudgery somewhat condensed my style.") However, Harte was dilatory in his work habits and, as a deadline reporter, he did not have much to recommend him ("If … a hole had to be filled in a jiffy, Harte wasn't worth a – !" said one former editor). The journalistic work for which he is best known – and which helped to launch both his literary career and Twain's – took place during his years writing for the specialty literary publications, the *Golden Era* and the *Californian*, which led to his editorship of the *Overland Monthly*. Established as a West Coast rival of the *Atlantic*, the *Overland Monthly* became the vehicle for Harte to develop his mastery of the art of stylish literary criticism, the parodying of famous novelists, and the short story. His success as a magazine editor (he was considered to be excellent in all facets of the job) was demonstrated not only in the writers he recruited to the publication but in his instantly successful short stories, "The Luck of Roaring Camp," "The Outcasts of Poker Flat," and others, which were reprinted in the East to great attention and acclaim.[31]

H. L. Mencken maintained that Bierce, Mencken's friend and fellow mocker of American pieties, was "the first writer of fiction ever to treat war realistically" – to describe soldiers, in Mencken's phrase, as "bewildered animals dying like hogs in Chicago."[32] Bierce – whose journalistic career began in San Francisco at the same time that Twain and Harte were using the city as their literary launching pad – is best remembered as "Bitter Bierce" whose savage barbs at the social and political establishment of his day have made him a favorite of iconoclasts and debunkers, and whose stories of the macabre and the bizarre have become a source of fascination for post-modernist scholars impressed with his clever epistemology and his plotting sleights-of-hand. Bierce was one of a handful of American writers whose reputations are associated with the Civil War, but Bierce is one of the few to have known battle. As a youthful enlistee in the Union Army, he gives some of the only personal, up-close, and often harrowing semi-fictional accounts from a participant in some of the war's most bloody battles at Shiloh, Chickamauga, and Missionary Ridge (in the Union Army, Bierce was repeatedly recognized for bravery under fire; he survived a near-fatal bullet wound in the skull; and he endured a long and painful period of rehabilitation).

Even as his stories of the supernatural and the Civil War appeared first in the periodicals where he worked – first for the San Francisco *Examiner*, then the *New York Journal*, and then *Cosmopolitan* magazine – and then as book compilations, Bierce continued to work as a journalist and columnist for Hearst. In 1881, Bierce published "What I Saw of Shiloh" in the San Francisco *Wasp*, and this began the recounting of his Civil War experiences in journalism and short stories, many of which first appeared in his work for the *San Francisco Examiner*. In Bierce's journalism and short fiction, one is impressed with his constant references to war and war's ever presence in his mind. Bierce used shock and allegory as key techniques in his writing, both in conveying the fear and the loneliness of battle in his war stories and in the tales of the supernatural that became his other specialty. Bierce's employment of foreboding and horror appears to have come from his recognition of the formula as marketable in their use in the Sunday *Examiner* feature stories. Bierce particularly must have noticed how often hangings were covered in the *Examiner* (ten alone in 1889) and in what sensationalistic detail. A favorite technique of his was to gather newspaper clippings of strange and mysterious occurrences, and then rewrite them as stories.[33]

Despite his mastery of the use of realistic detail in his Civil War fiction, Bierce never thought of himself as a realist, and he saw himself as a critic of the school. In his typically sardonic way, he once said to a fellow writer, "Stories are not true and you are too conscientious to make them seem true, and so mislead your fellow creatures. Try writing sermons, which are all true." At the same time, Bierce – unlike Harte – never used stock romantic frontier figures as part of his fiction. The western legend was, Bierce said, bosh. His fiction always relied on the technique he had mastered as a journalist and commentator – short, pithy observations about people and events, which evolved into narrations where irony, shock, and sarcasm dominated. In fact, Bierce's art must be seen in the context of the hoax tradition in journalism that was so popular at the time. ("Early one June morning in 1872 I murdered my father – an act which made a deep impression on me at the time," he began one story.)[34]

As with the emerging news formulas of the late nineteenth century, the literary realists were criticized for focusing too much on the negative. Although this criticism reached its peak with the naturalists, Twain and Howells were often accused of exploiting the baser side of human nature to capture readers. By today's standards, Howells and Twain kept a restrained and dignified tone to their "realistic" portrayals of life. However, this didn't keep their critics from complaining about the subject matter of Twain's and Howells' work (often in terms similar to their critiques of what they called the "gutter" press) and linking their books and their heterodox religious views to the great nineteenth-century debate over Darwinism and Christianity. (Howells' *The Rise of Silas Lapham*, opined one critic in the 1855 *Catholic World*, marked "a descent, a degradation" leading to an art that is "debased when it has fallen so low into realism … It is more probably the logic of the downward progress of godless science … It is the progress from man to apes, from the apes to the worms, from the worms to bacteria, from bacteria to – mud. It is the descent to dirt.")[35]

Ironically, this criticism in their day would become turned around in the years ahead when the realists – and particularly Howells – were criticized for focusing too much on the "smiling aspects" of life (as Howells once referred to his literary approach). As they grew older, Howells, Henry James, and others of the older "realistic" school protested the philistine aspects of the late nineteenth and early twentieth-century publishing business and its impact on those whom they saw as the heirs to their tradition. Even among the new breed of naturalist writers whom he championed (Crane and Norris, most notably), Howells was increasingly disparaged for his genteel approach and the focus upon middle-class manners in his literature. The older style family-owned magazines, such Howells' *Atlantic* and *Harper's*, were viewed as prudish and ossified compared to the new generation of progressive magazines, *McClure's*, *Collier's*, *Cosmopolitan*, *Everyday's*, and the *Arena*, that saw themselves as both barometers of cultural and literary trends and catalysts for political change. Howells and James fought to keep literature from becoming commodified, but more and more they found themselves alienated by the new publishing marketplace. James once wrote to his brother, the philosopher William, that he had given up the idea of ever becoming "a free-going and light-paced enough writer to please the multitude. The multitude, I am more and more convinced, has absolutely no taste." To Howells, he added, "The vulgar-mindedness of the public to which one offers the fruits of one's brain would chill the artist's breast if those fruits were not so sweet … One mustn't think of the public, *at all,* I find."[36]

The changes brought to American literature by Twain, Howells, Harte, Bierce, and Garland can be seen as a reflection of the changes that were happening within American newspapers as they evolved throughout the nineteenth century. The "realistic" nature of their literature – and its growth out of their journalistic work – must be viewed in the context of how writing within an increasingly commercialized and market-driven media industry was revolutionizing the popular arts during the period. The literary realists' focus upon ordinary life – or the "aesthetic of the common," as Howells put it – grew out of both the romantic assumptions about the citizenry and the common person, as reflected in the journalism and the poetry of Whitman and the idealistic editorials of Greeley, and the growing cynicism in the body politic about political and business institutions that were seen as corrupt and favoring a narrow elite.[37] The dual-mindedness of the American press when it came to arriving at a judgment about human nature – should human beings be seen as selfish, grasping opportunists eager to amass wealth and power or were they the good-hearted, public-spirited democrats who would cleanse the system if only given the chance? – can be seen in the literature of Twain and Howells as they struggled to define the nature of the American character in a time when optimistic assumptions about American society were being eroded by the wrenching developments of industrialization and corruption in high places. The literary realists acknowledged their debt to the romantic emphasis upon personal experience, the importance of the individual, the power of particularized description, and the fundamental morality of the average person. But so did the newsrooms of the nineteenth century as they evolved their mixed commitment to the "hard facts" of the news page that were combined with the reform values of the editorial page and then aggressively marketed to the common person in the hopes of selling as many cheap, mass-produced, and sensationalized editions of the newspaper as possible.

The debate about whether the literary realists were presenting a truly "real" picture of the world foreshadowed an argument that has come to obsess scholars and media critics of our time – is the press truly "objective," as it often claims for itself, or is this a myth and an impossible goal? The criticism that the literary realists did not achieve objectivity but only the "illusion of objectivity," as Lawrence Kolb has put it, is the same critique that has been applied to the news organizations that nurtured them. Howells, as the chief American realist and critical advocate for the movement, reflected this simple faith when he wrote that "an author is merely one who has had the fortune to remember more ... than other men. A good many wise critics will tell you that writing is inventing; but I know better than that; it is only remembering ... the history of your own life." Just as contemporary journalists are accused of naivety or disingenuousness in holding to an "objective" news philosophy by their post-modern critics, so, too, have the literary realists been accused of engaging in a "naïve subterfuge" by scholars. Amy Kaplan, for example, has judged the tradition of the American realists as a "history of failure" in adequately representing the social facts of American society and their works as "failed masterpieces." What this means is that the realists – despite their reputations as clear-eyed critics and social reformers in their time – have not proven to impress certain post-modern scholars as sufficiently progressive in the context of contemporary academic politics.[38]

NATURALISM, THE MOOD OF SCIENTIFIC PESSIMISM, AND THE COMING OF THE LITERARY "ANTI-HERO"

Stephen Crane believed in the value of real-life experience as the basis of literary production, and he experienced the down-and-out life to such a degree that it may have contributed to his early death. As a fledgling novelist and journalist in the 1890s, Crane took to heart the message of the literary realists – that it is real life that must be celebrated in any work of literature – by spending a number of years living with and chronicling the activities of transients, petty criminals, and other starving artists in the run-down Bowery section of New York City. After his literary star burned briefly before flaming out with his death at age twenty-nine, it has been speculated that the tuberculosis that killed him was contracted during, or at least exacerbated by, his years of poverty while exploring the dark side of human life in New York City.[39]

Crane's fatal fascination with the dispossessed and the downtrodden helped to make him one of the preeminent American naturalists, a literary school that grew out of American realism, and like that movement, is populated principally by journalists-turned-novelists. The best-known American naturalists, Crane, Dreiser, Norris, and London – as well as other journalist-literary figures that naturalism greatly influenced, such as Anderson, Hemingway, Steinbeck, Wright, Mencken, Kipling, Upton Sinclair, John Dos Passos, George Orwell, James T. Farrell, and Norman Mailer – all shared aspects of the naturalists' view of humans as creatures of heredity and environment who are locked in a stern, Darwinian struggle for existence and are buffeted about by the external forces of nature, implacable social and economic laws, and powerful inner compulsions.[40]

The definition of naturalism is something that is still debated by literary critics and analysts, and the naturalism of the American journalist-literary figures took very different shapes and forms. As it was with the realists, romanticism is blended into the naturalists' worldview – whether in the Homeric-like sagas of Norris' sweeping novels of the development of the West, the heroic battlefield "code" of Crane's wartime journalism and fiction, the Nietzschean-like supermen of London's adventure novels, or the romantic discontent of Carrie Meeber, Dreiser's fictional creature of the early consumer culture. In a sense, naturalism can be seen as a midway philosophy between the literary realism of the nineteenth century and twentieth-century existentialism. But while romanticism still lives within naturalism, it does so in ever fainter ways. The naturalists shared with the realists the mood of despair and unrest after the US Civil War that shook the faith of many in an all-loving God and delivered a blow in intellectual circles to Christian positivism and Emersonian idealism which had served for many as a substitute religion during the optimistic era of the early to mid-nineteenth century. In philosophical terms, the pessimistic outlook of the naturalists is viewed as the literary embodiment of the angst that settled over late nineteenth-century intellectual life – particularly as people applied to the social order the theories of Charles Darwin and his view that human beings evolved out of the animal world and were no different than other creatures in their needs, their instincts, and their capacity to adapt to environmental changes. Other factors that dampened the spirit of the age – the closing of the American frontier, the rise of institutions of industrialism and mass culture, corruption in politics and business, and an economy dominated by large trusts and prone to severe boom and bust cycles – led the naturalists to take on a hard-shelled and pessimistic philosophical stance to deal with the cruel exigencies of their world.[41]

But the examination of naturalism as a philosophical movement some-times neglects the role that modern journalism – and the naturalists' early experiences in the journalistic profession – played in the development of their worldview. It can be argued that the typical journalists' experience of the late nineteenth and early twentieth centuries was paramount in the development of the naturalists' tough-minded and often cynical view of the universe as a dog-eat-dog place where pragmatic and opportunistic attitudes about life were preferable to unconvincing religious explanations and the application of strict Victorian moral codes. In their sympathetic portrayals of the lives of real people in tough circumstances struggling to make the best of a bad lot of it, the naturalists reflected the values of the late nineteenth-century yellow press and its emphasis upon abnormal personalities, dramatic occurrences, heroic characters, sensational accounts of events, and colorful portrayals of the strivings of average people. The attempt to create a dramatic sweep of life in the sensationalized newspapers and magazines of the day tied into American jingoism, the cult of experience, the following of Thomas Carlyle's philosophy of heroic personalities making history, and Theodore Roosevelt's belief in the strenuous life as a way to conquer nature (and lesser peoples) – all elements that showed up in the naturalists' work. Norris, for example, once addressed a group of regional writers in San Francisco this way: "Give us stories now, give us men, strong, brutal men, with red-hot blood in 'em, with unleashed passions rampant in 'em, blood and bones and viscera ... It's life that we want, the vigorous, real thing, not the curious weaving of words and the polish of literary finish."[42]

Dreiser is the most explicit of the naturalists in pointing directly to his experiences in journalism as the foundation of his literary philosophy. As a young journalist working for the *Chicago Globe* in the early 1890s, Dreiser was deeply impressed by his colleagues who, he said, "looked upon life as a fierce, grim struggle in which no quarter was either given or taken, and in which all men laid traps, lied, squandered, erred through illusion: a conclusion with which I now most heartily agree." Dreiser, who had recently left the small-town Indiana home of his pious German Catholic father, said the viewpoint of his colleagues:

broadened me considerably and finally liberated me from moralistic and religionistic qualms ... To a certain extent they were confused by the general American passive acceptance of the Sermon on the Mount and the Beatitudes as governing principles, but in the main they were nearly all mistrustful of these things, and of conventional principles in general. They did not believe, as I still did, that there was a fixed moral order in the world which one contravened at his peril.[43]

Dreiser's newsroom experiences were reinforced by his reading of Julian Huxley, a prominent public advocate of the notion that Darwinian principles had supplanted religious explanations of life, and Spencer, who Dreiser said:

quite blew me, intellectually, to bits ... Hitherto, until I read Huxley, I had some lingering filaments of Catholic training about me, faith in the existence of Christ, the soundness of his moral and sociologic deductions, the brotherhood of man ... Now in its place was the definite conviction that spiritually one got nowhere, that there was no hereafter ... Man was a mechanism, undevised and uncreated, and a badly and carelessly driven one at that.

As Dreiser absorbed what he felt were these bleak truths about life, he went about his journalistic tasks, all the time finding his "low and hopeless" mood deepened by the sordid and cruel things he was required to report upon. "I was daily facing a round of duties which now more than ever verified all that I had suspected and that these books proved," he wrote. "... Suicides seemed sadder since there was no care for them; failures the same ... Also before my eyes were always those regions of indescribable poverty and indescribable wealth ... and when I read Spencer I could only sigh."[44]

Dreiser soon came to connect these philosophical conclusions about the futility of acting upon religious duty to his own moral code in ways that would be reflected in the actions of his literary characters – actions that led his books to be criticized as assaults upon traditional expectations of moral conduct. Dreiser came to advocate a "pagan" view of life, as he called it, and an ethical code that put natural gratification first. "It was useless for anyone to say to me 'Thou shalt not commit adultery' and expect me not to do so if a beautiful woman offered herself to me, my desires being what they were," he explained matter-of-factly in the autobiography of his early life, *Dawn*. " ... I, for one, did not propose that asserted moral law should interfere with my sharp human instincts." Again, Dreiser felt his rejection of moral restraints to be a function of the lessons that news reporting was teaching him. "I might be, as it were, a freak, a scoundrel, a villain," he wrote.

"Still, when I saw the large number of persons about me who seemed to have no moral scruples, and when I read the papers crowded with crime or social lapses, or visited the streets where people lived in horrible ignorance and poverty, or saw the rows of immoral houses and realized that nightly thousands of others were having intimate relations with women and girls outside these institutions, I could not help but feel that there was great confusion in the minds of many as to the authority of the asserted moral law; also that if there was a moral God, there certainly was a most powerful devil who busied himself building up ... these passions (that were) quite outside our willing."[45]

In moving toward a view of the modern world as a waste land – a view that would become solidified in the pessimistic literary and philosophical currents of the twentieth century – the naturalists were increasingly less moralists in their fiction (arguing for a world as it should be) than they were stoics (recognizing the futility and injustice of life and accepting it with resignation and even indifference). European naturalists such as Zola and Honore de Balzac were great literary influences in the period – and even journalists were encouraged (as Dreiser reports he was) to read them. (Balzac, said the young literary aspirant Dreiser, was one who "saw, thought, felt. Through him I saw a prospect so wide that it left me breath-less.") The implications of the psychological sciences, and the notions of humans in the grip of irrational and sexual drives, were being explored by William James, and Sigmund Freud was arriving on the scene. Dreiser and London harbored strong complaints about the economic and political workings of the world, and they became fervent social activists and political radicals, as did such later naturalists as Anderson, Steinbeck, Dos Passos, and Orwell.[46] But in Dreiser's fiction (particularly his early fiction) he stayed loyal to the tough-minded and detached creed that he found articu-lated in his early newsroom life, and his moralizing (such as about Carrie's permanent state of dissatisfaction within her acquisitive view of life or the cruelty of the social conventions that drove apart Lester Kane and Jennie in his second novel, *Jennie Gerhardt*) seems to be more commentary upon the futility of the American Dream in a culture of mass-produced dreams and accumulated wealth than it is a blueprint of hope that a person can do much to alter the conditions of alienation and anomie in modern mass society.

It was to be expected that the literary realists would be seen as a bridge to the naturalists – and particularly so since the realists also moved in the philosophical direction of the naturalists during their later lives. Although a disappointed idealist, Howells was never a full-fledged naturalist, and he didn't believe humans were helpless before their fate. But Howells never wavered in his support of the careers of Norris and Crane, and, agnostic as he was in his own religious beliefs, Howells had little trouble accepting their near total irreverence and iconoclasm. Twain also celebrated free will and the importance of moral choice – at least, in his greatest work, *Huckleberry Finn*. But as he grew increasingly embittered in his later years, Twain's philosophy took on a deterministic cast in his view of humans as engaged in a losing struggle dictated by the inherently tragic circumstances of life. ("That is human life," he wrote. "A child's first act knocks over the initial brick, and the rest will follow inexorably.") In his darkly pessimistic, late-life allegory, *The Mysterious Stranger*, Twain portrayed Satan as mock-ing humankind's "moral sense" as more cruel than the animals, laughing at humans as "a shabby, poor, worthless lot all around," and attacking Christianity as representing the height of human violence. ("Two or three centuries from now it will be recognized that all the competent killers are Christians.") Bierce, too, can be seen as holding something of a naturalistic philosophy, including an innate and outspoken loathing of conventional religion that only deepened with his growing cynicism. (Chance, Bierce once said, is a "malign and soulless Intelligence bestirring himself in earthly affairs with brute unrest" that never acts with goodwill.

It is "a brutal, blind design, like the unconscious malevolence of an idiot.")
Others of the literary realists, such as Harte and Eliot, also jettisoned belief
in orthodox Christianity (Harte taking refuge in the fatalism and the irony
to be found in the often tragic circumstances of frontier life; Eliot advocating a courageous embrace of life's suffering and a brave rejection of anything in religion that seemed incredible or required intellectual dishonesty)
and laid a foundation of disbelief that became commonplace not only in
the naturalists but in the even more heterodox and secular writers of the
later twentieth century.[47]

Even so, the American literary naturalists tended not to reflect the classic,
Zola-esque definition of naturalism in their fiction – even as they have come
to embody the American version of the definition. Fed on the myths of
democracy and individualism, it always has been difficult for Americans to
rid themselves of romantic idealism, and the American naturalists were no
different. It is easy to find contradictory elements in each of the great
American naturalists, such that one can find scholars who say that none
was a pure naturalist in the continental tradition. Dreiser's mysticism
became ever more apparent in his later philosophical writings as he searched
for a spiritual, unifying concept of universal truth to capture his notion of
the life force; London's quest for the Dionysian superman of Nietzsche
turned into a late-life study of C. G. Jung and mystical psychology; Norris'
naturalism was always mixed with his faith in the natural processes of life
and his belief in the unfolding goodness of evolution. Even Crane, although
the most unblinking pessimist among the four, suffused *The Red Badge of
Courage* with an impressionistic prose that gave an ethereal, unworldly
quality to the book's otherwise bleak atmosphere. It has been noted by
cultural historians how often intellectuals of the Victorian period – as they
grew bereft of personal belief in the old Christian formulas – were prone to
create counter-belief structures that found in science or Darwinism or
Socialism or other thought systems a substitute creed for traditional
Christian beliefs. The naturalists fall into this mold, too. Their fundamentally spiritual frame of mind remained intact, even if their overt philosophy
appeared to be godless and deterministic. As is the case with realism and
existentialism, the American literary naturalists' philosophy was often transformed so that its negative implications were turned into positive, spiritual
virtues in the same way that the grim and sensationalistic accounts of the
world's tragedies on the news pages can be transformed into the progressive
and optimistic exhortations of the typical editorial page. The jaded and
world-weary outlook of the modern newsroom – forbearance in the face of
the painful truths of mortality, the embrace of the here-and-now despite the

end that awaits all creatures – is often only a mask for a deep and pervasive faith in human beings and hope for the human condition. The naturalists may have elevated these intellectual inconsistencies to a literary level, but the source of their values is still to be found in the traditions of journalism.

The effect of Darwinism was making its way into journalism during this period, just as it was other areas of intellectual life, and journalism – in effect – was siding with Darwin. By the 1920s, when the Scopes trial, where a high-school biology teacher in Tennessee was put on trial for teaching evolution, made headlines throughout America, the game was virtually over, with only a handful of newspapers even in Tennessee siding with William Jennings Bryan and the cause of biblical literalists. The naturalists had tilled this field well in advance of the Scopes trial, and they can be seen as the literary inspiration for Mencken (who worked hand-in-hand with Clarence Darrow and Scopes' defense team) to advance his avowed goal of sabotaging the cause of fundamentalism and winning the day for secularism in America. Although James Gordon Bennett had made in-depth coverage of religion a feature of his *New York Herald* during the early Penny Press era, the discussion of religious matters was increasingly marginalized and banished to the back, church pages of the newspaper throughout the nineteenth century. Despite his claim to being a religious enthusiast, Bennett's religious views were far from mainstream, and his newspaper found itself at odds (in what came to be called the "Moral War") with religious and other establishment forces in New York for its sensationalized approach to news coverage. These early divisions in what today we call the "culture wars," which have pitted Christian traditionalists against secular and pluralistic forces in American society, caught newspapers in their up draft. As the news business professionalized throughout the late nineteenth- and early twentieth-century, the intellectual tradition of journalism (such as there is) increasingly was one where urbane and skeptical young people, often escaping small-town or pious backgrounds, could live free from religious restraints or constricting religious notions. Like Mencken (who made the downfall of fundamentalist Christianity a lifetime crusade), the naturalists tended to regard religious belief as an archaic remnant of a mythological past and to accept the truths of science as matters of fact and indisputable elements of a modern worldview. For the most part, they came to these conclusions with less pain and anxiety than that which seemed to plague many Victorians in letting go of the comforts of Christian doctrine. "I am a hopeless materialist," wrote London. "I see the soul as nothing else than the sum of the activities of the organism plus personal habits, memories, and experiences of the organism. I believe that when I am dead, I am dead. I believe that with my death I am just as much obliterated as the last mosquito you or I smashed."[48]

The trends in the publishing world during the era of the literary realists – toward a greater industrial organization, expansive economic growth, and commercialization of media companies – accelerated for the naturalists in the era between the US Civil War and World War I. The Industrial Revolution had some of its earliest effects on newspapers and periodicals, and the increased size, scope, and bureaucratization of publishing enterprises both expanded the opportunities for a few journalists and narrowed the work-life horizon for many others. For the handful of journalist-literary figures who followed in the celebrity tradition of Twain, the era proved to be a boon. But for typical reporters and editors, the transformation of journalism into big business diminished journalists' autonomy and turned reporting into a "career" that was dependent upon the highly regimented, bureaucratized, and marketplace-driven publications of the emerging era of mass audiences. At its best, art and industry were united in the new, progressive magazines operated by publishing innovators such as S. S. McClure and Norman Hapgood that flourished during the period of populism, progressivism, and muckraking – as well as the few newspapers, such as Dana's *New York Sun* or Scripps' feisty, pro-labor newspapers, that viewed journalism as a literate activity and a progressive force for change. But even at some of the best newspapers of the period, such as Pulitzer's *New York World,* organizational imperatives and commercial formulas drove the work life and the work product, and most reporters and editors operated as functionaries in service to the demands of their employers. Many of the stereotypes of the news business came into existence during this period – poorly paid and grumbling journalists being hired and fired at will, editors mercilessly hashing up reporters' copy, opportunistic reporters juicing up stories and exploiting human tragedies to create sensationalized headlines, pressured editors and reporters creating news if they couldn't find it, and fakers and ethical corner-cutters getting ahead in the business. The best-seller phenomenon and the overcrowded market for magazines also reduced the distinction between the newspaper world and the once high-brow field of literary publishing, and the elitist tradition in literature was submerged into a world where marketplace efficiencies, technological innovation, "scientific" management, and workaholic philosophies drove a harried media enterprise.[49]

For those few who came to benefit from it, the changing circumstances of American publishing in the years between the US Civil War and World

War I brought literary professionalism into vogue – along with the image of the urban reporter and foreign correspondent as a literary model and hero. This new intellectual credibility for high-profile journalists such as Crane and Richard Harding Davis created an easy pathway for these flamboyant figures to transform themselves into publishing enterprises. The competition by the tabloids and the burgeoning magazine marketplace created a bidding market for the service of well-known journalists; promising literary talents in the provinces were recruited to New York and the publishing centers by publishers such as McClure and Hearst; and publishing opportunities opened up with the cross-ownership and partnerships of newspapers, magazines, and publishing houses. In this environment, reporting came to be seen as a vital first step in a literary apprenticeship, and the reporter became the celebrated expert on real life. The exploits of Davis, who became the flamboyant foreign correspondent par excellence, and Crane, whose urban and war reporting often ran under his personal moniker, were the inspiration for a youthful Norris when he was recruited from California to New York by McClure in 1898, where Norris in turn "discovered" Dreiser while working as a reader for the Doubleday publishing house. Crane's straddling of the old world of the genteel journalist and the new world of the journalistic entrepreneur created a new kind of reporting ideal – an "artist" who blended the world of letters into the language of daily publications and fashioned a literary vision out of the creative tension inherent in the possibilities for the new forms of commercialized journalistic expression.[50]

The urbanity and cosmopolitanism found in the late nineteenth-century journalists who went on to become famous literary naturalists were a product, to some degree, of the higher formal educational standards that were coming to be found in the newsroom. Many of the large, land grant, state universities were founded in this period, and journalism – like other fields – was being heavily influenced by the democratization, secularization, and specialization of higher education in the US. Increasingly, journalism was drawing employees with college backgrounds. Crane, Dreiser, and London all attended college for a time (Crane at Lafayette College and Syracuse University, Dreiser for a year at Indiana University, London briefly at the University of California-Berkeley), and Norris nearly earned his degree at Berkeley. Some (such as Dreiser and London) were broadly educated enough to have a rudimentary grasp of the principles of philosophy, and they had been exposed enough to intellectual life to have absorbed significant elements of contemporary philosophical notions that became critical to their literary viewpoint. Norris was well-read – so well read, in fact, that his critics sometimes feel that his writing tends to reflect a self-conscious effort to manifest the techniques and the literary philosophy of Zola and the continental naturalists in his own works. It also was not unknown for some knowledge of the pessimistic philosophers of the nineteenth century to be found circulating in the newsroom. ("Read Schopenhauer, my boy, read Schopenhauer," Dreiser quotes his first city editor as telling him.) In fact, challenges to the optimistic nineteenth-century worldview found a welcome reception in the typical big-city newsroom, where a journalist such as Mencken was encouraged to explore the heterodox ideas of George Bernard Shaw and Friedrich Nietzsche (both of whom he authored books about).[51] Mencken's vigorous espousal of the atheistic, anti-Christian views of Nietzsche might have seen him run out of many American institutions. But the Baltimore *Sun*, where Mencken worked for much of his career, never hesitated to feature him in the newspaper. London's embrace of Nietzschean notions of an Aryan super race and Bierce's aggressively anti-Christian viewpoint never disqualified them from working for the Hearst newspapers of the period.

The news formulas of the ever larger, ever more commercial nineteenth-century newspapers reached a peak level of sensationalism – and in some cases, jingoism – at the very time the naturalists were making their mark. The fact that Crane built his career – both in newspapers and in literature – by focusing upon the seamy side of life was a function of the journalistic marketplace of the era. Crane's fame was at its height when he became a tool of Hearst and Pulitzer, who were using their news pages to foment conflict with Spain. Crane's willingness to carry out the political mission of his employers and his cynical view of journalistic standards are congruent with the detachment, philosophical barrenness, and stoicism he reflected in the naturalistic philosophy of his fiction. The journalistic mood of the time was to be skeptical of cant and political rhetoric and to take an adversarial stance against government and business – and to wrap it in a cynical worldview that became the acceptable stance in the newsroom. Although providing a breath of idealism for some, the emergence of "muckraking" and investigative reporting as a journalistic tool made other reporters (particularly those who didn't actually do any investigative reporting) feel even more disillusioned with politics, government, and self-dealing officials. If bad news was big news in the newspapers of the late nineteenth and early twentieth century, it was no surprise that the literary probing of the negative side of American life became the focus of the journalist-literary figures who came of age during the jolting recessions, the boom-and-bust cycles, and the consolidation of wealth that characterized the period. Meanwhile, human deviance – probed, analyzed, and sensationalized – became the grist of audience-building for many newspapers and filtered into the conventions for successful fiction as developed by the street-wise and market-savvy naturalists.[52]

The excesses of industrial capitalism of this period not only fostered a take-no-quarter, dog-eat-dog view of the economic world, but they also left journalists with a divided impulse to accept the hypocrisy and veiled brutality of American business rhetoric as an inexorable given in life and to want to do something about it. The naturalists, not surprisingly, reflected this oscillation between cynicism and reformist idealism, as did the news organizations where they worked. The muckraking movement had an important impact upon the naturalists – as it did (and continues to have) upon the American journalistic value system. A thorough-going cynic such as Bierce reached the pinnacle of his journalistic fame when he was sent to Washington, DC by Hearst to do published battle with Californian railroads trying to win major government subsidies; Crane tried his hand at muckraking the coal industry (but he didn't like it); Norris' novel, *The Octopus*, is considered to be a muckraking novel in its faintly fictional account of the Mussel Slough affair (a shoot-out between railroad agents and Californian ranchers upset with a railroad land grab); *The Jungle*, by the muckraking journalist Sinclair (who got his start as a writer of pot-boiler, dime-store novels), is a piece of fictionalized propaganda designed to publicize the abuses of labor and the violations of health standards in the meatpacking industry (it became a best-seller and spurred a campaign for federal health inspection laws). This economic and political backdrop deeply influenced the naturalist mindset as its proponents tried to reconcile their feelings about the philosophical futility of idealistic causes even as they argued for a better world.

Even more than muckraking, the increasingly imperialist ventures of the US and other western powers gave the naturalists a basis for portraying human beings as violent, self-willed, and in the grip of instinctual compulsions that they couldn't fully control. War coverage, which was transformed with the coming of the telegraph and the telephone and the market for immediately transmitted accounts of the battles of the US Civil and Spanish American wars, made it more likely that journalists would be directly exposed to the cruelties of war, and a number of the naturalists were. Crane, Norris, London (as well as Hemingway, Steinbeck, and Dos Passos) were all war correspondents and/or involved in military ancillary activities; later journalist-literary figures influenced by naturalism – Mailer (in the US Army on the Pacific front during World War II), Orwell (wounded in the

Republican cause in the Spanish Civil War) and H. H. Munro (known as "Saki", who died as a soldier in World War I) – fought as members of the military. The direct exposure to war deepened the already despairing tendencies of a number of the naturalists and reinforced their philosophical worldview of life as harsh, senseless, and fundamentally without meaning. In some cases, the naturalistic tone of their novels was modified by a romantic view of war (in Crane's *Active Service*, for example) or a celebration of the nobility found in the hopeless military cause (in Hemingway's *For Whom the Bell Tolls*). However, more often the naturalists' picture of war conveys a powerful message of futility and disillusionment. Whether this antipathy to the "ignorance, vainglory, pettiness, pompous triumph, and craven fear," as one critic describes Crane's critique of battle in the *Red Badge of Courage*, was in the naturalists' minds before they saw battle, or whether it was the cause of it, is open to debate.[53] But clearly the enticement of seeing warfare up close (many of the naturalists were recruited to be war correspondents based upon their literary reputation) did little to relieve their pessimistic outlook about life.

Journalistic ethics during the late nineteenth century were fairly no-holds-barred and contributed to the tolerant, relativistic, and even libertine moral outlook of the naturalists that made its way into their fiction. Professional journalistic instruction was only in its infancy in higher education, and formalized ethics codes, news organizations with promulgated ethical standards, and responsible notions of proper professional conduct were just beginning to make their way into the journalism of the time. Consistent with the negative image of the opportunistic reporter that has become a staple of popular literature, the naturalists tended to paint their journalistic characters as unfeeling and manipulative (Crane's Rufus Coleman in *Active Service*), disillusioned and detached (Kipling's Dick Heldar in *The Light That Failed*), apathetic and numb to pain (Anderson's Bruce Dudley in *Dark Laughter*) or cynical and world weary (Hemingway's Jake Barnes in *The Sun Also Rises*). The indifference toward traditional moral values expressed by these figures of the naturalists' imagination reflected broader literary currents, including the rise of the anti-hero in modern literature and the turning of the modern novel toward topics that used to be considered immoral, depraved, or shocking. The fact that the use of tabloid techniques and the practice of Yellow Journalism encouraged problematic behavior and dubious ethical conduct among journalists played a role in fixing the naturalistic attitude at the heart of modern journalism's adoption of its own version of the anti-hero as the reporter ideal.

DREISER, CRANE, AND BREAKING DOWN
THE BARRIERS OF CONVENTION

Dreiser was hardly the first novelist to build a tale around a young woman who strayed from prevailing standards of moral virtue, as he did in *Sister Carrie*. Crane did it, too, with his story of a New York prostitute, *Maggie: A Girl of the Streets*, as had other eighteenth- and nineteenth-century novelists such as Defoe, Gustav Flaubert, the Brontë sisters, Thomas Hardy, and Kate Chopin. However, Dreiser one-upped his predecessors, whose heroines were punished in one way or another for their transgressions, by rewarding his heroine, Carrie Meeber, for her decisions to live with men outside marriage and to engage in questionable moral behavior as a means to make it in the big city. Unlike Crane, who had Maggie ultimately pay with her life for her transgressions (she commits suicide), Dreiser defied the Victorian formula (a woman can sin – readers loved that – but she must be shown to pay the price) by having Carrie succeed as an actress. Dreiser's initial difficulties with the book – his publisher, Doubleday, did little to promote the book after trying unsuccessfully to get out of the contract – showed how much literary society was still wedded to Victorian and puritanical formulas at the turn of the twentieth century.[54]

The journalistic quality of Dreiser's fiction had long been noted, and derided in some cases, by critics and editors. One early reader at Harper and Brothers called *Sister Carrie* a "superior piece of reportorial realism – of high class newspaper work." (It wasn't a compliment; he recommended rejecting the manuscript.) A reviewer said the novel "tells of a common experience, as too often the daily newspapers witness." To add to the effect, Dreiser pasted in newspaper material throughout the manuscript, including "help wanted" advertisements from the *New York Journal*. Throughout the novel, newspapers play an ongoing role – most notably, in the narcotic effect they have upon George Hurstwood as he reads them in hotel lobbies while idling away his days in a downward spiral of apathy and unemployment. Newspapers had even played a role in the real-life story of *Sister Carrie*, where the plot was a loose version of what happened to Dreiser's sister, Emma, when she ran off with the married manager of a Chicago saloon, who stole money to set themselves up in New York City. The story became big news after the manager's wife complained to the press and caused great shame for Dreiser's family. Dreiser's use of long, inflated words in the novel (Fishkin says Dreiser was being imitative of the pompous diction in Chicago newspaper personality Eugene Fields' popular "Sharps and Flats" column but adopted the manner seriously rather than using it humorously) has led to criticism of him as a stylist to this day. However, Dreiser's training as a journalist meant that the writing where he "showed" the action (such as the scenes where Hurstwood is kicked out of his house by his wife and where Charlie Drouet confronts Carrie about her infidelity) are some of the most powerful in the novel and overwhelm his more affected "telling" passages (which, if one chooses, can be read ironically, as in the case where Dreiser moralizes about the choice of a young woman coming to the big city, who can either fall into saving hands or adopt cosmopolitan ways and go bad).[55]

Sister Carrie – which Dreiser wrote at age twenty-eight – is often considered the embodiment of the reporter's novel. Dreiser packed the book with the impressions he had experienced as a newcomer to Chicago, where he had come in 1887 to find work and join two of his sisters who lived there. He wove the observations of the eager and impressionable urban immigrant into the naturalists' vision of the cold, big-city world that was so captivating and yet so forbidding for people struggling to find a place in the new, industrialized megatropolises. While working at a variety of odd jobs, Dreiser grew frightened of the bigness and the impersonality of the city; at the same time he longed for the clothes and the good things of the life that he saw there. Convinced that his future lay in the world of journalism, he landed his first reporting job on the *Chicago Globe*. The editor who took a chance on him, John Maxwell, complained that Dreiser's early efforts were "awful stuff." But he helped Dreiser decide what to observe and how to write about it, and he hacked to the bone Dreiser's awkward but sometimes beautifully fleshed-out thoughts and nurtured the potential he found in Dreiser's occasionally polished observations.[56]

What Dreiser did best was to write color pieces that conveyed the feel and the mood of the urban landscape he found in his walks around the city streets and in his visits to the slums. Like his character, Carrie, Dreiser dreamed of fame and riches, but his dream was so powerful that he had manic-depressive episodes, sometimes exalting in his genius, sometimes sinking in despair at the hopelessness of his prospects. With his cumbersome prose style, he benefited from the unhurried attitude of the journalism of the 1890s, when newspapers had not yet fully adopted the fact-piled-on-fact ideal and some rambling was permissible. While Dreiser had a remarkable capacity for getting facts twisted, his employers found him effective at feature yarns, where he could speculate, digress and dramatize.[57]

By the time Dreiser moved to New York City, he was taking long mansion-viewing walks along Fifth Avenue, where he marveled at the fenced-in estates, the carriages, and the footmen, but often brooded about the narrow line that distinguished success from failure. When he found employment at Pulitzer's *New York World*, he was allowed only to write up brief squibs; when he arrived with a good story it was given to a regular reporter. Hired by the famed editor, Arthur Brisbane, Dreiser found he was working on space and paid by inches. The *World* editors discovered that whatever his feature-writing abilities, he was unable to grasp the curt and compressed techniques required at the *World*. This new form of journalism was to ultimately defeat him; he quit before he was let go by the newspaper for failing to grasp the quickly reported, once-over-lightly story formulas that Pulitzer used to beat the competition.[58]

After this experience, he worked as the editor of a magazine his musician brother Paul helped to start up, called *Ev'ry Month*, which was published by a music firm and ran a potpourri of popular songs, stories, and pictures, and then as an editor of women's magazines for the Butterick publications. As much as Dreiser hated the newspapers for their falsehoods and how they had treated him, he hated the popular magazines – including his own – for their conformities, the hypocrisies of convention, and the taste of the public for sweet nothings, and he took a cynical pleasure in editing them. When he visited an old friend, Arthur Henry, who had been his city editor during a brief stint on the *Toledo Blade*, Dreiser was initially unreceptive to Henry's encouragement that he start a novel. Henry (who had started a novel himself) persisted and Dreiser took out a piece of yellow paper and wrote down a title at random – "Sister Carrie". He later insisted he had no plot in mind. "My mind was a blank except for the name," he said.[59]

Dreiser seems to have had no inkling that he was writing a revolutionary work. He wrote with a tolerance for transgression that was natural to him. His mother had accepted immorality; some of his sisters had been immoral in the eyes of society (two, Mame and Sylvia, bore children out of wedlock; Dreiser lived for a time with Emma and her "husband" in New York City, where they had supported themselves by running a boarding house for women of dubious virtue), and he had come to believe that conventional morality was an enormous fraud. Luckily for Dreiser, Norris happened to be working as a reader-editor at Doubleday and Company when the manuscript was submitted. Recognizing a kindred artistic spirit, Norris talked Frank Doubleday's assistant into offering Dreiser a contract. But when Doubleday returned from Europe where he had been vacationing, he and his wife read the novel and decided that it was immoral and would not sell. Dreiser forced Doubleday to honor the contract, but at its publication in 1900 the publisher produced just enough copies to fulfill the agreement. Norris did his best to promote the book with reviewers, but to no avail – it bombed critically (although the book did get a few good reviews, including many in Europe). Dreiser was so crushed that he suffered an emotional breakdown, the first of what would be a lifetime pattern of nervous afflictions and publishing disappointments, including a delay in the publication of *Jennie Gerhardt* until he accepted major cuts of controversial passages, Harper's cancellation of his novel, *The Titan*, based upon the heavily researched and thinly disguised fictionalization of the life of the street car magnate, Charles Yerkes, because the realism was too uncompromising (the book was eventually published by another firm), and the suppression of another novel, *The Genius*, by anti-indecency forces in New York.[60]

For years, Dreiser had been fascinated by the kind of murder that regularly made headlines in American newspapers. In 1906, he found the perfect story for what would become his most successful novel, *An American Tragedy* – that of Chester Gillette, a straw boss in his wealthy uncle's skirt factory in Cortland, New York, who seduced and impregnated a pretty mill-hand and then murdered her after he became enamored of the daughter of a wealthy person in town. In plot terms, the main character, Clyde Griffiths, gets the idea for the murder by reading a story of a presumed double drowning in the Albany *Times-Union*. In depicting Griffiths' trial, Dreiser lifted some thirty pages nearly verbatim from old newspaper accounts of the court proceedings in Gillette's trial and the letters between the ill-fated lovers. Dreiser also engaged in reporting-research of his own by driving to Cortland to examine the homes of the wealthy and poor sections of town and the nearby factories, where clothing was manufactured. At one point, Dreiser actually rowed out onto the lake where Gillette had brought his girlfriend to drown her. In his search for authentic documentation, Dreiser arranged for the *New York World* to help him obtain a court order to see the death house at Sing Sing Prison where Gillette was to die.[61]

The living of the journalistic life as a moral and philosophical challenge to the prevailing religious outlook and Victorian moral code also was a trademark of Crane, whom Dreiser had enthusiastically published as a magazine editor. Crane's bohemian lifestyle and his cultivation of urban life in all its profligate variety were conscious rejections of the values that he had been raised with as the son of a Methodist preacher and an evangelistic mother. A key lesson that Crane took from the realists was to live life as it is, and he took up that challenge with a commitment few have seen then or since. In moving to New York City's Bowery district, Crane began fashioning city-scape pieces for the local newspapers while living the very life he was describing. "I decided that the nearer a writer gets to life the greater he becomes as an artist," he said. Fellow journalists told stories of how passing through the Bowery, Crane would dash off to talk with some stranger, tramp, or whore. Drawing upon an old journalistic tradition that can be traced to Nellie Bly and other "stunt" reporters, Crane donned the dress of a homeless person and joined a wintry breadline, from which he wrote a journalistic account, "The Men in the Storm." (He also wrote a "contrasting" sketch based on a dinner jacket-attired meal he spent with a New York millionaire.) An acquaintance who knew Crane had been ill-clad in the line asked him why he didn't put on more clothing. "How would I know how those poor devils felt if I was warm myself?" he responded. There were many stories of Crane's illness, his coughing, his not taking care of himself while living in the Bowery. When Crane wrote about the poor, he felt pity for his characters, but he also felt the irony of their plight and his tone was one of detachment.[62]

Crane's first attempt at publishing *Maggie*, about an ill-fated prostitute in New York, went nowhere. When one editor pointed out excessive adjectives and slaughtered infinitives, Crane cut him short: "You mean that the story's too honest?" The tone of the book came from Zola (whom Crane nonetheless found tiresome) and Flaubert. He insisted that in writing *Maggie* he had no other purpose than "to show people as they seemed to me. If that be evil, make the most of it." In his dispassionate and unsentimental view of Bowery life, Crane believed people were creatures of their environment, and he didn't judge them. "If one proves that theory one makes room in Heaven for all sorts of souls (notably an occasional street girl) who are not confidently expected to be there by many excellent people," he wrote. In the end, he printed the book at his own expense under a pseudonym (to avoid embarrassing his brothers and their prudish wives), but news stands and book stores wouldn't touch it.[63]

Crane's revolt from his conventional background began soon after his mother, who had taken up journalism after the death of Crane's father, involved the youthful Crane in his brother's reporting business, where she, Townley, and Stephen provided New Jersey seashore news to New York City newspapers. Besides her interest in journalism, Crane's mother was a temperance campaigner; she went to prayer meetings and believed firmly in the dangers of slipping from grace and eternal damnation. Crane said his interest in religion cooled off by about the time he was thirteen, and it was journalism that captured his imagination. Crane experienced the negative side of news reporting early on; he was fired from the *New York Tribune* for writing an article about a labor rally that embarrassed Whitelaw Reid, the owner of the *Tribune* and a vice-presidential candidate with Benjamin Harrison in 1892. Some of his *Tribune* colleagues, however, felt that by his firing Crane had been freed from mundane reporting; it "might be the making of him," said one.[64]

It was his Civil War novel, *The Red Badge of Courage*, which made Crane's literary reputation (and upon which it still largely rests). After finishing the book in the winter of 1893 to 1894, he tried to get it serialized, initially without success. Eventually, the book was published in the *Philadelphia Press* after being cut from 50,000 to 18,000 words for serial installments. The *Press* staff treated Crane as a writing hero (he reportedly received a standing ovation when he walked into the newsroom during the serialization of the book). Despite his literary success – the book was praised lavishly by critics who marveled at the fact that Crane could write so brilliantly about a war he had never seen – Crane never escaped the world of journalism, and he spent what would be his short life shuttling between journalism assignments while producing fiction on the side. When Crane traveled to Nebraska in 1895 en route to an assignment in Mexico, he surprised the young Cather with his slovenly dress and unkempt appearance. In Lincoln, he borrowed money from the managing editor of the local newspaper and tried to break up a fight at a bar, which he transposed into a short story, "The Blue Hotel." He muttered imprecations against journalism to the apprentice reporter, Cather, a junior at the University of Nebraska at the time. Cather never forgot what Crane said about how he needed the details "to filter through my blood, and then it comes out like a native product, but it takes forever."[65]

Crane's impressionistic writing and sketches made him less than the model journalist in the eyes of many of his colleagues. In many respects, Crane was a failure as a traditional reporter; he was unwilling to stick to bare facts or indulge in the breathless exaggerations that passed for reporting in his day. Many of the journalists he worked among found Crane a strange character, but he was so gentle and wistful that he was well liked – at least in the initial stages of his career. "He was not a persistent worker, because his body ... was ever too weak to bear continuous labor," wrote a fellow correspondent. "His brain never rested." Another described Crane as "one of the queerest" reporters he had ever known but was amazed at his ability to write prose effortlessly and without corrections. When the correspondents gathered in Puerto Rico at the end of the Cuban campaign, they voted Crane the best reporter covering the 1898 war against Spain. But as his celebrity grew, he became good copy himself, stirring wide reader interest, and he found that some journalists came to resent him. Some saw him as undisciplined and irresponsible, others envied his success and the freedom he was given by his employers to write what he wanted.[66]

The century-long tradition of romantic reputation surrounding star journalists seemed to apply perfectly to Crane's life. In the tradition of Coleridge, De Quincey, and Poe, Crane was always followed by gossip about his personal life – his drinking, his sex life, his decadence. But Crane courted his reputation by his flagrant and rebellious behavior performed in a body that was deteriorating in front of his friends and the public. Even while a youth in New Jersey he showed signs of ill-health, smoked incessantly, and had a hacking cough. He repeatedly told people he didn't expect to live long. Cather – convinced when she met him that he had a premonition of the shortness of his working days – remembered Crane's eyes as "dark and full of lustre and changing lights, but with a profound melancholy always lurking deep in them. They were eyes that seemed to be burning themselves out." Some biographers believe that Crane knew what was wrong with him, probably before he left New York to cover the Greco-Turkish War in 1897, and that his later Spanish-American War coverage offered him opportunities to "free himself" from life. During the campaign, he had a feverish approach to work, a risk-taking compulsiveness in his personal behavior, and a "grim flippancy" in his manner. A friend once noted to Crane that it was unfortunate that he and Kipling began to write at the same time. Crane responded: "Yes. I'm just a dry twig on the edge of the bonfire."[67]

Crane's critical standing has grown considerably in the years since his death. Much of this is because Crane's language is rich and figurative within its plain structure, particularly in its use of metaphors and its elegant turns of phrase. Although also a stylist, Crane believed in realism in his writing, and he subscribed to the modest stance of the journalist as a simple recorder of the world. "I try to give to readers a slice out of life; and if there is any moral or lesson in it, I do not try to point it out. I let the reader find it for himself." Crane said his chief responsibility was to tell the truth – but (in a way that endears him to post-modern critics) he readily acknowledged the limits of a journalist's ability to see the world objectively. "To keep close to this personal honesty is my supreme ambition," he said. "There is a sublime egotism in talking of honesty. I, however, do not say that I am honest. I merely say that I am as nearly honest as a weak mental machinery will allow."[68]

NORRIS, LONDON AND THE "RED-BLOODED SCHOOL" OF NATURALIST FICTION

As a Zola follower and militant naturalist (at least, in overt philosophy), Norris – who watched Crane from an admiring distance when both were covering the Spanish-American War in Cuba – felt the need to gain real-life experience, and after leaving college, he headed into the world with his philosophy that "the most difficult of all (things) for the intended novelist to acquire is the fact that life is better than literature." Working on the San Francisco *Wave*, he honed his skills of observation and was given great liberty under an editor sympathetic to his ambitions. He was already susceptible to the romantic myth of newspapers – he saw everyone around him as gruff but brilliant editors, shirt sleeves rolled up and barking orders, or young reporters immersing themselves in life and learning writing in the roughest of schools. An editor once said: "Frank never saw things with his eyes. He had no faculty of physical attention, but after having been to a place, exposed to its stimuli, he could describe it – on paper – with complete verisimilitude. I used to say that his pores served him as visual organs."[69]

After Norris was recruited to New York City as a young writer to work for *McClure's* magazine, he found himself on the precipice of becoming a propagandist and reformer, as would happen with Dreiser, London, Sinclair, and others who operated in the naturalistic tradition. But Norris turned out to be more interested in stories than reform. His background as the son of a wholesale jeweler had left him comparatively untouched by suffering, and his sense of the dramatic outweighed his social sympathies. "The moment … that the writer becomes really and vitally interested in his purpose his novel fails," he wrote. Sloppy as had been his journalistic research, he did prodigious amounts of it for his fiction. "You've no idea of the outside work on it," he once said of *The Octopus*. "I've been in correspondence with all kinds of people during its composition, from the Traffic Manager of a Western railroad to the sub-deputy-assistant of the Secretary of Agriculture at Washington."[70]

Norris often used vivid reporting to compensate for stylistic weaknesses in his works. In developing the narrative of *The Octopus*, Norris turned to material in the Mechanics Library and the files of the San Francisco newspapers to dig out the facts of the gun battle between San Joaquin Valley wheat farmers and railroad people, known as the Mussel Slough affair, around which he built the plot of the novel. In preparing the novel, Norris acted like a research worker, visiting the town of Tulare and watching the wheat farming in progress, producing index sheets for each character, tabulating and arranging notes, and creating a map of the country where his action was to take place. He researched the details of exploring and nursing in *A Man's Woman* and the impact of venereal disease in *Vandover and the Brute*. In *Blix*, he has the young writer express pleasure with a Kipling short story because of its use of engineering terms. In 1901, he observed the intricacies of the commodities market closely in anticipation of writing *The Pit*, and a New York stockbroker helped him learn the market since Norris had problems with math. In all his works, Norris piled up careful specifics in his writing. "No piece of information – mere downright acquisition of fact – need be considered worthless," he said. "Nothing is too trivial to be neglected."[71]

In *McTeague*, Norris – writing heavily under the influence of Zola – sought to probe the depths of human depravity and to deal with sex and brutality in a somewhat philosophical, rather than too specific, way. Norris' novel about a brutal and criminal dentist grew out of accounts of the stabbing death of a woman by her violent husband in the San Francisco newspapers. In preparing the book, Norris talked about his "aggressive faculty" for research, and he clearly valued scientific data, taking copious notes on dentistry, lycanthropy, criminal psychology, and atavism. He often went to libraries for information, and *McTeague* – like most of his novels – was long on particulars. However, in trying to maintain an objective and even an amoral attitude toward the story, Norris offended a number of critics, who found the book sordid and evil. "We must stamp out this breed of Norrises!" exclaimed one.[72]

Of all the naturalists, Norris – the Berkeley student – conveys the strongest sense that he has been to college. Despite his aversion to artsy culture, Norris' journalism had great aesthetic breadth, including reviews of art exhibits, architecture, and plays, interviews with artists and dramatists, critical essays on literature, and he often discussed aesthetic theories in his articles. A budding post-modernist of sorts, he noted that science can't give an accurate picture of life; that no two photographs will convey the same impression of actuality; that even the same artist will not see the same thing twice exactly. "Life itself is not always true, strange as it may seem, you may be able to say that life is not always true to life – from the point of view of the artist," he wrote. He was highly influenced by fashionable ideas of his time, particularly on race and evolution, and he came under the strong influence of Kipling in his interest in hereditary instinct. Norris said he preferred characters whose brains are "almost empty of thought ... as those of ... fine, clean animals." His love of the "atavistic, red-blooded brute" (which he shared with London) and his views about the superiority of Anglo-Saxon culture and the Aryan races (which he shared with London and Kipling) led to his enthusiasm for British and American imperialism and contributed to his strange and often contradictory political ideas, which found him advocating a form of populism and democratic reform on one hand while also subscribing to ideas about higher races exercising their responsibility to lead lesser peoples out of their primitivism.[73]

London, like Norris, fashioned his naturalism around a belief in Anglo-Saxon superiority and nineteenth-century philosophical notions of the superman. Called the successor to Norris in the "red-blooded school of America," London developed his naturalistic outlook as a teenager on a sealing expedition. Even before reading Darwin or Karl Marx, he saw the struggle to live among humans as similar to the struggle in the animal world. Arrested for vagrancy during his years as a tramp following a knock-about upbringing in and around Berkeley, California, London survived in a prison near Buffalo, New York, by joining "the oppressors to survive with the fittest," as he put it. The experience taught him about the "viciousness of trying to survive among the degraded," and he saw the Erie County Penitentiary as the "microcosm of racism and capitalism." A product of the Horatio Alger era that he so identified with (he was raised in near poverty by a spiritualist mother and a farmer-shopkeeper stepfather; it was only when he was in his early twenties that he learned his real father was a vagabond astrologer who had abandoned his mother), London went back to high school a number of years after he had dropped out and earned his degree. During this period, he became impressed with Marx's communist manifesto, which he felt explained his experience as a down-and-outer in society, and in 1896 joined the Socialist Labor Party in Oakland. London's socialism (like Norris' politics) suffered from a muddied philosophical basis – a glorification of the individual "superman," a blunt racism, a contempt for the lower orders and lesser breeds, and a love of romantic swashbuckling heroes. London came to feel a perverse satisfaction at knowing that he was irrelevant to the destiny of the species, that he could do anything he wished, and yet it would not affect the grim logic of Darwinian selection. "We are blind puppets at the play of great unreasoning forces," he said.[74]

London eventually got into the University of California at Berkeley, but he wasn't happy there and dropped out. During this period, he held a series of menial jobs – including working as a boiler and presser in a laundry – and then, hit by gold fever, he headed north in 1897 to the Klondike, where he stayed for one winter. When Harte's old magazine, *Overland Monthly*, bought one of his Alaska stories upon his return for $5, his writing career was on its way. The fashion for Kipling and social Darwinism had whetted the public appetite for the kinds of stories London was producing. Soon he was writing furiously and submitting his material relentlessly. He wrote 1,000 words a day, six days a week, and maintained a frantic pace, carried out in independent isolation. He refused to take newspaper work in his early days for fear it would restrict him (even though he did rely heavily upon newspaper articles for story ideas). "A reporter's work is all hack from morning till night ... It is a whirlwind life, the life of the moment, with neither past nor future, and certainly without thought of any style but reportorial style, and that certainly is not literature," said his protagonist in the semi-autobiographical novel, *Martin Eden.* "To become a reporter now, just as my style is taking form, crystallizing, would be to commit literary suicide."[75]

Eventually, after establishing himself as a popular author, London accepted an offer to contribute articles to the conservative Hearst press, the bugaboo of socialists. "Income was one thing, politics another," said London at the time, striking a note that he would live by as he balanced his socialist leanings with his love of money and the good life. Hearst was an excellent outlet for London's increasingly reactionary views of Aryan superiority and his belief in the right of a "superman" to live by his own moral rules. London's most famous story, *The Call of the Wild* – about a dog that reverts to a wolf-like existence in the north country – served for London as a myth about life and death and nature and as a saga of the human unconscious fused by the writer into the unsuppressed imagination of the beast. London himself became a follower of Jung and his theories of the "mythic subconscious," and psychologically-oriented critics have recognized the symbol of the wolf in London's art and his life as both the destroyer and preserver in ancient myth. In blending his naturalist and Darwinian beliefs, London did his best to blur the distinction between animals and humans in his writing. "You must not deny your relatives, the other animals," London once wrote. "Their history is your history."[76]

Naturalism's legacy was enhanced by the tragic early deaths of Crane, Norris (of appendicitis), and London (of a drug overdose) and the lore attached to their high risk, adventuring lifestyle. Their ethic of activism, intense professionalism, and a mixture of stoicism and epicureanism did much to establish the pose of the alienated twentieth-century artist and journalist in a century when even more wrenching and traumatic events were to rock the world. Kipling's vision of the dutiful and disciplined Aryan elite bringing technology and order to a world mired in cultural complacency and backwardness shared much with the naturalists, particularly Norris and London. Hemingway's books are filled with naturalistic themes even as he celebrates the occasions when humans appear to transcend their fate. Steinbeck was a thoroughgoing naturalist who, rather than growing depressed about it, was positively uplifted by the notion of humankind operating as biologically determined creatures in an indifferent universe. To see the human being as not at the center of the universe, but as a special animal that may survive only if it adapts, was for some readers drearily anti-humanistic, and yet Steinbeck believed it in a cheerfully untroubled fashion.[77]

At the same time, the naturalists' continued connection to journalism and mass-market publication conspired to dilute the naturalist ethic. The pressure to produce prefabricated writing to editorial prescriptions, the challenge of selling artistic works with bleak themes, the difficulty of successful and self-indulgent writers in maintaining such a tough-minded outlook on life – many of these problems were exacerbated by the hack-work formulas in which they had apprenticed, particularly the focus on criminal instinct and the always-popular theme of nature versus civilization. Their deterministic impulses were modified by the ever-present temptation – demanded by popular publication – to have their heroes triumph over the environment. Ironically, while seeking out life as it is lived, the naturalists – once they became celebrities – were pressured to negotiate an editorial ideal in advance so their trademark style could be marketed. The "real" world of the naturalists underwent a great deal of romanticizing and sensationalizing in the commercial marketplace. Eventually, naturalism took on the unreality of media engineering where, as Christopher Wilson has observed, seeking truth was turned into a convention of truthfulness. The naturalistic instinct to seek out "incredible" realism and to tout the romance of despair have become such a dominant voice in modern literary culture that it can be seen today to constitute an orthodox artistic viewpoint.[78]

Thus a modified naturalism has become imbedded in the consciousness of many modern writers as they spin out their literary themes against an inherited worldview of godlessness, disillusionment, stoic endurance, and psychological crisis. Art as a refuge against meaninglessness has become such a commonplace concept that it is often taken for granted as the contemporary artist's credo. To see the connections between the literary developments of the twentieth century and the lessons learned in the nineteenth-century newsroom is only one element in the story of modern art's turn to a pessimistic stance toward the universe. But journalistic values as a catalyst have played their role in this transition via the naturalists, and before them the realists, whose experiences in journalism played a powerful part in shaping their literary outlook and the development of the modern literary tradition.

CHAPTER 3

Reporters as novelists and the making of contemporary journalistic fiction, 1890–today: Rudyard Kipling to Joan Didion

A petty reason perhaps why novelists more and more try to keep a distance from journalists is that novelists are trying to write the truth and journalists are trying to write fiction.

– Graham Greene

Writing has laws of perspective, of light and shade, just as painting does, or music. If you are born knowing them, fine. If not, learn them. Then rearrange the rules to suit yourself.

– Truman Capote

That is what we are supposed to do when we are at our best – make it all up – but make it up so truly that later it will happen that way.

– Ernest Hemingway

Get your facts first, and then you can distort them as much as you please.

– Rudyard Kipling quoting Mark Twain

It is fair to say that Richard Wright found a journalist's way to become inspired to write his most critically acclaimed novel, *Native Son*. All across the floor of his New York City apartment in 1938, he spread hundreds of clippings that had been sent to him by friends about the murder trial of Robert Nixon, a young black man in Chicago who was accused of killing five women and raping others. Wright would read the clippings over and over again as a way to impress the story into his imagination. Ultimately he traveled to Chicago to help document the account he intended to write by visiting Nixon's defense attorneys, the Cook County Jail where Nixon was incarcerated and which contained the electric chair in which he was to die, and the Chicago public library, where Wright did research on similar cases.[1]

Wright was not the first celebrated novelist to use what is called "reportage" as the basis of a major piece of fiction. In fact, Wright saw himself as following in the footsteps of Theodore Dreiser, who had based his best-selling 1925 novel, *An American Tragedy*, on a real-life murder case, and whose earlier novels, *Sister Carrie*, *The Financier*, and *The Titan*, depended greatly upon the observations and experiences of his reporting career.[2] As a former reporter himself, it made sense that Wright would be drawn to the techniques of factual research, real-life observation, and the accumulation of empirical detail as the methods to give his writing the feeling of authenticity and a realistic atmosphere. And yet, Wright's novel, like Dreiser's, is generally not studied by scholars of literary journalism because – in the writing of it – Wright took too many creative liberties to have it considered to be non-fiction on the basis of contemporary standards of journalistic factuality.

Journalistic reporting as the basis for great literature is often recognized these days, if it is at all, as the contribution of the "new journalism" for which Tom Wolfe has so aggressively advocated. The contemporary variation of this movement began with the publication of Truman Capote's *In Cold Blood* in 1966 and has been carried on by a host of high-profile writers, including Wolfe, Norman Mailer, Hunter Thompson, Gay Talese, David Halberstam, John McPhee, Tracy Kidder, Joan Didion, Calvin Trillin, and Jane Kramer, among others. Capote, in particular, has been celebrated for the way he revived a flagging fiction-writing career by building a best-selling novel, *In Cold Blood*, around the reporting and the researching of the factual details of the murder of a Kansas family and then using the stylistic techniques of literary fiction to dramatize the story. The excitement generated by the "new journalism" movement has led some enthusiasts, most provocatively Wolfe, to declare that the contemporary novel has been captured by elitists and celebrators of arcane writing and has lost its relevance in comparison to the vital new practitioners of Wolfe's form of augmented journalism.[3]

In fact, Wolfe's and Capote's grand claims for "new journalism" tend to obscure the fact that the use of journalistic type reporting in the creation of fiction has a tradition that is as old as the novel itself. Since Daniel Defoe wrote *A Journal of the Plague Year*, *Robinson Crusoe*, and his other journal-istically inspired literary works, no period has been without its semi-fictional literary masterpieces forged out of the methodology of journalism – and which were often produced by novelists whose careers began in journalism.[4] It isn't just that reporting has served as the basis of so many journalistic novels; it is the impressive nature of the reporting and how often it masterfully enhanced what the journalist-literary figures had (and sometimes made up for what they had not) experienced first hand.

What Barbara Foley has called the "documentary" or "pseudo-factual" novel occupies a distinct kind of writing near the border between factual and fictional literature. However, the study of this phenomenon has often fallen between areas of scholarly specialization, and the examination of journalism's influence upon the fictional tradition is commonly resisted, ignored, or underestimated by literary scholars who are only rarely interested in trying to identify or analyze the journalistic elements of a piece of fiction, and scholars of what has become called "literary" or "narrative" journalism (many ex-journalists working in academic journalism or communication departments) who tend to want to preserve the journalism profession's traditional line of demarcation between fiction and non-fiction and to study only those literary works that meet the test of empirical validity outlined by Capote and Wolfe when they launched the "new journalism" movement.

The split between those who want to keep the study of literary non-fiction separate from fiction reflects another division that grew more apparent throughout the twentieth century – between writers who have aimed for a popular market and those who saw themselves as operating within a high literary tradition. Throughout the nineteenth, and into the twentieth century, as the study of literature professionalized within academic institutions and critical analysis became increasingly connected with literary theory, politicized literary criticism, and avant-garde movements of experimental writing, many of the journalist-literary figures became ever more aware that they were being judged by the standards of a highly specialized critical elite. The increased consciousness that they should be aiming for a "literary" audience and utilizing stylistic techniques that would impress an educated and exacting critical community can be seen in two pieces of writing by William Dean Howells and Stephen Crane that are often analyzed for what it means to write journalism, as compared to fictional literature, in the days since the industrialization of the commercial press.

The most famous of Howells' journalistic figures is Bartley Hubbard, who appears in Howells' novels *A Modern Instance* and *The Rise of Silas Lapham*, and who symbolizes all that Howells found "dishonest" about the nature of journalism in the nineteenth century. In *A Modern Instance*, Hubbard is described as a "poor, cheap sort of creature. Deplorably smart, and regrettably handsome. A fellow that assimilated everything to a certain extent, and nothing thoroughly. A fellow with no more moral nature than a base-ball." In the first chapter of *Silas Lapham*, where Hubbard is interviewing the paint merchant, Lapham, Howells uses a device where he intersperses pieces of the article that Hubbard would write about Lapham (about which Hubbard complained to his wife: "I couldn't let myself loose on him the way I wanted to. Confound the limitations of decency, anyway") with the cynical and manipulative thoughts that the novelist Howells recounts going on in Hubbard's mind. By juxtaposing fictional narrative with excerpts from Hubbard's flatteringly false and fulsome feature article about Lapham,

Howells was able to illustrate one of his major concerns about the trends in American writing, namely the increasingly close connection between nineteenth-century fiction and the devices of the popular newspaper (with Howells satirically demonstrating the superior "honesty" of the fictional portrayal).[5]

In a similar fashion, critics often have used Crane's 1897 short story, "The Open Boat," and its companion newspaper account in the *New York Press* of Crane's shipwreck while on the way to cover the preliminaries of the Spanish-American War to demonstrate the superiority of fiction-writing to conventional journalism. However, recent critiques of Crane's "The Open Boat" have challenged the notion that what makes a work journalistic is its factuality and what makes it literary is its fictionalization. Michael Robertson and Phyllis Frus have argued that the newspaper story, printed four days after Crane's rescue under the title "Stephen Crane's Own Story," and the short story, written within the next few weeks and published in *Scribner's* magazine, are both based on a factual recounting of events, and that the short story is no more fiction than the journalism article. Robertson maintains that what makes "The Open Boat" a superior piece of writing is not its imaginative or fictional basis but rather Crane's use of impressionistic scene painting, deliberate repetition in word use, and the employment of simile as stylistic device. And yet, for the purpose of this study, what may be most important to consider is the way that Crane had come to operate with a different notion of what was expected in a "high" literary account of an event and what was expected in a newspaper version. Crane's more prosaic newspaper story – arguably still a high-quality piece of newspaper writing – uses commonplace phrases and is modest in its overall aspirations, while the short story has a powerful impact despite its sometimes pretentious tone and self-conscious striving for stylistic effect. This appears to indicate that – rather than troubling himself about the fictional or non-fictional nature of his short story – Crane's greatest concern was in meeting the standards of the literary community that he was fully aware drew an important distinction between serious literature and writing aimed at a newspaper audience.[6]

This notion of Howells' and Crane's – that "literary" writing was and should be considered something superior to journalistic writing that met the commercial needs of newspapers or popular periodicals – solidified throughout the decades of the twentieth century. The writers of complex and erudite prose tended to follow the path of Henry James who – after a brief dalliance with the commercial press – came to see his success as appealing to a learned level of reader with sophisticated literary tastes and an appreciation for dense and prolix style. A few of the journalist-literary figures of the nineteenth and early twentieth centuries – George Eliot, George Bernard Shaw, Wallace Stevens, Virginia Woolf, E. M. Forster, Hart Crane, Eugene O'Neill, and Ernest Hemingway – joined the top ranks of literary figures who were studied for their psychologically complex themes and/or stylistic virtuosity and acclaimed as important writers by literary scholars and critics of serious literature. This tension – between writing with one eye on the popular marketplace and the other on the judgment of a loftier literary elite – had its roots in traditional British notions about "high" and "popular" literature and had caused considerable discomfort for such figures as Howells, William Thackeray, Edgar Allan Poe, Mark Twain, and other journalist-literary figures who craved acceptance by both the literary establishment and the popular marketplace. Still, despite these tensions, the "pseudo-factual" or "documentary" novel – with its foundation in journalistic reporting and research and writing methods – survived both within the scope of ambition of the journalist-literary figures and within the mainstream of fictional literature, although its status with scholars and critics has grown more problematic in recent years, given the growing appetite of the literary community for complex prose works that could be dissected within the context of literary theory and subjected to specialty analysis.

Time and again, it is the quality of the journalistic research that gives these "documentary" novels their strength and their durability. This is particularly striking in the novels where the authors weren't intimately familiar with the material through personal life experience or extended professional contact but still managed to produce works of great life-like texture, powerful verisimilitude, and deep knowledge of the ways of the world. It is no coincidence that the journalist-literary figures only rarely made their marks as exotic stylists, introspective examiners of the human psyche, or as confessional writers. Their fiction tended to be based upon the same writing philosophy and skills as their journalism: a careful attention to external things, a strong interest in matters outside of self and one's own psychology, a fascination with technical and occupational details, and a high level of competence in capturing the rhythms of human speech and the patterns in the way people live.

There are many stories of how the journalist-literary figures disciplined themselves in the rigors of accurate and precise observation. As a young writer in training, Hemingway has described the care he took to note the details of his daily activities and then to write them down – for instance, before boxing work-outs, when he would note the sensations of the gym while wrapping his hands – which Charles Fenton has described as Hemingway's way of exercising his belief that a writer must "see it, feel it, smell it, hear it." James Agee was so obsessed with capturing the "truth" of his accounts, such as in the posthumously published novel, *A Death in the Family*, about the trauma Agee experienced when he lost his father as a young boy, that he published little of a lengthy nature in his later years while devoting himself to perfecting the book. Conrad Richter repeatedly interviewed elderly people who were old enough to remember (or remember what their parents remembered) when Ohio was on the edge of the western frontier. "The characters I write about are immeasurably stronger and more interesting than myself," Richter once said. "That's why I am drawn to write about them, and try to picture and 'create' them."[7]

Consider some of what John Steinbeck, the son of a small-town financial official and a Stanford University dropout, had to learn to be able to give *The Grapes of Wrath* its earthy feel of nomadic tenant farming life: how to pull a piston and to repair a car, the way to use cotton-growing implements, the technique of slaughtering a pig, the different methods of evangelical preaching, the physical feel of a cotton field and the dusty Oklahoma countryside, the approaches to playing a fiddle and square dancing, the technical details of fruit growing and cultivation, and the slang terms and rhythms of speech of Oklahoma tenant farmers. Steinbeck gained some of this knowledge – plus a strong feel for the life of the working poor – during his stints of employment at manual jobs in breaks in his college years. But Steinbeck was "exceptionally unautobiographical" in much of his best work, as biographer Jackson J. Benson put it, and the carefully honed detail in his writing is most often the result of good reporting, careful observation, voluminous research, and a willingness to go out to where a story was to be found and to experience the ambience for himself.[8]

And yet, it also would be misleading to overestimate the similarities between journalism produced as journalism and the journalistic elements that infuse much of the fiction-writing of the journalist-literary figures, and they would be quick to note the many ways that the imaginative freedom in novel-writing leads to a richer and deeper exploration of the human experience. Hemingway, in fact, came to see newspapers as one of the main enemies of true expression, and particularly in the way that – through the use of industry conventions and formulas – they helped to dictate the way the culture came to view "acceptable" communication. Hemingway pointed to his friend and one-time writing inspiration Ring Lardner as a "writer tamed by journalism." In Hemingway's view, Lardner had failed to write the true language of his characters because he was restricted by the expression that was customarily used with newspaper and magazine editors worried about offending their audience. At a psychological level much deeper than the daily newspaper, Hemingway also came to believe that what limits people (and particularly writers) from authentic and honest expression is an almost instinctive sense of what it is one is supposed to feel and say in any given situation in order to fit within conventional moral, social, and workplace standards. In this respect, Hemingway actually believed in the opposite of what he is best known for – writing about the world in an "objective" journalistic short-hand style – and in comments he made repeatedly throughout his career, he rejected conventional journalism as having value beyond serving as an apprenticeship to a serious writing career.[9]

For Hemingway, the danger in what he came to call the "kinetographic fallacy" was the supposition that "we can get the best art by an absolutely true description of what takes place in observed action." Hemingway's approach to "transcending" the "kinetographic fallacy" was to use the creative imagination to present a picture of the world that penetrated more deeply into the texture of life than anything that journalism's one-dimensional methods of picturing reality could attain. One can see in Hemingway's fictional writings the many ways that he had greater freedom in the production of imaginative art – including the freedom to use extensive dialogue, to shape character development in a careful and psychologically revealing fashion, to engage in subjective commentary about life and the world, to use prose style for aesthetic effect, and to write in symbolic and evocative ways that signal a deeper meaning beneath the text. In particular, Hemingway liked to take real people from his life and then let his imagination reshape their characters and interactions. (Robert Cohn in *The Sun Also Rises*, for example, was Harold Loeb, Hemingway's real-life drinking companion and fellow novelist, while Lady Brett Ashley was Lady Duff Twysden, another friend from the Latin Quarter in Paris, and Mike Campbell was her boyfriend, Pat Guthrie. At one point in the novel, Hemingway transposes a real-life event – a bullfighter in Pamplona who cut off a bull's ear and gave it to Hemingway's wife, Hadley – into a scene where Lady Brett leaves a severed ear wrapped in a handkerchief in her hotel bureau drawer as a symbol of the end of her affair with Pedro Romero, the fictional bullfighter). Still, one can also see in his literature the inescapable effects of journalistic training and the reasons why Hemingway would also say, "Newspaper work will not harm a young writer and could help him if he gets out of it in time."[10]

As some of the journalist-literary figures began to become more lyrical and "poetic" in their writing style (a movement that became more pronounced throughout the twentieth century), they still tended to embrace in their prose what was genuine and substantial and fundamental to the human experience and the world of natural fact. Walt Whitman's phrase – that "logic and sermons never convince" and that there is more truth in "the damp of the night" – captures the journalist-literary figures' love of the external world, as does Whitman's advocacy of the alliterative and onomatopoetic sounds of hard-edged, practical Anglo-Saxon words ("A perfect writer would make words sing, dance, kiss, do the male and female act, bear children, weep, bleed, rage, stab, steal, fire cannon, steer ships, sack cities," Whitman once wrote). Over and over again, the journalist-literary figures articulated their joy in "reporting" upon what they had found manifest in their experiences, in their sensual perceptions, and in their encounters with the real people that they used as models for their literary characters. Even when they signaled that it was the "hidden meanings" in their work that mattered most, they didn't de-emphasize the use of concrete details in their writing. Both Hemingway and Willa Cather believed in writing by suggestion, and their writing style was influenced by their belief that they didn't want to overanalyze things or be too obvious in their meanings (Cather called it "the thing not named" in her writing, while Hemingway liked to compare his method to an iceberg where most of the meaning lies below the surface). Still, what she liked best about writing, Cather said, were the vividness and vigor of the English language, like the sound of a hammer striking an anvil.[11]

The lengths to which the journalist-literary figures would go to achieve a fullness of effect through the ambitious use of reporting techniques make fascinating tales in themselves. There are instances when the journalist-literary figures confounded the assumption that journalistic reporting provided the basis of their later fiction. Crane, for example, drafted his *Maggie, Girl of the Streets* before he moved to New York and wrote his famous newspaper sketches of the Bowery and the New York City slums. However, this was the exception to the rule that much of their fiction was constructed upon an edifice of journalistic research and reporting. The following novels and short stories, while often only parenthetically praised for the meticulousness of the reporting that went into them, are examples during and since the last decades of the nineteenth century of how the journalist-literary figures used their journalistic research skills to create the solid, factual underpinnings of their literary themes and the powerful descriptive impressions and vivid human characterizations that have put many of their novels in the pantheon of great literary works.

– Often underrated in Rudyard Kipling the novelist are the enormous reserves of "sympathetic imagination" that his years in journalism had helped him to develop (one critic called him the "artistic reporter of the Imperial England for posterity"). Whether it was soldiers or Indians or deck hands, Kipling had a hunger to "know" people who were different than he was. The irony is that Kipling the great "imperialist" worked so hard to get into the "heart" and "spirit" of others, including people of other cultures that the British had colonized. As a young reporter in India, Kipling saw mostly only the very rich and very poor among Indians, but in this fashion he did what journalists often do, which is to interpret the life of the high and the low for the middle. There was much comment in the English community about how often Kipling was seen around bazaars and wandering through the streets of the local cities where he acquired an immense knowledge of Indian ways, language, and customs. *Plain Tales from the Hills*, his evocative collection of short stories of colonial Indian life, was produced hastily as sketches to be used as "filler" and padding for his newspaper, the *Civil and Military Gazette*, and were very popular in India (where they were sold in railway stations).

Kipling was always eager to prove himself an initiate in the mysteries of trade, mechanics, soldiering, politics – any secret technique communicated by masters of their craft. Much of the fame of *Captains Courageous*, his novel about New England fishing life, rests on its use of detail, and it is undoubtedly his most impressive achievement of journalistic research. Kipling's accomplishment, with its rich descriptions of seascapes, its careful recounting of the dialogue and colloquy of the boat hands, and its convincing conveyance of the technical details of commercial fishing in the Atlantic Ocean, is even more praiseworthy, given that Kipling was an Englishman raised in India who lived only briefly in the United States. Like Steinbeck and Sinclair Lewis, Kipling benefited from the collaboration of an important source in the creation of his sea tale about a spoiled rich boy who falls from an ocean liner and is molded into a responsible young man by the New England fishing crew that rescues him. The help Kipling received from a local doctor, Dr. James Conland, was considerable. In their four visits (one to Boston and three to Gloucester, Massachusetts, covering fourteen days in all), they ate in sailors' eating houses along the wharfs, assisted tug masters in hauling their schooners around the harbors, examined charts and implements of navigation, went out with the boats and helped with the catch (where Kipling battled sea-sickness), and listened to the crews' tales and expressions and life philosophy. Kipling had uncanny skill in picking the brains of acquaintances and fashioning what they told him into convincing literary portraits, replete with details. However, he also said, "I have had miraculous escapes in technical matters which make me blush still.

Luckily the men of the seas and the engine-room do not write to the
Press, and my worst slip is still underided."[12]
– The verisimilitude in Lewis' portrait of American types and the extent
of the reporting he undertook to create authentic portraits of middle-class
life in 1920s and 1930s America is, in many respects, what has led to his
survival as a literary figure. There have been numerous criticisms of his
failings as a novelist, but what has earned him praise is the sociological
depth of his portrayal of early twentieth-century mainstream America
and the rich detail in the scenes of his small-town settings. Lewis was
let go in one of his first journalism jobs on the *Waterloo* (Iowa) *Daily
Courier*, at least in part because, as a small-town newspaper editorialist, he
was prone to writing meandering prose about literary and political and
philosophical questions. Part of his difficulty was that Lewis never found
a place in his daily journalism for the systematic observations he began to
catalog about local habits of speech, dress, and manners, which became
the grist for his later fiction. From his college days, Lewis liked to make
sociological expeditions to the places that he hoped to write about, and
he filled up notebooks with the details of what he observed. He was a
natural recorder of American speech; once, while in Paris sitting next
to some loquacious American tourists, his companion suggested that
he make notes. He said he didn't need to. The next day he repeated the
conversation verbatim from memory.

Lewis, in fact, did build his novels from the catalog of small-town types
that he had been keeping since his newspaper days. In *Arrowsmith*, one
of his most painstakingly researched novels, he wrote about a country
doctor who falls in love with medical research in part to respond to critics
who felt that George Babbitt, the archetypal small-town businessman
and booster in Lewis' earlier novel, was a shallow stereotype. In preparing
to write *Arrowsmith*, Lewis spent weeks with a medical investigator on a
West Indies cruise ship, pumping him for details about medical research
and reading intensively in bacteriology and epidemiology. Even though
he couldn't have tackled the book without the help of his collaborator,
Dr. Paul DeKruif, who had a PhD in bacteriology and had published an
outspoken book criticizing the medical profession which had cost him a
Rockefeller appointment, Lewis had a passion for research himself, and
he subjected DeKruif to his argumentative method of throwing out
bombastic statements and challenging the responses. In two months at
sea, the two men worked out everything, from a complete medical history
of the main characters to floor plans of hospitals and laboratories, and
Lewis made notes on everything, including their visit to the abandoned

town square of the plague-ridden San Lucia and a leper colony in Barbados. Lewis also used this immersion method in the preparation for *Elmer Gantry*, his book about American evangelism, where he attended two or three church services each week and read lots of religious books. But his most useful research was a weekly gathering of ministers in his Kansas City apartment, where he would probe their views on evangelism and theology and goad them with comments such as, "Why don't you tell your congregations that you are agnostics?" and, "You know you don't believe in God?"[13]

– *Death Comes for the Archbishop*, Cather's highly praised novel, was built, as with much good reporting, upon experiences and observations external to herself, including her travels as a tourist to the American Southwest and her fascination with historical research. M. Catherine Downs has noted how Cather fused her journalistic background and experiences into her fiction, including creating male protagonists that mimicked the male pseudonyms that convention required Cather adopt in some of her journalism, using prototypes of conventional "yellow" journalists in her early short stories, and adopting themes and plot lines that she produced or read in the newspapers during her career at the *Nebraska State Journal*, *Pittsburgh Leader*, and *Home Monthly* magazine. In her late-career novel about the cultural past of the Southwest, which many critics consider her best, Cather rewrote some of the historical material when it suited her artistic purposes. In fact, the book's dependence upon historical detail troubled some reviewers, who didn't know in what genre to place it. Cather's major written source was a Jesuit biography of the assistant to the archbishop of New Mexico in the mid-nineteenth century. In reality, the book was a composite of many sources and drew upon the talents that Cather had honed first as a journalist as well as a novelist: her pilgrimages to many of the Southwest's most dramatic archeological and religious sites, her correspondence and interviews with clerics and pioneers throughout the region, her fascination with the lives of New Mexican mission priests, her love of frescoes, her research into past figures of Southwest church history. As Cather (despite the strong barbs she often threw journalism's way) once said of her work for periodicals, "If I hadn't ... grasped the thrills of life, I would have been too literary and academic to even write anything worthwhile."[14]

– Journalists love the way Hemingway's journalistic use of language has come to define his fiction: the employment of short sentences and strong, one-syllable words, the concrete, muscular phrases, the wry, ironic dialogue, the terse, staccato rhythm of his prose, the deceptive simplicity of his vivid descriptions of scenery and action, and his "air of vast knowledgeability," as Fenton has put it. Critics and scholars, too, have been fascinated with journalism's influence upon Hemingway's fictional works. They have pointed to brief *Kansas City Star* vignettes that look forward to sections of *In Our Time*, as well as some of the longer, discursive pieces in the *Toronto Star* that were the basis for chapters in his first successful literary work. One chapter – about a procession of refugees evacuating eastern Thrace during the Greco-Turkish War – was reduced from a 343-word cabled scene in the *Toronto Star*, as Fenton, Frus, Shelley Fisher Fishkin, and other critics have analyzed it, to a 131-word passage with such journalese as "staggering" and "never ending" and "ghastly" stripped away and only a spare and vivid snapshot of the procession remaining. It was this technique that led Hemingway's friend, John Dos Passos, to describe Hemingway's writing style as "based on cablese and the King James Bible."[5]

However, it would be a mistake to presume that much of what Hemingway did as a fiction writer resembled his newspaper journalism except in external form. Hemingway's essay, "Pamplona in July," which was written for the *Toronto Star* magazine in 1923, demonstrates many of the elements of Hemingway's prose style: straight-forward, simple, declarative sentences, reliance on strong action verbs and the verb "to be", spare but elegant description, a powerfully conveyed sense of the action and color at the Spanish festival, and a confident, urbane tone that shows Hemingway as a young reporter very much in charge of his authorial voice. But it is apparent where Hemingway's journalism and his fiction are similar, and where they differ quite dramatically. In his early novel, *The Sun Also Rises*, which borrows a good deal of material from his Spanish travels and reporting about bullfighting, there are pages of verbal sparring among the characters (there is virtually no quoted dialogue in the journalism article), lengthy interior monologues, even plays on word-use in different foreign languages, not to mention a host of no-no's that would not be allowed in the daily journalism of Hemingway's time (open allusions to sex, aspersions cast on different cultures and ethnic groups, and references to impotence and venereal disease and other forbidden topics of the newspapers of that period). The slow, deliberate character development throughout the novel – much of it highly subtle and carried off through droll verbal exchanges – is matched by the dialogue itself, spare but so witty and fast-paced that it often seems like a script for the movies (many of which, such as *Casablanca*, were clearly influenced by the Hemingway style of conversation). In the novel, Hemingway went far beyond what a newspaper reporter would likely ever utilize to create some of the novel's most memorable lines ("Isn't it pretty to think so?", "It's no life being a steer", "I'm not going to be one of these bitches that ruins children"). The ironical allusions to life's great questions, often conveyed through the characters' oblique references to what they won't talk about directly – the pain underlying their hedonistic and aimless lives, the brave quips and verbal one-upmanship they employ to exercise control and to avoid looking squarely at their inner pain, the use of sex as a symbol of life's hopeless yearnings and alcohol as a truth serum to catalyze the action and lubricate the characters' brutally honest personal confrontations – have been pointed to by critics as examples of how Hemingway required the reader to read between the lines to see into the heart of a tragic vision that elevates the story beyond a journalist's tale of a bunch of drunks on holiday.[16]

Even though many of the scenes in the novel harken back to his journalism, *The Sun Also Rises* demonstrates a level of prose fluency that rises above the tried-and-true formulas that often limit journalistic writing. In "Pamplona in July," for example, Hemingway described the work of the bullfighter this way: "The bull turned like a cat and charged Algabeno and Algabeno met him with the cape. Once, twice, three times he made the perfect, floating, slow swing with the cape, perfectly, graceful, debonair, back on his heels, baffling the bull. And he had command of the situation. There never was such a scene at any world's series game." In the novel, this became:

Romero was taking (the bull) out with his cape. He took him out softly and smoothly, and then stopped and, standing squarely in front of the bull, offered him the cape. The bull's tail went up and he charged, and Romero moved his arms ahead of the bull, wheeling, his feet firmed. The dampened mud-weighted cape swung open and full as a sail fills, and Romero pivoted with it just ahead of the bull ... Each time he let the bull pass so close that the man and the bull and the cape that filled and pivoted ahead of the bull were all one sharply etched mass. It was all so slow and so controlled. It was as though he were rocking the bull to sleep. He made four veronicas like that, and finished with a half-veronica that turned his back on the bull and came away toward the applause, his hand on hip, his cape on his arm, and the bull watching his back going away.

Despite the need to discard some awkward similes and metaphors (A bull turning like a cat? Is it necessary to compare a bullfight to the World Series?), one can see the incipient outline of the fictional version in the original *Star* article. Still, the novel's prose has a finer, more flowing verisimilitude, not the least because Hemingway's writing is

more confident and refined – and because, it is clear, he was reaching
for a higher literary effect in the writing of his fictional version.[17]
– Steinbeck's *Grapes of Wrath*, his saga of the plight of migrant farmers
displaced by the Dust Bowl conditions of the 1930s, grew out of a series of
articles he wrote for a San Francisco newspaper. Steinbeck's insights into
the lives of the Oklahoma farmers who came to California only to face
exploitation and misery came about through repeated visits and interviews in migrant camps, detailed delving into the sociological documentation of the camps prepared by federal officials, and many days spent
with a federal social worker, Tom Collins, who knew and introduced
Steinbeck to the families, which he distilled into his fictional Joad family.
When he finished his reporting, Steinbeck wasn't sure what his next book
would be, but he knew it would be about a poor family he had observed
that was living in a house of willow branches, flattened cans, and paper,
with children suffering from malnutrition. In preparation for his newspaper series of Dust Bowl migrants, Steinbeck had purchased an old
bakery truck, outfitted it with food and blankets and utensils, and then
left for a tour of the San Joaquin Valley with Collins, the director of the
federal migrant camp program. An unexpected resource became the
reports written by Collins, which were filled with statistics, observations,
and even dialogue, that proved to be a gold mine of details and a
guidebook for Steinbeck's probing of migrant attitudes and actions.
In the novel much of the realistic feel of the names, incidents, and
expressions can be tied to Collins' reports as they were fictionalized
by Steinbeck. For his *San Francisco News* articles, Steinbeck also was
influenced by Collins' reports (which also were used by journalist Carey
McWilliams in his later book, *Factories in the Field*). Steinbeck was a
voracious researcher in the preparation of his other novels, too. To
assemble the background for his semi-autobiographical *East of Eden*,
based in part upon his family's past in the Salinas Valley, he went through
the files of the old *Salinas Index* to help charge his creative imagination.
He wanted matters of fact to be accurate down to the smallest reference
to people and events; at one point, he hired the city editor of the Salinas
paper to help him do research for the book.[18]
– Dos Passos envisioned the USA Trilogy (*The 42nd Parallel*, *1919*, *The Big
Money*) as a "series of reportages of the time," not a novel. But despite
incorporating non-fiction into the project, he viewed it as "sort of on
the edge between (fact and fiction), moving from one field to the other
very rapidly." Dos Passos also was writing journalism at the time for
the *New Republic*, *Fortune*, and *Esquire*, as well as a non-fiction book,

Orient Express, and journalistic backgrounding was an ingrained habit with him. His "Newsreel" sections of the trilogy involved a good deal of research, fact checking, and the examination of old newspapers. The trilogy contained a wealth of material from Dos Passos' journalism, according to Fishkin, including material from about a dozen articles and profiles he wrote for *New Masses* and *New Republic* in the 1920s and 1930s. "It sure does pay to put down what happens just as it does happen – I'm not at all sure that it isn't all anybody can do that's of any permanent value in a literary sense," he said. However, the nearness to real life grew into controversy when Harper's chose not to publish *1919* because it presented a too-derogatory profile of financier J. P. Morgan, who was involved in the company's financing. Dos Passos saw himself like Thackeray as "meddling in history" and writing the kind of prose that entailed "the presentation of the particular slice of history the novelist has seen enacted before his own eyes." Although experimental and avant-garde in its own way, the trilogy was viewed by Dos Passos as rooted in journalistic as well as artistic commentary, and he pushed for a commercially successful literature that wasn't simply belle lettres. The day of "the frail artistic enterprise, keeping alive through its own exqui-siteness, has passed," he said. "A play or book or a picture has got to have bulk, toughness and violence to survive in the dense clanging traffic of twentieth-century life."[9]

– Erskine Caldwell's work was so graphic that one editor called it "grotes-que overrealism." His reporting career had taught him to employ direct expression, economy of style, and material with intense emotional impact. He also had become fascinated with the underside of American life, and he liked to use violent, even repulsive detail. Caldwell battled editors who wanted him to delete material that was too sacrilegious or sexually explicit, and leftist critics grew frustrated at his mixture of nobility and degeneracy in his rural characters. He was crude and untutored as a writer (his grammar and sentence structure were terrible, and he relied heavily upon his first wife and others for editing). Famed Scribner's editor, Maxwell Perkins, hurried Caldwell out of New York after signing him; Perkins didn't want Caldwell involved in high-blown talk and cocktail parties. "Flustered and confused" writers like Caldwell "fluttered to their doom like moths to a flame" in New York City, Perkins said. Caldwell clearly fit into the camp of southern writers who made sport of "poor white trash," and his books were an uncomfortable mixture of buffoonery, social reform, and depravity. Some editors at Scribner's unsuccessfully opposed *Tobacco Road*'s publication; one was convinced its release would devastate the firm's textbook sales in the South. However, Caldwell was a committed social critic and political radical, and he engaged in serious investigative reporting even at the height of his novelist's fame. As a young reporter on the *Atlanta Journal*, Caldwell had arrived at the scene of a lynching before the body was cut down, and the experience left an indelible impression on him and helped to inspire one of his finest novels, *Trouble in July*. As a social realist with a taste for the surreal and grotesque, Caldwell's lean prose and studied portrayals of brutality made for some of his best fiction, and his account of a southern lynching was one of the most straightforward and effective novels he wrote. Even though there were those who described him as a "Breughel in prose," Caldwell eventually fell from favor with the critics and was written off as a sensationalist and a hack who finished his days writing for magazines like *Playboy, Cavalier, Dude, Swank*, and *Gent*.[20]

– The sociological research Wright did in Chicago for *Native Son* added depth and richness to the narrative, and his insights into the psychology of African-Americans and black and white racial patterns gave the public a disturbing taste of the alienation among members of the urban underclass. Wright acknowledged that he wanted the graphic realism in the book to "shock people, and I love to shock people." His characterization of Bigger Thomas – while clearly the portrait of an anti-hero – required a fictionalization that went well beyond what he learned of Robert Nixon's case and allowed Wright to express many of his personal frustrations and display his own anger at the injustices visited upon African-Americans. Although somewhat exaggerated from what actually happened in the Nixon case, Wright (a former communist journalist who never worked in the mainstream press) flogged the Chicago newspapers in the novel for their crude, racist coverage of Bigger Thomas' arrest and trial. Still, Wright's polemics against journalists (and communists) were far from the best parts of the novel. The strength of Wright's writing was in its psychological realism and the vivid way that he illuminated the inner turbulence of a marginalized, outcast personality. Wright's reporting and research – although augmented by his literary imagination and his own experiences as an alienated black man – gave *Native Son* its dramatic texture and its brutal, sometimes frightening honesty in confronting the racial divisions that still plague the US.[21]

– Agee's memorable accounts of the life of sharecroppers in the South (*Let Us Now Praise Famous Men*) and his moving story of his youthful reaction to his father's death (*A Death in the Family*) involved two different but equally intense kinds of reporting: reporting upon the circumstances of others' lives by living amidst them and reporting upon one's own past feelings by vividly recreating them on the printed page. *Let Us Now Praise Famous Men* grew out of a series of articles he wrote for (and which were rejected by) *Fortune* magazine. Agee and photographer Walker Evans obtained their material by traveling to Alabama and then living with a migrant family for three weeks in 1936. The book, published five years after the material in journalistic form was rejected, is a collage of Agee's writing styles, much of it self-consciously crafted, overwritten, and imitative of William Faulkner's prose. But mixed in are blindingly powerful and authentic pictures of the migrants' lives and the people whom Agee came to love and respect. Some critics have complained that the book's realistic intention was never attained, due to Agee's over-powering sense of guilt and his determination to idealize the share-croppers. But others have praised it as a compellingly honest portrayal of one man's efforts to come to grips with the social injustices and economic deprivation that plagued the nation during the Depression. *A Death in the Family* is a close-to-faithful account of Agee's recollections of the great tragic event of his boyhood embellished with a lyrical writing style that is much more accomplished than anything else he wrote. Agee's often-undisciplined writing habits and his ambivalence about his ambi-tion to see himself as a literary artist contributed to the fact that he never made a full break with journalism (he spent much of his career as a writer for *Time* and *Fortune*). Agee also struggled with grandiose writing goals and was never able to get his stylistic experiments under control in a way that satisfied him. It took a major effort by his publisher to assemble the disjointed manuscript and to forge it into the powerful form that was published after his death.[22]

– Richter also built his novels upon the painstaking research of a former journalist. When he was living or traveling in Pennsylvania, Ohio, or the desert Southwest, where he set most of his novels, Richter was constantly visiting libraries, historical societies, and courthouses, examining records and old newspaper stories. He compiled volumes of notes about inci-dents, places, and stories he found in historical material, the authentic language of earlier periods, and the usage of words and phrases as he heard them from local characters or read them in old clippings. Perhaps his finest book, *The Trees*, the first in his trilogy about settlers coming to Ohio, gained much of its richly atmospheric and true-to-its-time texture from this research, as well as the time that Richter and his wife traveled around Ohio in a house trailer, living among trees and trying to get the feel of them.

The reporter burned intensely in Richter all his life, and his notebooks and letters are filled with writing advice that he based upon his journalistic experiences. He once advised his daughter, a reporter with fiction-writing ambitions, to write her fictional stories like "you have been doing lately on news stories." He said the "indispensable element" in writing was "strength first and heart second," and he advocated paring all sentences and paragraphs to exact and essential words. With Richter, the oral tradition was always strong – he loved to read aloud to his wife and daughter – and he was obsessed with words and dialect and what common people past and present used in conversation. "Get a page of words that will describe each character," he wrote to his daughter. "Adjectives, nouns, verbs – then when you want to describe how your character says or does something, you have it right there." Richter kept pages of names: modern, old-fashioned, first names, last names, foreign names, as well as six large notebooks devoted to authentic characters, incidents, places, and objects. He used this material to create the world of frontier life vividly as he imagined it, dramatizing the natural heroism of his characters in a taut and graceful but not overly literary style. The American Southwest (where he spent much time because of his wife's health problems) was the scene of a number of his later books, and in one notebook, there is a five-page list of "Characters to See": sheep herders, cattle hands, well drillers, silver miners, ex-sheriffs, ministers, rangers, physicians, merchants, ranchers, and their spouses.[23]

– John Hersey's reputation as a journalist and a novelist developed hand-in-hand. His Pulitzer Prize-winning novel, *A Bell for Adano*, grew out of the material he collected while covering the aftermath of the fighting on the Italian front in World War II for *Life* magazine. The novel – which models its main character upon General George Patton – reflected the US military's agenda in trying to refashion a peaceful post-war society as Hersey observed it as a journalist. However, it was in his greatest work of literary non-fiction, *Hiroshima*, that Hersey most successfully blended the techniques of journalism, which he had refined as a *Time* and *Life* correspondent in China, Japan, and the Pacific front of World War II, with fictional models in ways that anticipated the "new journalism" movement of the 1960s and 1970s. Hersey's account of the survivors of the atomic blast at Hiroshima, which he based on six interviews conducted for the *New Yorker*, was written with a purposefully detached journalistic objectivity that gave the book much of its power. Hersey understood that certain subjects are so inherently emotionally intense that the best strategy is for the writer to let the story tell itself. Interestingly, Hersey's movement between the writing of fiction and the writing of journalism didn't keep him from emerging as a critic of the "new journalism" movement, which he viewed as dangerous in its blurring of the lines between fact and fiction and its claim that a literarily enhanced journalistic methodology could produce more meaningful literature.[24]

– Graham Greene's *The Quiet American*, his prescient novel predicting US involvement in the political and military unrest in Indochina, emerged from a number of reporting missions he undertook in the early 1950s for *The Times* of London and *Life* magazine. Interestingly, Greene's employer at *Life*, Henry Luce, embodied the faith in American goodness and its moral mission to save the world that Greene so adroitly critiqued in the novel. In *The Quiet American*, the character of Alden Pyle can be seen as a Luce disciple in the way he embodies the belief in the "absolute justice of American power," as Greene biographer Michael Shelden put it. Perhaps not surprisingly, *Life* – with a commissioning editor who was as eager as Luce to rid the world of the communist threat – didn't print anything of the Vietnam material that Greene submitted. Greene often went globe-trotting to find the settings of his novels, and Vietnam was just another of the many places he visited in search of the lush and forbidding backgrounds for his fiction. Greene's complex politics (some would say he was apolitical, forever changing his political stripes to vex the world and his readers) found him taking a tolerant view of the communist forces in Vietnam, at least in part because he saw the folly of the French effort to turn back the campaign of Ho Chi Minh. Greene was meticulous in his reporting – he spent six months researching an earlier piece about the British efforts to defeat the communist insurgency in Malaya, and he went on repeated military patrols (where, despite witnessing the brutal British tactics against the guerillas, he nevertheless endorsed them). In Vietnam, Greene also traveled with the military, and he never seemed to worry much about his personal safety (some would say he had a death wish). Greene's fascination with the corruption of expatriate life has always been on display in his novels, and the cynical journalist protagonist of *The Quiet American*, Thomas Fowler, contrasts (as Greene himself did) with the clean-cut American character, Pyle, whose "best and the brightest" image indicated that Greene foresaw how much damage a military campaign led by a lot of people with Pyle's naivety could do. However, Greene's success with *The Quiet American* worked against him as he tried to duplicate it, particularly late in his career. In *A Burnt-Out Case*, Greene spent three weeks researching his story at a leper colony in the old Belgian Congo, although the writing in the book indicated he was burned out himself (he suffered from pneumonia during much of the composition); in *The Comedians*, his 1966 novel about Haiti's Papa Doc Duvalier, he flew to Port-au-Prince and stayed for a couple of weeks at a large but nearly empty gingerbread hotel. As in Vietnam, he visited brothels, heard horror stories of the Tonton Macoutes, and soaked in the atmosphere (he also produced a short article about Papa Doc's reign of terror for the *Sunday Telegraph*). However, Papa Doc and the Tonton Macoutes never emerge as more than stick figures of a journalistic report. Ironically, Brown, the hotel-owner narrator of the book, refers to journalists who fly into a country for a short time, collect a few facts, then whip together articles with such titles as "The Nightmare Republic" – the exact title of the piece Greene (always aware of his dark and hypocritical side) submitted to the *Sunday Telegraph*.[25]

– James T. Farrell was another of the journalist-literary figures who seam-lessly blended his journalistic accomplishments into his fictional ones. Farrell supported himself in the late 1950s by writing thousands of unsigned editorials syndicated by the Alburn Bureau of Minneapolis for newspapers all around the country. His range was extensive – from sports commentary to politics to intellectual subjects – and he contri-buted to magazines, wrote a column in a Manhattan weekly, and produced criticism and essays on literary theory. His books – initially on baseball and travel – soon expanded into realistic fiction. One of the most distinctive literary forms is the one he evolved in the development of the characters Studs Lonigan (in his Studs Lonigan trilogy) and Danny O'Neill (in his five-book O'Neill–O'Flaherty series) – objective, attuned to the vernacular idiom of real-life characters, powerfully immediate. Farrell held up Dreiser and Hemingway as his models – but critics accused him of writing without artistry and relying too much on detail and uncut dialogue. They complained his Dreiser-influenced naturalism was too close to stenography, newspaper reporting, and undiscriminating documentation, which sometimes read like case studies or sociology. But part of Farrell's philosophy was to let life speak – and he was unapologetic for the journalistic influences in his writing.[26]

– Capote is one of the few journalist-literary figures to resurrect a slumping fiction career by turning to journalism and turning it into one of the great marketing and artistic triumphs of twentieth-century literature. The publication of Capote's *In Cold Blood* in 1966 brought him the fame that he had hungered for in a career that was long on celebrity glitz but light on literary accomplishments. Capote is now known as the founder of a genre – the true crime novel – that, in fact, Capote didn't found, but which his masterful use of public relations and self-promotion has guaranteed will be associated with him. Capote had long believed that non-fiction could be as compelling as fiction, and that one of the major reasons that it wasn't was because it was often produced by journalists rather than a writer in control of fictional techniques. "Journalism always moves along on a horizontal plane, telling a story, while fiction – good fiction – moves vertically, taking you deeper and deeper into character and events," he said. With most of his early novels only modest critical successes, Capote had kept his career going by doing magazine journalism, and he seemed the unlikeliest of reporters when he arrived in the Kansas town of Holcomb after reading in the *New York Times* about the unexplained murder of a local ranching family, the Clutters, and deciding to do a series on it for the *New Yorker*. Initially, the members of the ranching and farming community did not know what to make of the swish mannerisms and the high, lilting voice of the diminutive Capote, who was a regular guest on television talk shows and the country's most prominent openly gay celebrity. Even though he was often rebuffed in his quest for details and information by authorities and friends of the family, Capote operated with a determined professionalism that ultimately bore fruit. He and novelist Harper Lee, a childhood friend whom Capote took along as a research partner, would not take notes for fear of scaring off sources but would return to their hotel at night and transcribe the day's interviews from memory; he doggedly traveled the back roads to interview farmers in their homes; and his persistence finally won over many townspeople, who came to find him charming and invited him into their confidence.

Yet it was when the two suspects who were eventually convicted of the murders – Perry Smith and Dick Hickok – were arrested that Capote realized that he had more than a magazine series on his hands. In convincing the two to give him intimate details of their lives and crimes, Capote was able to follow through on the project's design – namely to use the facts he could dig up through diligent record searching and exhaustive interviewing as the journalistic underpinning of his work. In making the book "immaculately factual," as he put it, Capote's skills as a novelist were put to good use; he wrote with a lyric intensity and created a dramatic narrative that came straight out of fictional tradition. Although small inventions and factual discrepancies can be found (Capote believed his techniques allowed him some freedom to juxtapose events for dramatic effect, re-create conversations, and even speculate about what his characters were thinking), journalists, as a group, were bowled over by the accomplishment, and the book served as the inspiration to turn Capote's techniques into a genre form.[27]

- Like Capote, Mailer's dream of being remembered as a great novelist has become overshadowed by the acclaim he has earned as a journalist. Mailer's early successes as a fiction writer – most notably with *The Naked and the Dead*, his fictionalized account of his experiences as a soldier in the Pacific in World War II – were considerably greater than Capote's, and nobody would have considered him to be a failed novelist when he turned his attention to the practice of "new journalism" in the late 1960s. However, Mailer's fiction was always infused with a raw, journalistic tone, and his greatest achievements were in the production of vivid, realistic prose (such as in *The Naked and the Dead*) rather than the self-consciously stylized, experimental fiction of his mid-career. From the start, Mailer's writing roots were connected to journalism, although he never worked formally in the daily newspaper business (he was one of the original founders of the weekly *Village Voice*, however, and he wrote a column for it). His novel about a murderous husband, *American Dream*, was written on deadline and serialized in *Esquire* in 1964. Without a high-profile fictional hit in the years after *The Naked and the Dead*, Mailer – like Capote – jump-started his career by recognizing that something different was happening in the world of novel-writing and that his journalistic strengths might play into it. With *The Armies of the Night* (1968) – which launched Mailer into the Vietnam War protest as well as the "new journalism" movement – Mailer could claim (like Capote) that he had helped to invent a new genre. His use of the third person to describe himself was self-deprecating only rhetorically, and by inserting himself into the narrative, he sought to create a new public persona for himself. Perhaps Mailer's greatest achievement in the genre of literary non-fiction has been his account of the period leading up to the execution of Utah killer, Gary Gilmore. Mailer did not make himself a figure in *The Executioner's Song* – for a change – and most critics found this refreshing. His spare and haunting account was a triumph of research, interviewing, and riveting story-telling, and it won him a cascade of critical praise and honors. As one critic wrote: "At long last, Mailer has used his immense narrative powers, a true gift of the gods, the way they are meant to be used: to tell a story that is not about himself."[28]
- Didion, who began her career at *Vogue* magazine, is a writer who – despite a prolific output of fiction – has tended to impress critics more with her literary journalism than her novels with their bleak landscapes and their depressive protagonists. Like Wolfe, who has received anything

but universal acclaim since he turned to writing novels (*Bonfire of the Vanities, I am Charlotte Simmons*), Didion finds herself most appreciated for the texture and effectiveness of her terse, but fluent, non-fictional prose and her capacity to capture local settings with atmospheric details. The opening passage of the first essay in *Slouching Toward Bethlehem* – about the trial of a southern California woman for staging the murder of her husband – includes this celebrated sentence:

The San Bernardino Valley lies only an hour east of Los Angeles by the San Bernardino Freeway but is in certain ways an alien place: not the coastal California of the subtropical twilights and the soft westerlies off the Pacific but a harsher California, haunted by the Mojave just beyond the mountains, devastated by the hot dry Santa Ana wind that comes down through the passes at 100 miles an hour and whines through the eucalyptus windbreaks and works on the nerves.

Didion's novels are constructed with, if anything, even more spare sentences and blunt, journalistic prose. However, Didion's efforts to capture the damaged psyches and empty lives of her fictional protagonists have a hollow and evanescent quality. This is clear, for instance, when *Play It As It Lays*, one of her best-reviewed novels, where the nihilistic main character is an imagined one, is compared to the richly textured portrait she develops of a real person, such as the murderess, Lucille Miller, in her essay, "Some Dreamers of the Golden Dream," in *Slouching Toward Bethlehem*.[29] Throughout the decades, the journalist-literary figures have incorporated the many things they had learned in journalism into their novel-writing. This has not gone unnoticed by critics and scholars. However, there is often only begrudging appreciation for the degree to which their novels and their literature were made great through the inclusion of journalistic research material and the use of techniques that had been imported from their work as journalists. This doesn't in itself require one to alter the commonplace view that journalism is a craft as opposed to an art form and an activity that should generally be judged inferior to the art of fiction-writing. But the powerful journalistic elements that infuse so many of the journalist-literary figures' best novels – and their use of journalistic practices as the methodology for the creation of a powerful core within their literary achievements – should make one at least pause before asserting a singular claim for fictional techniques as the only way to attain literary greatness in prose.

CHAPTER 4

The taint of journalistic literature and the stigma of the ink-stained wretch: Joel Chandler Harris to Dorothy Parker and beyond

There is no more unhappy being than a superannuated idol.

– Joseph Addison

All the critics who could not make their reputations by discovering you are hoping to make them by predicting hopefully your approaching impotence, failure and generally drying up of natural juices. Not a one will wish you luck.

– Ernest Hemingway

That's my trouble. I don't think I have anything to say any more. And yet, I am like an old tailor. Put a needle and thread into my hand and a piece of cloth and I begin to sew … I want to write every day, even if I don't have anything to say.

– John Steinbeck

Editing should be, especially in the case of old writers, a counseling rather than a collaborative task.

– James Thurber

Ambrose Bierce, like many of the journalist-literary figures who came before him, could be called a "hack of genius" – a phrase which has been applied to Daniel Defoe by one of his biographers but which is a fitting appellation for the heirs of Defoe who toiled away in journalism, used the lessons learned there to go on to greater literary success, and today are recognized as lasting, if not always universally acclaimed, wordsmiths and literary figures.[1] However, Bierce, cynic and self-loather that he was, would almost certainly have rejected the complimentary "genius" half of the label.

Bierce once demonstrated his low opinion of his literary skills in an outburst to a woman novelist who was goading him for writing only short stories, not novels, and not fulfilling his potential as a writer. Bierce almost flew at her, proclaiming that he was not a great literary writer but was a failure, a mere journalist, a hack. Later, he was reported to have said, "I have the supremest contempt for my books – as books. As a journalist I believe I am unapproachable in my line; as an author, a slouch!"[2]

Toward the end of his career, in demonstrating his contempt even for his achievements as a journalist, Bierce quarreled bitterly with his son about his desire to quit school and to follow in his father's footsteps and become a newspaper reporter. Some people would have been flattered by his son's intentions – but not Bierce. "I will say this for my own profession, horribly I hate it," he once wrote. It was a calling that was "almost a disgrace to belong to." (Perhaps the saddest commentary on Bierce's jaundiced view of a journalism career was its prophetic quality: his youngest son, Day, with whom he quarreled so violently, was ultimately shot to death in a lover's quarrel just a few days after he quit his reporter's job at the *Red Bluff Sentinel*, and the story was carried in salacious detail in the competing press; his other son, Leigh, a journalist with Hearst's *New York Morning Journal*, was a womanizer whose lack of discipline worried Bierce, and Leigh ultimately died from pneumonia during a wild drinking binge after delivering Christmas presents to children for the newspaper.)[3]

The tension Bierce felt between his journalistic accomplishments and his sense of literary failure is at the core of a struggle that plagued a number of the journalist-literary figures who found journalism irresistibly appealing throughout their careers, but whose self-respect plummeted whenever they engaged in "mere" journalism. This issue became a particularly critical one in the later career years of those who returned to journalism after their fiction-writing powers waned. But for others, too, their sense of themselves as half-journalist and half-novelist never abated, and they oscillated throughout their writing lives between journalism with its gravitational pull on them and the challenge of writing fiction that they (and many of the critics) believed was the only place to achieve true literary greatness.

A few of the journalist-literary figures were proud throughout their lives to call themselves journalists – "I am a journalist first and last," H. G. Wells once said – and looked with regard upon periodical journalism's positive impact upon a writing career. For example, William Dean Howells, despite his repeated denigration of the commercial journalism business, sometimes looked back with regret that he hadn't more fully explored the world of newspaper reporting – which he said could have shown him "many phases of life" – instead of deciding that poetry and literature were more interesting. Margaret Fuller gave up her editorship at the *Dial*, the transcendentalist newspaper on which she worked with Ralph Waldo Emerson and other high-culture luminaries, to take a staff position on the *New York Tribune*, where editor Horace Greeley encouraged her to do investigative reporting into the social problems of poverty and immigration and helped her to turn her murky prose into something more direct and concrete. The strongest leftist social activists among the journalist-literary figures, including Upton Sinclair and Charlotte Gilman Perkins, always viewed their novels as a form of propagandistic writing and as a means to convey a social message that was of much greater importance to them than aesthetic accomplishment. In a different fashion, this was the view for a time of Rudyard Kipling, whose journalism for conservative publications and whose editing of a British troop newspaper in South Africa during the Boer War became a major late-life preoccupation as his artistic concerns became submerged under his ever more strident political views. (Kipling believed that, by correcting proofs, sub-editing, and writing copy on the troop newspaper, he was renewing his youth. "Never again will there be such a paper. Never again such a staff. Never such fine larks," he wrote of the experience.)[4]

The hunger for the real-life experiences that journalism could bring, even to an already successful literary figure, was the motivation for Ernest Hemingway, John Steinbeck, Jack London, Erskine Caldwell, Graham Greene, Evelyn Waugh, and others to seek out overseas reporting assignments and/or to use journalism as a means to explore the world and to continue to keep open to new life situations at a time when many writers find it difficult to stay in touch with real people and real emotions. This drive was so strong in some – such as Steinbeck and John Dos Passos – that they were relatively nonplussed by the pummeling they took from critics for taking newspaper and periodical assignments and went cheerfully about writing journalism or whatever worked for them. Others – such as the muckraker journalist, Ida Tarbell – held up the fact-based mission of journalism as superior to fiction (even though she tackled fiction-writing with her own novel, *The Rising of the Tide*), as she indicated in her assessment of the magazine investigations of fellow muckraker, David Graham Phillips, which she felt were based too much on "emotion and imagination" rather than factual research. "Mr. Phillips was more a novelist than a journalist," Tarbell said. "He should be judged by the field in which he worked, not by that in which some other people work."[5]

In perhaps the most dramatic statement of them all, E. M. Forster, an accomplished and critically respected novelist, decided to quit writing fiction during the last forty-six years of his career and to devote himself to topical and journalistic subjects – because, he said, he believed it to be more stimulating and socially important than novel-writing. Bored with the conventions of fiction, Forster said that the upheavals in society, psychology, and physics were too powerful for a form of writing that requires stability in all three. "I shall never write another novel – my patience with ordinary people has given out," he said. "But I shall go on writing." Forster's simple, direct, and sensible journalism drew a large audience as he churned out non-fiction articles and commentaries throughout his later career, and – along with his broadcasts on the BBC – made him a popular symbol of liberal values. Interestingly, his comment in *A Passage to India*, his last and most popular novel, has sometimes been applied to his reasons for quitting fiction-writing. "Most of life is so dull that there is nothing to be said about it and the books and talk that would describe it as interesting are obliged to exaggerate, in the hope of justifying their own existence," he wrote.[6]

As a general rule, the view of the literary critical establishment and many biographers has been that, by taking journalistic assignments throughout their careers or returning to journalism in their waning years, the journalist-literary figures shortchanged their literary promise, and that the intermittent practice of journalism and other "lesser" writing activities was often a sign that their literary confidence or their writing powers had flagged. Sometimes the picture was one of pathos: an aging and insecure Ring Lardner, under pressure to, but fearful of trying to, tackle a novel, finding comfort in the production of his syndicated national newspaper column; or Bret Harte, in experiencing the literary version of the burned-out reporter's dilemma, recycling the same successful short story and journalistic formulas but never stretching beyond what had worked in the past; or E. B. White, with his sense of himself as a frightened writer thwarted by anxieties and phobias, clinging to magazine routines until he struck upon children's writing as the way to leave his literary mark; or Caldwell, his fictional talents in decline, displaying his diminished skills under lurid covers on drug-store racks, pursuing journalistic assignments, and chasing Hollywood screenwriting jobs. In their later years, some of the greatest novelists among the journalist-literary figures – including Mark Twain, Stephen Crane, Theodore Dreiser, Sherwood Anderson, and Steinbeck – decided to do something other than crank out bad novels and devoted much of their time to journalism as a way to cling to the writer's life.

There are examples of the journalism of the journalist-literary figures that are recognized by literary scholars as timeless contributions to their writing careers – but there aren't many. George Orwell's *Homage to Catalonia*, his dramatic account of his involvement in the Spanish Civil War, is one of the better-known examples. It is only one of his many essays, critical articles, and other non-fiction works that are, for the most part, held in high esteem by critics across the board, and Orwell is one of the few of the journalist-novelists (along with Defoe, Twain, Wells, Hemingway, Jonathan Swift, and William Thackeray) whose journalistic output has received serious attention on the level of their fiction from a wide spectrum of the scholarly community. Of course, Orwell's legacy hardly rests upon his journalistic work alone (as is also true of Twain and the others), and it is unlikely that their journalism would receive such attention today if they hadn't also written acclaimed fiction. Orwell's enduringly popular novels, *1984* and *Animal Farm*, for example, have continued to exercise their hold on the modern fancy (even, it is interesting, as 1984 has come and gone and can no longer be used as a metaphor for the future). Although Orwell saw journalism as highly honorable, vitally important, and socially engaging, it is likely that he understood the risks of having his literary reputation rest solely upon it (which may explain, in part, why he worked so furiously to complete *1984* in the months before his death).[7]

Ironically, one of the strongest reinforcements of the view of novel-writing as a superior writing activity has come from the many journalist-literary figures whose intermittent and continued practice of journalism offered a spectre of mediocrity that hung over their image of themselves as evolved literary figures. Since at least the early nineteenth century, when views of what constituted "high" and "popular" forms of prose-writing had become solidified, literary scholars and critics have maintained a strong bias toward fiction, and they have tended to hold novels in higher esteem than they do even the best non-fiction (or short stories, for that matter). It is remarkable how often the journalist-literary figures themselves concurred in the critical dismissal of their journalism, and how much they had internalized the view that journalism was an inferior pursuit to the writing of fiction. White referred to his journalistic self as a "minor poet" and "lack wit" who wrote only of "the trivial matters of the heart" and the "inconsequential" things of life. At other times, they used unflattering assessments of their colleagues' work that they believed was too "journalistic," as Dos Passos once said of Sinclair Lewis' books, or a sign that one had become a "tradesman" of letters, as Virginia Woolf once described J. B. Priestley. Djuna Barnes, who worked as a stunt reporter for a number of New York newspapers before turning to experimental fiction and identifying herself with James Joyce, Ezra Pound, T. S. Eliot, and Gertrude Stein, adopted the "high" art view of her former profession (she called her journalism "rubbish"), as did Willa Cather, who was particularly resistant to the commercial elements of periodical journalism as she grew older. "Journalism is the vandalism of literature," she once said. "It has brought to it endless harm and no real good. It has made art a trade."[8]

No one could recognize better than an ex-journalist how involvement in journalism could threaten literary risk-taking – the lazy reliance upon writing formulas, the import of ingrained habits into one's literature, the fear of straying outside the bounds of safe expression and a tried-and-true writing purview. Journalism of any period also can seem time-bound, with references to long-forgotten current affairs and preoccupations with events and people that don't matter anymore. While any artist is tempted to repeat the things that have brought him or her success, the journalist-literary figures had a special handicap – they knew the temptation of easy accomplishment within the norms and routines of their old profession. Thackeray made many disparaging comments about his journalistic writing throughout much of his career, even while he practiced it ("This indiscriminate literary labor, which obliges a man to scatter his intellects upon so many trifles ... has been the ruin of many a man of talent since Fielding's time"). Woolf, whose main source of income until 1925 was reviewing and essay writing in newspapers, referred to her journalism as "brain prostitution" and "intellectual harlotry"; Edgar Allan Poe described his editorial work as "the miserable life of literary drudgery to which I now, with a breaking heart, submit." Lardner's editor at Scribner's, Maxwell Perkins, once said of him: "Ring was not, strictly speaking, a great writer. The truth is he never regarded himself seriously as a writer. He always thought of himself as a newspaperman, anyhow."[9]

The emergence of the so-called "new" journalism of the 1960s, and the growing embrace by serious writers of the practice of "literary" journalism and its study by contemporary scholars, has altered this viewpoint somewhat, but only in certain quarters. In fact, it is a testimony to how fiction-writing has been valued over journalism to consider how many of the journalist-literary figures who are now noted for their accomplishments other than novel-writing nonetheless have tried to make their mark in the field of fiction. Perhaps the most notable in this regard were the muckrackers of the late nineteenth and early twentieth centuries who – while celebrated today for their reform journalism that contributed to the progressive politics of that era – tried their hand at novel-writing with only marginal success. With the exceptions of Sinclair's *The Jungle* (about the abuses in the meat-packing industry that helped spur the passage of federal food and drug safety laws) and Phillips' *The Great God Success* (often viewed as a thinly disguised fictional account of Joseph Pulitzer's life, which it probably was not), most of these fictional works, including books by Tarbell, Lincoln Steffens (*Moses in Red*), Ray Stannard Baker (*Hempfield*),

Will Irwin (*Youth Rides West*), and William Allen White (*In Our Town*) are little read today. A number of other journalist-literary figures, well-regarded for their work outside of novel-writing, had only nominal success with their novels in the minds of literary critics and scholars. These include Bret Harte (*Gabriel Conroy*), Henry Adams (*Esther*), W. E. B. Du Bois (*The Quest of the Silver Fleece*), Ben Hecht (*Erik Dorn*), Floyd Dell (*Moon-Calf*), and the critic Edmund Wilson (whose *The Memoirs of Hecate County* took a particularly tough beating when he tried to enter the fiction arena himself). Even in recent times, when the so-called "new" or "literary" journalism has been much in vogue, it is remarkable to see how many of the prominent literary journalists have turned to novel-writing at some point in their careers, led by Tom Wolfe, Joseph Mitchell (*Old Mr. Flood*), Gloria Emerson (*Loving Graham Greene*), Rex Reed (*Personal Effects*), Hunter Thompson (*Rum Diary*), David Halberstam (*One Very Hot Day*), Calvin Trillin (*Floater*), Jimmy Breslin (*The Gang That Couldn't Shoot Straight*), and Pete Hamill (*The Deadly Piece*). (A few of the most celebrated contemporary narrative journalists have held the line at non-fiction-writing, such as John McPhee, Gay Talese, and Tracy Kidder, and not strayed into imaginative writing.) "It's hard to explain what an American dream the idea of writing a novel was" during his growing-up years, explained Wolfe. "... The Novel was no mere literary form. It was a psychological phenomenon. It was a cortical fever."[10]

But if one looks at the lifelong journalistic production of the journalist-literary figures as an historical group, it is possible to come to the conclusion that their journalism should receive more attention and be treated with more respect than it often is. One can make a case that the good quality non-fiction the journalist-literary figures produced – particularly, in some cases, in their late careers – should be better recognized for having enhanced their legacies more than the continued production of poor novels may have diminished them. Although often only peripherally noted by literary critics, some of the journalism produced by a number of the journalist-literary figures, even after they had made their reputations as novelists or fiction-writers, was solidly executed, and in some cases exceeded in quality the critically-dismissed fiction of what has become viewed as their declining years. In fact, one cannot help wondering whether, if creatively executed journalism had been more respected by the literary establishment, a number of the journalist-literary figures might have embraced their pursuit of journalistic projects more intensively and broadened our view of what constitutes meaningful writing and important literary production in the evaluation of a writing life.

It is remarkable how often the journalist-literary fictionists worked against the grain of literary opinion, and how often (if one chooses to look for it) high-quality writing can be found in the journalism they produced after they had established their literary reputations. It can be argued that such journalist-novelists as Dreiser, Anderson, Steinbeck, Dos Passos, Rebecca West, Richard Wright, and Norman Mailer contributed to literature more with the journalism they produced in their late careers than in their late-career fiction. For example, in the later collection of magazine essays that grew out of his political causes, *Puzzled America*, which poignantly portrayed the lives of people in northern factory towns and southern sharecropping country during the Great Depression, Anderson demonstrated a powerful talent as an interviewer and a skill at vividly conveying the human pathos that he found in the circumstances of joblessness and deprivation; while as journalism, Steinbeck's *Sea of Cortez* (written with his biologist friend, Edward F. Ricketts) and *Travels with Charley* can be viewed as at least as successful as his last novel, *Winter of Our Discontent* (which was serialized in the supermarket magazine, *McCall's*). Wright's travelogues and his journalism about Spain (*Pagan Spain*) in the last years of his career rival his much-heralded autobiography, *Black Boy*, and some of his early-career journalism, such as his story about the impact of Joe Louis' 1935 defeat of Max Baer upon African-American crowds in Harlem. ("From the symbol of Joe's strength they took strength, and in that moment all fear, all obstacles were wiped out, drowned. They stepped out of the mire of hesitation and irresolution and were free! Invincible! A merciless victor over a fallen foe! Yes, they had felt all that for a moment ... And then the cops came.")[11] In addition, a host of artfully crafted, non-fictional social and political commentaries and travelogues by a number of the journalist-literary figures can be (although only occasionally are) viewed as integral elements of the body of their literary production as a whole. These include works by Defoe (*A Tour thro' the Whole Island of Great Britain*), Fielding (*The Journal of a Voyage to Lisbon*), Washington Irving (*The Alhambra*), Charles Dickens (*American Notes for General Circulation*), Stevenson (*The Amateur Emigrant*), Twain (*Innocents Abroad, Roughing It, Life on the Mississippi*), Wells (*A Short History of the World*), London (*The People of the Abyss*), G. K. Chesterton (*Orthodoxy*), Hilaire Belloc (*The Path to Rome*), Forster (*Alexandria*), C. S. Forester (*The Voyage of the Annie Marble*), Priestley (*English Journey*), V. S. Pritchett (*Marching Spain*), Aldous Huxley (*The Doors of Perception*), Dos Passos (*Orient Express*), Greene (*Lawless Roads*), Waugh (*Robbery Under Law*), Mary McCarthy (*Medina*), and Nelson Algren (*Notes from a Sea Diary*).

Although they also wrote some inferior and eccentric journalism and non-fiction late in life, the memoirs of Dreiser (*Book About Myself* and *Dawn*) and Hemingway (*A Moveable Feast*) are arguably more satisfying reads than much of their later fiction. Rebecca West's *Meaning of Treason*, about the post-World War II Nazi trials, Martha Gellhorn's war and global reporting, C. D. B. Bryan's Vietnam War-related journalism, and Christopher Dickey's and Renata Adler's topical non-fiction have garnered as much or more attention than much of their very interesting fiction in a century when journalistic literature has become very popular.

Not all of the journalist-literary figures subjected themselves to self-laceration when they continued to practice the journalist's craft. A few fell into a middle camp – neither condemning their journalistic experiences nor overly praising them – and tended toward a pragmatic approach to the ongoing practice of journalism and/or a relaxed view of journalism's impact upon their writing lives. For these writers – who include Belloc, Chesterton, Pritchett, Thomas De Quincey, William Cullen Bryant, John Greenleaf Whittier, Walt Whitman, Joel Chandler Harris, P. G. Wodehouse, Malcolm Muggeridge, Margaret Mitchell, Carl Sandburg, Langston Hughes, Katherine Anne Porter, James T. Farrell, Eudora Welty, John Hersey, Gore Vidal, and Elie Wiesel – journalism served as a place on their writer's resume, an interesting experience that they valued and enjoyed but held lightly, and an activity that they sometimes were willing to continue practicing despite their success in other literary venues. For those who practiced journalism simultaneously with their other writing endeavors, such as Harris and Hughes, journalism provided them with income, security, and professional structure and kept them in touch with their audience and the issues of their day. Hughes and Harris, for example, both enjoyed immense popularity with their respective audiences for their respective literary characters, Hughes' "Simple", whose commentaries amused readers of the *Chicago Defender* for twenty-three years, and Harris' "Bre'r Rabbit" and the other Uncle Remus characters, whom Harris popularized while maintaining his job as an editorial writer for the *Atlanta Constitution*. Although it is his poetry that he is best-remembered for by the literary community, Hughes' popular following in his lifetime was based on his column, "Here to Yonder," and his conversations with "Simple" and another character, "Madame," that he produced for the black press. Harris' stories, written originally as newspaper sketches for a largely white southern audience, developed a widespread following when his Uncle Remus tales were reprinted in book form. Both Hughes and Harris enjoyed the ongoing dialogue with, and the continuing

creation of, their characters, and they were able to perform both their journalistic and literary tasks with little professional conflict throughout most of their
careers. At the same time, both recognized in their different ways (Hughes
because he took his poetry more seriously than his journalism; Harris because
he believed the importance of his figures resided in the genre of folk tales
more than the genre of serious literature) that they were operating in a
journalistic tradition that some didn't take seriously, and suffered little
when those efforts were judged not to have attained literary greatness.[12]

This matter-of-fact approach to journalism as a useful, but not particularly
dramatic, precursor to, or parallel activity with, a fiction-writing career was
shared by Welty, who had little negative to say about her early opportunity
in the daily press. Like Mitchell, another southern woman, Welty was only
able to secure work on the society page – in Welty's case, as a part-time
correspondent for the *Memphis Commercial Appeal*, for which she covered
society news in her hometown of Jackson, Mississippi. Welty wrote about
society events with a *Vanity Fair* magazine style of cleverness and irony, and
she found the work pleasant – even if it was confined to the less serious region
of the newspaper. "All they let a woman do in those days was society – for
any paper," she said. "I was trying to make a living. You got paid space rates,
that is, by the time they pasted all your columns together ... you got something like $3.65. But it was worth doing for me." Welty's close friend, the
Texas-born Porter, escaped her provincial southern environment by securing
a reporting job on the *Rocky Mountain News* in Denver. However, she, too,
took a pragmatic view of her journalism career, and she found her advertising
column, "Let's Shop with Suzanne," useful to her lifestyle more than her
professional ambitions (largely because it provided her with some extra
income and allowed her to visit clothing stores and to keep her wardrobe
up-to-date).[13]

In contrast, it is in today's literary environment – where the practice of
what has been called "new" journalism is touted for its artistic potential by the
journalism community but where the judgment of what makes "literature"
has largely become the domain of the literary scholarly community – that
the debate about the possibilities of including high-quality journalism within
the literary canon has often reached hot-house levels. One can look to the
troubled psyche of Mailer, for example, to see how the dynamic of the literary
figure in a delicate dance with the journalist within has been played out in
high-profile public fashion. Mailer's literary career (like that of Capote's) was
revived when he turned from writing traditional fiction to his much-touted
hybrid form of journalistic literature. However, despite Mailer's celebration
of this new form of journalistic "art," his work is filled with slighting

references to the place of journalism versus the lofty stature of literature. (Critics have wondered, for example, whether Mailer was engaging in multiple ironies in his exchange in *Armies of the Night* with poet Robert Lowell, where Lowell condescendingly refers to Mailer as the best journalist in America instead of the best writer, as Mailer tells Lowell that he prefers to think of himself.) Mailer, never unaware of his public image or what others thought of him, has often found himself reacting to the purist views of a literary community that were summed up by his friend and fellow novelist, James Jones, who wrote to Mailer after he launched his column for the *Village Voice*, "I still believe there are great books in you. Great books. If you can ever get them out. But I certainly doubt very much if you'll ever do it while writing a fucking column for the *Village Voice*."[14]

   Perhaps it took egos such as Mailer's and Wolfe's to bring the issue full circle – to help launch the field of contemporary literary journalism, then to claim, as Wolfe did, that it has displaced fiction as the highest point of writing accomplishment in the contemporary literary world, and finally to take up writing novels, too, as in Wolfe's case. And yet, in Mailer's case, his fictional experimentations often disguised the fact that his greatest strengths may be that of a reporter and journalist and that his greatest legacy may be as a pioneer in changing the way journalism was done as opposed to having a great influence upon the novel-writing tradition. Only two of Mailer's fictional novels probably have much chance of standing the test of time – *The Naked and the Dead* (done in the realistic war-novel tradition of Leo Tolstoy and Dos Passos) and *Why Are We in Vietnam?* (a stylistic experiment that grows out of the "gonzo" tradition of 1960s alternative journalism). On the other hand, his role as a journalistic innovator – in helping to found the *Village Voice* and then establish what was meant by underground, anti-establishment journalism, in his personalized and contextualized coverage of political conventions and war protest, and in his role as a cultural critic and social analyst – may rank him as a late twentieth-century commentator in the H. L. Mencken tradition, and his major contribution may be in the way he helped to encourage other journalists to push beyond the boundaries of standard reporting conventions. Although some traditionalists have complained of his approach to political coverage ("This isn't writing," said one editor. "It's just smearing anything on the page that comes into his head"), Mailer's coverage of the 1960 Democratic convention for *Esquire* – done in a highly personal, idiosyncratic style built around his role as a participant – had a big impact upon other political journalists. Mailer's new style of political writing reached its apex in his best-selling, book-length account of his experiences at the 1968 Democratic and

Republican national conventions – *Miami and the Siege of Chicago*. Mailer's approach to political writing "went through journalism like a wave," said his friend, Hamill. "Something changed. Everybody said, 'Uh oh. Here's another way to do it.' Mailer had altered the form, and you said, 'Okay. It's not the same, and you've got to deal with that.'"[15]

The temptation for the established journalist-literary figures to turn to, or turn back to, journalism – whether pure journalism, or some hybrid form – has always been considerable. Money (Mailer, with his six wives and nine children always needed it), the opportunity to become involved in the world, the desire to stay in the public spotlight, the belief that there are public issues that need their attention – all have been strong incentives for a number of the journalist-literary figures. Both Thackeray and Dickens, who wrote many of their best-known novels as magazine serials on deadline, wrestled with the grinding demands of magazine editorships that caused them serious complications in their later years. Some – including White, Robert Benchley, Dorothy Parker, James Thurber, and James Agee – were employed for significant portions of their careers at magazines and/or newspapers that they tried to juggle with other literary pursuits; others (such as Dreiser and Howells) spent many exhausting years as editors of periodical publications before they could devote themselves full-time to writing, then returned to the production of journalism as a late-career focus. Interestingly, only a few of the most prominent of the journalist-literary figures really put journalism behind them once they had established their literary reputation – as did Cather and George Eliot, for example – and avoided journalism altogether after becoming successful novelists.

Two of the most intriguing figures to return to journalism were Anderson and Caldwell, who became small-town newspaper owners late in their careers. Anderson's ownership of two small Virginia newspapers allowed him to revive a lagging career and to excel as a journalist and a cultural commentator. The preference shown by literary critics for "pure" fiction – and their tendency to discount the literary accomplishments linked to strong reporting – is amply demonstrated in the critical judgments made about Anderson's career. It is virtually uncontested among his critics and biographers that Anderson's writing skills deteriorated after the publication of his early stories and novels. However, in many ways, Anderson's career followed an inverse pattern of many others of the journalist-literary figures. Anderson (an advertising executive and business magazine editor before he turned to fiction-writing) needed a place to write free of the pressure he felt from the critics, and he became a conventional journalist late in life after buying up a pair of small weekly newspapers near his retirement home in the Virginia countryside.

Some of his most successful, albeit journalistic, writing appears in his news-papers (such as his brilliantly mordant interview with then Secretary of Commerce Herbert Hoover), and biographer Irving Howe feels that, in his later non-fiction, Anderson demonstrated a better ear for dialogue than in his fiction. Even in his early novels and short stories, Anderson's skills as a journalist have been greatly underestimated (particularly as they went into building the key characters of *Winesburg, Ohio* and *Poor White*, two of his much-admired early fictional efforts). In the non-fictional *Puzzled America* and *Poor White*, a psychological drama set against the backdrop of a Midwestern town transforming itself into an industrial city, Howe sees Anderson as playing an important role in chronicling America's transition from an agrarian to an industrial society, and he says Anderson should receive more credit than he has for his role as a journalist and sociological commentator.[16]

For Caldwell – who bought a group of weekly newspapers in South Carolina, ostensibly to give his preacher-father a chance to fulfill his dream to be a journalist – the responsibility for the money-losing publications weighed heavily upon him. Like Dickens, who found an editorial position for his father on his newspaper, Caldwell took his family duties seriously. However, it meant he had to spend a good deal of time helping his father with advertising, distribution, and staff problems. "All I have to worry about is doing another book, running four weekly newspapers in South Carolina, and such odds and ends," he wrote at one point. Yet Caldwell is an example of a writer whose forays back into journalism made a difference even as he was under attack for resorting to cheap sensationalism and hack fictional techniques to spur sales of his novels. His 1934 series for the *New York Post* on the plight of sharecroppers in the Deep South during the Depression allowed him to put to journalistic use the material that he had used in the fictional *Tobacco Road* and *God's Little Acre*. Using his outspokenly reform-oriented father as a guide in his reporting, Caldwell garnered nationwide attention with his extensive investigative examination of rural poverty, including leading local reporters on a tour of the harsh conditions after the nearby *Augusta* (GA) *Chronicle* questioned whether such suffering really existed.[17]

As with Anderson and Caldwell, the contact some journalist-literary figures maintained with the world of regular journalism had positive benefits within the negatives. A number came to rely upon writing – including taking periodical assignments or positions – as a way of life and sometimes as a way to just keep functioning in the world. Journalism provided an outlet to keep their egos intact, to help deal with the vicissitudes of their personal lives, and to ward off the emotional void by maintaining the continuity of meaningful production. There are those who believe that the alcoholic Agee was able to retain a semblance of mental balance thanks to the support of, and the latitude granted him by, the Luce publications (*Time* and *Fortune*) over the years, even as he struggled with the frustrations of having the expression of his radical social views often curtailed or censored. Other writers, too, benefited from their involvement in regular journalistic work after they had established their literary reputations, although with sometimes mixed results. The depressive James Boswell gained mental health benefits, as well as much-needed ego satisfaction, from his regular appearances as a newspaper commentator. This was also the case with a variety of other troubled and alcoholic personalities (Poe, Parker, Benchley, Thurber, O. Henry, John O'Hara) who needed both the income and the support system that writing for periodicals provided them. And yet, despite the benefits to the psyche and the soul, most of the journalist-literary figures had to face a largely dismissive critical community whenever they took up the practice of journalism. This was typified in the case of Steinbeck, who wrote hundreds of thousands of words of journalism but little fiction late in his career – the reception to which can be summed up by one critic who asked why it was that Steinbeck had "succumbed to the fatal itch and joined the gaggle of columnists."[18]

So what are some of the other reasons the journalist-literary figures kept at journalism, or took it up again, even after they had made their reputations as novelists?

– Once the forms of journalism have been mastered, it is like riding a bike again to return to the practice. Generally speaking, a new piece of fiction-writing requires at least a modicum of originality in content as well as style and voice. In journalism, the style and form are often dictated by the standards of the publication with only limited deviation allowed. Since the content in journalism is taken from the real world, the "angle" is often the only imaginative application necessary for the journalist and the rest can be filled in by reporting.

– The journalist-literary figures were in demand as writers not only by the journalism organizations of their day but also by literary agents, Hollywood producers, stage adapters, and speakers' bureaus. Celebrity journalism has had a long history in the US and the British Isles, and the journalist-literary figures had to actively resist the opportunities that came their way in order to maintain their focus on serious literature. That they often took up the offers is as much a commentary on the commercialization of literature in modern society as it is on their artistic will power.

- The money in journalism was quick and easy. There were more outlets for journalism that paid than for fiction, and journalism could be produced quickly and for fast cash. Stephen Crane, for example, was less ashamed of the hastily produced journalism articles than the poor fiction that he cranked out on his deathbed as a way to pay off the bills for his extravagant, end-of-life lifestyle ("There was born into an unsuspecting world a certain novel called 'Active Service,' full and complete in all its shame," Crane said of his last novel. "... May Heaven forgive it for being so bad").[19] Reviewing has been a particularly alluring activity, since a literary reputation can be traded upon for remuneration and used for settling scores and keeping one's name before the public.
- Journalism offers the possibility of involvement in the exciting issues of the day. The journalist-literary figures – almost all avid devourers of life experience – often found the lure of a "front row seat on history" difficult to resist, particularly when journalistic assignments gave them a chance to head off to the hot spots of the world. This also gave many of them a chance to break away from the complexities of their personal and family lives and find diversion and stimulation in travel to exotic and dangerous places.
- In their forays back into journalism, the journalist-literary figures often convinced themselves that they were pioneering new literary forms – which was only true in a few cases. Commonly, they were embellishing basic journalism with the stylistic flourishes and freedom of commentary that their literary status afforded them. Some hoped that the "elevated" journalism they were producing might be embraced as great literature. But often those who like to read non-fiction are less patient with literary experimentation than readers of art, and that has been particularly the case with critics who (at least until recent years) have shown a pronounced bias toward fictional literature.
- In a few cases, a journalist and a non-fiction essayist or commentator, such as Joseph Addison and Richard Steele or Samuel Johnson or William Hazlitt or A. J. Liebling or Mencken, is remembered for creating literature out of the forms of journalism, but it usually took an exclusive focus on non-fiction and essay-writing to accomplish it. The social commentary of Mencken (who abandoned his half-hearted efforts at fiction and playwrighting in his youth) was recognized in his time in the same way that the essays of Johnson (who didn't even know what to call fiction-writing, including his own) were acclaimed in his. In some ways, the journalist-literary figures who never harbored ambitions to write fiction had a harder time convincing critics that their non-fiction – without

any fictional production to buttress it – was worthy of lasting attention. But in other ways, they have benefited from the lack of fictional material to which their journalism can be compared.

- Certain kinds of writing – most notably short stories and humor writing – invited stronger contacts with periodical publishers than novel-writing, at least in the years after serialized novels largely disappeared from periodicals. Those journalist-literary figures who limited their fictional production to humor and/or short stories usually had to find magazines or journals to publish them before they were collected into book form. These relationships often led to journalistic opportunities – columns, syndication, essay-writing, reporting assignments – that kept their literary and their journalistic work-life intimately linked.

- One reason that journalism has sometimes felt like a consolation activity for the journalist-literary figures has been the ease of editorial acceptance and the lesser standards for journalistic publication they found once their reputations were secure. As it is with most popular and well-established writers, the journalist-literary figures faced a lower bar to the publication of their later novels and non-fiction, no matter what their quality, and seldom did publishers hold them to the tougher evaluations that might have been applied to an unproven novelist or writer. (Mailer, for example, once forced *Esquire* to agree not to change a word that he wrote for the magazine.)[20]

So why was it that so many of the journalist-literary figures felt so terribly about themselves when they resorted to writing journalism? Was it simply the lower regard that the culture and the critics held for journalism as opposed to fiction and imaginative literature? Or was more at work? Here are some of the additional reasons why the journalist-literary figures may have suffered from a loss of esteem (both self and social) whenever they took up journalism.

- Lack of education and/or social pedigree often led to a serious lack of confidence in themselves as true literary successes. Since the eighteenth century, journalism has been an attractive occupation for ambitious young people from modest backgrounds who hope to use it to rise in the world. Many of the journalist-literary figures weren't from the privileged classes, either in terms of social status, education, or financial position. This often left them with feelings of insecurity, and it was easy for them to view journalism as a writing activity for interlopers, literary impostors, and those on the lower social rungs of life. Defoe never forgave the snubs he received from Swift and others in Swift's social circle who regarded Defoe as a crude man from the trading classes who operated out

of opportunism and a grudge against the political and religious establishment; Howells never forgot his intimidating meeting with the "Brahmins"
of east coast literature who "anointed" him (in thoroughly condescending
fashion) as their successor; Twain spent months processing his chagrin
from a much-chronicled dinner attended by Emerson, Oliver Wendell
Holmes, and Henry W. Longfellow, where Twain's "tall tale" about the
three fell flat in front of a crowd of literary worthies; London's sense of
himself as a bastard child of neglect translated into a grandiose mission to
compensate for it with literary and financial success of any kind;
Anderson's self-consciousness about his lack of schooling and poor grammar and spelling never left him throughout his writing days; Wright always
saw life through the lens of a poor black man from the segregated South
who could not forget his experiences of racism and marginalization from
white American society no matter where he moved. While all discovered in
journalism the avenue to literary success, most never shook a sense of
financial and emotional insecurity and the feeling that journalism provided
only a precarious hold against life's vicissitudes, and a slightly disreputable
one at that.[21]

– Those whose family backgrounds were not so humble were prone to
internalize the elitist view of journalism as a not fully respectable profession that was held in the "better" quarters of society. The gentlemanly
"airs" of Harte and the dandy dressing of Richard Harding Davis, for
example, always seemed a bit ridiculous to their colleagues, but they
reflected a desire to remake the image of the journalist into a more proper
one. Lardner's lack of self-confidence and pretensions to social acceptance were reflected in his settling amid the estates of Long Island and his
participation in the *Great Gatsby*-like social life there (he lived next door
to the mansion of Herbert Bayard Swope, the editor of the New York
World, that Lardner's friend, F. Scott Fitzgerald, made the model for the
novel); Agee, Mailer, and Benchley, with their Harvard educations, all
wrestled with insecurities about their rightful place in society, and their
rebellions can be seen in the context of the emotional turbulence fostered
by issues of self-worth in young men from modest backgrounds who
found themselves dealing with Ivy League privilege; the Harvard-edu-
cated Dos Passos and the Yale-educated Lewis skirted direct or lengthy
employment in the journalistic world, to some degree because their
literary ambitions had been established in an Ivy League environment
where journalism was considered suspect; Hemingway, who never wrote
about his growing-up years because, he said, "I did not want to hurt
living people," was haunted by the sense that beneath his respectable

suburban upbringing as a doctor's son lurked issues of family dysfunc-
tion, suicide, and psychological imbalance; Mitchell never forgot her
snubbings as an ingenue by Atlanta society, or Parker the fact that her
upper-class Jewish family could never penetrate beyond the edges of
Wasp social circles; Capote straddled the worlds of his strange, almost
surrealistic small-town southern family, with its aspirations to an eccentric
gentility, and the glitter of Manhattan social life, and his beginnings at the
New Yorker introduced him early on to the ways of a magazine which
coveted an elite readership; Wolfe came from a southern prep school
background, and his dapper dress can be seen as a serious statement or
a satiric spoof on journalism's pretensions to social dignity. Stories of
lost family birthrights, evaporated fortunes, and/or forgotten family soci-
etal connections played a role in the upbringings of Swift, Fielding, Poe,
Thackeray, Twain, Harte, Kipling, Lardner, and Cather, and all had an
acutely developed sense of the class stratifications of society and of how
journalism could help one both compensate for, and lose, economic and
social standing and all the attendant issues that went with it.[22]

– Journalism provided pathways to climb the economic ladder for the
journalist-literary figures, but it didn't always diminish their preoccupation
with issues of social mobility that became a populist focus in their literature. Dreiser – who suffered from the poverty and ostracism of his family
by the "good people" of his small town Indiana upbringing – became a
major literary spokesperson for those from humble backgrounds seeking to
rise in society. These themes were echoed in varying fashion by others who
had grown up in rural settings, such as Eliot and Hamlin Garland, who
were fascinated with the impact of changing economic, political, and
technological forces on the people of both the countryside and the city.
Lardner grew up in a moneyed home but suffered the shock of his father's
losing much of his business fortune, thus forcing him to go to work at a
relatively early age in a trade (a baseball writer) that had little more social
status at the time than the uneducated athletes that he covered, and his
short stories often focus on the ludicrous aspects of social pretension. Both
Thackeray and Howells hungered for success, but both also recognized its
ultimate hollowness, as did Dreiser in his portrayals of Jennie in *Jennie
Gerhardt* and Clyde Griffiths in *An American Tragedy*, who in their different ways both fell victim to the desire to rise in society without fully
understanding the way society operates.[23]

– So many of the journalist-literary figures came from abused or deprived
childhoods, suffered early life crises, or had to set out on their own at such
an early age that they came with deep emotional scars to their journalism

work – and later to their novel-writing. A sense of personal abandonment was probably the most common experience among this group. They included Bierce, whose hatred for his emotionally distant parents took on epic, literary proportions in the parenticide themes of his writing; Wright, with a father who abandoned the family and a mother and grandmother who were religious fanatics that left Wright feeling like a damned and worthless young person, documented this in *Black Boy*; Capote, whose father seldom visited him and whose mother didn't want him for portions of his youth, framed *In Cold Blood* in terms of the parallels between his own deprived childhood and that of the killer, Perry Smith. Although starting off life in relatively stable circumstances, Swift, Thackeray, Twain, Harte, Crane, Agee, Parker, and Dos Passos all lost their fathers when they were relatively young and dealt with the family and economic turmoil that came with it; Poe, O. Henry, Woolf, Mitchell, Porter, and Parker lost their mothers at an early age, and Eliot, McCarthy, and Conrad Aiken witnessed the deaths of both parents before they had left home; Benchley was deeply affected by the death of his brother in the Spanish-American War, as were De Quincey, J. M. Barrie, George S. Kaufman, and Jack Kerouac at the passing of beloved siblings during their childhoods. In all these cases, the journalist-literary figures were haunted by a sense of loss, unworthiness, and anxiety that both fueled and undermined their literary progress, and it was particularly easy for them to project their insecurities onto the practice of journalism, with its uncertain standing with the social and literary establishment and what they viewed as the stable ranks of society.[24]

– The price of making it in the "school of journalism" often meant that the journalist-literary figures' writing was considered suspect when it was popularly embraced or did not meet the political, ideological, or literary standards of the critical establishment. As literary gatekeepers and advocates for the realistic and naturalistic styles of writing, critics and editors such as Howells and Mencken often proved to be good friends and mentors of their fellow journalist-literary figures, but that didn't stop other, more intellectually and academically oriented critics from dismissing their work as too pedestrian, too straightforward, or too successful with the masses. Their connections with the popular press – Bierce and London's work for Hearst, the continued employment of Harte and Kipling and Crane by newspapers throughout their careers, the 1920s *New Yorker* and Algonquin Round Table crowd (Lardner, White, Thurber, Parker, Benchley, O'Hara, Edna Ferber, Marc Connelly, Alexander Woollcott), the challenges to the literary establishment by the "new journalists" of the 1960s and 1970s – were sometimes the target of criticism, or more often their work simply was not taken seriously in the critical circles where avant garde ideas ruled. The literarily refined Oscar Wilde, for example, once said of Kipling that his:

> mere lack of style in the story-teller gives an odd journalistic realism to what he tells us. From the point of view of literature Mr. Kipling is a man of talent who drops his aspirates. From the point of view of life he is a reporter who knows vulgarity better than anyone has ever known it ... He is our best authority on the second rate.[25]

– As the twentieth century brought with it ever more esoteric literary fads and the professionalization of literary criticism within the academic community, many of the journalist-literary figures became self-conscious about the unschooled nature of their prose and concerned that clear and direct written communication wasn't particularly valued by the literary world anymore. This trend had begun in the nineteenth century with those who criticized Harte for never succeeding in forms beyond the popular short story or complained that Twain had frittered away too much of his talent doing journalism. Bierce, who was routinely written off as a journalist and a writer of short fiction for the newspapers, responded with a rousing defense of the short story and challenged those who called the novel the greater feat – but his defensiveness was unmistakable. By the 1940s, White and Thurber had come to believe that they would probably never be taken seriously by the literary establishment for not venturing beyond humor, cultural commentary, and fanciful and children's literature; Benchley wrote himself off as a failed literary funny man who deserved the fate of a life as a minor Hollywood movie actor; Lewis bitterly fended off the charges of those who complained of the crudities of his style and his overfondness for sociological detail; Lardner was dismissed as a chronicler of the shallow American personality type with an ear for popular speech; and Parker anguished over her inability to finish a novel and her talent for what was often considered light verse and frivolous themes. ("Write novels, write novels, write novels – that's all they can say," Parker complained. "Oh, I do get so sick and tired, sometimes.") Even Mencken damned his friend Dreiser with what some would see as faint praise for his journalistic habits. ("'An American Tragedy' as a work of art, is a colossal botch, but as a human document it is searching and full of a solemn dignity," Mencken wrote. "... What other American novelist could have done it? His method, true enough, is the simple, bald one of the reporter – but of *what* a reporter! ... (The book) is clumsy. It lacks all grace. But it is tremendously moving.")[26]

- Even as they attained fame and literary stature, many of the journalist-literary figures felt most at home in the company of journalists. Many continued to practice journalism because it fit with their self-image and made them feel professionally at home, even though they often suffered from guilt for taking away time from their more literary efforts. Thackeray regularly dined with the editors and journalists at his long-time employer, *Punch*, long after he had attained the status of great Victorian novelist; Caldwell in his later years found welcome congeniality among newspaper and radio folk at the Tucson Press club where he drank, shot pool, and played poker; Thurber hung out with newspaper people at their favorite watering holes, whether they were in Columbus, Ohio, Paris, or New York City. Some, such as Steinbeck, even thought of journalism as an heroic activity (despite the fact that Steinbeck's early journalism experience amounted to being fired as a cub reporter for the New York *American*), and he often commented that – even as a famous author – he took pride in thinking of himself as a journalist.[27]

- Particularly when they felt trapped by their need for ready money and/or a job, many of the journalist-literary figures viewed journalism as a fall-back whenever circumstances required. Bierce, for example, left the San Francisco *Argonaut* in July 1880, intending to break forever from "journalism's tainted ink" by going to work for a mining company in South Dakota. When it didn't work out, he returned to San Francisco, broke and exhausted and looking to journalism to put him back on his feet. In the 1960s, O'Hara, whose novels had sold more than twenty million copies, nonetheless took up writing a column, "My Turn," for Long Island *Newsday*, which he described as aimed at "the Lawrence Welk people" for whom he proposed to say a few good words. But many editors dropped the column after it was syndicated, complaining of its poor quality, and O'Hara soon gave it up. Still he said, "I'll turn up on a newspaper somewhere. I always do," adding that, "I have never been convinced that my drawing power is permanent. One of these days the people will get fed up and I will be back writing obits for Guild scale. That's why I keep my hand in."[28]

Magazines in particular have served as half-way homes for some of the journalist-literary figures as they aged, offering them opportunities to straddle the fields of journalism and fiction and the latitude to call the shots on what they wanted to write. The established journalist-literary figures were perfect matches for the general interest and literary magazines of their eras since they came with a ready-made celebrity and a name that was a draw for readership. And yet only occasionally did a journalist-literary figure who established his or her fame as a novelist do memorable work for magazines, and (with the possible exception of Orwell) the magazine non-fiction of the journalist-literary figures has only in recent years begun to be seen by some literary critics as more than incidental to their fictional production. A number of the journalist-literary figures left an important mark at the magazines they founded or where they worked – Howells at the *Atlantic* and *Harper's*, Agee at *Time* and *Fortune*, Mencken at the *Mercury* and the *Smart Set* – but their best writing was often accomplished in spite of, and not as a result of, the demands of the magazines. (Magazine writing, of course, could also tarnish a reputation if it was a man's magazine or a true adventure magazine, such as Hemingway and Caldwell wrote for in their later years.)

In journalistic lore, the one place that challenges the image of the perishable nature of magazine journalism was the *New Yorker* under the editorships of Harold Ross and William Shawn, where White, Thurber, and Benchley were employed for long stretches and where a number of the other journalist-literary figures were regulars in the magazine's pages and occasionally took staff positions. If any magazine in the US has achieved the ideal of Poe it would be the *New Yorker*, and no magazine in literary history has probably offered a writing home and paycheck to such a broad collection of distinguished journalistic writers. Some of its admirers consider the magazine – particularly in its early years – literature in and of itself, and some of its features (such as the "Talk of the Town" column, often produced by White) have been held up as important literary achievements in the tradition of Johnson, Addison and Steele, Hazlitt, and Leigh Hunt. Ross was famously loyal and highly forgiving of his writers – and very dependent upon them for their judgments and for giving the magazine the tone it was noted for. This was particularly the case with White, whom Ross wooed, flattered, and courted back to the magazine on a number of occasions, and White ultimately settled for a lifetime relationship with the publication. But White also felt that he tended to cling to the magazine as a safety net, and he regularly upbraided himself for the fact that he wasn't more ambitious and willing to tackle the serious novel. Many people (most notably Ross) felt that the *New Yorker's* personality and White's writing talents (Ross thought White the master at the short form vignette, the odd or understated observation, the soft parody, the insightful but self-effacing bit of philosophizing) were the perfect match. But in his gentle, self-deprecating way one can sense in White's correspondence that he suffered from a sense of disappointment in himself as a writer and, in his more whimsical moments, tended to include himself in his view (as articulated in his children's books) that all creatures are products of their environments and that one shouldn't lament when one couldn't rise above one's fundamental nature and passed from the scene without leaving a more permanent mark in life.

At the same time, Ross' tolerance for his long-time writers was distinctively in evidence in his willingness to employ and support Thurber and Benchley as their writing careers – and their personal lives – headed downhill. The *New Yorker*'s reputation as a "golden coffin", as it was for White, applied in a different way for Thurber and Benchley as their lives lurched out of control, and they needed all the support that they could get from their friends. Thurber's affection for the *New Yorker*, which reflected his feeling that it gave him the opportunity to grow and find himself as a writer, turned bitter and contentious at the end. His blindness, his alcoholism, and his increasing paranoia led Thurber to submit cynical and humorless pieces which the magazine often rejected – and which Thurber reacted to in an acerbic and curmudgeonly fashion. Benchley also stretched Ross' good will for many years when, while occupying the magazine's position as theater reviewer, he spent most of his time in Hollywood, dealing with his movie career. Although Benchley's reviews remained upbeat and generous, his own alcoholism was making him an increasingly erratic and unreliable employee – and Ross (with great reluctance) finally severed the relationship in 1940. It can be argued that, as comic writers, Thurber and Benchley had little else to prove. But they, like White, felt that they had not done what was necessary for literary greatness, and they often looked to their continued association with the magazine as evidence of it.[29]

The cynicism and world-weariness that accompanied continued involvement in journalism was often a trademark of the careers of the literary journalists. Greene, in the tradition of Howells and Dreiser before him, took on the taxing job of helping to produce a periodical as he was establishing and trying to maintain a literary reputation. In Greene's case, his position as literary editor of the short-lived *Night and Day* magazine, intended to be an English version of the *New Yorker*, lasted only six months, coming to an end when the magazine folded in 1937. But Greene didn't exit the job before he had committed a disastrous journalistic mistake, losing a libel suit with Shirley Temple which cost him in a serious financial way. Greene was prone to taking on very demanding journalistic tasks – for example, in 1932, he began regular book reviewing, mostly for the London *Spectator* – which meant a prodigious load of reading (often of inferior books) and the task of saying something intelligent about them. Greene's disciplined reading and his steady stream of polished reviews (he reviewed 142 titles, for example, from 1932 to 1933) didn't keep him from working at his literary and novel writing, but the strain was considerable. (By 1935, he had also become the *Spectator*'s film reviewer; between 1935 and 1939 he delivered his assessments of more than 400 films.) Greene's propensity for "hit and run" journalism throughout his career gave him a great deal of satisfaction, particularly as it let him settle scores and enabled him to see himself as a commentator upon his age. But little of what he wrote of a journalistic nature is read now, and one biographer faults Greene for spending too much time in his later years writing letters to the press or articles on subjects of passing interest.[30]

Greene's friend, Waugh, also continued to be seduced by the lure of quick journalistic money throughout his writing years. From the start of his career, Waugh looked upon journalism with a jaundiced but whimsical and pragmatic eye. His flip advice to aspiring newspaper people when sent out on a story was "to jump to your feet, seize your hat and umbrella and dart out of the office with every appearance of haste to the nearest cinema ... (there to sit) for an hour or so and smoke a pipe." Always the opportunist, Waugh was willing to write for the marketplace and sell magazine and newspaper editors an article on any topic, no matter how slight, with the goal of getting people talking about him. ("You do this by forcing your way into the newspaper" one way or the other, he advised.) After the publication of *Decline and Fall* made him a celebrity, London periodicals competed heavily for his services, and he did book reviews and light features in the *Daily Express*, the *Graphic*, the *Daily Mail*, *Week-End Review*, *John Bull*, and the *American Bookman and Architectural Review*. But his laziness and his temperamental ways made him unpopular with editors. (One editor complained about an article Waugh penned – ironically about boredom – and wrote back: "It is – to be frank – rather a hastily put-together job; it reads as if it were a manufactured paper on a topic about which the author really cared very little;" another editor complained of paying Waugh for "one of the most uninteresting and uninspired contributions it has ever been my misfortune to publish.") When his agent confronted him with complaints such as these, Waugh responded, "You can't tell me a thing I don't know about the low quality of my journalism" (although he was never willing to accept a reduction in price for his work, no matter how poor it was).[31]

O'Hara, too, filled his later years with journalistic tasks, even though – while he labored at journalism quite seriously – he was not particularly good at it. O'Hara – who struggled throughout his career to hold a job as a daily reporter, first for the *Pottsville* (PA) *Journal* before moving through a series of jobs at *Time* and a variety of New York daily newspapers – always managed to carry the air of the newspaper reporter about him, even when he began to make a national name for himself as a contributor to the *New Yorker* and then as a best-selling novelist. Former colleagues described how O'Hara, as the editor of an arts and commentary magazine in Pittsburgh, would come into the office, take off his coat and loosen his tie, mount his chair like a horse, and then start tapping out much of the copy that filled the magazine. However, O'Hara never developed the touch that allowed a good columnist to establish a rapport with an audience. In columns and reviews he wrote for *Newsweek, Collier's,* and the *Trenton Times-Advertiser* that he undertook during his career as a novelist, he was prone to air prejudices, drop names, focus on idiosyncratic trivialities, and write truculent prose.[32]

Journalists, scholars, and other writers have consistently rated Orwell's journalism as high on the literary scale and some of their favorite of his written work. And yet, one can see in Orwell the toll that continued involvement in journalism took on his career and his life. Orwell's journalistic production was monumental despite the fact that he struggled against a lung disease (which developed into full-blown tuberculosis) that eventually took his life at age forty-six. One can measure Orwell's workaholic nature and his diligent approach to writing about the issues of the world (as well as how he dealt with painful emotions) by his prodigious journalistic production the year after his first wife died – 130 essays and reviews for a variety of publications. Orwell has often been seen as a vehement idealist who was willing to sacrifice everything – his health, his security, his career – for his beliefs, and a person who saw journalism as a key conduit in carrying out that mission. In fact, with the writing and the publication of his most famous novels toward the end of his life, Orwell can be seen as someone who put off his fictional projects for his journalistic tasks – and, because he has been so widely admired for his integrity as a cultural commentator, critics have complained less about this than with others of the journalist-literary figures. Still, Orwell also occasionally indulged in the same literary subterfuges as Defoe and his literary heirs, and a number of Orwell's works occupy a border zone between fact and fiction (for example, critics have never been able to be sure how much of the novel *Down and Out in Paris and London* should be considered to have come from his imagination or real experience or exactly how much of *Burmese Days* to consider a novel and how much a thinly-disguised memoir).[33]

The ongoing participation by the journalist-literary figures in the world of journalism has been both a blessing and a curse in the ways posterity has come to view their accomplishments. If one can say that the liberalized definition of journalism (or what many now call literary journalism) has been a boon to writing talents in the UK and the US, it equally can be argued that there have been a number of careers whose downward direction has been accelerated thanks to a continued connection to journalism. Conversely, the journalist-literary figures – who, almost by definition, have commonly been tugged in contrary directions – have done much to show that the categorization of writing into genres does not always do justice to the range and scope of fine writing. In the tradition of Defoe, who had no fixed idea of which literary specialization he was functioning in, the written legacy of the journalist-literary figures is the ultimate statement and the final testimony to the success of their efforts at literary expression, no matter how they may have crossed writing modes in accomplishing it. To call the journalist-literary figures half-journalists, half-fictionalists is in itself a simplification since many of the works of the authors in this study occupy multiple positions on the spectrum between journalism and fiction. Still, the blended products of both traditions, and the hybrid careers of those who straddled these fields, have enriched American and British literary history, even as they have sometimes confounded those who (including, on occasion, the journalist-literary figures themselves) tend to use the word journalism as if it was an epithet and to identify the profession of journalist as synonymous with second-rate achievement.

Epilogue. The future of journalistic fiction and the legacy of the journalist-literary figures: Henry James to Tom Wolfe

> No art that is not understood by the people can live or ever did live a single generation.
>
> – Frank Norris

> Our American professors like their literature clear and cold and pure and very dead.
>
> – Sinclair Lewis

> It is so hard to be clear. Only a fool is willfully obscure.
>
> – John Steinbeck

> The press ... is the watchdog of civilization, and the watchdog happens to be ... in a chronic state of rabies.
>
> – Henry James

In both his time and ours, the stylistically complex novelist Henry James has served as the literary intellectual's bulwark against the crudities and the low-brow nature of popular culture and the popular press that James came to loathe. James' views about the press were reflected in his recondite literary philosophy and his opaque writing strategies. But they also grew out of personal experience.

In 1875, the youthful James had arranged to be a correspondent on manners, people, and the arts for the *New York Tribune* during his travels to Europe. But his editor, Whitelaw Reid, didn't like the lengthy and discursive style of James' "letters" and wrote to him that they should be more "newsy" and written less on "topics too remote from popular interests to please more than a select few of our readers." An offended James ended the relationship, writing back: "I am afraid I can't assent to your proposal ... I know the sort of letter you mean – it is doubtless the proper sort of thing for the *Tribune* to have ... I am too finical a writer and I should be constantly becoming more 'literary' than is desirable."[1]

James can be seen as embodying in his literary outlook the division that now exists between a literary scholarly establishment – where James' digressive, difficult, and thickly textured prose is widely studied and admired – and others of the journalist-literary figures who, in many cases, have been banished to the sidelines of critical and scholarly consideration. A number of journalist-literary figures still rank high in the estimation of literary critics and scholars. But unlike James, their plain-spoken writing style and their belief in clear, candid, and direct prose that can easily be communicated to a popular audience works against them in the "post-modern" world of literary scholarship where density in style and allusiveness in content are appreciated for the opportunities they give for scholarly interpretation and specialist analysis.

Interestingly, James' distaste for the superficialities and the typecasting of commercial journalism (this is reflected in a series of journalistic characters in his fiction, such as Merton Densher in *The Wings of a Dove*, Henrietta Stackpole in *The Portrait of a Lady*, and George Flack in *The Reverberator*) was shared by many of the journalist-literary figures themselves. Despite being deemed a "realist" like Mark Twain and William Dean Howells in his early fictional efforts, James came to represent a new trend in fictional writing that would be embraced by contemporary readers and scholars who have come to value text that is weighty, prolix, and subtle in meaning and structure. His fellow journalist-literary figures watched this development with a certain wry amusement (Henry Adams has been credited with saying that James tended to chew more than he had bitten off; H. G. Wells called James' style "an elephant attempting to pick up a pea"). But even so, a number of the journalist-literary figures were strongly influenced by James' serpentine sentences and hypersensitivity to human psychology and manners. James Thurber, for example, once referred to "the great God James" and paid homage to his highly wrought style by calling it an influence that almost overwhelmed him. However, Thurber said that what ultimately made him successful as a writer was getting Jamesian patterns out of his prose and adopting the precision and clarity that he had learned from his friend and mentor, E. B. White. "The influence I had to fight off in writing was that of Henry James," Thurber wrote, "and the influence that helped me most" was that of White.[2]

This contest within Thurber's creative faculty has come to define the dilemma for the advocates of journalistic literature, squeezed as they are between a literary establishment that has grown fascinated with ambiguous writing styles and specialized literary theories and a professional journalism world that is no longer the first obvious choice for young writers interested in an apprenticeship for a serious fiction-writing career.

Circumstances have changed since the period when many of the prominent British and American journalist-literary figures produced their best-known literary works in connection with their journalism careers. Fewer of today's most prominent fiction writers have come up through the newsrooms of journalistic organizations than did their literary predecessors, and few could be said to know a lot about the world of journalism (or care, in many cases).

Ironically, this has happened, at least in part, because journalism as a profession has risen in terms of social esteem, monetary rewards, and the possibilities for wider literary success, and professional journalism – and particularly deadline-based journalism – is less and less the place where successful novelists look to get their start and to test their fiction-writing ambitions. Many of today's contemporary journalists who began their writing career on newspapers and periodicals have been able to stay in the field of journalism and still gain financial success by moving into the wider publishing world and expanding their purview to book-length journalistic and non-fiction topics. Such prominent journalists as John McPhee, Gay Talese, Gloria Steinem, Susan Orlean, Jane Kramer, Richard Rodriguez, Tracy Kidder, and Frances Fitzgerald have stayed on the best-seller lists without moving into the field of fiction-writing. The contemporary "new journalists"–Tom Wolfe, Truman Capote, Norman Mailer, Hunter Thompson, Joan Didion – are more admired, in many respects, for their book-length explorations of non-fictional topics written with a literary flair than their full-fledged fictional creations, and a few university English departments treat "new journalism" as a serious field of contemporary literature. There are daily or ex-daily journalists who are writing popular but serious fiction – Pete Dexter, William Kennedy, Tom Robbins, Tim O'Brien, Anna Quindlen, Tobias Wolff, Martin Amis, Julian Barnes, and Gail Godwin, among others – but none has gained the broad public stature of the most renowned of the earlier generations of journalist-literary figures, who achieved their fame before trends in publishing and commercialized and electronic media communications had reshaped the celebrity landscape.

The phenomenon of fewer widely saluted fiction-writing masters with backgrounds in journalism at a time when journalistic writing has become more respectable and commercially sought out is almost certainly no coincidence. The opportunities to stay in journalism and not necessarily feel as compromised within it as did an Ambrose Bierce or Ring Lardner or James Agee have been fed by a number of developments in the writing field: the greater opportunities for journalists to market their talents to book agents and publishing houses, the expanded appetite within the publishing world for writers who can turn developments in politics, foreign affairs, business, entertainment, and sports into blockbuster non-fiction books and celebrity biographies, the public's increased taste for "true life" topics and expansive, narrative dramas in their reading, the greater respectability of book-length journalistic non-fiction among critics, and the big-money book contracts available to celebrity journalists. Some have gone so far as to call this the age of narrative journalism, what with the public's great and growing appetite for high-quality non-fiction books.

At the same time, the "high art" aspirations of up-and-coming fiction writers can be nourished without having to find an apprenticeship in the marketplace of commercial journalism. Contemporary fiction writers-to-be have ample opportunity to develop their writing talents in nurturing environments far from the exigencies of the newsroom. The rise of creative writing programs in university English departments and the possibilities for writers to make a living teaching fiction and literary writing in academic posts have created a milieu where literary hopefuls have few incentives to scramble for a living in journalism jobs. Not only do university writing programs offer funding and support for hundreds of would-be novelists, poets, and playwrights, they also have pushed many into the sphere of influence of academic literary programs where they are exposed to fashionable literary theories and tools of scholarly analysis. In these surroundings, literary celebrity increasingly means becoming established within a tight and largely self-sufficient world of academic literature and scholarship where broad-scale popularity is not considered a necessary or even a desirable thing. Except for the occasional writer who crosses over from the academic to the public arena – Robert Penn Warren or Joyce Carol Oates or Vladimir Nabokov – the contemporary literary figures who are highly regarded among academic literary scholars are often little known to the public at large, and their reputations are dwarfed by such writers of popular block-buster fiction as Stephen King, John Grisham, Tom Clancy, Dean Koontz, Jean Auel, and Judith Krantz, who are creations of the commercial book-publishing culture and are of little interest to serious literary scholars.

This division between the culture of academic literary achievement and the culture of popular literary success has become mediated by a handful of celebrity journalist-literary figures who have ruminated publicly about the impact of these changes on the production of high-quality fiction and non-fiction. Wolfe took a much-discussed shot at the literary establishment in 1989 when he offered the view that contemporary fiction writers have failed because they have retreated from realism and produced instead absurdist fables, self-indulgent and self-referencing tales, and pointless exercises in minimalism. In Wolfe's view, the only way for fiction to recover its traditionally dominant role was for novelists to take up the journalist's task of reporting and to revive realism by utilizing the journalist's zest for recorded fact and instinct for the big story. "Any literary person who is willing to look back over the American literary terrain of the past twenty five years ... will admit that in at least four years out of five the best nonfiction books have been *better literature* than the most highly praised books of fiction," Wolfe concluded.[3]

In firing back at Wolfe, as did Robert Towers, the former chairman of the writing program at Columbia University in the *New York Times Book Review*, Wolfe was accused of having read very little fiction of recent years and of refusing to be specific in backing up his claims. Towers responded with a list of "flourishing realists" among successful contemporary novelists, including Don DeLillo, John Updike, Philip Roth, Anne Tyler, Russell Banks, Richard Ford, Mona Simpson, Mary Gordon, Raymond Carver, and Bobbie Ann Mason. These authors have been documenting the shifting mores, status symbols, and appetites of Middle America "with an exuberance and exactitude that fully match Mr. Wolfe's," Towers wrote. Towers went on to say that there has been no mass defection from realism among serious young writers, as Wolfe contended. In his attack on the literary establishment, Towers said, Wolfe has "confused" the writing programs from which many writers now emerge with the more scholarly academic programs "where the challenge of the difficult text has an enormous appeal to a certain type of intellectual."[4]

In many ways, this debate has said more about the changing landscape of commercial journalism and the scholarly literary environment than it has achieved in providing a decisive answer as to which writers should be considered the proper heirs to the tradition of literary realism. Behind Wolfe's position looms the world of multi-million-dollar book contracts, mega blockbuster bestsellers, and publicity and promotional machines that have made a talented ex-journalist such as Wolfe into a popular celebrity. Towers' was the voice, in turn, of the academic culture of English literary departments and university creative-writing programs that lay claim to the creation and maintenance of the literary canon through the production of scholarship, literature created in a campus or campus-connected environment, and the network of academic journals and literary magazines that anoint new literary stars and spread the word about the latest trends in criticism. In these university writing programs, there is a steady stream of young writers nurtured in a comfortable milieu of creative-writing classes and fellow students who share the same aspirations, grants, and teaching fellowships. Moderating this are the prominent literary reviews – the *New York Review of Books*, the *New York Times Book Review*, the *Atlantic Monthly*, *Harper's* – that draw for their contributions upon other artists, academic specialists, or other prominent critics who move with varying degrees of influence within the circles of the contemporary literary elite.

In today's commercialized, professionalized, and highly specialized world, with big media vying with academic institutions for everything from the career opportunities they offer to the allegiance of the public, few big-name novelists have risen to success in the same fashion as the journalist-literary figures of the past. Of the new "realists" mentioned by Towers, only three have had a bit of journalism or journalism-related experience (DeLillo as an advertising copy-writer in the 1960s, Updike as a writer for the *New Yorker* in the mid-1950s, and Mason briefly as a local journalist and writer for movie and television magazines). The other seven have spent their careers in academic teaching posts, in writer-in-residence programs, and/or as recipients of literary fellowships, or in other employment outside journalism (such as working in book stores or university libraries).[5] By living within this cocoon of university writing programs, writing workshops, public readings and reading tours, subsidies from book awards, and a network of fellowship programs designed to free them to write, it is no wonder that there is often little incentive for today's hopeful writers to look to the newsroom as a training ground.

This, in a sense, points to a key element in Wolfe's complaint – but one which Wolfe's own literary life tends to contradict. Many of the journalist-literary figures went downhill after they achieved success but found that they had little of life's "real" material to work with anymore. Frank Norris – who felt that he suffered himself from this phenomenon – wrote tellingly of what happens when a writer goes "soft" and trades in the material of the real world for the seductions of artistic success. In his story, "Dying Fires," Norris recounts the tale of a young California journalist, Overbeck, who has a novel accepted and then is offered a position with the New York publishing house (as happened to Norris). But Overbeck soon falls in with a literary crowd made up of people who talk about the "tendencies" of new writers who are "more subtle than Henry James." Soon Overbeck catches on to the lingo and is flattered by those who praise his work as having more harmony than the "sublimated journalese" of Bret Harte and Rudyard Kipling. However, after his second novel is turned down by his old publishers and then issued by a small artsy publishing house, his literary circle soon loses interest in him. Overbeck goes back to California in the vain hope of rekindling his artistic passion. "The fire that the gods had allowed him to snatch, because he was humble and pure and clean and brave, had been stamped out beneath the feet of minor and dilettante poets," Norris wrote.[6]

Norris spares no derision in his tale – but the moral to his story has not been the one that has directed the fate of many of the contemporary journalist-literary figures. Wolfe's solution to this dilemma – to get out into the world and to "report," to gather up information and experiences, and to fill the writer's basket with material from "real life" – is almost a nostalgic one. From his New York City apartment, Wolfe himself should know something about the dangers of creative isolation. Although the results of research and interviewing have continued to be built into his novels, Wolfe's own preoccupations have become anything but what "real" people are concerned with (*Bonfire of the Vanities* focuses upon the divisions between the luxury-living fast life and the impoverished and criminal world of the country's capital of entertainment sensationalism, New York City; *I am Charlotte Simmons* is a novel about what campus life might be like if college students were as indulged, dissolute, and sex-obsessed as a 70-plus-year-old writer might like to imagine).

In addition, while there are writers who succeed across the spectrum of today's specialized literary and commercial publishing worlds (Toni Morrison and Salman Rushdie come to mind), it is the rare person who can pull it off, and for reasons that Wolfe illustrates in his own writing. The contemporary focus on style encourages writers with literary pretensions to develop a distinct prose signature rather than relying upon content alone to carry a narrative. Despite his plea for a more realistic literature, Wolfe is one of the most self-consciously stylized writers of our time, with his artistic voice relying upon prose flourishes, clever embellishments, and a fast-paced and self-consciously hip writing style (Mailer once said of Wolfe that he may be "the hardest working show-off the literary world has ever seen"). This growing divergence between the straightforward, utilitarian writing required in the media industries and the textured, elliptical, rhythmic, and/or poetic prose style admired in literary circles has created a chasm between popular literature and that which is successful with academic critics, and some fans of literary journalism as well. A few of the later journalist-literary figures – most notably Agee, Ernest Hemingway, Sherwood Anderson, Virginia Woolf, and Conrad Richter – were involved in the stylistic revolution in modern literary prose, as was Stephen Crane with his impressionistic *Red Badge of Courage*. But many of the journalist-literary figures were not notable stylists, and some, such as Theodore Dreiser and Sinclair Lewis, were admired despite their widely acknowledged stylistic lapses.[7]

As one who apprenticed in the newsroom of the old *New York Herald Tribune*, Wolfe can still celebrate the old-fashioned virtues of researching and reporting (for example, he offered someone as old-hat and out-of-fashion as Lewis as his model of the reporter-fictionist). But Wolfe has been kidding himself if he believes that today's publishers, critics, or the book audience would probably be interested in anything like Lewis' excessively reported, sociologically detailed, often painfully slow-moving portrayals of life as it was really lived in small-town, provincial America. Wolfe's own career is an acknowledgement that the reach for stylistic "effect" – and the choice of topics that will appeal to publishers and a reading public eager for glittery, fashionable, and sensationalized themes – has dwarfed the market for fiction that relies too much on the fundamentals of journalistic realism and tried-and-true journalistic reporting techniques alone.

What Wolfe also doesn't address is the changed environment of today's newsrooms that has altered their traditional role as the training-ground for some of the country's top literary talent. Commercial, deadline-based journalism is quite frequently no longer a place where a premium is put upon written communication or where editors place their focus upon the prose content of the printed page. Throughout the twentieth century, the job of the journalist was transformed by technological and economic changes that have turned contemporary media organizations into enterprises that are as much about conglomerate growth, business synergies, stock-market performance, digital convergence, and the advance of electronic culture as they are about the doing of journalism. In this environment, news packaging and visual presentation, the race for the instantaneous communication of information, career promotion, and the seeking after celebrity journalism positions are increasingly becoming top priorities of news workers and the unearthing of facts and the crafting of words secondary activities. Loren Ghiglione, in noting the decline in newspaper and book reading in American culture, has said, "Despite what we newspaper Neanderthals wish to believe about the majesty of print, the age of literate readers – readers of newspapers, serious literature, and books – is passing ... Perhaps the time has come to admit that print has fallen prey to television, computers, videos, and Nintendo."[8]

Not only has the nature of journalism jobs and journalistic organizations changed, so has the system that confers literary and marketplace success. The incentives for a writer with serious literary aspirations to leave regular journalism employment are still there, but the reasons for abandoning journalistic writing for fiction-writing are considerably less than they have been. While the market for non-fiction books has grown greatly, the chances of an unknown writer placing a serious first novel with an established commercial publisher are slim. In today's megabucks world of conglomerate publishing houses and chain bookstores marketing blockbuster novels, the sums paid to established popular novelists can be so great that it will tend to suck up much of the investment that could be made in first-time, unproven novelists. The Catch-22 of contemporary publishing success – that author reputation, marketing potential, and popular audience appeal are the major gauges of a manuscript's publishability – dramatically reduces the chances of an unknown journalist producing a critically and/or financially successful serious novel. Internet publishing – with the opportunities for authors to circumvent traditional publishing gate-keepers and put their work directly before a web audience – is still in its infancy, but the record of authors gaining recognition and serious critical acclaim for web-based work is a very limited one so far.

That a few writers continue to move from the newsroom to broader publishing success is a testimony to the persistence of the tradition of the journalist-turned-novelist – even if one cannot name a contemporary one who has achieved the iconic status of a Twain or a Crane or a Hemingway or a Charles Dickens in their time. Outside of the better-known literary journalist figures – a number of whom also have written widely reviewed (although not always critically acclaimed) fictional works – there are a cadre of contemporary novel-writers who have sustained themselves at least for a time in journalism jobs and who have developed important reputations in certain literary circles. An older generation of contemporary American fiction writers – including Kennedy, Dexter, O'Brien, Elie Wiesel, Doris Betts, Ward Just, Ivan Doig, Susan Cheever, E. Annie Proulx, and Robert Olen Butler – are best-known for their fictional works, even though they have also labored in the vineyards of journalism. On the other side of the Atlantic, a contingent of prominent contemporary novelists and poets from the British Isles, including Amis, Barnes, Angela Carter, Angela Lambert, Craig Raine, James Fenton, William Boyd, Jonathan Meades, A. A. Gill, Sean French, Tibor Fischer, Mark Lawson, and Giles Foden, have worked on Fleet Street for leading periodicals, often in arts, television, and restaurant reviewing, or for musical publications (Tony Parsons, Julie Burchill). Scattered among these folks are other well-known literary personalities whose resumes have included stints in journalism (including Updike, Robbins, Barbara Kingsolver, Tom Stoppard, and Anne Lamott), as well as electronic media personalities or scriptwriters (Meades, Lambert, Jim Lehrer, Michael Frayn, Jim Crace, Muriel Gray, Nora Ephron) who also have written fictional prose works that have received attention.

The changed career prospects for the aspiring novelist who might be considering spending time in journalism is well-illustrated in the career trajectory of Robert Stone, whose kinetic fiction about the Vietnam War era and the countercultural characters of the 1960s and 1970s has made him the "apostle of (the) strung out," as one critic described him. Stone secured a copyboy job at the *New York Daily News* in the late 1950s and early 1960s, where he also wrote captions, reported on sporting events, and grew fascinated by the hard-boiled reporters around him. However, Stone – who was grateful to the *Daily News* for "having enough repellant aspects to scare him off a newspaper career forever," in the words of one biographer – soon quit to support himself through a succession of menial jobs before he was accepted into the writing program at Stanford University. After that – and with the completion of his first novel, *A Hall of Mirrors* – Stone, the one-time bohemian and writing vagabond, was able to find a lifetime of support in a series of writer-in-residence programs and faculty creative-writing posts at Princeton, Amherst, Stanford, University of Hawaii at Manao, Harvard, University of California-Irvine, New York University, University of California-San Diego, Johns Hopkins, and Yale.[9]

Besides the opportunities that academic writing posts and writer-in-residence programs offer, the taste of the academic and critical literary world has come to influence the journalist-literary figures themselves in other important ways. In his introduction to the book's fiftieth anniversary edition, Mailer treated the young author that he was when he wrote *Naked and the Dead* in slighting terms. "He was naïve, he was passionate about writing, he knew very little about the subtler demands of a good style, he did not have a great deal of restraint, and he burned with excitement as he wrote," Mailer said of his younger self. "He hardly knew whether he should stand in the shadow of Tolstoy or was essentially without talent. He was an amateur." Even though it can be argued (as I would) that *The Naked and the Dead* is a success exactly because of the influence of Tolstoy upon it, Mailer clearly had more respect for his "mature" work of stylistic experimentation in *Why Are We in Vietnam?* or his pioneering but self-consciously "new" journalistic *The Armies of the Night*, where his indulgences of technique and efforts at prose poetry are more impressive to him than the straightforward and vivid prose of his youth. In reading Mailer's later works, one encounters places where he, like so many contemporary writers, is striving too hard to make a stylistic impression. His most journalistically successful work – *The Executioner's Song* – has been praised largely because Mailer, for once, got out of the way and let the story tell itself.[10] However, the fact that Mailer and the critical literary establishment might come to agreement on what amounts to "mature" writing success may be no surprise either, given the growing entanglements of literary careerism, specialized literary scholarship and criticism, and literary and artistic tastes forged in the rarified atmosphere of academia.

It is perhaps to be expected, then, that the journalist-literary figures would have come to occupy a tenuous foothold in the pantheon of literary greats whose ranks are being reshuffled by the changing trends of literary criticism and scholarship. Brian McCrea, in his book *Addison and Steele Are Dead*, claims that today's academic critics have found little to analyze in the clear prose style of the many journalist-literary figures who championed writing plainly to a mass audience and spurned communication that was pretentious, obfuscating, or overly learned. Addison and Steele (whose philosophy was, "Hard and crabbed Words are to be avoided because they obscure clarity") have become "useless" from the standpoint of post-World War II academic criticism, McCrea argues, and have fallen on the wrong side of the enforced division in academia between "high" and "popular" art. There is room for a journalist-literary figure to retain scholarly popularity, such as Jonathan Swift does, as long as that person is seen as producing equivocal texts which elude final interpretation. But the academic world lacks the traditional common sense that Swift celebrated, McCrea argues, and Swift probably would be "amazed and troubled" by the "Scriblerian pedantry that underlies the notion of an English department and a PhD in English."[11]

Thomas Strychacz, like McCrea, has argued that as literary studies have been professionalized, many of its theories and definitions have grown up to protect the scholarly profession. As journalism reached its peak of influence toward the end of the nineteenth century – when a reporter-writer such as Crane was widely celebrated as a "high priest of experience" and the journalist-literary figures were reaching the pinnacle of success in a growing market of mass publications – the rise of the modern university came along to change the ground rules of literary achievement. Beginning in the period after the US Civil War, the expanding university system emerged as a place where communities of intellectuals took refuge against what they saw as the erosion of high culture in a society awash in popular forms of news and entertainment. The key to maintaining an exclusive critical outlook was to define higher knowledge as something that needed institutionalized training, the ability to interpret texts in the context of literary theory, and the mastery of specialized terminology.[12]

In this atmosphere the journalist-literary figures have frequently been found lacking when it comes to the political and literary standards that have been utilized in much literary criticism dating back to the 1930s, when it became common for critics to put a priority on a writer's political viewpoint or the avant-garde nature of his or her aesthetic principles. A writer such as Willa Cather, for example, who grew more politically conservative throughout her life and impatient with the new trends in literary analysis, increasingly has found her works evaluated in political terms by critics radicalized by the Great Depression or through the prism of heightened attention to issues of gender and sexual orientation. (Cather, for example, has become a figure of fascination for gay and women's studies scholars, even though she herself preferred men to women writers and destroyed much of her correspondence as an apparent discouragement to the scholarly examination of her private life or the pursuit of questions about her sexuality.) John Steinbeck, who was originally embraced by the left, was increasingly chastised by leftist-oriented critics when his later writings proved him to be anything but a social or political radical in outlook, as well as by critics who found his writing too sentimental for their taste. As American and British universities have become bastions of multiculturalism and diversity politics, a host of writers – including a number of the journalist-literary figures – have been re-evaluated for the acceptability of their views on race, gender, culture, militarism, and other political questions. Twain's use of racial epithets and his portrayal of the runaway slave Jim in *Huckleberry Finn* have embroiled him in repeated protests against the use of his literature in the classroom. Hemingway's macho attitudes and insensitive comments about a host of groups have made him a target for academic literary critics and members of women's studies departments. Kipling is seldom studied in the university anymore except as a symbol of imperialism and cultural arrogance that deserves little but strong censure. Even among those favored by journalists themselves, the witty and iconoclastic H. L. Mencken has been "discovered" to have been a racist (hardly a surprise to even the casual peruser of his writings) and someone who managed to insult virtually every group that is now thought of as victimized by western history.[13]

Twain's pummeling at the hands of novelist Jane Smiley is a classic case of how badly the journalist-literary figures have fared under the pressures of contemporary literary revisionism. In her 1996 article in *Harper's*, Smiley argued that *Huckleberry Finn* "has little to offer in the way of greatness" and only has been treated as such because of "meretricious" reasoning by critics who have misguidedly tried to make the book out to be an important statement against racism. "To invest *The Adventures of Huckleberry Finn* with 'greatness' is to underwrite a very simplistic and evasive theory of what racism is and to promulgate it," Smiley wrote. " … No matter how often the critics place in context Huck's use of the word 'nigger,' they can never fully excuse or fully hide the deeper racism of the novel." Smiley's thesis is that Twain appears to believe – like many Americans – that it is enough to oppose racism simply by embracing a black person as a friend and as a human being, as Huck does with Jim. Smiley said this gesture means little to many African-Americans, who understand racism as a way of structuring American society, and that a book such as Harriet Beecher Stowe's *Uncle Tom's Cabin*, which advocates for something to be done to correct the institutional inequities of racism, should be valued above *Huckleberry Finn*.[14]

Smiley's indictment displays the vehemence in which contemporary critics can put politics and political correctness above considerations of aesthetics, artistic vision, and historical perspective. Huck, who as a poor white southern boy living before the Civil War had nothing of Smiley's modern political sophistication, is certainly no contemporary liberal – nor was Twain in many respects. But Huck does "act" courageously, and in ways that are consistent with the limited life vision of his character. With his sentimental view of his Missouri upbringing, his brief service with the Missouri troops opposing the Union Army, and his insulting statements about Native Americans in other works, Twain is no model of contemporary political correctness, let alone the authoritative commentator on the state of American race relations. But to imply, as Smiley does, that *Huckleberry Finn* should be dropped from the literary canon because "propagandists" have used it for political purposes that she finds offensive is in itself the triumph of politicized critical judgment. Smiley has her complaints about the places where she finds *Huckleberry Finn* to be a "failure" in artistic terms, but in not applying the same aesthetic standards to Stowe's *Uncle Tom's Cabin*, with its own propagandistic melodrama and its one-dimensional, good-or-evil characters, she confesses to a taste for weak literature with a strong moral polemic over literature that may not satisfy the political purist but was created with artistic purpose first in mind. (Smiley might also have made more of the fact that Stowe, too, was a creature of her time. Although a vehement abolitionist, she believed that blacks, once freed, should be returned to Africa to set up their own homeland.)[15]

Times have changed greatly since the days of Twain's journalistic apprenticeship, and one can only imagine the many ways that his hard-scramble, real-world literary vision does not satisfy the residents of literary academia. The idea of commercial journalism as an incubator for literary talent can be expected to find only passing sympathy in a world where academic writing programs, literary fellowships, and visiting teaching posts beckon (ironically, an academic world that Smiley herself works in and has satirized in her novel, *Moo*).[16] In today's specialized and careerist world, where big media, big academia, and big-time publishing dominate the literary and the journalistic scene, there appear to be fewer possibilities for the ascendance of the great writing personality to capture the public imagination. The journalism being produced today offers some opportunities for exposure, but most often for writers who are willing to try to gain the attention of the electronic media and to make their peace with the demands of the blockbuster publicity world of contemporary publishing and a mass media environment that has elevated movie, business, sports figures, and rock musicians far above any mere wordsmith in cultural status. The reduced celebrity profile of the typically successful serious writer in an electronic age when the stars celebrated on ESPN Live, "Entertainment Tonight," MTV, and *People* magazine occupy center stage may not be a bad thing for the psyche of the individual writer and the uncontaminated pursuit of art, but it has diminished the influence of serious writing on the public consciousness.

Perhaps in eras to come, critics will look to today's journalist-literary figures and decide that the legacy of journalistic literature's impact on the development of the literary tradition has continued unabated through our age, and we will continue to see journalism as a place where artistic talent has been cultivated and encouraged. There are those who believe that the high-quality, book-length non-fiction being produced today – in combination with journalism's contribution to literary trends via the "new" or "literary" journalism – will more than compensate for the lack of widely acclaimed and popularly embraced serious fiction-writers who have emerged from the journalistic workplace.[17] The tradition of great writing has survived many changes in the media marketplace and the world of scholarship and criticism, and the shape of journalistic literature in the future and the critical judgments about it are still questions for posterity. One can only hope that the interplay between these two vital and important fields – journalism and fiction-writing – will continue to provide a rich tableau for the nourishment of the literary tradition in whatever manner it unfolds.

One only has to be around a group of writers and critics to be reminded of the ironies that abound in any evaluation of the impact of journalistic literature upon the public consciousness and the collective artistic imagination. Such was the case in 2003 when a symposium of French and American writers and scholars gathered in Florida to discuss the direction of literature in their respective cultures. For the Americans, the names that got them excited were the French literary scholars and apostles of post-modernism and textual deconstruction, Michel Foucault and Jacques Derrida, as well as the cerebral works of Simone de Beauvoir, Alain Robbe-Grillet, and Albert Camus (the only journalist-literary figure in that group). The French, on the other hand, indicated that the American writers who have been most important to them included almost exclusively journalist-literary figures (Hemingway, Steinbeck, Jack London, Erskine Caldwell, Upton Sinclair, and Richard Wright), as well as a number of the "tough guy" writers of mystery and detective novels, including one-time journalists Raymond Chandler and Horace McCoy. "We all seek our opposite, don't we?" commented the organizer of the conference, Alec Hargreaves. However, beyond the fact that Americans have often looked to Europe for guidance in high culture while Europeans have been fascinated with American popular culture, there might be another message to be taken from the symposium. People from all over the world continue to love to read the journalist-literary figures (Twain, London, Hemingway, and Steinbeck are still among the hundred top best-selling American authors today), and their "stealthy literature" appears to be continuing to impress itself on the popular imagination, no matter what the prevailing literary fashions.[18]

Appendix. The major journalist-literary figures: their writings and positions in journalism

Here are the journalistic professional experiences and the literary accomplishments of the major British and American journalist-literary figures:

DANIEL DEFOE (1660–1731). Editor, Defoe's London *Review* (1704–1713); Editor, *Mercator* (1713–1714); Editor, *Flying Post* (1715); Contributor, *Dormer's Newsletter* (1715–1719); Editor, *Mercurius Politicus* (1716–1721); Editor and contributor, *Mist's Weekly Journal* (1716–1724); Editor, *Mercurius Britannicus* (1718–1719); Editor, *Manufacturer* (1719–1720); Editor, *Whitehall Evening Post* (1719–1721); Editor, *Daily Post* (1719–1725); Contributor, *Applebee's Weekly* (1722–1726); Editor, *Political State* (1729–1730). Literary works: *Robinson Crusoe* (1719); *Moll Flanders* (1722); *A Journal of the Plague Year* (1722); *Roxana* (1724); *Tour thro' the Whole Island of Great Britain* (1724, 1725, 1727); *The Life of Jonathan Wild* (1725).

JONATHAN SWIFT (1667–1745). Contributor, *Tatler* (1709); Editor, *Examiner* (1710–1711). Literary works: *A Tale of a Tub* (1704); *Gulliver's Travels* (1726); *A Modest Proposal* (1729).

JOSEPH ADDISON (1672–1719). Contributor, *Tatler* (1709–1711); Editor, *Whig Examiner* (1710); Co-founder and co-editor, *Spectator* (1711–1712, 1714); Contributor, *Guardian* (1713); Editor, *Freeholder* (1715–1716); Editor, *Old Whig* (1719). Literary works: *Cato* (play, 1713).

DELARIVIÉRE MANLEY (1672–1724). Editor, *Female Tatler* (1709–1710); Editor, *Examiner* (1711). Literary works: *The Lost Love* (play, 1696); *The Secret History of Queen Zarah* (1705); *Atalantis* (1709–1710).

RICHARD STEELE (1672–1729). Writer and editor, London *Gazette* (1707–1710); Founder and editor, *Tatler* (1709–1711); Co-founder and co-editor, *Spectator* (1711–1712, 1714); Editor, *Guardian*, (1713); Editor, *Englishman* (1713–1715); Editor, *Lover* (1714); Editor, *Reader* (1714); Editor, *Town-Talk* (1715–1716); Editor, *Plebian* (1719); Editor, *Theater* (1720). Literary works: *The Christian Hero* (1701); *The Tender Husband* (play, 1705).

ELIZA HAYWOOD (1693–1756). Editor, *Female Spectator* (1744–1746); Editor, *Parrot* (1746). Literary works: *Love in Excess* (1719–1720); *Jemmy and Jenny Jessamy* (1753).

BENJAMIN FRANKLIN (1706–1790). Editor and publisher, *New England Courant* (1722–1723); Publisher and editor, *Pennsylvania Gazette* (1729–1748); Publisher, *General Magazine* (1741). Literary works: *Poor Richard, An Almanack* (1732); *Autobiography of Benjamin Franklin* (1791, 1818).

HENRY FIELDING (1707–1754). Co-editor, *Champion* (1739–1740); Editor, *True Patriot* (1745–1746); Editor, *Jacobite's Journal* (1747–1748); Editor, *Covent-Garden Journal* (1752). Literary works: *Joseph Andrews* (1742); *Tom Jones* (1749); *Amelia* (1751); *The Life of Jonathan Wild* (1754); *The Journal of a Voyage to Lisbon* (1755).

SAMUEL JOHNSON (1709–1784). Contributor, *Birmingham Journal* (1732–1733); Contributor and sub-editor, *Gentleman's Magazine* (1738–1744); Editor, *Rambler* (1750–1752); Contributor, *Adventurer* (1753–1754); Editor, *Idler* (1758–1760). Literary works: *An Account of the Life of Mr. Richard Savage* (1744); *The History of Rasselas* (1759, 1768).

TOBIAS SMOLLETT (1721–1771). Contributor, *Monthly Review* (1751–1752); Editor, *Critical Review* (1755–1762); Editor, *British Magazine* (1761–1763); Editor, *Briton* (1762–1763). Literary works: *The Adventures of Roderick Random* (1748); *The Adventures of Peregrine Pickle* (1751); *The Expedition of Humphry Clinker* (1771).

FRANCES BROOKE (1724–1789). Editor, *Old Maid* (1755–1756). Literary works: *The History of Lady Julia Mandeville* (1763).

OLIVER GOLDSMITH (1730–1774). Reviewer, *Monthly Review* (1757); Contributor, *Critical Review* (1759); Editor, *Bee* (1759); Contributor, *Public Ledger* (1760–1761); Editor, *Lady's Magazine* (1761). Literary works: *The Citizen of the World* (1762); *The Vicar of Wakefield* (1766); *She Stoops to Conquer* (play, 1773).

THOMAS PAINE (1737–1809). Editor and contributor, *Pennsylvania Magazine* (1775–1776). Literary works: *Common Sense* (1776).

JAMES BOSWELL (1740–1795). Contributor, *London Chronicle* (1763–1774); Part-owner, contributor, and columnist, *London Magazine* (1769–1785). Literary works: *Ode to Tragedy* (poetry, 1761); *Dorando, A Spanish Tale* (1767); *Journal of a Tour to the Hebrides with Samuel Johnson* (1785); *The Life of Samuel Johnson* (1791); *Boswell's London Journal, 1762–1763* (1950).

RICHARD BRINSLEY SHERIDAN (1751–1816). Contributor, *Englishman* (1779); Co-founder and contributor, *Political Herald* (1785–1786). Literary works: *The Critic* (play, 1779).

PHILIP FRENEAU (1752–1832). Contributor, *United States Magazine* (1779); Co-editor and contributor, *Freeman's Journal* (1781–1783); Editor, *New York Daily Advertiser* (1790–1791); Editor, *National Gazette* (1791–1793); Editor, *Jersey Chronicle* (1795–1796); Editor, *Time-Piece, and Literary Companion* (1796–1798). Literary works: *The British Prison-Ship* (1781); *A Voyage to Boston* (poetry, 1775).

WILLIAM GODWIN (1756–1836). Contributor, *English Review* (1783); Contributor, *New Annual Register* (1784–1791); Contributor, *Political Herald* (1785–1786). Literary works: *Political Justice* (1793); *The Adventures of Caleb Williams* (1794).

SUSANNA HASWELL ROWSON (1762–1824). Editor, *Boston Weekly Magazine* (1802–1805). Literary works: *Charlotte* (1791).

SAMUEL TAYLOR COLERIDGE (1772–1834). Contributor, London *Morning Chronicle* (1793–1795); Editor, *Watchman* (1796); Correspondent and writer, London *Morning Post* (1797–1803); Contributor, *Courier* (1804–1817); Contributor, *Edinburgh Review* (1808); Editor, *Friend* (1809–1810). Literary works: "Kubla Khan, A Vision in a Dream" (poetry, 1816); *Specimens of the Table Talk of Samuel Taylor Coleridge* (1835).

CHARLES LAMB (1775–1834). Writer and editorial assistant, *Albion* (1801); Writer, London *Morning Chronicle* (1801); Writer, London *Morning Post* (1801–1802); Contributor, *Reflector* (1811–1812); Contributor, *Gentleman's Magazine* (1813); Contributor, *Champion* (1813); Contributor, London *Examiner* (1812–1814); Essayist and contributor, *London Magazine* (1820–1825); Contributor, *Englishman's Magazine* (1831). Literary works: *Tales from Shakespeare* (with Mary Lamb, 1807); *A Tale of Rosamund Gray and Old Blind Margaret* (1798).

WILLIAM HAZLITT (1778–1830). Parliamentary reporter, London *Morning Chronicle* (1812–1814); Contributor, London *Examiner* (1814–1816); Contributor, *Champion* (1814–1817); Contributor, *Edinburgh Review* (1815–1824); Reviewer, *The Times* of London (1817); Contributor, *Edinburgh Magazine* (1817–1818); Co-editor, *Yellow Dwarf* (1818); Contributor, *London Magazine* (1820). Literary works: *The Round Table* (with Leigh Hunt, 1817); *Table-Talk* (1821, 1822).

WASHINGTON IRVING (1783–1859). Contributor, *New York Morning Chronicle* (1802–1803); Columnist, *Corrector* (1804); Co-editor, *Salmagundi* (1807–1808); Editor, *Analectic Magazine* (1812–1814). Literary works: *The Sketch Book* (1819–1820); *The Alhambra* (1832).

LEIGH HUNT (1784–1859). Drama critic, *The News* (1805–1807); Editor, London *Examiner* (1808–1821); Editor, *Reflector* (1811–1812); Editor, *Literary Pocket Book* (1818–1822); Editor, *Indicator* (1819–1821); Editor, *Liberal*

(1822–1823); Editor, *Companion* (1828); Editor, *Chat of the Week/Tatler* (1830–1832); Editor, *Leigh Hunt's London Journal* (1834–1835); Editor, *Monthly Repository* (1837–1838); Editor, *Leigh Hunt's Journal* (1850–1851). Literary works: *The Round Table* (with William Hazlitt, 1817); *A Legend of Florence* (play, 1840).

THOMAS DE QUINCEY (1785–1859). Editor, *Westmorland Gazette* (1819); Contributor, *London Magazine* (1821–1825); Contributor, *Blackwood's* magazine (1826–1845); Contributor, *Edinburgh Saturday Post* (1827–1828); Contributor, *Tait's Edinburgh Magazine* (1834–1846); Contributor, *North British Review* (1846–1848); Contributor, *Hogg's Instructor* (1851–1852). Literary works: *Confessions of an English Opium Eater* (1823); *Walladmor* (1825); *Klosterheim* (1832).

WILLIAM CULLEN BRYANT (1794–1878). Co-editor, *New York Review and Atheneum* magazine (1825–1826); Reporter and editor-in-chief, *New York Evening Post* (1826–1878). Literary works: *Thanatopsis* (poetry, 1821); *Tales of Glauber-Spa* (with others, 1832).

THOMAS CARLYLE (1795–1881). Contributor, *Edinburgh Review* (1827–1831); Contributor, *Westminster Review* (1830–1853); Contributor, *Fraser's* magazine (1830–1875). Literary works: *Sartor Resartus* (1836); *On Heroes* (1841).

LORD MACAULAY (THOMAS BABINGTON, 1800–1859). Contributor and essayist, *Edinburgh Review* (1825–1844). Literary works: *Pompeii* (poetry, 1819); *History of England* (1849–1861).

HARRIET MARTINEAU (1802–1876). Contributor, *Monthly Repository* (1822–1832); Staffer and contributor, London *Daily News* (1852–1866); Contributor, *Edinburgh Review* (1859–1864). Literary works: *Deerbrook* (1839).

LYDIA MARIA CHILD (1802–1880). Editor, *National Anti-Slavery Standard* (1841–1843). Literary works: *Hobomok* (1824); *The Rebels* (1825).

DOUGLAS JERROLD (1803–1857). Co-founder and contributor, *Punch* magazine (1841–1857); Founder and Editor, *Illuminated Magazine* (1843–1844); Editor, *Jerrold's Shilling Magazine* (1845–1848); Sub-editor, London *Daily News* (1846); Editor, *Lloyd's Weekly Newspaper* (1852–1857). Literary works: *More Frightened than Hurt* (play, 1821); *The Life and Adventures of Miss Robinson Crusoe* (1846).

JOHN GREENLEAF WHITTIER (1807–1892). Editor, *American Manufacturer* (1829); Editor, *Haverhill* (MA) *Gazette* (1830, 1836); Editor, *New England Weekly Review* (1830–1832); Editor, *Emancipator and Anti-Slavery Record* (1837); Editor, *Pennsylvania Freeman* (1838–1840); Editor, *Middlesex Standard, Essex Transcript* (1844–1846); Contributing editor,

National Era magazine (1847–1860); Contributor, *Atlantic Monthly* magazine (1857–1882). Literary works: *Lays of My Home* (poetry, 1843); *Leaves from Margaret Smith's Journal* (1848–1849).

EDGAR ALLAN POE (1809–1849). Reviewer and assistant editor, *Southern Literary Messenger* (1835–1837); Co-editor, *Burton's Gentleman's Magazine* (1839–1840); Literary editor, *Graham's* magazine (1841–1842); Staff member, *New York Evening Mirror* (1844–1845); Editor and part-owner, *Broadway Journal* (1845–1846). Literary works: *Tales by Edgar A. Poe* (1845).

MARK LEMON (1809–1870). Contributor, *Bentley's Miscellany* (1837–1838); Co-founder and editor, *Punch* (1841–1870); Founder and contributor, *Illustrated London News* (1842–1870); Sub-editor, London *Daily News* (1846); Editor, *London Journal* (1857–1858). Literary works: *The Enchanted Doll* (1849).

MARGARET FULLER (1810–1850). Editor, *Dial* (1839–1842); Columnist, reporter, reviewer, foreign correspondent, *New York Tribune* (1844–1850). Literary works: *Summer on the Lakes* (1843); *Woman in the Nineteenth Century* (1845).

WILLIAM THACKERAY (1811–1863). Founder and editor, *National Standard* (1833–1834); Contributor, *Fraser's* (1834–1847); Paris correspondent, London *Constitutional* (1836–1837); Contributor to *The Times* of London, *Westminster Review*, and *New Monthly* magazine (1838–1840); Contributor, *Punch* (1842–1851); Correspondent and political reporter, London *Morning Chronicle* (1844–1846); Editor, *Cornhill* magazine (1860–1863). Literary works: *Vanity Fair* (1847–1848); *The Book of Snobs* (1848); *Pendennis* (1848–1850); *The History of Henry Esmond* (1852); *The Newcomes* (1853–1855); *The Adventures of Philip* (1862).

FANNY FERN (SARA PAYSON PARTON, 1811–1872). Columnist, *Boston Olive Branch* (1851–1853), *Boston True Flag* (1851–1853), *New York Musical World and Times* (1852–1853), *Philadelphia Saturday Evening Post* (1854), *New York Ledger* (1856–1872). Literary works: *Ruth Hall* (1855); *Rose Clark* (1856).

CHARLES DICKENS (1812–1870). Reporter, *Mirror of Parliament* (1832–1834); Political reporter, London *Morning Chronicle* (1834–1836); Editor, *Bentley's Miscellany* magazine (1836–1839); Editor, London *Daily News* (1846); Founder and Editor, *Household Words* magazine (1850–1859); Founder and Editor, *All the Year Round* magazine (1859–1870). Literary works: *The Pickwick Papers* (1836–1837); *Sketches by Boz* (1837); *Oliver Twist* (1838); *Barnaby Rudge* (1841); *American Notes for General Circulation* (1842); *Life and Adventures of Martin Chuzzlewit* (1842–1844); *Hard Times* (1854);

204   *Appendix. The major journalist-literary figures*

Little Dorrit (1855–1857); *A Tale of Two Cities* (1859); *Great Expectations* (1861).

HENRY MAYHEW (1812–1887). Co-founder, contributor, and editor, *Figaro in London* (1831–1838); Co-founder, *Thief* (1832); Co-founder and contributor, *Punch* (1841–1845); Founder and contributor, *Iron Times* (1845–1846); Contributor, *Illustrated London News* (1848); Contributor, London *Morning Chronicle* (1849–1850); Editor, *Comic Almanac* (1850–1851); Contributor, *Edinburgh News and Literary Chronicle* (1851); Editor, *Morning News* (1859). Literary works: *The Greatest Plague of Life* (with Augustus Mayhew, 1847); *London Labour and the London Poor* (1851–1852, 1861–1862).

GEORGE HENRY LEWES (1817–1878). Contributor, *Monthly Repository* (1837–1838); Contributor, *Westminster Review* (1840–1856); Co-editor, London *Leader* (1851–1854); Editor, *Fortnightly Review* (1865–1866). Literary works: *A Biographical History of Philosophy* (1845–1846); *The Noble Heart* (play, 1850).

FREDERICK DOUGLASS (1817–1895). Editor and owner, *North Star* (1847–1851); Editor and owner, *Frederick Douglass' Paper* (1851–1860); Editor, *Douglass' Monthly* magazine (1858–1863); Part-owner and correspondent, *New National Era* (1870–1874). Literary works: *The Heroic Slave* (1859); *Life and Times of Frederick Douglass* (1881).

GEORGE ELIOT (MARY ANN EVANS, 1819–1880). Contributor, *Coventry Herald and Observer* (1846–1847); Editor and contributor, *Westminster Review* (1852–1854); Contributor, London *Leader* (1855–1856). Literary works: *Adam Bede* (1859); *Felix Holt* (1866); *Middlemarch* (1871–1872); *Daniel Deronda* (1876).

JAMES RUSSELL LOWELL (1819–1891). Editor, *Atlantic Monthly* (1857–1861); Editor, *North American Review* (1864–1872). Literary works: *The Biglow Papers* (1848).

WALT WHITMAN (1819–1892). Contributor, *Long Island Patriot* (1831); Owner and editor, *Long Islander* (1838–1839); Contributor, *Long Island Democrat* (1839–1841); Editor and contributor, *New York Aurora and Evening Tatler* (1842); Editor, *New York Statesman* (1843); Editor, *New York Democrat* (1844); Contributor, *Long Island Star* (1845–1846); Editor, *Brooklyn Daily Eagle* (1846–1848); News editor, *New Orleans Crescent* (1848); Editor, *Brooklyn Daily Freeman* (1848–1849); Editor, *Brooklyn Daily Times* (1857–1859). Literary works: *Leaves of Grass* (poetry, 1855); *Specimen Days* (1892).

JOHN RUSKIN (1819–1900). Publisher, *Fors Clavigera: Letters to the Workmen and Laborers of Great Britain* (1871–1884). Literary works: *Salsette and Elephanta* (poetry, 1839); *Time and Tide* (1867).

EDWARD EVERETT HALE (1822–1909). Co-editor, *Christian Examiner* (1857–1861); Associate editor, *Army Navy Journal* (1863); Editor, *Old and New* magazine (1869–1875); Editor, *Lend a Hand Record* (1886–1897); Editor *New England Magazine* (1889); Editor, *Peace Crusade* magazine (1899). Literary works: *The Man Without a Country* (1865); *Susan's Escort* (1895).

BAYARD TAYLOR (1825–1878). Contributor, *New York Tribune* (1847–1875). Literary works: *El Dorado* (1850); *Hannah Thurston* (1863); *John Godfrey's Fortunes* (1864).

GEORGE MEREDITH (1828–1909). Co-founder and contributor, *Monthly Observer* (1848–1849); Journalist, *Ipswich Journal* (1858–1868); Contributor and war correspondent, London *Morning Post* (1862–1901); Editor and contributor, *Fortnightly Review* (1867–1868). Literary works: *Beauchamp's Career* (1876); *The Egoist* (1879).

CHARLES DUDLEY WARNER (1829–1900). Editor and assistant editor, *Hartford Press* (1860–1867); Editor and co-owner, *Hartford Courant* (1867–1900). Literary works: *The Gilded Age* (with Mark Twain, 1873).

REBECCA HARDING DAVIS (1831–1910). Associate editor, *New York Tribune* (1869–1875). Literary works: *Margret Howth* (1862); *John Andross* (1874).

ARTEMUS WARD (CHARLES FARRAR BROWNE, 1834–1867). Writer, *Boston Carpet-Bag* (1851–1853); Local editor, *Toledo Commercial* (1853–1857); Local editor, *Cleveland Plain Dealer* (1857–1860); Writer, *Vanity Fair* (beginning in 1860). Literary works: *Artemus Ward, His Book* (1865).

WILLIAM MORRIS (1834–1896). Founder and editor, *Oxford and Cambridge Magazine* (1856); Contributor, *Justice* magazine (1883–1890); Contributor, *Commonweal* magazine (1885–1890). Literary works: *News from Nowhere* (1890).

MARK TWAIN (SAMUEL CLEMENS, 1835–1910). Typesetter and writer, *Hannibal* (MO) *Journal* (1850–1852); Typesetter and writer, *Muscatine* (IA) *Journal* (1854); Reporter, *Territorial Enterprise*, Virginia City, Nevada (1862–1864); Reporter, *San Francisco Daily Morning Call* (1864); Correspondent, *Sacramento Union* (1866); Managing editor, *Buffalo Express* (1869–1871). Literary works: *The Celebrated Jumping Frog of Calaveras County, and Other Sketches* (1867); *Innocents Abroad* (1869); *Roughing It* (1872); *The Gilded Age* (with Charles Dudley Warner, 1873); *The Adventures of Tom Sawyer* (1876); *Ah, Sin* (play with Bret Harte, 1877); *Life on the Mississippi* (1883); *The Adventures of Huckleberry Finn* (1884); *A Connecticut Yankee in King Arthur's Court* (1889); *Pudd'nhead Wilson* (1894); *Editorial Wild Oats* (1905); *The Mysterious Stranger* (1916); *Letters from the Earth* (1962).

BRET HARTE (1836–1902). Printer, writer, assistant editor, *Northern Californian*, Union (Arcata), CA (1857–1860); Contributor and columnist, *Golden Era* magazine (1857–1861); Contributor, *Atlantic Monthly* (1863–1874); Contributor, *Californian* (1864–1867); California correspondent, *Springfield* (MA) *Republican* and *Boston Christian Register* (1866–1867); Editor, *Overland Monthly* (1868–1871). Literary works: *The Luck of Roaring Camp, and Other Sketches* (1869); *Gabriel Conroy* (1876); *Ah, Sin* (play with Mark Twain, 1877).

WILLIAM DEAN HOWELLS (1837–1920). Writer and critic, *Ohio State Journal* (1851–1860); Contributor, *Jefferson* (OH) *Sentinel* (1852); Legislative correspondent and city editor, *Cincinnati Gazette* (1857); Columnist, *Cleveland Herald* (1858); Columnist, *Boston Daily Advertiser* (1862–1864); Sub-editor, *Nation* (1865); Assistant editor and editor-in-chief, *Atlantic* (1866–1881); Columnist, *Harper's Monthly* (1886–1891, 1900–1920); Editor, *Cosmopolitan* (1892). Literary works: *Their Wedding Journey* (1871); *The Undiscovered Country* (1880); *A Modern Instance* (1881); *The Rise of Silas Lapham* (1884); *A Hazard of New Fortunes* (1889); *The Quality of Mercy* (1892); *A Traveler from Altruria* (1892–1893); *Through the Eye of the Needle* (1907); *My Mark Twain* (1910).

HENRY ADAMS (1838–1918). Washington, DC correspondent, *Boston Daily Advertiser* (1860–1861); London correspondent, *New York Times* (1861–1862); Editor and contributor, *North American Review* (1868–1877). Literary works: *Esther* (as Francis Snow Compton, 1884); *The Education of Henry Adams* (1907).

AMBROSE BIERCE (1842–1914). Columnist and managing editor, *San Francisco News Letter and California Advertiser* (1867–1872); Writer and sub-editor, San Francisco *Wasp* (1876–1886); Columnist, San Francisco *Examiner* (1887–1898); Washington, DC correspondent, *New York Journal* and *New York American* (1896–1909). Literary works: *Tales of Soldiers and Civilians* (1891); *The Devil's Dictionary* (1911).

HENRY JAMES (1843–1916). Writer, *Nation* and *Atlantic Monthly* (1866–1869); Art critic, *Atlantic Monthly* (1871–1872); Correspondent, *New York Tribune* (1875–1876). Literary works: *The Wings of a Dove* (1902).

GEORGE WASHINGTON CABLE (1844–1925). Columnist and reporter, *New Orleans Picayune* (1870–1871); Contributor, *Scribner's* (1873–1875). Literary works: *Old Creole Days* (1879); *The Grandissimes* (1880).

GEORGE R. SIMS (1847–1922). Staffer, *Fun* (1874–1877); Columnist, *Referee* (1876–1922); Investigative reporter, London *Daily News* (early 1880s); Contributor, *Pictorial World* (beginning 1881). Literary works: *How the Poor Live* (1883), *Dorcas Dene, Detective* (1897, 1898).

JOEL CHANDLER HARRIS (1848–1908). Typesetter, *Macon* (GA) *Telegraph* (1866); Staffer, *Crescent Monthly* magazine (1866–1867); Staff writer, *Monroe* (GA) *Advertiser* (1867–1870); Associate editor, *Savannah Morning News* (1870–1876); Editor, columnist, and staff writer, *Atlanta Constitution* (1876–1900). Literary works: *Uncle Remus, His Songs and His Sayings* (1880).

JACOB RIIS (1849–1914). Police reporter, *New York Tribune* (1878–1890); Police reporter, *New York Evening Sun* (1890–1899). Literary works: *How the Other Half Lives* (1890); *The Children of the Poor* (1892); *Neighbors: Life Stories of the Other Half* (1914).

ROBERT LOUIS STEVENSON (1850–1894). Contributor, *Cornhill, Macmillan's,* and *London Magazine* (1873–1879). Literary works: *Treasure Island* (1883); *Kidnapped* (1886); *Dr. Jekyll and Mr. Hyde* (1886); *The Amateur Emigrant* (1895).

EUGENE FIELD (1850–1895). Reporter and writer, *St. Louis Evening Journal, St. Joseph Gazette, St. Louis Times-Journal, Kansas City Times, Denver Tribune* (1873–1883); Columnist, *Chicago Morning News* (1883–1895). Literary works: *Culture's Garland* (1887).

EDWARD BELLAMY (1850–1898). Journalist, *New York Evening Post* (1871–1872); Editorial writer and reviewer, *Springfield* (MA) *Union* (1872–1877); Publisher, *Springfield Daily News* (1880–1881). Literary works: *Looking Backward* (1888).

E. W. HOWE (1853–1937). Owner and publisher, *Atchison* (KS) *Globe* (1877–1910); Editor, *E. W. Howe's Monthly* (1911–1933). Literary works: *The Story of a Country Town* (1883).

L. FRANK BAUM (1856–1919). Reporter, *New York World* (1873–1875); Editor, *New Era,* Bradford, PA (1876); Editor, *Saturday Pioneer,* Aberdeen, SD (1889–1891); Reporter, *Chicago Post* (1891). Literary works: *The Wonderful Wizard of Oz* (1900).

GEORGE BERNARD SHAW (1856–1950). Reviewer, *Pall Mall Gazette* (1885–1888); Music critic, *Dramatic Review* (1886); Art and music critic, *London World* (1886–1894); Music columnist, *London Star* (1888–1890); Theatre critic, *Saturday Review* (1895–1898). Literary works: *Cashel Byron's Profession* (1886); *Arms and the Man* (play, 1894); *Man and Superman* (play, 1905).

IDA TARBELL (1857–1944). Associate and managing editor, *Chautauquan* (1883–1901); Mid-level and associate editor and contributor, *McClure's* magazine (1894–1906); Co-founder and associate editor, *American Magazine* (1906–1915). Literary works: *The Rising of the Tide* (1919).

GERTRUDE ATHERTON (1857–1948). Columnist, San Francisco *Examiner* (1891). Literary works: *The Doomswoman* (1893); *Black Oxen* (1923).

EDITH NESBIT (1858–1924). Co-editor, *Neolith* magazine (1907–1908). Literary works: *Five Children and It* (1902); *The Story of the Amulet* (1906).

CHARLES W. CHESNUTT (1858–1932). Reporter, Dow Jones and Co. (1883); Reporter and columnist, *New York Mail and Express* (1883); Contributor, *New York Independent* (1889–1891). Literary works: *The Conjure Woman* (1899); *The House Behind the Cedars* (1900); *The Marrow of Tradition* (1901).

PAULINE HOPKINS (1859–1930). Section editor, *Colored American* (1900–1904). Literary Works: *Contending Forces: A Romantic Illustrative of Negro Life North and South* (1900).

CHARLOTTE PERKINS GILMAN (1860–1935). Contributor, *People* newsweekly (1885–1887); Contributor, *Women's Journal* (1885–1887); Contributor, *New England Magazine* (1892); Co-editor, *Impress* (1894–1895); Founder and editor, *Forerunner* (1909–1916). Literary works: *The Yellow Wallpaper* (1899); *What Diantha Did* (1910); *The Man-Made World* (1911); *Herland* (1915).

JAMES M. BARRIE (1860–1937). Writer and reviewer, *Nottingham Daily Journal* (1883–1884). Literary works: *Better Dead* (1888); *Peter Pan* (play, 1904); *Peter and Wendy* (1911).

HAMLIN GARLAND (1860–1940). Reviewer, *Boston Evening Transcript* (1885–1892). Literary works: *Main-Traveled Roads* (1891); *A Spoil of Office* (1892); *A Member of the Third House* (1892); *Jason Edwards* (1892); *Prairie Folks* (1893).

ABRAHAM CAHAN (1860–1951). Co-editor, *Neie Tseit* (1886); Editor, *Arbeiter Zeitung* (1891–1894); Editor, *Die Zunkunf* (1893–1894); Reporter, *New York Commercial Advertiser* (1897–1901); Co-founder and editor, *Jewish Daily Forward* (1897, 1903–1951). Literary works: *Yekl* (1896); *The Rise of David Levinsky* (1917).

VICTORIA EARLE MATTHEWS (1861–1907). Writer for *Brooklyn Eagle, New York Times, New York Herald, New York Mail and Express, National Leader, Detroit Plaindealer,* and *Southern Christian Recorder* (starting in the 1880s); Associate editor and contributor, *Woman's Era* (1894–1897). Literary works: *Aunt Liddy* (1893).

O. HENRY (WILLIAM SYDNEY PORTER, 1862–1910). Contributor, *Detroit Free Press* (1887); Columnist, Houston *Daily Post* (1895); Contributor, *Pittsburgh Dispatch* (1901–1902); Contributor, *New York World* (1903–1906). Literary works: *The Four Million* (1906); *Heart of the West* (1907); *The Voice of the City* (1908).

IDA B. WELLS-BARNETT (1862–1931). Editor, *Living Way* (1887–1889); Editor, *Memphis Free Speech* (1889–1892); Part-owner and contributing

editor, *New York Age* (1892–1893); Editor, *Conservator* (1895–1917).
Literary works: *The Memphis Diary of Ida B. Wells* (1995).
RICHARD HARDING DAVIS (1864–1916). Reporter, *Philadelphia Record*
(1886); Reporter, *Philadelphia Press* (1886–1889); Reporter, *New York
Evening Sun* (1889–1891); Managing editor, *Harper's Weekly* (1891–1893);
Associate editor, *Harper's New Monthly Magazine* (1893); Correspondent,
New York Journal (1895–1897); Greco-Turkish War correspondent, *The
Times* of London (1897); Spanish-American War correspondent, *New
York Herald* (1898), *The Times* of London (1898), *Scribner's* (1898); Boer
War correspondent, *New York Herald* and London *Daily Mail* (1899–
1900); Russo-Japanese War correspondent, *Collier's* (1904); World War I
correspondent, Wheeler Syndicate, *New York Times, Collier's* (1915–1916).
Literary works: *Gallegher and Other Stories* (1891); *Cinderella and Other
Stories* (1896); *Ranson's Folly* (1902); *The Red Cross Girl* (1912).
NELLIE BLY (ELIZABETH COCHRAN, 1864–1922). Reporter, *Pittsburgh
Dispatch* (1885–1887); Reporter, *New York World* (1887, 1893–1895);
Reporter, *Chicago Times-Herald* (1895); Reporter, *New York Evening
Journal* (1912–1922). Literary Works: *Ten Days in a Mad House* (1887);
Nellie Bly's Book: Around the World in Seventy-Two Days (1890).
NEIL MUNRO (1864–1930). Contributor, *London Globe* (1880s);
Contributor, *Falkirk Herald* (1880s); Journalist, *Scottish News* (1881–1893);
Journalist, *Greenock Advertiser* (1893); Journalist and editor, *Glasgow News*
and *Glasgow Evening News* (1918–1927). Literary works: *John Splendid*
(1898).
SUI SIN FAR (EDITH MAUDE EATON, 1865–1914). Contributor, *Land of
Sunshine* (1896–1900), *Overland* (1899), *Good Housekeeping* (1908–1910),
Westerner (1909–1910), *Independent* (1909–1912), *Delineator* (1910), *New
England Magazine* (1910–1912). Literary works: *Mrs. Spring Fragrance* (1912).
RUDYARD KIPLING (1865–1936). Reporter and writer, *Civil and Military
Gazette*, Lahore, India (1882–1889); Assistant editor and correspondent,
Pioneer, Allahabad, India (1887–1889); Associate editor and correspondent,
Friend, Bloemfontein, South Africa (1900). Literary works: *Plain Tales
from the Hills* (1888); *The Light That Failed* (1891); *The Jungle Book* (1894);
Captains Courageous (1897); *The Man Who Would Be King* (1898); *Stalky
and Company* (1899); *Kim* (1901); *Puck of Pook's Hill* (1906).
LINCOLN STEFFENS (1866–1936). Reporter and assistant city editor, *New
York Evening Post* (1892–1897); City editor, *New York Commercial
Advertiser* (1897–1901); Writer and editor, *McClure's* (1901–1906).
Literary works: *Moses in Red* (1926); *Autobiography of Lincoln Steffens*
(1931).

VIOLET HUNT (1866–1942). Writer and columnist, *Pall Mall Gazette* and other publications (1890s). Literary works: *A Hard Woman* (1895); *Affairs of the Heart* (1900).

GEORGE ADE (1866–1944). Reporter, *Lafayette* (IN) *Call* (1890); Reporter, *Chicago Record* (1893–1900). Literary works: *Fables in Slang* (1899).

H. G. WELLS (1866–1946). Founder and editor, *Science Schools Journal* (1888); Reviewer, *Saturday Review* (1895–1897). Literary works: *The Time Machine* (1895); *The Invisible Man* (1897); *The War of the Worlds* (1898); *A Short History of the World* (1922).

DAVID GRAHAM PHILLIPS (1867–1911). Reporter, *Cincinnati Times-Star* (1887); Reporter, *Cincinnati Commercial Gazette* (1887–1890); Reporter, *New York Sun* (1890–1893); Feature writer, investigative reporter, foreign correspondent, *New York World* (1893–1902). Literary works: *The Great God Success* (as John Graham, 1901).

ARNOLD BENNETT (1867–1931). Assistant editor and editor, *Woman* (1893–1900); Columnist, *New Age* (1908–1910); Director, *New Statesman* (1915). Literary works: *Riceyman Steps* (1923).

FINLEY PETER DUNNE (1867–1936). News writer, *Chicago Evening News* (1888); Political writer and city editor, *Chicago Times* (1888–1889); Reporter and Sunday editor, *Chicago Tribune* (1889–1891); Political writer and columnist, *Chicago Herald* (1891–1892); Managing editor and editorial page editor, *Chicago Journal* (1897–1900); Part-owner and editor, *New York Morning Telegraph* (1902–1904); Editor and writer, *Collier's Weekly* (1902–1919); Co-founder and contributor, *American Magazine* (1906–1913); Columnist, *Metropolitan Magazine* (1911). Literary works: *Observations by Mr. Dooley* (1902).

ELIZABETH JORDAN (1867–1947). Reporter, *New York World* (1890–1900); Editor, *Harper's Bazaar* (1900–1913). Literary works: *Tales of the City Room* (1898); *May Iverson's Career* (1914).

KATHARINE GLASIER (1867–1950). Columnist and editor, *Labour Leader* (1904–1909, 1916–1921). Literary works: *Husband and Brother* (as Katharine St. John Conway, 1894); *Aimee Furness, Scholar* (as Katharine St. John Conway, 1896).

LAURA INGALLS WILDER (1867–1957). Household editor and contributing editor, *Missouri Ruralist* (1911–1924). Literary works: *Little House on the Prairie* (1935).

WILLIAM ALLEN WHITE (1868–1944). Editor, *El Dorado* (KS) *Republican* (1890–1891); Reporter, *Kansas City Journal* (1891–1892); Reporter, *Kansas City Star* (1892–1895); Owner and editor, *Emporia* (KS) *Gazette* (1895–1944); Co-founder, *American Magazine* (1906). Literary works: *In Our Town* (1906).

W. E. B. DU BOIS (1868–1963). Founder and editor, *Moon Illustrated Weekly* (1905–1906); Founder and editor, *Horizon* magazine (1908–1910); Editor, *Crisis* magazine (1910–1934). Literary works: *The Souls of Black Folks* (1903); *The Quest of the Silver Fleece* (1911).

HUTCHINS HAPGOOD (1869–1944). Reporter and writer, *New York Commercial Advertiser* (1897–1900); Reporter and writer, *Chicago Evening Post* (beginning in 1904); Writer, *New York Globe* (1912–1913). Literary works: *The Spirit of the Ghetto* (1902); *Enemies* (play with Neith Boyer, 1916), *A Victorian in the Modern World* (1939).

EVELYN SHARP (1869–1955). Contributor, *Manchester Guardian* (1903–1933); Editor, *Votes for Women* (1912–1918). Literary works: *The Making of a Schoolgirl* (1897), *All the Way to Fairyland* (1898), *The Other Side of the Sun* (1900), *Rebel Women* (1910).

FRANK NORRIS (1870–1902). South African correspondent, *San Francisco Chronicle* (1895–1896); Copywriter, San Francisco *Wave* (1896–1898); War correspondent, S. S. McClure's Syndicate (1898–1899). Literary works: *Moran* (1898); *McTeague* (1899); *Blix* (1899); *The Octopus* (1901); *The Pit* (1903); *Vandover and the Brute* (1914); *The Best Short Stories of Frank Norris* (1998).

SAKI (H. H. MUNRO, 1870–1916). Political satirist, *Westminster Gazette* (1896–1902); Foreign correspondent, London *Morning Post* (1902–1908). Literary works: *The Toys of Peace, and Other Papers* (1919); *The Square Egg, and Other Sketches* (1924).

MIRIAM MICHELSON (1870–1942). Reporter, *San Francisco Call* (1890s). Literary works: *A Yellow Journalist* (1905); *In the Bishop's Carriage* (1913); *The Better Half* (1918).

RAY STANNARD BAKER (1870–1946). Reporter, *Chicago Record* (1892–1898); Reporter, *McClure's* (1898–1906); Reporter and Co-founder, *American Magazine* (1906–1915). Literary works: *Hempfield* (as David Grayson, 1915).

HILAIRE BELLOC (1870–1953). Co-founder, *Paternoster Review* (1889); Literary editor, London *Morning Post* (1905–1910), Editor, *Eye Witness* (1911–1912); Editor, *Land and Water* (1914–1920). Literary works: *The Path to Rome* (1902); *Mr. Petre* (1925).

STEPHEN CRANE (1871–1900). New Jersey correspondent, *New York Tribune* (1891–1892); Correspondent, *New York Herald* (1891–1894); Contributor, *New York Journal* (1896); War correspondent, *New York Press* (1896–1897); Greco-Turkish War correspondent, *New York Journal* (1897); Spanish-American War correspondent, *New York World* and *New York Journal* (1898). Literary works: *Maggie: A Girl of the Streets* (1893);

The Red Badge of Courage (1895); *The Open Boat, and Other Tales of Adventure* (1898); "The Blue Hotel" (1898); *Active Service* (1899); *Wounds in the Rain* (1900).

JAMES WELDON JOHNSON (1871–1938). Founder and co-editor, *Daily American*, Jacksonville, FL (1895–1896); Editorial writer, *New York Age* (1914–1924). Literary works: *The Autobiography of an Ex-Colored Man* (1912).

THEODORE DREISER (1871–1945). Reporter, Chicago *Globe* (1892); Reporter, St. Louis *Globe-Democrat* (1893); Reporter, St. Louis *Republic* (1893–1894); Reporter, *Toledo Blade* (1894); Reporter, Pittsburgh *Dispatch* (1894); Reporter, *New York World* (1895); Editor, *Ev'ry Month* magazine (1895–1897); Contributor, *Success* magazine (1898); Editor, *Smith's Magazine* (1905–1906); Editor, *Broadway Magazine* (1906–1907); Editor, *Delineator* magazine (1907–1910); Co-editor, *American Spectator* magazine (1932–1934). Literary works: *Sister Carrie* (1900); *Jennie Gerhardt* (1911); *The Titan* (1914); *The Genius* (1915); *Free and Other Stories* (1918); *A Book About Myself* (1922); *An American Tragedy* (1925); *Dawn* (1931); *Tragic America* (1931); *The Bulwark* (1946); *The Stoic* (1947).

PAUL LAURENCE DUNBAR (1872–1906). Editor, *Dayton Tatler* (1889–1990); Temporary editor, *Indianapolis World* (1895); Guest editor, *Chicago Tribune* (1903). Literary works: *The Sport of the Gods* (1902).

WILLA CATHER (1873–1947). Reporter, columnist, and reviewer, *Nebraska State Journal* (1893–1896); News editor and drama critic, Pittsburgh *Daily Leader* (1896–1901); Writer and managing editor, *McClure's* (1906–1911). Literary works: *O Pioneers!* (1913); *One of Ours* (1922); *Death Comes for the Archbishop* (1927).

WILL IRWIN (1873–1948). Sub-editor and editor, San Francisco *Wave* (1899–1900); Reporter and Sunday editor, *San Francisco Chronicle* (1900–1904); Reporter, *New York Sun* (1904–1906); Correspondent, *New York Tribune* (1915). Literary works: *Youth Rides West* (1925); *The Making of a Reporter* (1942).

G. K. CHESTERTON (1874–1936). Contributor, London *Daily News* (1901–1913); Contributor, *Illustrated London News* (1905–1936); Co-editor, *Eye Witness* (1911–1912); Editor, *New Witness* (1912–1923); Contributor, London *Daily Herald* (1913–1914); Editor, *G. K.'s Weekly* (1925–1936). Literary works: *The Napoleon of Notting Hill* (1904); *Orthodoxy* (1908); *The Ball and the Cross* (1909); *Tales of Long Bow* (1925); *The Return of Don Quixote* (1926).

ZONA GALE (1874–1938). Reporter, *Milwaukee Evening Wisconsin* (1895–1896); Reporter, *Milwaukee Journal* (1896–1901); Reporter, *New York Evening World* (1901–1903). Literary works: *Miss Lulu Bett* (1920).

THERESA MALKIEL (1874–1949). Reporter, *New York Call* (1909). Literary works: *The Diary of a Shirtwaist Striker* (1910).

ROBERT FROST (1874–1963). Reporter, Lawrence (MA) *Daily American* (1895). Literary works: *North of Boston* (poetry, 1914); *A Way Out* (play, 1929); *Stories for Lesley* (1984).

MARY HEATON VORSE (1874–1966). Contributor to *New Republic, McClure's, Harper's, Atlantic Monthly, Good Housekeeping, Woman's Home Companion* (1903–1912); Co-editor and contributor, *Masses* (1912–1917). Literary works: *Strike!* (1930).

ALICE DUNBAR-NELSON (1875–1935). Co-editor and writer, *A. M. E. Review* (1913–1914); Founder and co-editor, *Wilmington* (DE) *Advocate* (1920); Founder, co-editor and columnist, *Pittsburgh Courier* (1926, 1930); Columnist, *Washington Eagle* (1926–1930). Literary works: *The Goodness of St. Racque, and Other Stories* (1899).

JACK LONDON (1876–1916). Russo-Japanese War correspondent, Hearst Newspapers (1904); Mexican Revolution correspondent, *Collier's* (1914). Literary works: *The People of the Abyss* (1903); *The Call of the Wild* (1903); *The Sea-Wolf* (1904); *Martin Eden* (1909).

SHERWOOD ANDERSON (1876–1941). Contributor, *Agricultural Advertising* and *Reader* (1903–1904); Publisher and editor, *Commercial Democracy* (1907–1909); Editor, *Smyth County News* and *Marion Democrat*, Marion, VA (1927–1929); Co-founder, *American Spectator* (1932). Literary works: *Winesburg, Ohio* (1919); *Poor White* (1920); *Dark Laughter* (1925); *Puzzled America* (1935).

DON MARQUIS (1878–1937). Reporter, *Washington Times* (1900–1902); Copy desk editor, Philadelphia *North American* (1902); Associate editor, *Atlanta News* (1902–1904); Editorial writer, *Atlanta Journal* (1904–1907); Associate editor, *Uncle Remus' Home Magazine* (1907–1909); Reporter, *New York American* and *Brooklyn Daily Eagle* (1909–1912); Columnist, *New York Sun* (1912–1922), Columnist, *New York Tribune* (1922–1925). Literary works: *Danny's Own Story* (1912); *Carter, and Other People* (1921); *Archy and Mehitabel* (1927).

CARADOC EVANS (1878–1945). Editor, *Ideas* (1915–1917); Sub-editor, London *Daily Mail* (1917–1923); Acting editor, *T. P.'s Review* (1923–1929). Literary works: *My People* (1915); *My Neighbors* (1919); *Nothing to Pay* (1930).

H. L. MENCKEN (1878–1956). Reporter, Sunday editor, city editor, editor, *Baltimore Herald* (1899–1906); News editor, Baltimore *Evening News* (1906); Sunday editor, editor, columnist, and political correspondent, Baltimore *Sunpapers* (1906–1916, 1919–1941, 1948); Co-editor, *Smart Set* magazine (1914–1923); Creator and co-editor, *Parisienne* (1915); Creator and co-editor, *Saucy Stories* (1916); Columnist, New York *Evening Mail* (1917–1918); Creator and co-editor, *Black Mask* (1920); Co-founder and editor, *American Mercury* (1924–1933). Literary works: *A Book of Burlesques* (1916); *Newspaper Days* (1941); *Christmas Story* (1946).

CARL SANDBURG (1878–1967). Associate editor, *Lyceumite* (1906–1907); Reporter, *Milwaukee Journal, Milwaukee Daily News, Milwaukee Sentinel* (1909); Columnist and contributor, Milwaukee *Social Democratic Herald* (1911–1912); Reporter and columnist, *Milwaukee Leader* (1911–1912); Reporter, *Chicago Evening World* (1912); Associate editor, *System* magazine (1913); Editor, *American Artisan and Hardware Record* (1913–1914); Writer and reporter, *Day Book* (1913–1917); Editorial writer, *Chicago Evening American* (1917); Reporter, *Chicago Daily News* (1917–1932); War correspondent and news manager, Newspaper Enterprise Association (1918–1919). Literary works: *Chicago Poems* (poetry, 1916); *Rootabaga Pigeons* (1923); *Home Front Memo* (1943).

JOHN MASEFIELD (1878–1967). Literary editor, *Speaker* magazine (1903); Staff member, *Manchester Guardian* (1904–1905). Literary works: *Salt-Water Ballads* (poetry, 1902); *Tragedy of Nan* (play, 1908); *Sard Harker* (1924).

UPTON SINCLAIR (1878–1968). Contributor, *Army and Navy Weekly* (1897); Contributor (pulp fiction), Street and Smith publications (1897–1900); Columnist and contributor, *Appeal to Reason* (1904–1921); Editor and publisher, *Upton Sinclair's Magazine* (1918–1919). Literary works: *The Jungle* (1906).

WALLACE STEVENS (1879–1955). Reporter, *Reading* (PA) *Times* (1898); Reporter, *New York Tribune* (1900–1901). Literary works: *Three Travelers Watch a Sunrise* (play, 1916); *Harmonium* (poetry, 1923); *The Necessary Angel* (poetry, 1951).

JAMES BRANCH CABELL (1879–1958). Copy-editor, *Richmond* (VA) *Times* (1898); Harlem reporter, *New York Herald* (1899–1900); Reporter, *Richmond News* (1900–1901); Co-founder and contributor, *Reviewer* (1921–1924); Co-founder, *American Spectator* (1932). Literary works: *Jurgen* (1919).

E. M. FORSTER (1879–1970). Contributor, *Egyptian Mail* (1917–1918); Literary editor, *Daily Herald* (1920–1921). Literary works: *Alexandria* (1922); *A Passage to India* (1924).

DAMON RUNYON (1880–1946). Reporter and office assistant, *Pueblo* (CO) *Evening Press* (1895–1898); Sports reporter, *Pueblo Chieftan* (1900), *Colorado Springs Gazette* (1901), *Denver News* (1905), *Denver Post* (1905), and *San Francisco Post* (1906); Sports reporter, *Rocky Mountain*

News (1906–1910); Sports reporter, columnist, and war correspondent, *New York American* (1911–1934); Columnist and feature writer, King Features and International News Service (1918–1945); Film producer, RKO and Twentieth Century-Fox (1942–1943). Literary works: *Guys and Dolls* (1931).

FRANKLIN P. ADAMS (1881–1960). Columnist, *Chicago Journal* (1903–1904); Columnist, *New York Evening Mail* (1904–1913); Columnist, *New York Tribune* (1914–1921); Columnist, *New York World* (1922–1931); Columnist, *New York Herald Tribune* (1931–1937); Columnist, *New York Post* (1938–1941). Literary works: *Overset* (1922); *So There!* (1923).

P. G. WODEHOUSE (1881–1975). Columnist and contributor, *Globe* (1901–1909); Drama critic and contributor, *Vanity Fair* (1915–1919). Literary works: *Psmith, Journalist* (1915); *My Man Jeeves* (1919); *Showboat* (lyrics for musical, 1927).

VIRGINIA WOOLF (1882–1941). Reviewer, *Guardian* (1904–1906), *Times Literary Supplement* (1905–1935). Literary works: *Mrs. Dalloway* (1925).

SUSAN GLASPELL (1882–1948). Reporter, *Des Moines Daily News* and *Des Moines Capital* (1899–1901). Literary works: *The Visioning* (1911); *Alison's House* (play, 1930).

GEORGE JEAN NATHAN (1882–1958). Reporter, *New York Herald* (1905); Drama critic, *Outing* and *Bohemian* magazines (1906–1908); Theater critic, *Smart Set* (1909–1923); Co-founder, co-editor, theater critic and columnist, *American Mercury* (1924–1930); Co-founder, *American Spectator* (1932). Literary works: *The American Credo* (with H. L. Mencken, 1920).

ARTHUR RANSOME (1884–1967). War correspondent, London *Daily News* (1916–1919) and *Manchester Guardian* (1924–1934). Literary works: *Swallows and Amazons* (1930).

RING LARDNER (1885–1933). Reporter, *South Bend Times* (1905–1907); Sports reporter, *Chicago Inter-Ocean, Chicago Examiner, Chicago Tribune* (1907–1910); Mid-level editor, *Sporting News* (1910–1911); Sportswriter, *Boston American* (1911); Sportswriter, *Chicago American* (1911–1912); Sportswriter, *Chicago Examiner* (1912–1913); Columnist, *Chicago Tribune* (1913–1919); Writer, Bell Syndicate (1919–1927); Radio columnist, *New Yorker* (1932–1933). Literary works: *You Know Me Al* (1916); *The Love Nest, and Other Stories* (1926).

SINCLAIR LEWIS (1885–1951). Reporter, Oberlin (OH) *Herald* (1903); Night rewrite editor, New Haven (CT) *Journal Courier* (1904); Reporter, Waterloo (IA) *Daily Courier* (1908); Reporter, San Francisco *Evening Bulletin* (1909); Staffer, Associated Press, San Francisco (1909–1910); Assistant editor, *Adventure* magazine (1912); Columnist, *Newsweek* magazine (1937–1938);

Columnist, *Esquire* magazine (1945). Literary works: *Main Street* (1920); *Babbitt* (1922); *Elmer Gantry* (1927); *Arrowsmith* (1935); *It Can't Happen Here* (1935).

SOPHIE TREADWELL (1885–1970). Feature writer, *San Francisco Bulletin* (1908–1914); Foreign correspondent, *Harper's Weekly* (1915); Reporter, *New York American* and *New York Tribune* (1920s). Literary works: *Lusita* (1931); *One Fierce Hour and Sweet* (1959).

ANNA LOUISE STRONG (1885–1970). Journalist, *Advance* (1905–1906); Journalist, *Seattle Daily Call* (1918); Features editor and writer, *Seattle Union Record* (1918–1921); Foreign correspondent, *Hearst's International* (1921); Founder and contributor, *Moscow* (Russia) *Daily News* (1930–1932). Literary works: *Wild River* (1943).

JOHN REED (1887–1920). Contributor, correspondent, and sub-editor, *American Magazine*, *Masses*, *Metropolitan* magazine (1910–1920). Literary works: *Insurgent Mexico* (1914); *Tamberlaine* (poetry, 1917); *Ten Days that Shook the World* (1919).

ALEXANDER WOOLLCOTT (1887–1943). Reporter and drama critic, *New York Times* (1909–1922); Reporter, *Stars and Stripes* (1917–1918); Drama critic, *New York Herald* (1922–1925); Drama critic, *New York World* (1925–1928); Columnist, *New Yorker* (1928–1943). Literary works: *The Channel Road* (play with George Kaufman, 1929).

EDNA FERBER (1887–1968). Writer, *Appleton* (WI) *Daily Crescent* (1902–1904); Reporter, *Milwaukee Journal* (1905–1908); Political reporter, *Chicago Tribune* (1912). Literary works: *Dawn O'Hara* (1911); *The Royal Family* (play with George Kaufman, 1927); *Cimarron* (1930).

ROSE WILDER LANE (1887–1968). Reporter and feature writer, *San Francisco Bulletin* (1914–1918); Correspondent, *Woman's Day* (1965). Literary works: *Let the Hurricane Roar* (1933); *Free Land* (1938).

FLOYD DELL (1887–1969). Reporter, *Davenport* (IA) *Times* (1905); Reporter, *Tri-City Workers' Magazine* (1905); Reporter, *Davenport Democrat* (1906–1907); Writer and literary editor, *Chicago Evening Post* (1908–1913); Managing editor and contributor, *Masses* (1913–1917); Associate editor, *Liberator* (1918–early 1920s). Literary works: *Moon-Calf* (1920).

HEYWOOD BROUN (1888–1939). Reporter, *New York Morning Telegraph* (1910–1911); Reporter, *New York Sun* (1911); Copy-editor, sports writer, drama critic, and war correspondent, *New York Tribune* (1912–1921); Writer, *New York World* (1921–1928); Writer, *New York Telegram*, later *World-Telegram* (1928–1939); Founder and president, Newspaper Guild (1933–1939); Writer, *New York Post* (1939). Literary works: *The Boy Grew Older* (1922); *The Sun Field* (1923); *Gandle Follows His Nose* (1926).

EUGENE O'NEILL (1888–1953). Reporter, *New London* (CT) *Telegraph* (1912); Co-founder, *American Spectator* (1932). Literary works: *Ah, Wilderness!* (play, 1933).

RAYMOND CHANDLER (1888–1959). Reporter, London *Daily Express* and *Bristol Western Gazette* (1908–1912); Reporter, *Los Angeles Express* (1919). Literary works: *The Big Sleep* (1939).

ROBERT BENCHLEY (1889–1945). Reporter and desk editor, *New York Tribune* (1915–1918); Writer and managing editor, *Vanity Fair* magazine (1914–1921); Journalist, *Tribune Magazine* (1919–1920); Sub-editor and reviewer, *Life* magazine (1920–1929); Drama reviewer, *New Yorker* (1927–1940). Literary works: "The Treasurer's Report" (movie short, 1928); *The Benchley Roundup* (1954).

GEORGE S. KAUFMAN (1889–1961). Columnist, *Washington Times* (1912–1913); Columnist, *New York Evening Mail* (1914–1915); Theater reporter, *New York Tribune* (1915–1917); Theater critic, *New York Times* (1917–1930). Literary works: *Dulcy* (play with Marc Connelly, 1921); *The Royal Family* (play with Edna Ferber, 1927); *The Channel Road* (play with Alexander Woollcott, 1929).

HOWARD SPRING (1889–1965). Reporter, *South Wales Daily News* and *Yorkshire Observer* (1911–1915); Reporter, *Manchester Guardian* (1919–1931); Book critic, London *Evening Standard* (1931–1938). Literary works: *My Son, My Son!* (1938).

CONRAD AIKEN (1889–1973). American correspondent and columnist, *Athenaeum* and *London Mercury* (1916–1922); Reviewer for *New Republic*, *Chicago Daily News*, *North American Review*, *Criterion*, and other periodicals (1916–1958); Contributing editor, *Dial* (1917–1918); London correspondent, *New Yorker* (1934–1936). Literary works: *Earth Triumphant* (poetry, 1914); *Blue Voyage* (1927).

CHRISTOPHER MORLEY (1890–1957). Editor, *Ladies' Home Journal* (1917–1918); Columnist, *Philadelphia Evening Public Ledger* (1918–1920); Columnist, *New York Evening Post* (1920–1924); Contributing editor, *Saturday Review of Literature* (1924–1941). Literary works: *Parnassus* (1917).

CONRAD RICHTER (1890–1968). Reporter, *Johnstown* (PA) *Journal* (1910); Editor, *Patton* (PA) *Daily Courier* (1910); Reporter, *Pittsburgh Dispatch* (1911); Sports reporter, *Johnstown Leader* (1911–1912). Literary works: *The Trees* (1940); *The Fields* (1946); *The Town* (1950).

JOSEPHINE LAWRENCE (1890–1978). Staff writer and editor of Household department, *Newark Sunday Call* (1915–1946); Columnist and women's page editor, *Newark Sunday News* (1946–1970). Literary works: *Head of the Family* (1932).

KATHERINE ANNE PORTER (1890–1980). Reporter, *Rocky Mountain News* (1918–1919). Literary works: *Ship of Fools* (1962).

MARC CONNELLY (1890–1980). Reporter, *Pittsburgh Press and Gazette Times* (1908–1916); Reporter, *New York Morning Telegraph* (1916–1921). Literary works: *A Souvenir from Qam* (1965); *Dulcy* (play with George Kaufman, 1921).

ZORA NEALE HURSTON (1891–1960). Reporter, *Pittsburgh Courier* (1952); Journalist, *Fort Pierce* (FL) *Chronicle* (1957–1959). Literary works: *Their Eyes Were Watching God* (1937).

HENRY MILLER (1891–1980). Proofreader, *Chicago Tribune*, Paris edition (1932); Co-editor, *Booster* (later *Delta*) magazine (1937–1938); European editor, *Phoenix* (1938–1939); Continental editor, *Volontes* (1938–1939). Literary works: *Tropic of Cancer* (1934).

AGNES SMEDLEY (1892–1950). Correspondent, *Frankfurter Zeitung* (1928–1932); Contributor, *Asia, New Republic, Nation, New Masses, Vogue, Life, New York Call, Birth Control Review* (1920s and 1930s). Literary works: *Daughter of Earth* (1929).

JOSEPHINE HERBST (1892–1969). Staffer, *Smart Set* (as Carlotta Greet, early 1920s); Writer, *American Mercury* (1920s and 1930s); Writer, *Scribner's* (early 1930s); Writer, *New Masses* (1930s); Correspondent, *New York Post* (1935). Literary works: *Rope of Gold* (1939).

JAMES M. CAIN (1892–1977). Journalist and writer, *Baltimore American* (1917–1918); Reporter, Baltimore *Sun* (1919–1923); Editorial writer, *New York World* (1924–1931); Managing editor, *New Yorker* (1931). Literary works: *The Postman Always Rings Twice* (1934); *The Embezzler* (1944).

HUGH MACDIARMID (C. M. GRIEVE, 1892–1978). Reporter, *Montrose Review* (1920–1929); Journalist, *Vox* (1929); Staffer, *Unicorn Press* (1941–1943). Literary works: *Annals of the Five Senses* (poetry, 1923); *Some Day* (play, 1923).

ARCHIBALD MACLEISH (1892–1982). Associate editor, *New Republic* (1920); Staff member, *Fortune* (1929–1938). Literary works: *Streets in the Moon* (poetry, 1926); *J. B.* (play, 1958).

DJUNA BARNES (1892–1982). Reporter, *Brooklyn Eagle* (1913); Contributor, *Munsey's, Dial, Vanity Fair, New Republic, New Yorker, Smart Set* (1913–1931). Literary works: *Ryder* (1928); *Nightwood* (1936).

REBECCA WEST (CICELY ISABEL FAIRFIELD, 1892–1983). Reviewer, *Freewoman* and *New Freewoman* (1911–1912); Contributor and staff member, *Clarion* (1912–1914); World War II war trials correspondent, London *Daily Telegraph* and *New Yorker* (1946–1947); Correspondent, House Un-American Activities committee, *Sunday Times* of London and

U.S. News and World Report (1954); South African correspondent, *Sunday Times* (1960). Literary works: *The Return of the Soldier* (1918); *The Meaning of Treason* (1947).

JOHN P. MARQUAND (1893–1960). Reporter, *Boston Transcript* (1916); Feature writer, *New York Herald Tribune* (1919–1920). Literary works: *The Late George Apley* (1937).

DOROTHY PARKER (1893–1967). Editorial staffer, *Vogue* (1916–1917); Editorial staffer, *Vanity Fair* (1917–1920); Reviewer, *New Yorker* (1925–1927). Literary works: *Laments for the Living* (1930).

VERA BRITTAIN (1893–1970). Contributor, *Time and Tide* (1922–1928); Contributor, *Yorkshire Post, Manchester Guardian* (late 1920s and 1930s). Literary works: *The Dark Tide* (1923); *Testament of Youth* (1933); *Testament of Friendship* (1940).

JAMES THURBER (1894–1961). Reporter and columnist, *Columbus Dispatch* (1921–1924); Reporter, Paris edition, *Chicago Tribune* (1925–1926); Reporter, *New York Evening Post* (1926); Writer, sub-editor, *New Yorker* (1927–1961). Literary works: *Is Sex Necessary?* (with E. B. White, 1929); *My Life and Hard Times* (1933); *The Last Flower* (1939); *The Years with Ross* (1959).

DOROTHY THOMPSON (1894–1961). Correspondent, International News Service, *New York Post, Philadelphia Public Ledger, Christian Science Monitor* (1920–1924); Berlin correspondent, *Philadelphia Public Ledger* (1924–1928). Literary works: *I Saw Hitler!* (1932); *Concerning Vermont* (1937).

ALDOUS HUXLEY (1894–1963). Staff member, *Athenaeum* (1919); Staff member, Conde Nast publications (1919–1923); Drama critic and staff member, *Westminster Gazette* (1920–1924). Literary works: *Brave New World* (1932); *The Doors of Perception* (1954); *Island* (1962).

BEN HECHT (1894–1964). Reporter, *Chicago Journal* (1910–1914); Reporter, columnist, *Chicago Daily News* (1914–1923); Publisher, *Chicago Literary Times* (1923–1924). Literary works: *Erik Dorn* (1921); *Front Page* (play with Charles MacArthur, 1928).

CHARLOTTE HALDANE (1894–1969). Social editor and reporter, *Daily Express* (1921–1926); Editor and contributor, *Women's Day* (1939–1940); Producer, BBC (1943–1950s). Literary works: *Man's World* (1926).

J. B. PRIESTLEY (1894–1984). Columnist, *Bradford Pioneer* (1913); Contributor, *Yorkshire Observer* (1919); Theater reviewer, London *Daily News* (1923); Broadcaster, BBC (1940–1944); Columnist, *New Statesman* (1956–1960). Literary works: *The Good Companions* (1929); *Dangerous Corner* (play, 1932); *English Journey* (1934); *The Image Men* (1969).

CHARLES MACARTHUR (1895–1956). Reporter, *Oak Leaves*, Oak Park, IL (1915); Reporter, City Press news service (1916); Reporter, *Chicago*

Herald-Examiner (1919–1921); Reporter, *Chicago Tribune* (1921–1924); Reporter, *New York American* (1924–1927). Literary works: *Front Page* (play with Ben Hecht, 1928); *Johnny on a Spot* (play, 1942).

EDMUND WILSON (1895–1972). Reporter, *New York Evening Sun* (1916–1917); Managing editor, *Vanity Fair* (1920–1921); Associate editor and drama critic, *New Republic* (1926–1931); Book reviewer, *New Yorker* (1944–1948). Literary works: *Memoirs of Hecate County* (1946).

GEORGE SAMUEL SCHUYLER (1895–1977). Associate editor, *Messenger* (1923–1928); Columnist, editorial writer, associate editor, and foreign correspondent, *Pittsburgh Courier* (1924–1966); Special correspondent, *New York Evening Post* (1931); Correspondent and national news editor, *New York Evening Post* (1931–1972); Editor, *National News* (1932); Editor, *Review of the News* (1967–1977). Literary works: *Black No More* (1931).

ROBERT SHERWOOD (1896–1955). Drama critic, *Vanity Fair* (1919–1920); Movie critic and subeditor, *Life* (1920–1928); Literary editor, *Scribner's* (1928–1930). Literary works: *Abe Lincoln in Illinois* (play, 1940).

JOHN DOS PASSOS (1896–1970). Co-founder and contributor, *New Masses* (1926–1934); Contributor, *New Republic, Common Sense* (late 1920s–early 1930s); Overseas correspondent, *Life* (1932, 1945, 1948). Literary works: *Three Soldiers* (1921); *Manhattan Transfer* (1925); *Orient Express* (1927); *The 42nd Parallel* (1930); *1919* (1932); *The Big Money* (1936).

HORACE MCCOY (1897–1955). Reporter and columnist, *Dallas Dispatch* (1919–1920); Reporter and sports editor, *Dallas Journal* (1920–1929); Contributor and editor, *Dallasite* (1929–1930). Literary works: *They Shoot Horses, Don't They?* (1935); *No Pockets in a Shroud* (1937).

DOROTHY DAY (1897–1980). Reporter and columnist, *New York Call* (1916–1917); Assistant editor and writer, *Masses* (1917); Writer and editor, *Liberator* (1921–1923); Writer, *New Orleans Item* (1923–1924); Founder, publisher, and columnist, *Catholic World* (1933–1980). Literary works: *The Eleventh Virgin* (1924).

MYRA PAGE (DOROTHY MARKEY, 1897–1993). Writer, *Daily Worker, New Masses, Working Woman, Southern Worker* (1930s and beyond). Literary works: *Gathering Storm* (1932); *Moscow Yankee* (1935).

WINIFRED HOLTBY (1898–1935). Contributor and director, *Time and Tide* (1924–1935); Literary critic, *Good Housekeeping* (1933–1935). Literary works: *The Crowded Street* (1924); *South Riding* (1936).

HART CRANE (1899–1932). Reporter, *Cleveland Plain Dealer* (1919); Reporter, *Fortune* (1930–1931). Literary works: *The Bridge* (poetry, 1930).

ERNEST HEMINGWAY (1899–1961). Reporter, *Kansas City Star* (1917–1918); Reporter and European correspondent, *Toronto Star* (1920–1924);

Correspondent covering Spanish Civil War for North American Newspaper Alliance (1937–1938); War correspondent in China (1941) and Europe (1944–1945). Literary works: *In Our Time* (1925); *The Sun Also Rises* (1926); *A Farewell to Arms* (1929); *Green Hills of Africa* (1935); *For Whom the Bell Tolls* (1940); *The Old Man and the Sea* (1952); *A Moveable Feast* (1964); *By-line, Ernest Hemingway* (1967).

C. S. FORESTER (1899–1966). Spanish Civil War and European correspondent, *New York Times* (1937–1940). Literary works: *The Voyage of the Annie Marble* (1929); *The African Queen* (1935).

E. B. WHITE (1899–1985). Reporter, United Press and American Legion News Service (1921); Reporter and columnist, *Seattle Times* (1922–1923); Writer and sub-editor, *New Yorker* (1926–1985); Columnist, *Harper's* (1938–1943). Literary works: *Is Sex Necessary?* (with James Thurber, 1929); *Stuart Little* (1945); *Charlotte's Web* (1952); *The Second Tree from the Corner* (1954).

MARGARET MITCHELL (1900–1949). Reporter and columnist, *Atlanta Journal* (1922–1926). Literary works: *Gone with the Wind* (1936).

JAMES HILTON (1900–1954). Columnist and reviewer, *Irish Independent* and London *Daily Telegraph* (1921–1932). Literary works: *Lost Horizon* (1933); *Good-bye Mr. Chips* (1934).

MERIDEL LE SUEUR (1900–1996). Journalist, *Daily Worker* (mid-1920s); Contributor, *New Masses* (mid 1920s–early 1940s); Founder and co-editor, *Midwest Magazine* (mid 1930s). Literary works: *Salute to Spring and Other Stories* (1940); *Women in Breadlines* (1977); *The Girl* (1979); *I Hear Men Talking and Other Stories* (1984); *Harvest Song* (1990); *The Dread Road* (1991).

V. S. PRITCHETT (1900–1997). Writer, *Christian Science Monitor* (1923–1926); Literary critic, *New Statesman, Nation* (1926–1965). Literary works: *Marching Spain* (1928); *The Spanish Virgin and Other Stories* (1930); *Nothing Like Leather* (1935); *Dead Man Leading* (1937); *On the Edge of the Cliff* (1979); *A Careless Widow and Other Stories* (1989).

JOHN GUNTHER (1901–1970). Reporter, European and Near East correspondent, *Chicago Daily News* (1922, 1924–1936); Asian correspondent, North American Newspaper Alliance (1937–1939); European correspondent, NBC (1939); Correspondent in Europe, Latin America, US, *Look* magazine (1940–1941, 1943–1945); Writer, *New York Herald Tribune* (1948, 1950). Literary works: *Inside Europe* (1936); *The Lost City* (1964).

LANGSTON HUGHES (1902–1967). Contributor, *Crisis* (1921–1969); Madrid correspondent, *Baltimore Afro-American* (1937); Columnist, *Chicago Defender*, Associated Negro Press, *New York Post* (1942–1965).

Literary works: *Not Without Laughter* (1930); *The Ways of White Folks* (1934); *Shakespeare in Harlem* (1942); *The Best of Simple* (1961); *Simple's Uncle Sam* (1965).

JOHN STEINBECK (1902–1968). Reporter, *New York American* (1926); World War II correspondent in North Africa and Italy, *New York Herald Tribune* (1943); Correspondent, *Saturday Review* (1952–1969); Correspondent, *Louisville Courier-Journal* (1956–1960); Vietnam War correspondent, *Newsday* (1966–1967). Literary works: *Tortilla Flat* (1935); *In Dubious Battle* (1936); *Of Mice and Men* (1937); *The Grapes of Wrath* (1939); *The Sea of Cortez* (with Edward F. Ricketts, 1941); *Cannery Row* (1945); *East of Eden* (1952); *Travels with Charley* (1962).

GEORGE ORWELL (ERIC BLAIR, 1903–1950). Producer, BBC (1941–1943); Literary editor and columnist, *Tribune* of London (1943–1947); World War II correspondent, London *Observer* (1945). Literary works: *Down and Out in Paris and London* (1933); *Burmese Days* (1934); *Homage to Catalonia* (1938); *The Lion and the Unicorn* (1941); *Animal Farm* (1945); *1984* (1949).

EVELYN WAUGH (1903–1966). Reporter, London *Daily Express* (1927); Foreign correspondent, London *Daily Express, Graphic,* and *The Times* of London (1930); Foreign correspondent, London *Daily Mail* (1935–1936, 1961–1962); Foreign correspondent, London *Daily Telegraph* (1947). Literary works: *Scoop* (1938); *Robbery Under Law* (1939); *Brideshead Revisited* (1945); *The Loved One* (1948).

JAMES GOULD COZZENS (1903–1978). Associate editor, *Fortune* (1938). Literary works: *Guard of Honor* (1948).

ERSKINE CALDWELL (1903–1987). Reporter, *Jefferson* (GA) *Reporter* (1921); Sports reporter, *Augusta* (GA) *Chronicle* (1921); Reporter, *Atlanta Journal* (1925–1926); Book reviewer, *Charlotte Observer, Houston Post,* and *Atlanta Journal* (1926); War correspondent, *Life, PM,* and CBS (1932); Investigative reporter, *New York Post, Daily Worker, Fortune* (1934–1935); Owner of four South Carolina newspapers, *Allendale Citizen, Hampton County Guardian, Jasper County Record, Beaufort Times* (1943–1944). Literary works: *Tobacco Road* (1932); *God's Little Acre* (1933); *Journeyman* (1935); *You Have Seen Their Faces* (with Margaret Bourke-White, 1937); *Trouble in July* (1940).

MALCOLM MUGGERIDGE (1903–1990). Staff member and foreign correspondent, *Manchester Guardian* (1930–1932); Assistant editor, *Calcutta Statesman* (1934–1935); Staff member, London *Evening Standard* (1935–1936); Washington, DC correspondent and deputy editor, London *Daily Telegraph* (1946–1947, 1950–1952); Editor, *Punch*

(1953–1957). Literary works: *Picture Palace* (1934, 1987); *Winter in Moscow* (1934).

A. J. LIEBLING (1904–1963). Sports reporter, *New York Times* (1925–1926); Sports reporter, *Providence Journal and Evening Bulletin* (1926–1930); Reporter, *New York World* (1930–1931); Feature writer, *New York World-Telegram* and *Journal* (1931–1935); Staff writer, *New Yorker* (1935–1963). Literary works: *The Earl of Louisiana* (1961); *The Press* (1961).

JAMES T. FARRELL (1904–1979). Contributor and Drama critic, *Partisan Review* and *Partisan Review and Anvil* (1934–1936); Columnist, *Socialist Call* (1936–1937); Syndicated editorial writer, Alburn Bureau of Minneapolis (1956–1958). Literary works: *Studs Lonigan: A Trilogy* (1935).

S. J. PERELMAN (1904–1979). Writer, *Judge* magazine (1925–1929); Writer, *College Humor* magazine (1929–1979); Writer, *New Yorker* and other magazines (1929–1979). Literary works: *Parlor, Bedlam and Bath* (with Quentin Reynolds, 1930); *One Touch of Venus* (play with Ogden Nash, 1943).

GRAHAM GREENE (1904–1991). Writer and sub-editor, *The Times* of London (1926–1930); Film critic, *Night and Day* magazine (1937); Indochina correspondent, *New Republic* (1954). Literary works: *Brighton Rock* (1938); *Lawless Roads* (1939); *The Power and the Glory* (1940); *The Heart of the Matter* (1948); *The End of the Affair* (1951); *The Quiet American* (1955); *A Burnt-Out Case* (1961); *The Comedians* (1966).

WILLIAM L. SHIRER (1904–1993). European correspondent, *Chicago Tribune* (1925–1932); European correspondent, *New York Herald* (1934); Correspondent, CBS radio (1935–1947); Columnist, *New York Herald Tribune* (1942–1948); Commentator and writer, Mutual Broadcasting System (1947–1993). Literary works: *The Traitor* (1950); *The Rise and Fall of the Third Reich* (1960).

TESS SLESINGER (1905–1945). Assistant editor, *Menorah Journal* (1928–1932); Book reviewer, *New York Post* (1920s). Literary works: *The Unpossessed* (1934); *Time: The Present* (1935).

JOHN O'HARA (1905–1970). Reporter, *Pottsville (PA) Journal* (1924–1926); Reporter, *New York Herald Tribune* (1928); Writer, *Time* (1928); Contributor, *New Yorker* (1928–1967); Managing editor, *Pittsburgh Bulletin-Index* (1933). Literary works: *Appointment in Samarra* (1934); *Butterfield 8* (1935); *Hope of Heaven* (1938).

RICHARD WRIGHT (1908–1960). Contributor, *New Masses* (1934–1941); Co-founder and contributor, *New Challenge* magazine (1937); Editor, Harlem bureau, *Daily Worker* (1937–1938). Literary works: *Native Son* (1940); *Black Boy* (1945); *Pagan Spain* (1957).

IAN FLEMING (1908–1964). Moscow correspondent, Reuters (1929–1933); Reporter, *The Times* of London (1939); Foreign news service manager, Kemsley/Thomson Newspapers (1945–1959). Literary works: *From Russia, with Love* (1957).

JOSEPH MITCHELL (1908–1996). Reporter, *New York World* (1929–1930); Reporter, *New York Herald-Tribune* (1930–1931); Reporter, *New York World-Telegram* (1931–1938); Staff writer, *New Yorker* (1938–1996). Literary works: *Old Mr. Flood* (1948); *Joe Gould's Secret* (1965).

MARTHA GELLHORN (1908–1998). Staffer, *New Republic* (1927–1936); War correspondent, *Collier's* (1937–1946); War correspondent, *Guardian* (1966–1967). Literary works: *Liana* (1944); *The Wine of Astonishment* (1948); *The Face of War* (1959); *The Weather in Africa* (1978); *The View from the Ground* (1986).

WILLIAM MAXWELL (1908–2000). Staff writer, *New Yorker* (1936–1976). Literary works: *The Folded Leaf* (1945); *So Long, See You Tomorrow* (1980).

JAMES AGEE (1909–1955). Reporter, *Fortune* (1932–1937); Reviewer and reporter, *Time* (1939–1948); Columnist and writer, *Nation* (1942–1948). Literary works: *Let Us Now Praise Famous Men* (1941); *A Death in the Family* (1957).

NELSON ALGREN (1909–1981). Co-editor, *New Anvil* (1939–1941); Writer for *Esquire* and other magazines (1941–1981); Columnist, *Chicago Free Press* (1970). Literary works: *Somebody in Boots* (1935); *Never Come Morning* (1942); *The Man with the Golden Arm* (1949); *Notes from a Sea Diary* (1965).

EUDORA WELTY (1909–2001). Reporter, *Jackson* (MS) *Daily News* (1930); Society page correspondent, *Memphis Commercial Appeal* (1933–1935); Staffer and contributor, *Southern Review* (1934–1939). Literary works: *Losing Battles* (1970); *The Optimist's Daughter* (1972).

PETER DE VRIES (1910–1993). Editor, community newspaper, Chicago, IL (1931); Staff member, *New Yorker* (1944–1987). Literary works: *Comfort Me with Apples* (1956); *The Tents of Wickedness* (1959).

RUTH MCKENNEY (1911–1972). Reporter, *Akron Beacon-Journal* (1932–1933); Feature writer, *New York Post* (1934–1936). Literary works: *My Sister Eileen* (1938); *Industrial Valley* (1943); *Jake Home* (1943).

MARY MCCARTHY (1912–1989). Reviewer, *New Republic* (1933–1934); Reviewer, *Nation* (1933–1937); Editor and Drama critic, *Partisan Review* (1937–1962). Literary works: *The Group* (1963); *Medina* (1972).

STUDS TERKEL (1912–). Host, Wax Museum, WFMT-Radio, Chicago (1945–1991); Moderator, TV program, *Stud's Place* (1950–1953). Literary works: *Working* (1974); *Talking to Myself* (1977); *The Good War* (1984).

DYLAN THOMAS (1914–1953). Reporter, *South Wales Daily Post* (1931–1932); Reviewer, *Herald of Wales* (1931–1932). Literary works: *Portrait of the Artist as a Young Dog* (1940); *Under Milk Wood* (play, 1954); *Adventures in the Skin Trade, and Other Stories* (1955).

JOHN HERSEY (1914–1993). Writer, sub-editor, overseas correspondent, *Time* (1937–1944); Correspondent and sub-editor, *Life* (1944–1945); Writer, *New Yorker* (1945–1993). Literary works: *A Bell for Adano* (1944); *Hiroshima* (1946).

W.C. HEINZ (1915–2008). Copy aide, reporter, feature writer, war correspondent, sports columnist, *New York Sun* (1937–1950). Literary works: *The Professional* (1958); *The Surgeon* (1963).

MARY LEE SETTLE (1918–2005). Assistant editor, *Harper's Bazaar* (1945); Correspondent, *Flair* magazine (1950–1951). Literary works: *The Love Eaters* (1954); *The Kiss of Kin* (1955); *Prisons* (1973); *Blood Tie* (1977); *The Scapegoat* (1980); *The Killing Ground* (1982).

CHARLES BUKOWSKI (1920–1994). Columnist, *Open City* and *LA Free Press* (mid-1950s to mid-1970s). Literary works: *Post Office* (1971); *Hot Water Music* (1983).

DICK FRANCIS (1920–). Racing correspondent, London *Sunday Express* (1957–1973). Literary works: *For Kicks* (1965).

JACK KEROUAC (1922–1969). Sports reporter, Lowell (MA) *Sun* (1942). Literary works: *On the Road* (1957); *The Dharma Bums* (1958).

KURT VONNEGUT, JR. (1922–2007). Police reporter, Chicago City News Bureau, Chicago, IL (1946–1947). Literary works: *Cat's Cradle* (1963); *Slaughterhouse-Five* (1969).

BRENDAN BEHAN (1923–1964). Broadcaster, Radio Eireamm (1951–1953); Columnist, *Irish Press* (1954–1955). Literary works: *The Hostage* (play, 1958); *The Scarperer* (1964).

NORMAN MAILER (1923–2007). Co-founding editor and columnist, *Village Voice* (1955–1956). Literary works: *The Naked and the Dead* (1948); *An American Dream* (1964); *Why Are We in Vietnam?* (1967); *Miami and the Siege of Chicago* (1968); *The Armies of the Night* (1968); *The Executioner's Song* (1979).

TRUMAN CAPOTE (1924–1984). Office assistant, *New Yorker* (1943–1944); Writer, *New Yorker* (1955–1979). Literary works: *Other Voices, Other Rooms* (1948); *Breakfast at Tiffany's* (1958); *In Cold Blood* (1966).

ART BUCHWALD (1925–2007). Columnist, *New York Herald Tribune*, Paris edition (1949–1952); Columnist, *New York Herald Tribune* and *Los Angeles Times* syndicates (1952–2007). Literary works: *A Gift from the Boys* (1958).

GORE VIDAL (1925–). Contributor to *Esquire*, *New York Review of Books*, *New Statesman* (1964–2003). Literary works: *Myra Breckinridge* (1968); *Burr* (1974).

RUSSELL BAKER (1925–). Reporter, foreign correspondent, and London bureau chief, Baltimore *Sun* (1947–1953); Columnist and reporter in Washington, DC bureau, *New York Times* (1954–1962). Literary works: *Our Next President* (1968); *The Upside-Down Man* (1977); *Growing Up* (1982).

TONY HILLERMAN (1925–). Reporter, *Borger* (TX) *News Herald* (1948); City editor, Lawton (OK) *Morning Press-Constitution* (1948–1950); Political reporter, United Press International, Oklahoma City, OK (1950–1952); Bureau manager, UPI, Santa Fe, NM (1952–1954); Political reporter and executive editor, Santa Fe *New Mexican* (1954–1963). Literary works: *The Fly on the Wall* (1971); *A Thief of Time* (1988).

GEORGE PLIMPTON (1927–2003). Editor and contributor, *Paris Review* (1953–2003); Associate editor, *Horizon* (1959–1961); Contributing editor, *Sports Illustrated* (1967–1994); Associate editor and contributor, *Harper's* (1972–1994). Literary works: *Paper Lion* (1966); *The Curious Case of Sidd Finch* (1987).

LILLIAN ROSS (1927–). Staff writer, *New Yorker* (1949–present). Literary works: *Picture* (1952); *Vertical and Horizontal* (1963).

ROGER KAHN (1927–). Reporter and sportswriter, *New York Herald Tribune* (1948–1955); Writer, *Sports Illustrated* (1955); Sports editor, *Newsweek* (1956–1960); Editor-at-large, *Saturday Evening Post* (1963–1969). Literary works: *The Boys of Summer* (1972); *But Not to Keep* (1979); *The Seventh Game* (1982).

RICHARD VASQUEZ (1928–1990). Reporter, *Santa Monica* (CA) *Independent* (1959–1960); Reporter, *San Gabriel* (CA) *Valley Daily Tribune* (1960–1965); Feature writer, *Los Angeles Times* (1970–1981). Literary works: *Chicano* (1972); *The Giant Killer* (1978); *Another Land* (1982).

MAYA ANGELOU (1928–). Writer, *Ghanian Times* and Ghanian Broadcasting Corp. (1963–1966); Features editor, *African Review* (1964–1966). Literary works: *I Know Why the Caged Bird Sings* (1970); *Still I Rise* (poetry, 1978).

WILLIAM KENNEDY (1928–). Columnist, Glen Falls (NY) *Post Star* (1949–1950); Reporter and writer, Albany *Times-Union* (1952–1956, 1963–1970); Assistant managing editor and columnist, *Puerto Rico World Journal* (1956); Correspondent, Time-Life publications (1957–1959); Managing editor, San Juan (Puerto Rico) *Star* (1959–1961); Book editor, *Look* (1971). Literary works: *The Ink Truck* (1969); *Ironweed* (1984).

ELIE WIESEL (1928–). Correspondent, *L'Arche* (Paris, France, 1949–1952), *Yedioth Ahronoth* (Tel Aviv, Israel, 1952–1956), and *Jewish Daily Forward* (1957–today). Literary works: *Night* (1958); *Dawn* (1961); *The Accident* (1962).

PETER MAAS (1929–2001). European reporter, *New York Herald Tribune* (1951–1955); Reporter, *Collier's* (1955–1956); Senior editor, *Look* (1959–1962); Senior editor, *Saturday Evening Post* (1963–1966). Literary works: *King of the Gypsies* (1975); *Made in America* (1979).

LARRY L. KING (1929–). Newspaper reporter in Hobbs, NM (1949), Midland, TX (1950–1951), Odessa, TX (1952–1954); Radio news director, KCRS, Midland, TX (1951–1952); Editor, *Capitol Hill* magazine (1965). Literary works: *The One-Eyed Man* (1966); *Confessions of a White Racist* (1971); *The Old Man and Lesser Mortals* (1974); *The Best Little Whorehouse in Texas* (play with Peter Masterson, 1977).

KEITH WATERHOUSE (1929–). Writer and columnist, London *Daily Mirror* (1951–1986); Columnist, London *Daily Mail* (1986–today). Literary works: *Billy Liar* (1959); *Jubb* (1964).

GLORIA EMERSON (1930–2004). Women's page reporter, *New York Times* (1957–1960); Foreign correspondent, *New York Times* (1964–1972). Literary works: *Winners and Losers* (1976); *Loving Graham Greene* (2000).

JIMMY BRESLIN (1930–). Sportswriter, New York *Journal American* (1950–1963); Sportswriter and columnist, *New York Herald Tribune* (1963–1967); Columnist, *New York Post* (1968–1969); Columnist, *New York Daily News* (1978–1988); Columnist, *New York Newsday* (1988–1995). Literary works: *The Gang That Couldn't Shoot Straight* (1969); *.44* (with Dick Schaap, 1978).

DONALD BARTHELME (1931–1989). Reporter, *Houston Post* (1951–1953). Literary works: *Snow White* (1967).

TOM WOLFE (1931–). Writer and reporter, *Springfield* (MA) *Union* (1956–1959); Reporter and Latin American correspondent, *Washington Post* (1959–1962); Reporter, writer, and contributing editor, *New York Herald Tribune* (1962–1966); Writer, *New York World Journal Tribune* (1966–1967); Contributing editor, *Esquire* (1977–present); Contributing writer, *Harper's* (1978–1981). Literary works: *The Electric Kool-Aid Acid Test* (1968); *The Bonfire of the Vanities* (1987); *I am Charlotte Simmons* (2004).

JOHN MCPHEE (1931–). Associate editor, *Time* (1957–1964); Staff writer, *New Yorker* (1965–today). Literary works: *Coming into the Country* (1977).

MIKE ROYKO (1932–1997). Reporter, Chicago North Side Newspapers (1956); Reporter and mid-level editor, Chicago City News Bureau (1956–1959); Reporter, columnist, and associate editor, *Chicago Daily News*

(1959–1978); Columnist, *Chicago Sun-Times* (1978–1984); Columnist, *Chicago Tribune* (1984–1997). Literary works: *Boss* (1971).

GAY TALESE (1932–). Writer, *New York Times* (1953–1965). Literary works: *The Kingdom and the Power* (1969).

DAN WAKEFIELD (1932–). Staff writer, *Nation* (1956–1959); Contributing editor, *Atlantic Monthly* (1968–1980). Literary works: *Island in the City* (1959); *Going All the Way* (1970).

JOHN UPDIKE (1932–). Reporter-writer, *New Yorker* (1955–1957). Literary works: *Rabbit, Run* (1960).

DORIS BETTS (1932–). Journalist, *Statesville* (NC) *Daily Record* (1950–1951); Journalist, *Chapel Hill* (NC) *Weekly and News-Leader* (1953–1954); Journalist, *Sanford* (NC) *News Leader* (1956–1957); Journalist, *North Carolina Democrat*, Raleigh, NC (1960–1962); Editor, *Sanford News Leader* (1962). Literary works: *The River to Pickle Beach* (1972); *Beasts of the Southern Wild and Other Stories* (1973).

MICHAEL FRAYN (1933–). Reporter and columnist, *Manchester Guardian* (1957–1959); Columnist, London *Observer* (1962–1968). Literary works: *The Russian Interpreter* (1966); *Noises Off* (play, 1982); *Headlong* (1999); *Spies* (2002).

WILLIE MORRIS (1934–1999). Editor-in-chief, *Texas Observer* (1960–1962); Editor and Executive editor, *Harper's* (1963–1971). Literary works: *North Toward Home* (1967); *Yazoo* (1971); *Last of the Southern Girls* (1973); *Terrains of the Heart* (1981).

DAVID HALBERSTAM (1934–2007). Reporter, West Point *Daily Times Leader* (1955–1956); Reporter, *Nashville Tennessean* (1956–1960); Reporter and foreign correspondent, *New York Times* (1960–1967); Contributing editor, *Harper's* (1967–1971). Literary works: *One Very Hot Day* (1968); *The Best and the Brightest* (1972).

JOAN DIDION (1934–). Writer, *Vogue* (1956–1963). Literary works: *Slouching Towards Bethlehem* (1968); *Play It as It Lays* (1970).

GLORIA STEINEM (1934–). Contributing editor, *Glamour* magazine (1962–1969); Co-founder and contributing editor, *New York* magazine (1968–1972); Co-founder, editor, and columnist, *Ms.* magazine (1972–1987). Literary works: *Outrageous Acts and Everyday Rebellion* (1983); *Moving beyond Words* (1993).

JIM LEHRER (1934–). Reporter, *Dallas Morning News* (1959–1961); Reporter, columnist, and city editor, *Dallas Times Herald* (1961–1970); Executive producer and correspondent, KERA-TV, Dallas (1970–1972); Public affairs coordinator, PBS-TV (1972–1973); Co-anchor and anchor, MacNeil/Lehrer News Hour, Newshour with Jim Lehrer, PBS-TV

(1975–today). Literary works: *Viva Max!* (1966); *Crown Oklahoma* (1989); *The Last Debate* (1995).

E. ANNIE PROULX (1935–). Publisher and Editor, *Behind the Times* newspaper in rural Vermont (1984–1986). Literary works: *The Shipping News* (1993).

PETE HAMILL (1935–). Reporter, columnist, and editor, *New York Post* (1960–1963, 1965–1967, 1969–1974, 1988–1993); Contributing editor, *Saturday Evening Post* (1964–1965); Editor, *Mexico City News* (1986–1987). Literary works: *The Deadly Piece* (1979); *A Drinking Life* (1995).

CALVIN TRILLIN (1935–). Writer and columnist, *Time* (1960–1963, 1996–today); Staff writer, *New Yorker* (1963–1982); Columnist, *Nation* (1978–1985); Columnist, King Syndicate (1986–1995). Literary works: *American Fried* (1974); *Floater* (1980).

WARD JUST (1935–). Reporter, Waukegan (IL) *News-Sun* (1957–1959); Reporter and London correspondent, *Newsweek* (1959–1962); Foreign correspondent, *Washington Post* (1965–1970). Literary works: *Nicholson at Large* (1975); *The Weather in Berlin* (2002); *An Unfinished Season* (2004).

C. D. B. BRYAN (1936–). Editor, *Monocle* magazine (early 1960s). Literary works: *P. S. Wilkinson* (1965); *The Great Dethriffe* (1970); *Friendly Fire* (1976); *Beautiful Women, Ugly Scenes* (1983).

TOM ROBBINS (1936–). Writer and copy-editor, *Richmond* (VA) *Times-Dispatch* (1960–1962); Copy-editor, *Seattle Times* and *Seattle Post-Intelligencer* (1962–1963); Reviewer and art critic, *Seattle Magazine* (1964–1968). Literary works: *Even Cowgirls Get the Blues* (1976).

HUNTER S. THOMPSON (1937–2005). Sportswriter, *Playground News*, Ft. Walton, FL (1956–1957); Caribbean correspondent, *Time* (1959); Caribbean correspondent, *New York Herald Tribune* (1959–1960); South American correspondent, *National Observer* (1961–1963); West Coast correspondent, *Nation* (1964–1966); Columnist, *Ramparts* (1967–1968); Columnist, *Scanlan's Monthly* (1969–1970); National Affairs editor, *Rolling Stone* (1970–1984); Global Affairs correspondent, *High Times* (1977–1982); Media critic, San Francisco *Examiner* (1985–1990); Editor-at-large, *Smart* (1988). Literary works: *Hell's Angels* (1966); *The Rum Diary* (1998).

TOM STOPPARD (1937–). Reporter and critic, *Western Daily Press*, Bristol (1958–1960); Reporter, *Bristol Evening World* (1958–1960). Literary works: *Rosencrantz and Guildenstern Are Dead* (play, 1966); *Lord Malquist and Mr. Moon* (1966); *Night and Day* (play, 1978).

GAIL GODWIN (1937–). Reporter, *Miami Herald* (1959–1960). Literary works: *The Perfectionists* (1970); *The Odd Woman* (1974).

RICHARD RHODES (1937–). Contributing editor, *Harper's* (1970–1974); Contributing editor, *Playboy* (1974–1980); Contributing editor, *Rolling Stone* (1988–1993). Literary works: *The Inland Ground* (1970); *The Last Safari* (1980); *Sons of the Earth* (1981); *Dark Sun* (1995).

ROBERT STONE (1937–). Copy aide, caption writer, and sports correspondent, *New York Daily News* (1958–1960); Writer, *National Mirror* (1965–1967). Literary works: *A Hall of Mirrors* (1967); *Dog Soldiers* (1974).

JANE KRAMER (1938–). Founder and editor, *Morningsider*, New York City (1961–1962); Writer, *Village Voice* (1962–1963); Contributor and staff writer, *New Yorker* (1963–today). Literary works: *The Last Cowboy* (1978); *Unsettling Europe* (1980).

REX REED (1938–). Film critic, *Holiday* (1965–1969), *Women's Wear Daily* (1965–1969), *New York Daily News* (1971–1975), *New York Observer* (beginning in the 1990s), and other publications. Literary works: *Do You Sleep in the Nude?* (1968); *Personal Effects* (1986).

RENATA ADLER (1938–). Writer and reporter, *New Yorker* (1962–1968, 1970–1982); Film critic, *New York Times* (1968–1969). Literary works: *Speedboat* (1976); *Pitch Dark* (1983); *Reckless Disregard* (1986).

AUBERON WAUGH (1939–2001). Editorial writer, London *Daily Telegraph* (1960–1963); Columnist, *Catholic Herald* (1963–1964); Columnist, International Publishing (1963–1967); Commentator and columnist, London *Spectator* (1967–2001); Commentator, *Private Eye* (1970–1986); Editor, London *Literary Review* (1986–2001). Literary works: *The Foxglove Saga* (1961); *Path of Dalliance* (1963).

EDNA BUCHANAN (1939–). Reporter, *Miami Herald* (1970–1988). Literary works: *The Corpse Had a Familiar Face* (1987); *Contents under Pressure* (1992).

IVAN DOIG (1939–). Editorial writer, Lindsay-Schaub Newspapers, Decatur, IL (1963–1964); Assistant editor, *Rotarian*, Evanston, IL (1964–1966). Literary works: *This House of Sky* (1978).

JOHN BERENDT (1939–). Editor and columnist, *Esquire* (1961–1969, 1982–1984); Senior editor, *Holiday* (1969); Editor, *New York* (1977–1979). Literary works: *Midnight in the Garden of Good and Evil* (1994).

ANGELA CARTER (1940–1992). Journalist, *Croydon Advertiser* (1965–1966). Literary works: *Several Perceptions* (1968).

MARSHALL FRADY (1940–2004). Correspondent, Newsweek (1966–1967); Staff writer, *Saturday Evening Post* (1968–1969); Contributing editor, *Harper's* (1969–1971); Writer, *Life* (1971–1973); Correspondent, ABC-TV News and *Nightline* program (1979–2004). Literary works: *Wallace* (1968); *Southerners* (1980).

ANGELA LAMBERT (1940–2007). Assistant editor, *Modern Woman* (1962); Reporter and presenter, Independent Television News (1972–1976); Reporter and presenter, Thames Television (1976–1988); Feature writer, *Independent* (1990–2007). Literary works: *Love among the Single Classes* (1989); *A Rather English Marriage* (1992).

MICHAEL HERR (1940–). Vietnam correspondent, *Esquire* (1967–1969). Literary works: *Dispatches* (1977).

L. J. DAVIS (1940–). Investigative reporter, contributing editor, contributor, *Harper's, Buzz, New Republic, Mother Jones, Penthouse* magazines (1980–today). Literary works: *Whence All But He Had Fled* (1968); *Cowboys Don't Cry* (1969); *Bad Money* (1982).

EDMUND WHITE (1940–). Staff writer, Time, Inc. (1962–1970); Senior editor, *Saturday Review* (1972–1973). Literary works: *Forgetting Elena* (1973); *Nocturnes for the King of Naples* (1978); *The Beautiful Room is Empty* (1988); *The Married Man* (2000).

FRANCES FITZGERALD (1940–). Contributor to *New Yorker* and other publications (1964–today). Literary works: *Fire in the Lake* (1972).

BOBBIE ANN MASON (1940–). Writer, *Mayfield* (KY) *Messenger* (1960); Writer, *Movie Life, TV Star Parade* (1962–1963). Literary works: *Shiloh and Other Stories* (1982); *Feather Crowns* (1993).

PHILIP CAPUTO (1941–). Local and foreign correspondent, *Chicago Tribune* (1969–1977). Literary works: *A Rumor of War* (1977); *DelCorso's Gallery* (1983).

ROY BLOUNT, JR. (1941–). Reporter and sports columnist, *Decatur-DeKalb* (GA) *News* (1958–1959); Reporter, New York *Morning Telegraph* (1961); Reporter, *New Orleans Times-Picayune* (1963); Reporter, editorial writer, and columnist, *Atlanta Journal* (1966–1968); Staff writer, associate editor, and contributor, *Sports Illustrated* (1968–1975). Literary works: *One Fell Soup* (1982); *Now, Where Were We?* (1989).

NORA EPHRON (1941–). Reporter, *New York Post* (1963–1968); Columnist, contributing editor, and senior editor, *Esquire* (1972–1973, 1974–1976); Contributing editor, *New York* (1973–1974). Literary works: *Scribble, Scribble* (1979); *Heartburn* (1983).

RON POWERS (1941–). Journalist and critic, *St. Louis Post-Dispatch* (1963–1969); Sports reporter, reporter, and critic, *Chicago Sun-Times* (1969–1977); Critic, WMAQ-TV, Chicago, WNET-TV, New York City, CBS News (1977–1988). Literary works: *Face Value* (1979); *Flags of Our Fathers* (with James Bradley, 2000).

JOE MCGINNISS (1942–). Reporter, *Port Chester* (PA) *Daily Item* (1964); Reporter, *Worcester* (MA) *Telegram* (1965); Reporter, *Philadelphia*

Bulletin (1966); Columnist, *Philadelphia Inquirer* (1967–1968). Literary works: *Fatal Vision* (1983).

PETE DEXTER (1943–). Reporter, *West Palm Beach Post* (1971–1972); Columnist, *Philadelphia Daily News* (1972–1984); Columnist, *Sacramento Bee* (1985–2000s). Literary works: *Paris Trout* (1988); *The Paperboy* (1995).

HOWELL RAINES (1943–). Reporter, *Birmingham Post-Herald* (1964–1965); Staff writer, WBRC-TV, Birmingham, AL (1965–1967); Reporter, *Tuscaloosa News* (1968–1969); Film critic, *Birmingham News* (1970–1971); Political editor, *Atlanta Constitution* (1971–1974); Political editor, *St. Petersburg Times* (1976–1979); Atlanta bureau, London bureau chief, Washington, DC bureau chief, editorial page editor, executive editor, *New York Times* (1979–2003). Literary works: *Whiskey Man* (1977); *Fly Fishing Through the Midlife Crisis* (1993).

SUSAN CHEEVER (1943–). Reporter, *Tarrytown* (NY) *Daily News* (1971–1972); Religion and lifestyle editor, *Newsweek* (1974–1978). Literary works: *Home before Dark* (1984); *Doctors and Women* (1987).

SARA DAVIDSON (1943–). Reporter and correspondent, *Boston Globe* (1965–1969). Literary works: *Loose Change* (1977); *Friends of the Opposite Sex* (1984).

MOLLY IVINS (1944–2007). Reporter, *Houston Chronicle, Minneapolis Star-Tribune, Texas Observer* (1970–1976); Reporter, *New York Times* (1976–1980); Columnist, *Dallas Times-Herald* and other newspapers (1980–2007). Literary works: *Molly Ivins Can't Say That, Can She?* (1991).

RICHARD RODRIGUEZ (1944–). Editor, Pacific News Service; Contributing editor, *Harper's, Los Angeles Times, US News and World Report*, PBS-TV's "News Hour" (early 1980s–today). Literary works: *The Hunger of Memory* (1982).

CRAIG RAINE (1944–). Book editor, *New Review* (1977–1978); Poetry editor, *New Statesman* (1981). Literary works: *Haydn and the Valve Trumpet* (1990); *History: The Home Movie* (1994).

ANNIE DILLARD (1945–). Columnist, *Living Wilderness* (1973–1975); Contributing editor, *Harper's* (1973–1985). Literary works: *Tickets for a Prayer Wheel* (poetry, 1974); *Pilgrim at Tinker's Creek* (1974); *The Living* (1992).

TRACY KIDDER (1945–). Contributing editor, *The Atlantic* (1982–today). Literary works: *Soul of a New Machine* (1997).

TOBIAS WOLFF (1945–). Reporter, *Washington Post* (six months in early 1970s). Literary works: *The Barracks Thief* (1984); *This Boy's Life* (1989).

ROBERT OLEN BUTLER (1945–). Editor and reporter, *Electronic News* (1972–1977); Editor, *Energy News* (1975–1985). Literary works: *Sun Dogs*

(1982); *On Distant Ground* (1985); *A Good Scent from a Strange Mountain* (1992).

TIM O'BRIEN (1946–). Reporter, *Washington Post* (1973–1974). Literary works: *The Things They Carried* (1990).

JULIAN BARNES (1946–). Assistant literary editor and TV critic, *New Review* (1977–1981); TV critic, London *Observer* (1979–1981); Deputy literary editor, *Sunday Times* of London (1982–1986); London correspondent, *New Yorker* (1990–1995). Literary works: *Flaubert's Parrot* (1985); *A History of the World in 10 ½ Chapters* (1989).

ANITA SHREVE (1946–). Journalist, *US* magazine, *Quest*, *Newsweek*, *Viva* magazine; Journalist in Nairobi, Kenya (1970s and 1980s). Literary works: *Eden Close* (1989).

JIM CRACE (1946–). TV producer and writer, Khartoum, Sudan (1968–1969); Freelance journalist contributing to London *Telegraph* and other newspapers (1970–1987). Literary works: *Continent* (1986); *The Gift of Stones* (1988); *Being Dead* (2000).

JONATHAN MEADES (1947–). Staff writer, *Time Out* magazine (1976–1978); Staff writer, London *Observer* (1978–1979); Staff writer, *Architectural Review* (1979–1980); Editor, *Event* (1981–1982); Features editor, London *Tatler* (1982–1987); Restaurant critic, *The Times* of London (1986–2001). Literary works: *Filthy English* (1984); *Pompey* (1993); *The Fowler Family Business* (2002).

DAVE BARRY (1947–). Reporter, West Chester (PA) *Daily Local News* (1971–1975); Reporter, Associated Press (1975–1976); Columnist, *Miami Herald* (1983–today). Literary works: *Dave Barry is Not Making This Up* (1994); *Tricky Business* (2002).

STEPHEN HARRIGAN (1948–). Senior editor, *Texas Monthly* (1983–1991). Literary works: *Aransas* (1980); *Jacob's Well* (1984); *The Gates of the Alamo* (2000).

MARTIN AMIS (1949–). Editorial assistant, Fiction and poetry editor, *Times Literary Supplement* (1972–1975); Assistant literary editor, Literary editor, *New Statesman* (1975–1979). Literary works: *The Information* (1995).

JAMES FENTON (1949–). Columnist, Assistant literary editor, editorial staff writer, *New Statesman* (1971–1973, 1976–1978); German correspondent, London *Guardian* (1978–1979); Theater critic, *Sunday Times* of London (1979–1984); Literary critic, *The Times* of London (1984–1986); Correspondent, *Independent* (1986–1988); Columnist, *Sunday Independent* (1990–today). Literary works: *Memory of War* (1982).

BARRY SIEGEL (1949–). Staff writer, *L.A. Weekly* (1972); West Coast editor, *Women's Wear Daily* (1973–1976); Correspondent and reporter, *Los Angeles Times* (1976–today). Literary works: *A Death in White Bear Lake* (1990); *Shades of Gray* (1992); *The Perfect Witness* (1998).

CHRISTOPHER DICKEY (1951–). Reporter, foreign correspondent, Sunday magazine editor, book world assistant editor, and columnist, *Washington Post* (1974–1986); Foreign bureau chief, regional editor, and columnist, *Newsweek* (1993–today). Literary works: *With the Contras* (1986); *Innocent Blood* (1997); *The Sleeper* (2004).

ANNA QUINDLEN (1952–). Reporter, *New York Post* (1974–1977); Reporter, *New York Times* (1977–1995); Columnist, *Newsweek* (1999–today). Literary works: *One True Thing* (1994).

WILLIAM BOYD (1952–). TV critic, *New Statesman* (1981–1983). Literary works: *A Good Man in Africa* (1982).

CARL HIAASSEN (1953–). Reporter, *Cocoa Today*, FL (1974–1976); Reporter and columnist, *Miami Herald* (1976–today). Literary works: *Tourist Season* (1986).

TONY PARSONS (1953–). Journalist, *New Musical Express* (1976–1979), *Arena* (1986–1996), London *Daily Telegraph* (1990–1996), London *Daily Mirror* (1996–today). Literary works: *The Boy Looked at Johnny* (with Julie Burchill, 1978); *Platinum Logic* (1981); *Man and Boy* (1999).

TIMOTHY EGAN (1954–). Reporter, *Seattle Post-Intelligencer* (1980s); Northwest correspondent, *New York Times* (1987–today). Literary works: *The Good Rain* (1990); *Breaking Blue* (1992); *The Winemaker's Daughter* (2004); *The Worst Hard Time* (2006).

A. A. GILL (1954–). TV and restaurant critic, *Sunday Times* of London; Contributor, *Vanity Fair, Gentleman's Quarterly*. Literary works: *Sap Rising* (1997); *Starcrossed* (1999).

ANNE LAMOTT (1954–). Staff writer, *WomenSports* (1974–1975). Literary works: *Crooked Little Heart* (1997).

SUSAN ORLEAN (1955–). Reporter, *Willamette Week*, Portland, OR (1979–1983); Staff writer, *Boston Phoenix* (1983–1986); Contributing editor, *Rolling Stone* and *New Yorker* (1987–today). Literary works: *The Orchid Thief* (1998).

BARBARA KINGSOLVER (1955–). Writer, Tucson newspapers, *Nation, Progressive, Smithsonian* magazine (1985–1987). Literary works: *Bean Trees* (1988).

MURIEL GRAY (1958–). Presenter, BBC Radio (1980s); TV personality and owner of a television network, Ideal World (1993–2005). Literary works: *The Trickster* (1995); *Furnace* (1996); *The Ancient* (2000).

BENILDE LITTLE (1958–). Journalist, *Newark Star-Ledger* (1982–1985); Journalist, *People* magazine (1985–1989). Literary works: *Good Hair* (1996); *The Itch* (1998); *Acting Out* (2003).

RICK BRAGG (1959–). Reporter on Alabama newspapers, *Talladega Daily Home, Jacksonville News, Anniston Star, Birmingham News* (1977–1989); Reporter, *St. Petersburg Times* (1989–1993); Reporter, *Los Angeles Times* (1993); Reporter, *New York Times* (1994–2003). Literary works: *All Over but the Shootin'* (1997).

CRISTINA GARCIA (1959–). Reporter, researcher, and Miami bureau chief, *Time* (1983–1988). Literary works: *Dreaming in Cuban* (1992).

SEAN FRENCH (1959–). Theater critic, British *Vogue* (1981–1986); Deputy literary editor and TV critic, *Sunday Times* of London (1981–1986); Film critic, *Marie Claire* (1981–1987); Deputy editor, *New Society* (1986–1988); Columnist, *New Statesman* (1987–2000). Literary works: *The Imaginary Monkey* (1993); *Dreamer of Dreams* (1995); *Beneath the Skin* (with wife, Nicci Gerrard under joint pseudonym, Nicci French, 2000).

TIBOR FISCHER (1959–). Correspondent, London *Daily Telegraph* (1988–1990). Literary works: *Under the Frog* (1992); *The Thought Gang* (1994).

JULIE BURCHILL (1960–). Journalist, *New Musical Express* and contributor to *Spectator, Daily Mail, Sunday Times* of London (mid-1970s–2006). Literary works: *The Boy Looked at Johnny* (with Tony Parsons, 1978); *Ambition* (1989).

JIM LYNCH (1961–). Reporter in Alaska, investigator with columnist Jack Anderson, legislative and Puget Sound reporter, *Seattle Times* and Portland *Oregonian* (mid-1980s to early 2000s). Literary works: *The Highest Tide* (2005).

MARK LAWSON (1962–). Writer and critic, *Independent* (1986–2007). Literary works: *Bloody Margaret* (1991); *Idlewood* (1996); *Going Out Live* (2001).

JESS WALTER (1965–). Investigative reporter, Spokane *Spokesman-Review* (nine years, beginning in early 1990s). Literary works: *The Zero* (2006).

ANDREA LOUIE (1966–). Reporter, *Akron Beacon Journal* (1989–1993); Editor, Market News Service (1995–2001); Literary critic, *Chicago Tribune* (1997–today). Literary works: *Moon Cakes* (1995).

GILES FODEN (1967–). Assistant editor, *Times Literary Supplement* (1993–1997); Deputy literary editor, London *Guardian* (mid-1990s to mid-2000s). Literary works: *The Last King of Scotland* (1998).

COLSON WHITEHEAD (1970–). Writer and television critic, *Village Voice* (for a number of years beginning in the early 1990s). Literary works: *The Intuitionist* (1999); *John Henry Days* (2001); *Apex Hides the Hurt* (2006).

Notes

INTRODUCTION

1. Bjorn Larsson, *Long John Silver* (1995; reprint, London: Harvill Press, 1999), 133.
2. Grahame Smith, *The Novel and Society: Defoe to George Eliot* (London: Batsford, 1984), 56; Diana Spearman, *The Novel and Society* (London: Routledge and Kegan Paul, 1966), 56, 66, 69.
3. Mark Kinkead-Weekes, "Johnson on 'The Rise of the Novel,'" in Isobel Grundy, ed., *Samuel Johnson: New Critical Essays* (London: Vision Press, 1984), 70–77; Lawrence Lipking, *Samuel Johnson: The Life of an Author* (Cambridge, MA: Harvard University Press, 1998), 174; Iain Finlayson, *The Moth and the Candle: A Life of James Boswell* (London: Constable, 1984), 168.
4. Barbara Foley, *Telling the Truth: The Theory and Practice of Documentary Fiction* (Ithaca, NY: Cornell University Press, 1986), 25–41.
5. Tom Wolfe, "Stalking the Billion-Footed Beast: A Literary Manifesto for the New Social Novel," *Harper's* (Nov., 1989): 45–56; Robert Towers, "The Flap Over Tom Wolfe: How Real Is the Retreat from Realism?" *New York Times Book Review* (Jan. 28, 1990): 15–16. There is a need for historical perspective whenever one refers to the "new" journalism. Besides the period of the 1960s and 1970s, a form of what was then called the "new" journalism was practiced during the period of the Penny Press newspapers in the 1830s, the crusading journalism of Hearst and Pulitzer in the 1880s and 1890s, and the "Yellow" journalism of a slightly later period. See Phyllis Frus, *The Politics and Poetics of Journalistic Narrative: The Timely and the Timeless* (Cambridge, England: Cambridge University Press, 1994), 134–136; Karen Roggenkamp, *Narrating the News: New Journalism and Literary Genre in Late Nineteenth-Century American Newspapers and Fiction* (Kent, OH: Kent State University Press, 2005), xii.
6. George Plimpton, "Ernest Hemingway," in Van Wyck Brooks, ed., *Writers at Work: The Paris Review Interviews* (New York: Viking, 1963), 225.
7. Ian Watt, *The Rise of the Novel* (Berkeley: University of California Press, 1964); Lennard J. Davis, *Factual Fictions: The Origins of the English Novel* (1983; reprint, Philadelphia: University of Pennsylvania Press, 1996); Richard I. Cook, *Jonathan Swift as a Tory Pamphleteer* (Seattle: University of Washington Press, 1967); Foley, *Telling the Truth*; Frus, *Politics and Poetics of Journalistic Narrative*;

William Dow, "Documentary Fictions: Testimonies of 'Truth,'" in James Agee's *Let Us Now Praise Famous Men*" (Paper delivered to First International Conference on Literary Journalism, Nancy, France, May 19, 2006); Shelley Fisher Fishkin, *From Fact to Fiction: Journalism and Imaginative Writing in America* (Baltimore: The Johns Hopkins University Press, 1985); Michael Robertson, *Stephen Crane, Journalism, and the Making of Modern American Literature* (New York: Columbia University Press, 1997); Jean Marie Lutes, *Front-page Girls: Women Journalists in American Culture and Fiction, 1880–1930* (Ithaca, NY: Cornell University Press, 2006); Brian McCrea, *Addison and Steele Are Dead: The English Department, Its Canon, and the Professionalization of Literary Criticism* (Newark: University of Delaware Press, 1990); Thomas Strychacz, *Modernism, Mass Culture, and Professionalism* (Cambridge, England: Cambridge University Press, 1993); Smith, *Novel and Society*; Spearman, *Novel and Society*. See also Paula Rabinowitz, *They Must Be Represented: The Politics of Documentary* (New York: Verso, 1994) and William Stott, *Documentary Expression and Thirties America* (New York: Oxford University Press, 1973).

8. Michael Allen, *Poe and the British Magazine Tradition* (New York: Oxford University Press, 1969); Richard Pearson, *W. M. Thackeray and the Mediated Text: Writing for Periodicals in the Mid-nineteenth Century* (Aldershot, England: Ashgate, 2000); Virgil Grillo, *Charles Dickens' Sketches by Boz: End in the Beginning* (Boulder: The Colorado Associated University Press, 1974); John M. L. Drew, *Dickens the Journalist* (New York: Palgrave Macmillan, 2003); Louis L. Cornell, *Kipling in India* (London: Macmillan, 1966); M. Catherine Downs, *Becoming Modern: Willa Cather's Journalism* (London: Associated University Presses, 1999); Charles A. Fenton, *The Apprenticeship of Ernest Hemingway: The Early Years* (1954; reprint, New York: Viking, 1958); Roggenkamp, *Narrating the News*; Christopher P. Wilson, *The Labor of Words: Literary Professionalism in the Progressive Era* (Athens: University of Georgia Press, 1985); John Gross, *The Rise and Fall of the Man of Letters: Aspects of English Literary Life Since 1800* (London: Weidenfeld and Nicolson, 1969); Thomas Berry, *The Newspaper in the American Novel 1900–1969* (Metuchen, NJ: Scarecrow Press, 1970); Howard Good, *Acquainted with the Night: The Image of Journalists in American Fiction, 1890–1930* (Metuchen, NJ: Scarecrow Press, 1986); Loren Ghiglione, "The American Journalist: Fiction Versus Fact," in John B. Hench, ed., *Three Hundred Years of the American Newspaper* (Lunenburg, VT: Stinehour, 1991): 445–463.

9. Chris Anderson, ed., *Literary Nonfiction: Theory, Criticism, Pedagogy* (Carbondale: Southern Illinois University Press, 1989); Chris Anderson, *Style as Argument: Contemporary American Nonfiction* (Carbondale: Southern Illinois University Press, 1987); Thomas Connery, ed., *A Sourcebook of American Literary Journalism: Representative Writers in an Emerging Genre* (New York: Greenwood, 1992); John C. Hartsock, *A History of American Literary Journalism: The Emergence of a Modern Narrative Form* (Amherst: University of Massachusetts Press, 2000); Iona Italia, *The Rise of Literary Journalism in the Eighteenth Century: Anxious Employment* (London: Routledge, 2005); Paul Many, "Toward a History of Literary Journalism," *Michigan Academician* 24 (1992):

359–369; John Hellman, *Fables of Fact: The New Journalism as New Fiction* (Urbana: University of Illinois Press, 1981); John Hollowell, *Fact and Fiction: The New Journalism and the Nonfiction Novel* (Chapel Hill: The University of North Carolina Press, 1977); Kevin Kerrane and Ben Yagoda, eds., *The Art of Fact: A Historical Anthology of Literary Journalism* (1997; reprint, New York: Touchstone, 1998); Barbara Lounsberry, *The Art of Fact: Contemporary Artists of Non Fiction* (New York: Greenwood, 1990); Norman Sims, *True Stories: A Century of Literary Journalism* (Evanston, IL: Northwestern University Press, 2007); Norman Sims, ed., *The Literary Journalists* (New York: Ballantine, 1984); Norman Sims, ed., *Literary Journalism in the Twentieth Century* (New York: Oxford University Press, 1990); Norman Sims and Mark Kramer, eds., *Literary Journalism: A New Collection of the Best of American Nonfiction* (New York: Ballantine, 1995); Richard Keeble and Sharon Wheeler, eds., *The Journalistic Imagination: Literary Journalists from Defoe to Capote and Carter* (London: Routledge, 2007); Edd Applegate, *Literary Journalism: A Biographical Dictionary of Writers and Editors* (Westport, CT: Greenwood, 1996); R. Thomas Berner, *The Literature of Journalism: Text and Context* (State College, PA: Strata, 1998); Kate Campbell, ed., *Journalism, Literature, and Modernity* (Edinburgh: Edinburgh University Press, 2000); Jean Chance and William McKay, eds., *Literary Journalism: A Reader* (Belmont, CA: Wadsworth, 2001); Everette E. Dennis, *Other Voices: The New Journalism in America* (New York: HarperCollins, 1974); Louis Dudek, *Literature and the Press: A History of Printing, Printed Media, and Their Relation to Literature* (Toronto: Ryerson, 1960); Michael L. Johnson, *The New Journalism: The Underground Press, the Artists of Nonfiction, and Changes in the Established Media* (Lawrence: University of Kansas Press, 1972); Arthur J. Kaul, *American Literary Journalists, 1945–1995* (Detroit: Gale Research, 1997); James Emmett Murphy, *The New Journalism: A Critical Perspective* (Association for Education in Journalism and Mass Communication, 1974); Warren C. Price, *The Literature of Journalism: An Annotated Bibliography* (Minneapolis: University of Minnesota Press, 1959); Edwin H. Ford, *A Bibliography of Literary Journalism in America* (Minneapolis: Burgess, 1937); Ronald Weber, *The Literature of Fact: Literary Non-fiction in American Writing* (Athens: Ohio University Press, 1980); Ronald Weber, *Hired Pens: Professional Writers in America's Golden Age of Print* (Athens: Ohio University Press, 1997); W. Ross Winterowd, *The Rhetoric of the 'Other' Literature* (Carbondale: Southern Illinois University Press, 1990); Daniel C. Hallin, "The Passing of 'High Modernism' of American Journalism," *Journal of Communication* 42:3 (Summer, 1992): 14–25; D. L. Eason, "The New Journalism and the Image-World: Two Modes of Organizing Experience," *Critical Studies in Mass Communication* 1:1 (March, 1984): 51–65; Robert Boynton, ed., *The New New Journalism: Conversations with America's Best Nonfiction Writers on Their Craft* (New York: Vintage, 2005).

10. Hartsock, *Literary Journalism*, 204–245; John C. Hartsock, "'Literary Journalism' as an Epistemological Moving Object within a Larger 'Quantum' Narrative," *Journal of Communication* 23:4 (October, 1999): 432–450; John C. Hartsock, "The

Critical Marginalization of American Literary Journalism," *Critical Studies in Mass Communication* 15:1 (March, 1998): 61–84; Roggenkamp, *Narrating the News*, xv.

11. Frus, *Politics and Poetics of Journalistic Narrative*, 2–4, 8–10.

12. Good, *Acquainted with the Night*, 77; Berry, *Newspaper in the American Novel*; Mark Twain (Samuel Clemens), "How I Edited an Agricultural Paper," in *Editorial Wild Oats* (1905; reprint, Freeport, NY: Books for Libraries Press, 1970), 66; John Graham (David Graham Phillips), *The Great God Success* (New York: Frederick A. Stokes, 1901), 11.

13. Frus, *Politics and Poetics of Journalistic Narrative*, 2–4, 8–10.

14. Hartsock, *Literary Journalism*, 114–119, 138; Frus, *Politics and Poetics of Journalistic Narrative*, 2–4, 8–10; Foley, *Telling the Truth*, 25–41; Lounsberry, *Art of Fact*, xi–xviii; Mark Kramer, "Breakable Rules for Literary Journalists," in Sims and Kramer, *Literary Journalism*, 24–25; Kerrane and Yagoda, *Art of Fact*, 13–16.

15. I was made aware of these scholarly and critical divisions when I attended the "First International Conference of Literary Journalism" in Nancy, France in May, 2006. The scholars in attendance bonded in terms of our common recognition of how important the role of "literary" or "narrative" journalism (as some in attendance hoped to define the field) or "journalistic literature" (as I was pushing for) has been in their respective professional cultures, and how it has tended to be overlooked by the scholars in the more traditional fields of literature, journalism, and communication in all of our countries. But even with these common viewpoints, we engaged in intense discussions of how we defined the terms that have been applied to the role of journalism within the literary tradition, and it gave us a greater understanding of the complexities of terminology and their application in the journalistic, literary, and scholarly worlds.

16. By using the terms in this way, I hoped to avoid the problem, for example, of studying Truman Capote's *In Cold Blood* because it is widely accepted as a piece of non-fiction-writing (although it takes some creative liberties with the facts) while ignoring Theodore Dreiser's *An American Tragedy* or Richard Wright's *Native Son* because – while their books were inspired by real-life crimes and are the product of much journalistic-style research – both authors stretched their accounts in ways that have been largely deemed to have made the works more fictional than factual in nature. The author would contend that Dreiser and Wright should be considered important journalist-literary figures because of the influence that their journalistic experiences and their use of the methods and techniques learned in journalism had upon all their writings and because of the literary quality of some of their journalism, as well as their journalistically-inspired fiction, semi-fiction, or semi-non-fiction, whatever one chooses to call it. See W. A. Swanberg, *Dreiser* (New York: Scribner's, 1965), 253–254, 269–271, 276–277; Margaret Walker, *Richard Wright/Daemonic Genius: A Portrait of the Man/A Critical Look at His Work* (New York: Warner, 1988), 121–126; Hartsock, *Literary Journalism*, 197–198.

17. Although it falls into one of my other areas of scholarly specialization (media and religion), I would invite one to examine the recent writings of Daniel A. Stout, the co-editor of the *Journal of Media and Religion*, about the need to

apply the biographical method more frequently in media studies and the use of cultural biography as a valuable new genre available to researchers. See Stout, "Media and Religion: The Promise of Cultural Biography," *Journal of Media and Religion* 5:3 (2006): 141–146.

18. David S. Reynolds, *Walt Whitman's America: A Cultural Biography* (1995; reprint, New York: Vintage, 1996), 271, 321, 334.

19. J. A. Simpson and E. S. C. Weiner, eds., *The Oxford English Dictionary*, second edition, volume viii (Oxford, England: Clarendon Press, 1989), 280–281; Paul Fussell, *Samuel Johnson and the Life of Writing* (New York: Harcourt Brace Jovanovich, 1971), 38–39; Donald Greene, "Samuel Johnson, Journalist," in Donovan H. Bond and W. Reynolds McLeod, eds., *Newsletters to Newspapers: Eighteenth-Century Journalism* (Morgantown: The School of Journalism, West Virginia University, 1977), 87.

20. Simpson and Weiner, *Oxford English Dictionary*, second edition, volume viii, 280–281.

21. Nationmaster.com.Encyclopedia: Journalist; Fussell, *Samuel Johnson*, 38–39; Greene, "Samuel Johnson, Journalist," 88.

22. Simpson and Weiner, *Oxford English Dictionary*, second edition, volume x, 564; Foley, *Telling the Truth*, 114: Davis, *Factual Fictions*, 42–70.

23. Simpson and Weiner, *Oxford English Dictionary*, second edition, volume viii, 1027, 1029.

24. Arthur and Barbara Gelb, *O'Neill: Life with Monte Cristo* (2000; reprint, New York: Applause, 2002), 348–349; Joan Richardson, *Wallace Stevens: The Early Years 1879–1923* (New York: Morrow, 1986), 127–129; Joan Richardson, *Wallace Stevens: The Later Years 1923–1955* (New York: Morrow, 1988), 124–125, 166–167.

25. Gary Scharnhorst, *Charlotte Perkins Gilman* (Boston: Twayne, 1985), 45, 48–49, 89, 93, 104; Michael Shelden, *Graham Greene: The Enemy Within* (New York: Random House, 1994), 331–332; Irving Howe, *Sherwood Anderson* (Toronto: George J. McLeod, 1951), 219–220; Genevieve Moreau, *The Restless Journey of James Agee* (New York: Morrow, 1977), 112; Kenneth S. Lynn, *Hemingway* (1987; reprint, Cambridge, MA: Harvard University Press, 1996), 444–449; Townsend Ludington, *John Dos Passos: A Twentieth Century Odyssey* (New York: Dutton, 1980), 122, 184, 191–192; Mark Schorer, *Sinclair Lewis: An American Life* (New York: McGraw-Hill, 1961), 92, 142, 178, 213, 218, 769; Marion Meade, *Dorothy Parker: What Fresh Hell Is This?* (1988; reprint, New York: Penguin, 1989), 67–68, 224, 254; William A. Bloodworth, Jr., *Upton Sinclair* (Boston: Twayne, 1977), 37–39; Leon Harris, *Upton Sinclair: American Rebel* (New York: Thomas Y. Crowell, 1975), 177; Dan B. Miller, *Erskine Caldwell: The Journey from Tobacco Road* (New York: Knopf, 1995), 222, 224, 267; Wayne Mixon, *The People's Writer: Erskine Caldwell and the South* (Charlottesville: University Press of Virginia, 1995), 94–95; Sylvia Jenkins Cook, *Erskine Caldwell and the Fiction of Poverty: The Flesh and the Spirit* (Baton Rouge: Louisiana State University Press, 1991), 48, 67–68; Edwin H. Cady, *The Road to Realism: The Early Years 1837–1895 of William Dean Howells* (Syracuse, NY: Syracuse University Press, 1956), 21, 87, 180; Swanberg, *Dreiser*, 393, 406, 475; Richard Lingeman, *Theodore Dreiser: An*

American Journey 1908–1945 (New York: G. P. Putnam's, 1990), 467–469; James Lundquist, *Theodore Dreiser* (New York: Frederick Unger, 1974), 14; Ellen Moers, *Two Dreisers* (New York: Viking, 1969), 47–56; Andrew Sinclair, *Jack: A Biography of Jack London* (New York: Pocket, 1977), 33, 79, 128; Michael Shelden, *Orwell: The Authorized Biography* (New York: HarperCollins, 1991), 3, 229, 264–269; Gregory Wolfe, *Malcolm Muggeridge: A Biography* (Grand Rapids, MI: Eerdmans, 1995), 94–95, 98–99; Douglas Clayton, *Floyd Dell: The Life and Times of an American Rebel* (Chicago: Ivan R. Dee, 1994), 15–17; Lincoln Steffens, *The Autobiography of Lincoln Steffens* (New York: Harcourt, Brace, 1931), 526; David Levering Lewis, *W. E. B. DuBois: Biography of a Race 1868–1919* (New York: Henry Holt, 1993), 39; Jeffrey Meyers, *Edmund Wilson: A Biography* (Boston: Houghton Mifflin, 1995), 149, 158, 221–225; Carol Gelderman, *Mary McCarthy: A Life* (New York: St. Martin's, 1988), 73–79, 295; Colin Wilson, *Bernard Shaw: A Reassessment* (New York: Atheneum, 1969), 64–68, 75–79; Audrey Williamson, *Bernard Shaw: Man and Writer* (New York: Crowell-Collier, 1963), 35–39; Julia Briggs, *A Woman of Passion: The Life of E. Nesbit, 1858–1924* (London: Hutchinson, 1987), 62–85; Tim Hilton, *John Ruskin: The Early Years 1819–1859* (New Haven, CT: Yale University Press, 1985), 151, 203, 224, 240, 262; Tim Hilton, *John Ruskin: The Later Years* (New Haven, CT: Yale University Press, 2000), 70–71, 354–359; Edgar M. Branch, *James T. Farrell* (New York: Twayne, 1971), 27; Philip Henderson, *William Morris: His Life, Work and Friends* (New York: McGraw-Hill, 1967), 148–149, 241–243, 253–300; Vincent Brome, *J. B. Priestley* (London: Hamish Hamilton, 1988), 249–252, 255–256; Judith Cook, *Priestley* (London: Bloomsbury, 1997), 128–132, 185–186, 192; Carl Rollyson, *Rebecca West: A Life* (New York: Scribner, 1996), 29–30, 63, 106; Victoria Glendenning, *Rebecca West: A Life* (London: Weidenfeld and Nicolson, 1987), 99–101; Michael Foot, *H. G.: The History of Mr. Wells* (London: Doubleday, 1995), 9, 16, 22–23, 33, 44–45, 51, 53–54, 59, 67, 71, 86; Richard Hauer Costa, *H. G. Wells* (Boston: Twayne, 1985), 49–51, 61–78; Laurence Thompson, *The Enthusiasts: A Biography of John and Katharine Bruce Glasier* (London: Victor Gollancz, 1971), 68–69, 88–103, 230–243; Penelope Niven, *Carl Sandburg: A Biography* (New York: Scribner's, 1991), 133–138, 184, 228; Richard Crowder, *Carl Sandburg* (New York: Twayne, 1964), 39–40, 61–62; "C(hristopher) M(urray) Grieve (Hugh MacDiarmid)," *Contemporary Authors Online* (Gale, 2004); Anne Janette Johnson, "Dorothy Day," *Contemporary Authors Online* (Gale, 2003); "Ruth McKenney," *Contemporary Authors Online* (Thomson Gale, 2007); "Josephine (Frey) Herbst," *Contemporary Authors Online* (Gale, 2002); Roxanne Harde, "Mary Heaton Vorse," *Dictionary of Literary Biography, Volume 303: American Radical and Reform Writers, First Series* (Gale, 2004), 359–368; "Myra Page," *Contemporary Authors Online* (Thomson Gale, 2006); Jeff Berglund, "Meridel LeSueur," *Dictionary of Literary Biography, Volume 303: American Radical and Reform Writers, First Series* (Gale, 2004), 238–246; "Agnes Smedley," *Contemporary Authors Online* (Gale, 2003); www.tenant.net (Theresa Malkiel). For other important women literary figures, including socialist and radical writers, see Charlotte Nekola and Paula Rabinowitz, eds., *Writing Red: An Anthology of Women Writers, 1930–1940* (New York: The Feminist Press at The City University of New York, 1987) and Lutes, *Front-Page Girls*.

26. Frederick Schyberg, *Walt Whitman* (New York: Columbia University Press, 1951), 167; Bettina L. Knapp, *Walt Whitman* (New York: Continuum, 1993), 35; Justin Kaplan, *Walt Whitman: A Life* (New York: Simon and Schuster, 1980), 233–240, 281–287, 311–316, 359–364; Joan Acocella, *Willa Cather and the Politics of Criticism* (New York: Vintage, 2000), 9–10, 39, 43, 45–58, 79, 95; Hermione Lee, *Willa Cather: A Life Saved Up* (1989; reprint, New York: Virago, 2000), 10–12, 57–59, 70, 72–73, 192; James Woodress, *Willa Cather: A Literary Life* (1987; reprint, Lincoln: University of Nebraska Press, 1989), 141–143; Gerald Clarke, *Capote: A Biography* (1988; reprint, New York: Ballantine, 1989), 44–46, 60, 62–64, 93, 111–112, 128–129, 153, 276; Paul Mariani, *The Broken Tower: A Life of Hart Crane* (1999; reprint, New York: Norton, 2000), 60–61, 63, 67, 101–102, 114, 130, 137–140, 158, 206; Nicola Beauman, *E. M. Forster: A Biography* (New York: Knopf, 1994), 14–15, 70, 94–95, 119–121; Gerald Nicosia, *Memory Babe: A Critical Biography of Jack Kerouac* (1983; reprint, Berkeley: University of California Press, 1994), 102, 142, 154–155, 220, 456, 493; Lutes, *Front-Page Girls*, 146; Jo R. Mengedoht, "Dorothy Thompson," *Dictionary of Literary Biography, Volume 29: American Newspaper Journalists, 1926–1950* (Gale, 1984), 343–350; "Edmund White," *Contemporary Authors Online* (Thomson Gale, 2004).

27. The methods and other details of this survey can be found in Doug Underwood and Dana Bagwell, "Journalists with Literary Ambitions No Less Satisfied with Their Jobs," *Newspaper Research Journal* 27 (Spring 2006): 75–83; and Doug Underwood and Dana Bagwell, "Newspapers as Launching Pads for Literary Careers: A Study of How Today's Literary-Aspirants in the Newsroom Feel About Daily Journalism's Role in Developing Literary Talent" (Paper delivered to the Newspaper Division of the Association for Education in Journalism and Mass Communication, San Francisco, CA, August, 2006). Along with many of the journalist-literary figures that are listed in this appendix, Norman Sims, the longtime scholar of "literary" or "immersion" journalism, mentions these writers, among others, in his recent history of literary journalism: Josh Billings, Petroleum Nasby, Opie Read, Tillie Olsen, Meyer Berger, St. Clair McKelway, Malcolm Cowley, Richard West, Al Stump, Timothy Crouse, Gail Sheehy, Susan Sheehan, John Sack, Barry Lopez, Peter Matthiessen, V. S. Naipaul, Paul Theroux, John Gregory Dunne, Jonathan Raban, Nicholas Lemann, Mark Singer, Ted Conover, David Remnick, Michael Paterniti, Adrian Nicole Le Blanc, Joe Nocera, Doug Whynott, Jonathan Harr, Walt Harrington, and Stanley Booth. Sims, *True Stories*.

28. This global interest in the connection between journalism and literature was reflected in the diversity of attendance at the "First International Conference of Literary Journalism" in Nancy, France in 2006 and the follow-up conference in Paris in 2007. At the 2006 conference, I was particularly appreciative of two papers by scholars from the United Kingdom who attempted to explain why literary journalism is little studied in the contemporary British writing world despite its historically rich tradition. Jenny McKay said the university academy

sees journalism as a functional, professional form of writing and has never considered journalism to be a branch of literature. Mckay, "Reporting: A Hidden Genre" (Paper delivered to First International Conference on Literary Journalism, Nancy, France, May 19, 2006). Susan Greenberg speculated that the dearth of literary journalism studies in the UK has to do with the split between "high" and commercially oriented writing that occurred in the minds of the intelligentsia during the Romantic period; a strong British bias that literature by definition means fiction; and a smaller total audience than in the US for literary journalism. Greenberg, "Beyond Journalism: Teaching Non-fiction-Writing in the UK," Ibid.

29. Notes taken from presentation of Michele Weldon, Medill School of Journalism, AEJMC panel on writing trends, August, 2006, San Francisco, CA. See also Chris Harvey, "Tom Wolfe's Revenge," *American Journalism Review* (Oct. 1994): 40–46; Roy Peter Clark and Don Fry, "Return of the Narrative," *Quill* (May 1994): 10–12; Carl Sessions Stepp, "Going Long in a No-Jump World," *American Journalism Review* (Jan./Feb. 1993): 1–5; Roy Peter Clark, "A New Stage for the News," *Washington Journalism Review* (Mar. 1984): 46–47.

30. John Marshall, "Fact and Fiction," *Seattle Post-Intelligencer* (Oct. 29, 2006): D-1.

31. Joseph B. McCullough and Janice McIntire-Strasburg, eds., *Mark Twain at the Buffalo Express: Articles and Sketches by America's Favorite Humorist* (DeKalb: Northern Illinois Press, 1999), xx–xxiii, xlii–xliiii; Edgar M. Branch, *The Literary Apprenticeship of Mark Twain* (Urbana: University of Illinois Press, 1950), 154.

CHAPTER 1 JOURNALISM AND THE RISE OF THE NOVEL, 1700–1875

1. Peter Martin, *A Life of Boswell* (1999, reprint, London: Phoenix Press, 2000), 401.

2. Ibid., 341, 494.

3. Richard West, *Daniel Defoe: The Life and Strange, Surprising Adventures* (1998; reprint, New York: Carroll and Graf, 2000), 218; John Ginger, *The Notable Man: The Life and Times of Oliver Goldsmith* (London: Hamish Hamilton, 1977), 115, 121, 145; Stephen Gwynn, *Oliver Goldsmith* (1935; reprint, London: Thornton Butterworth, 1937), 141; Martin, *Life of Boswell*, 292; Jenny Uglow, "Fielding, Grub Street, and Canary Wharf," in Jeremy Treglown and Bridget Bennett, eds., *Grub Street and the Ivory Tower: Literary Journalism and Literary Scholarship from Fielding to the Internet* (New York: Clarendon-Oxford University Press, 1998), 4–6. Between 1700 and 1760, there were over 900 periodicals circulating in Britain, and in 1728 there were 100 operating in London alone, according to Uglow.

4. Pearson, *W. M. Thackeray*, 103–104; D. J. Taylor, *Thackeray: The Life of a Literary Man* (New York: Carroll and Graf, 2001), 103–109, 198–199; Allen, *Poe*, 20–22; Fred Kaplan, *Dickens: A Biography* (1988; reprint, Baltimore: Johns Hopkins University Press, 1998), 49–50. Kenneth Silverman notes that there was a 600 percent multi-plication of American periodicals between 1825 and 1850. Kenneth Silverman, *Edgar*

A. Poe: Mournful and Never-ending Remembrance (1991; reprint, New York: Harper Perennial, 1992), 99.

5. Stanley T. Williams, *The Life of Washington Irving*. 2 volumes (New York: Oxford University Press, 1935), 114, 192–193 (vol. I), 116–117, 203, 208, 213 (vol. II); Allen, *Poe*, 35, 101, 110, 188; Donald McQuade, Robert Atwan, Martha Banta, Justin Kaplan, David Minter, Cecelia Tichi, and Helen Vendler, eds., *The Harper American Literature* (New York: Harper and Row, 1987), x, 348–406. However, it should be noted that scholars now point to other American novelists of this period – in particular the novelists Susannah Rowson (whom I also include as a journalist-literary figure) and Hannah Webster Foster – as important figures in the development of the American fiction-writing tradition.

6. Grillo, *Boz*, 46–48.

7. Allen, *Poe*, 101, 103; Oswald Doughty, *Perturbed Spirit: The Life and Personality of Samuel Taylor Coleridge* (London: Associated University Presses, 1981), 457.

8. Pearson, *W. M. Thackeray*, 123.

9. Taylor, *Thackeray*, 135–136.

10. Ibid., 420.

11. Spencer L. Eddy, Jr., *The Founding of The Cornhill Magazine* (Muncie, IN: Ball State University Publications, 1970), 21.

12. Allen, *Poe*, 137, 148–149, 183–184.

13. Doughty, *Perturbed Spirit*, 105–106.

14. Watt, *Rise of the Novel*, 71.

15. West, *Daniel Defoe*, 266–277.

16. Robert Giddings, *The Tradition of Smollett* (London: Methuen and Company, 1967), 47, 49–50; Foley, *Telling the Truth*, 55, 66, 71, 115; Clive T. Probyn, *English Fiction of the Eighteenth Century 1700–1789* (London: Longman, 1987), 15; George M. Kahrl, *Tobias Smollett: Traveler-Novelist* (Chicago: University of Chicago Press, 1945), 152; Smith, *Novel and Society*, 66; Uglow, "Fielding, Grub Street, and Canary Wharf," 4–6.

17. Spearman, *Novel and Society*, 50–51; Foley, *Telling the Truth*, 119.

18. Hugh Walker, *The English Essay and Essayists* (New York: Dutton, 1915), 101; Cook, *Jonathan Swift*, 112; West, *Daniel Defoe*, 86–117, 209.

19. Davis, *Factual Fictions*, 76, 88–89, 91, 168, 171; Thomas R. Cleary, *Henry Fielding: Political Writer* (Waterloo, Ontario: Wilfrid Laurier University Press, 1984), 119.

20. Davis, *Factual Fictions*, 125, 131, 134; West, *Daniel Defoe*, 84; Ian A. Bell, *Henry Fielding: Authorship and Authority* (London: Longman, 1994), 150–154.

21. Davis, *Factual Fictions*, 155–156, 166; West, *Daniel Defoe*, 237.

22. Watt, *Rise of the Novel*, 42, 49, 56–57, 99, 101, 103–104; Spearman, *Novel and Society*, 55.

23. Victoria Glendinning, *Jonathan Swift* (London: Hutchinson, 1998), 101; West, *Daniel Defoe*, 49, 100; Bertrand A. Goldgar, *The Curse of Party: Swift's Relations with Addison and Steele* (Lincoln: University of Nebraska Press, 1961), 97–98; Cook, *Jonathan Swift*, xv–xvi, xxiv–xxv, 84–85.

24. Davis, *Factual Fictions*, 89, 166–167; West, *Daniel Defoe*, 69–85.

25. West, *Daniel Defoe*, 166, 180–181, 203–204; John F. Ross, *Swift and Defoe: A Study in Relationship* (Berkeley: University of California Press, 1941), 10–36.

26. West, *Daniel Defoe*, 165, 218; Ross, *Swift and Defoe*, 8–10.

27. Donald Thomas, *Henry Fielding* (London: Weidenfeld and Nicolson, 1990), 147–158, 298–375; Frans Pieter Van Der Voorde, *Henry Fielding: Critic and Satirist* (New York: Haskell House, 1966), 27–28, 30, 38; Bell, *Henry Fielding*, 83; Cleary, *Henry Fielding*, 5–6, 119–121, 158–159; Uglow, "Fielding, Grub Street, and Canary Wharf," 10; Martin C. and Ruthe R. Battestin, *Henry Fielding: A Life* (London: Routledge, 1989), 327, 446–606; Brian McCrea, *Henry Fielding and the Politics of Mid-eighteenth Century England* (Athens: University of Georgia Press, 1981).

28. Davis, *Factual Fictions*, 193, 197, 199; Giddings, *Tradition of Smollett*, 58; Henry Fielding, *The History of Tom Jones* (1749; reprint, Middlesex, England: Penguin, 1975), 435–439; Battestin and Battestin, *Henry Fielding*, 328; Thomas, *Henry Fielding*, 222; Bell, *Henry Fielding*, 149.

29. Thomas, *Henry Fielding*, 149, 248, 262, 269; Battestin and Battestin, *Henry Fielding*, 327–328, 401, 403; Davis, *Factual Fictions*, 156, 195, 201–209; Van Der Voorde, *Henry Fielding*, 33, 36–37, 41; Cleary, *Henry Fielding*, 10, 217, 240, 243, 265, 267, 269–271.

30. Davis, *Factual Fictions*, 9, 194; Uglow, "Fielding, Grub Street, and Canary Wharf," 13; R. P. C. Mutter, ed., "Introduction" to Fielding, *Tom Jones*, 11; Fielding, *Tom Jones*, 435–439, 657. Although Fielding's definition seems to fit exactly with the modern description of the serious novel, it appears that Fielding was sometimes using the term "novel" in a derogatory sense and did not fully apply it to his own work. Fielding goes into a lengthy explanation of how the authors of "the romances and novels with which the world abounds" have failed to demonstrate anything more than a "pruritus, or rather ... a looseness of the brain" and complains that society often lumps all "historical writers, who do not draw their materials from records" into the same camp. However, Fielding did not succeed in convincing the prudish Johnson, nor did it keep future moralists from criticizing the book. For example, Colonel Newcome, in Thackeray's 1854 *The Newcomes*, praises Johnson but denounces *Tom Jones* and *Joseph Andrews* as "disgraceful things." "As for that Tom Jones – that fellow that sells himself, sir – by heavens, my blood boils when I think of him! I wouldn't sit down in the same room with such a fellow, sir," he added. W. M. Thackeray, *The Newcomes*, volume one in *Complete Works of William Makepeace Thackeray* (New York: Collier and Son, 1902), 41.

31. Bell, *Henry Fielding*, 101–102, 124, 168; Uglow, "Fielding, Grub Street, and Canary Wharf," 11.

32. Thomas, *Henry Fielding*, 152, 275, 344–347, 352–354; Van Der Voorde, *Henry Fielding*, 38; Uglow, "Fielding, Grub Street, and Canary Wharf," 17–18; Cleary, *Henry Fielding*, 291–293, 296–297; Battestin and Battestin, *Henry Fielding*, 144, 537–539, 543–555, 563.

33. Robert Donald Spector, *Tobias George Smollett* (Boston: Twayne, 1989), 3, 14, 17, 27, 31, 34, 44, 60, 83; Giddings, *Tradition of Smollett*, 13–14, 73–91, 122, 163–173;

Kahrl, *Tobias Smollett*, 80, 152; James G. Basker, *Tobias Smollett: Critic and Journalist* (Newark: University of Delaware Press, 1988), 188; Smith, *Novel and Society*, 61, 63.

34. Ginger, *Notable Man*, 129, 164–172, 317–324; www.ourcivilization.com/ smartboard/shop/goldsmith/about.html; www.samueljohnson.com/goldsmith. html.

35. Martin, *Life of Boswell*, 217, 271–272, 287, 337, 371, 393–397, 412, 475–476; A. Russell Brooks, *James Boswell* (New York: Twayne, 1971), 54, 56.

36. Greene, "Samuel Johnson, Journalist," 87; Martin, *Life of Boswell*, 128, 217, 232–233, 287, 297–298, 337, 426–431, 477, 479.

37. Richard B. Schwartz, *Boswell's Johnson: A Preface to the Life* (Madison: The University of Wisconsin Press, 1978), 93; John J. Burke, Jr., "But Boswell's Johnson Is Not Boswell's Johnson," in John A. Vance, ed., *Boswell's Life of Johnson: New Questions, New Answers* (Athens: The University of Georgia Press, 1985), 178.

38. Schwartz, *Boswell's Johnson*, 50, 52, 62, 100–101.

39. Frederick Pottle, "The Life of Boswell," in Harold Bloom, ed., *Dr. Samuel Johnson and James Boswell* (New York: Chelsea, 1986), 33; Paul J. Korshin, "Johnson's Conversation in Boswell's *Life of Johnson*," in Greg Clingham, ed., *New Light on Boswell: Critical and Historical Essays on the Occasion of the Bicentenary of The Life of Johnson* (Cambridge, England: Cambridge University Press, 1991), 179–181, 183, 185–186, 195; William R. Siebenschuh, "Boswell's Second Crop of Memory: A New Look at the Role of Memory in the Making of the *Life*," in Vance, *Boswell's Life of Johnson*, 95; Adam Sisman, *Boswell's Presumptuous Task* (London: Hamish Hamilton, 2000), xviii, 28, 36, 149, 159; William R. Siebenschuh, *Fictional Techniques and Factual Works* (Athens: University of Georgia Press, 1983); 56, 62, 64–65; Martin, *Life of Boswell*, 475.

40. Siebenschuh, *Fictional Techniques*, 54, 73–74, 84, 147–150; Korshin, "Johnson's Conversation," 178; Sisman, *Boswell's Presumptuous Task*, 114, 227; Brooks, *James Boswell*, 73; Greg Clingham, "Truth and Artifice in Boswell's *Life of Johnson*," in Clingham, *New Light on Boswell*, 208–209.

41. Greene, "Samuel Johnson, Journalist," 88, 96–98; Fussell, *Samuel Johnson*, 38–39; Donald Greene, *Samuel Johnson* (New York: Twayne, 1970), 71–72; Lipking, *Samuel Johnson*, 165.

42. Steven Lynn, *Samuel Johnson after Deconstruction: Rhetoric and The Rambler* (Carbondale: Southern Illinois Press, 1992), 9; Paul Fussell, "'The Anxious Employment of a Periodical Writer,'" in Bloom, *Dr. Samuel Johnson*, 92, 100–101; W. Jackson Bate, *Samuel Johnson* (New York: Harcourt Brace Jovanovich, 1975), 222, 290; Lipking, *Samuel Johnson*, 146, 148, 169; Greene, "Samuel Johnson, Journalist," 93, 95–96; Fussell, *Samuel Johnson*, 76–77; John Wain, *Samuel Johnson* (New York: Viking, 1974), 152, 163; Robert Donald Spector, *Samuel Johnson and the Essay* (Westport, CT: Greenwood, 1997), 193–194; Isobel Grundy, "Samuel Johnson: Man of Maxims?," in Grundy, *Samuel Johnson*, 18–19.

43. Greene, "Samuel Johnson, Journalist," 93; Fussell, "'Anxious Employment,'" 90–91; Wain, *Samuel Johnson*, 153; James Boswell, *The Life of Samuel Johnson*, ed.

Frank Brady, (1791; reprint, New York: Signet, 1968), 169; Spector, *Samuel Johnson*, 193–194.

44. Greene, "Samuel Johnson, Journalist," 91; Spector, *Samuel Johnson*, 8; Bate, *Samuel Johnson*, 203–205; McCrea, *Addison and Steele Are Dead*, 12; Lipking, *Samuel Johnson*, 150; Davis, *Factual Fictions*, 76, 88–89, 91; Carey McIntosh, *The Choice of Life: Samuel Johnson and the World of Fiction* (New Haven, CT: Yale University Press, 1973), 20, 26, 30; Kinkead-Weekes, "Johnson," 72–74, 81.

45. Grillo, *Boz*, 1–5, 11, 13, 22, 55, 71, 82, 92, 123, 157, 188, 208, 210, 214.

46. Kaplan, *Dickens*, 97–103.

47. Archibald C. Coolidge, Jr., *Charles Dickens as Serial Novelist* (Ames: Iowa State University Press, 1967), 46, 50, 91, 97, 99–101.

48. Kaplan, *Dickens*, 305–309; Drew, *Dickens the Journalist*, 124, 128, 131, 176–178.

49. Kaplan, *Dickens*, 195–202.

50. Ibid., 197–198, 264–269, 304–310, 414, 429–432, 489–90, 531.

51. Coolidge, *Charles Dickens*, 93; Pearson, *W. M. Thackeray*, 135.

52. Taylor, *Thackeray*, 93, 131; Pearson, *W. M. Thackeray*, 53.

53. Gordon N. Ray, ed., *William Makepeace Thackeray: Contributions to the Morning Chronicle* (Urbana: University of Illinois Press, 1955), xi–xii, xvii, 255; Pearson, *W. M. Thackeray*, 21, 32–42, 61, 65, 67, 137, 167–170, 198; W. M. Thackeray, *The Adventures of Philip* (1862; reprint, London: Macmillan, 1905), 517; Edgar F. Harden, *Thackeray the Writer: From Journalism to Vanity Fair* (New York: St. Martin's, 1988), 33; W. M. Thackeray, *The History of Pendennis: His Fortunes and Misfortunes/His Friends and His Greatest Enemy* (1850; reprint, New York: Oxford University Press, 1994).

54. Pearson, *W. M. Thackeray*, xii–xiii, 8, 11, 13, 137, 152, 154, 164, 166, 192; Harden, *Thackeray the Writer*, 117–118; Taylor, *Thackeray*, 178, 198; Thackeray, *Pendennis*, 416.

55. Taylor, *Thackeray*, 221, 235, 240–241, 250, 252, 255; Pearson, *W. M. Thackeray*, 31, 82–83, 86.

56. Eddy, *Cornhill Magazine*, 12, 19, 48–49; Taylor, *Thackeray*, 419–433.

57. Allen, *Poe*, 97; Calhoun Winton, "Richard Steele, Journalist," in Bond and McLeod, *Newsletters to Newspapers*, 26; Silverman, *Edgar A. Poe*, 198–200.

58. Silverman, *Edgar A. Poe*, 145; Allen, *Poe*, 38, 138, 178.

59. Allen, *Poe*, 83–84; Silverman, *Edgar A. Poe*, 152, 171–174, 205, 209, 297–298.

60. Allen, *Poe*, 54, 167; Silverman, *Edgar A. Poe*, 120–121, 145.

61. Allen, *Poe*, 141, 148–149, 188; from the Introduction to *Great Tales and Poems of Edgar Allan Poe* (New York: Washington Square, 1962), xi.

62. Silverman, *Edgar A. Poe*, 110, 112, 171–173.

63. Allen, *Poe*, 10, 12, 23–24, 29–30, 35, 87, 92–93, 97, 101, 110, 188.

64. Silverman, *Edgar A. Poe*, 119–121, 146, 155; Allen, *Poe*, 67.

65. Silverman, *Edgar A. Poe*, 188–190, 244–247, 271–277.

66. Allen, *Poe*, 189–190; Silverman, *Edgar A. Poe*, 191, 202, 209, 222–225, 234, 394, 396–397, 408, 423–424, 432.

67. Gordon S. Haight, *George Eliot and John Chapman* (New Haven, CT: Yale University Press, 1940), 12–13, 40, 49; Kathryn Hughes, *George Eliot: The Last*

Victorian (New York: Farrar, Straus and Giroux, 1998), 83, 98–101, 103, 107–108, 118–120.

68. Haight, *George Eliot*, 69–70, 97–101.
69. Ibid., 68, 97–100, 102; David Williams, *Mr. George Eliot: A Biography of George Henry Lewes* (London: Hodder and Stoughton, 1983), 107.
70. Williams, *Mr. George Eliot*, 34, 165, 169–170, 231; Gross, *Rise and Fall of the Man of Letters*, 68–75.
71. Zachary Leader, "Coleridge and the Uses of Journalism," in Treglown and Bennett, *Grub Street*, 22–40.
72. Ibid., 23, 27–28, 38; Doughty, *Perturbed Spirit*, 99–107, 133, 340–341, 354–355, 357, 434.
73. George L. Barnett, *Charles Lamb* (Boston: Twayne, 1976), 39, 43, 50, 52.
74. Ibid., 44, 89, 91–92, 94–98, 104, 108–109, 113; Winifred F. Courtney, *Young Charles Lamb 1775–1802* (London: Macmillan, 1982), 311–313.
75. Barnett, *Charles Lamb*, 44, 91–93, 95–96, 98, 108, 113; Courtney, *Young Charles Lamb*, 314.
76. Leader, "Coleridge," 29; Grevel Lindop, "De Quincey and the Edinburgh and Glasgow University Circles," in Treglown and Bennett, *Grub Street*, 43, 45, 52; Grevel Lindop, *The Opium-Eater: A Life of Thomas De Quincey* (London: J. M. Dent and Sons, 1981), 259–260, 284–286.
77. Lindop, *Opium-Eater*, 144, 146, 157, 202–203, 239, 241–243, 254; Lindop, "De Quincey," 45; Doughty, *Perturbed Spirit*, 553.

CHAPTER 2 LITERARY REALISM, 1850–1915

1. Mark Twain, *Life on the Mississippi* (1877; reprint, New York: Signet, 1961), 53; John Lauber, *The Making of Mark Twain: A Biography* (New York: Farrar, Straus and Giroux, 1985), 113.
2. Mark Dawidziak, ed., *Mark My Words: Mark Twain on Writing* (New York: St. Martin's, 1996), 103.
3. Branch, *Literary Apprenticeship of Mark Twain*, 153.
4. Ernest Marchand, *Frank Norris: A Study* (1942; reprint, New York: Octagon, 1964), 53, 203.
5. Christopher Smith, ed., *American Realism* (San Diego, CA: Greenhaven Press, 2000), 26–27, 41; Richard O'Connor, *Bret Harte: A Biography* (Boston: Little, Brown, 1966), 7; Margaret Duckett, *Mark Twain and Bret Harte* (Norman: University of Oklahoma Press, 1964), 9, 312–332.
6. Smith, *American Realism*, 43; Theodore Dreiser, *A Book About Myself* (New York: Boni and Liveright, 1922).
7. William Dean Howells, *My Mark Twain: Reminiscences and Criticisms* (1910; reprint, Baton Rouge: Louisiana State University, 1967), 38; Lars Ahnebrink, *The Beginnings of Naturalism in American Fiction: A Study of the Works of Hamlin Garland, Stephen Crane, and Frank Norris with Special Reference on Some European Influences, 1891–1903* (New York: Russell and Russell, 1961), 11, 80–85.

8. Smith, *American Realism*, 14, 166; Anthony Channell Hilfer, "The Small Town in American Realism," in Smith, *American Realism*, 167, 175; Ahnebrink, *Beginnings of Naturalism*, 69, 80–87.

9. Smith, *American Realism*, 15; Sydney H. Bremer, "The Rise of the City in American Realism," in Smith, *American Realism*, 178.

10. Smith, *American Realism*, 18.

11. Mark Twain, *The Adventures of Huckleberry Finn* (1884; reprint, New York: Laurel, 1971), 209.

12. Smith, *American Realism*, 19.

13. Howells, *My Mark Twain*, 26.

14. Herbert J. Gans, *Deciding What's News: A Study of CBS Evening News, NBC Nightly News, Newsweek, and Time* (1979; reprint, New York: Vintage, 1980), 42–52.

15. Cady, *Road to Realism*, 180; Edmund Reiss, Afterword in Twain, *A Connecticut Yankee in King Arthur's Court* (1889; reprint, New York: Signet, 1963), 324–325; Justin Kaplan, *Mr. Clemens and Mark Twain: A Biography* (New York: Simon and Schuster, 1966), 265, 347; Ron Powers, *Mark Twain: A Life* (2005; reprint, New York: Free Press, 2006), 374–375.

16. Margaret Sanborn, *Mark Twain: The Bachelor Years: A Biography* (New York: Doubleday, 1990), 73–75, 79–80; Philip Ashley Fanning, *Mark Twain and Orion Clemens: Brothers, Partners, Strangers* (Tuscaloosa: The University of Alabama Press, 2003), 23, 25–27.

17. McCrea, *Addison and Steele Are Dead*, 106; Gladys Carmen Bellamy, *Mark Twain as a Literary Artist* (Norman: University of Oklahoma Press, 1950), 86, 89; McCullough and McIntire-Strasburg, *Mark Twain at the Buffalo Express*, xl; Lauber, *Making of Mark Twain*, 110, 115–116; Sanborn, *Mark Twain*, 185–186; Branch, *Literary Apprenticeship of Mark Twain*, 62.

18. Lauber, *Making of Mark Twain*, 141–143; McCullough and McIntire-Strasburg, *Mark Twain at the Buffalo Express*, xi; Branch, *Literary Apprenticeship of Mark Twain*, 113, 153–154; Andrew Hoffman, *Inventing Mark Twain: The Lives of Samuel Longhorne Clemens* (New York: Morrow, 1997), 95; Sanborn, *Mark Twain*, 253.

19. Kaplan, *Mr. Clemens and Mark Twain*, 162–164.

20. Everett Emerson, *Mark Twain: A Literary Life* (Philadelphia: University of Pennsylvania Press, 2000), 132–139, 144–145; Fishkin, *From Fact to Fiction*, 78; Powers, *Mark Twain*, 465, 471–474.

21. Kaplan, *Mr. Clemens and Mark Twain*, 347; Powers, *Mark Twain*, 184.

22. Rodney D. Olsen, *Dancing in Chains: The Youth of William Dean Howells* (New York: New York University Press, 1991), 137–138; Smith, *American Realism*, 10.

23. Kenneth Eble, *William Dean Howells, Second Edition* (Boston: Twayne, 1982), 2–3, 11; Kenneth S. Lynn, *William Dean Howells: An American Life* (1970; reprint, New York: Harcourt Brace Jovanovich, 1971), 54–55; Olsen, *Dancing in Chains*, 36–37, 44; Clara Kirk and Rudolf Kirk, *William Dean Howells* (New York: Twayne, 1962), 22; Cady, *Road to Realism*, 49.

24. Olsen, *Dancing in Chains*, 47, 104–115; Kirk and Kirk, *William Dean Howells*, 28; Eble, *William Dean Howells*, 24–25; Amy Kaplan, *The Social Construction*

of American Realism (Chicago: University of Chicago Press, 1988), 20; Cady, *Road to Realism*, 69–71; Lynn, *William Dean Howells*, 78.

25. Olsen, *Dancing in Chains*, 188–189; Eble, *William Dean Howells*, 32; Cady, *Road to Realism*, 84.

26. Eble, *William Dean Howells*, 43, 84; Cady, *Road to Realism*, 117–119, 132–133.

27. Robertson, *Stephen Crane*, 18–20, 22–23; Cady, *Road to Realism*, 208.

28. Lynn, *William Dean Howells*, 158–160; Cady, *Road to Realism*, 166–167.

29. Axel Nissen, *Bret Harte: Prince and Pauper* (Jackson: University Press of Mississippi, 2000), xv, 97; Gary Scharnhorst, *Bret Harte: Opening the American Literary West* (Norman: University of Oklahoma Press, 2000), 43; Gary Scharnhorst, *Bret Harte* (New York: Twayne, 1992), 118.

30. Nissen, *Bret Harte*, 33, 37–39, 98.

31. Scharnhorst, *Bret Harte*, 3, 78–86, 92–112; Nissen, *Bret Harte*, 60; Scharnhorst, *Opening the American Literary West*, 37–69, 86.

32. Lawrence I. Berkove, *A Prescription for Adversity: The Moral Art of Ambrose Bierce* (Columbus: The Ohio State University Press, 2002), 30, 83; Richard Saunders, *Ambrose Bierce: The Making of a Misanthrope* (San Francisco: Chronicle, 1985), 62.

33. Berkove, *Prescription for Adversity*, 21, 23, 46, 76, 83, 87, 113, 115; Richard O'Connor, *Ambrose Bierce: A Biography* (Boston: Little, Brown, 1967), 22–23, 29–30, 41–42, 163, 180; Carey McWilliams, *Ambrose Bierce: A Biography* (Hamden, CT: Archon, 1967), 226, 307.

34. Berkove, *Prescription for Adversity*, 94, 136, 142–143, 151; O'Connor, *Ambrose Bierce*, 120, 124, 132–133.

35. Ambrose Bierce, *The Enlarged Devil's Dictionary* (1906; reprint, Garden City, New York: Doubleday, 1967), 237; Smith, *American Realism*, 40; Harold H. Kolb, *The Illusion of Life: American Realism as a Literary Form* (Charlottesville: The University Press of Virginia, 1969), 45; *The Catholic World*, Issue XLII, Nov., 1885.

36. Franklin Walker, *Frank Norris: A Biography* (1932; reprint, New York: Russell and Russell, 1963), 79, 169–171; R. W. Stallman, *Stephen Crane: A Biography* (New York: Braziller, 1968), 125; Robertson, *Stephen Crane*, 20–21; Swanberg, *Dreiser*, 92, 161; F. O. Matthiessen, *Theodore Dreiser* (Toronto: George J. McLeod, 1951), 57.

37. Smith, *American Realism*, 12.

38. Kolb, *Illusion of Life*, 34; Cady, *Road to Realism*, 204; David E. Shi, "American Realism in the Postmodern Age," in Smith, *American Realism*, 188; Kaplan, *Social Construction of American Realism*, 9.

39. Christopher Benfey, *The Double Life of Stephen Crane* (New York: Knopf, 1992), 15, 229–230; Linda H. Davis, *Badge of Courage: The Life of Stephen Crane* (Boston: Houghton Mifflin, 1998), 272–273.

40. Paul Civello, *American Literary Naturalism and Its Twentieth Century Transformations: Frank Norris, Ernest Hemingway, Don DeLillo* (Athens: The University of Georgia Press, 1994), 1–5, 72, 74, 76, 91, 93–96, 105, 110; Marchand, *Frank Norris*, 52.

41. Mary Lawlor, *Recalling the Wild: Naturalism and the Closing of the American West* (New Brunswick, NJ: Rutgers University Press, 2000), 85, 157–158, 194; Yoshinobu Hakutani, *Young Dreiser: A Critical Study* (Cranbury, NJ: Associated University Presses, 1980), 20–21; Shawn St. Jean, *Pagan Dreiser: Songs from American Mythology* (Cranbury, NJ: Associated University Presses, 2001), 37; Ahnebrink, *Beginnings of Naturalism*, 11–15.

42. Lawlor, *Recalling the Wild*, 90.

43. Dreiser, *Book About Myself*, 69–70.

44. Ibid., 457–459; Hakutani, *Young Dreiser*, 125.

45. Theodore Dreiser, *Dawn: An Autobiography of Early Youth* (1931; reprint, Santa Rosa, CA: Black Sparrow Press, 1998), 551–553.

46. Everett Carter, *Howells and the Age of Realism* (Hamden, CT: Archon, 1966), 234, 237, 271. See also Donald Pizer, *Realism and Naturalism in Nineteenth Century American Literature* (Carbondale: Southern Illinois University Press, 1966); Dreiser, *Book About Myself*, 75, 411; Matthiessen, *Theodore Dreiser*, 61.

47. Mark Twain, *The Mysterious Stranger and Other Stories* (1916; reprint, New York: Harper and Brothers, 1922, 1950), 20, 26–27, 50–51, 81, 111; Carter, *Howells and the Age of Realism*, 234; Marchand, *Frank Norris*, 206–208; Roy Morris, Jr., *Ambrose Bierce: Alone in Bad Company* (New York: Oxford University Press, 1995), 205; Richard O'Connor, *Jack London; A Biography* (Boston: Little, Brown, 1964), 14, 100, 104; Hughes, *George Eliot*, 279–280.

48. Edward J. Larson, *Summer for the Gods: The Scopes Trial and America's Continuing Debate over Science and Religion* (New York: BasicBooks, 1997), 94, 125, 256–257; Charles Child Walcutt, *American Literary Naturalism, A Divided Stream* (Minneapolis: University of Minnesota Press, 1956), 90.

49. Wilson, *Labor of Words*, 27–41, 47–49, 58–59, 61, 79.

50. Ibid., 16–18, 22, 58; Moers, *Two Dreisers*, 18; Robertson, *Stephen Crane*, 6, 56–57.

51. Walker, *Frank Norris*, 96–101; Dreiser, *Book About Myself*, 75; Carl Bode, *Mencken* (Carbondale: Southern Illinois University Press, 1969), 55.

52. Moers, *Two Dreisers*, 21.

53. Walcutt, *American Literary Naturalism*, 81.

54. Matthiessen, *Theodore Dreiser*, 61.

55. Swanberg, *Dreiser*, 19–20, 59, 83, 253–254, 277, 286–287, 297; Robertson, *Stephen Crane*, 185, 187–188, 192; Moers, *Two Dreisers*, 21, 29, 210; Fishkin, *From Fact to Fiction*, 97–98.

56. Richard Lehan, *Theodore Dreiser: His World and His Novels* (Carbondale: Southern Illinois University Press, 1969), 54; Philip L. Gerber, *Theodore Dreiser* (New York: Twayne, 1964), 67; Hakutani, *Young Dreiser*, 194; Swanberg, *Dreiser*, 23–26, 35, 37.

57. Robert Penn Warren, *Homage to Theodore Dreiser* (New York: Random House, 1971), 17; Swanberg, *Dreiser*, 37–41; Matthiessen, *Theodore Dreiser*, 24–25, 56, 66; Hakutani, *Young Dreiser*, 69.

58. Swanberg, *Dreiser*, 65–68; Gerber, *Theodore Dreiser*, 67.

59. Swanberg, *Dreiser*, 67–68, 70–72, 82, 119–135; Hakutani, *Young Dreiser*, 128–130, 174; James Lundquist, *Theodore Dreiser* (New York: Frederick Unger, 1974), 28; Matthiessen, *Theodore Dreiser*, 55–56, 174.

60. Swanberg, *Dreiser*, 11, 20, 59, 83, 86–92, 100–105, 144, 172, 203–204; Robert H. Elias, *Theodore Dreiser: Apostle of Nature* (Ithaca, NY: Cornell University Press, 1948), 113–115; Lehan, *Theodore Dreiser*, 211; Hakutani, *Young Dreiser*, 50; Lingeman, *Theodore Dreiser*, 40–41, 95–98, 127–140.

61. Swanberg, *Dreiser*, 253–254, 277, 286–287, 294, 297; Robertson, *Stephen Crane*, 192.

62. Davis, *Badge of Courage*, 79–81; Stallman, *Stephen Crane*, 85, 94, 99; Robertson, *Stephen Crane*, 95–96, 177–210; John Berryman, *Stephen Crane* (1950, reprint, Cleveland: World Publishing, 1962), 92; James B. Colvert, *Stephen Crane* (San Diego: Harcourt Brace Jovanovich, 1984), 44.

63. Stallman, *Stephen Crane*, 67, 69, 73–74; H. Wayne Morgan, *Writers in Transition: Seven Americans* (New York: Hill and Wang, 1963), 6.

64. Stallman, *Stephen Crane*, 9, 13; Milne Holton, *Cylinder of Vision: The Fiction and Journalistic Writing of Stephen Crane* (Baton Rouge: Louisiana State University Press, 1972), 21; Colvert, *Stephen Crane*, 36–37; Davis, *Badge of Courage*, 51.

65. Stallman, *Stephen Crane*, 93–94, 129–132; Colvert, *Stephen Crane*, 74–78.

66. Morgan, *Writers in Transition*, 3; Stallman, *Stephen Crane*, 88, 107–108; Berryman, *Stephen Crane*, 33, 94; Edwin H. Cady, *Stephen Crane* (Boston: Twayne, 1980), 22–23.

67. Cady, *Stephen Crane*, 55; Benfey, *Double Life of Stephen Crane*, 121; Davis, *Badge of Courage*, 103, 106, 274; Colvert, *Stephen Crane*, 35–36; Marston LaFrance, *A Reading of Stephen Crane* (London: Clarendon Press, 1971), 174; Thomas Beer, *Stephen Crane: A Study in American Letters* (New York: Knopf, 1923), 233. The footnotes that refer to Beer should reflect that everything he says about Crane be judged carefully, since he apparently fabricated letters of Crane's and invented stories and romances. Davis, *Badge of Courage*, x.

68. Holton, *Cylinder of Vision*, 80–81; Morgan, *Writers in Transition*, 13–14.

69. Lawlor, *Recalling the Wild*, 91; Joseph R. McElrath, Jr., *Frank Norris Revisited* (New York: Twayne, 1992), 14; Walker, *Frank Norris*, 127; William B. Dillingham, *Frank Norris: Instinct and Art* (Lincoln: University of Nebraska Press, 1969), 32; Stallman, *Stephen Crane*, 354.

70. Walker, *Frank Norris*, 127, 129, 139, 255–257, 265, 267; Dillingham, *Frank Norris*, 51; Robert W. Schneider, *Five Novelists of the Progressive Era* (New York: Columbia University Press, 1965), 116–117; Marchand, *Frank Norris*, 17–18, 94; McElrath, *Frank Norris Revisited*, 14.

71. Dillingham, *Frank Norris*, 44–45, 74, 127–128; Warren French, *Frank Norris* (New York: Twayne, 1962), 82; Marchand, *Frank Norris*, 49; Walker, *Frank Norris*, 246–250, 253.

72. Barbara Hochman, *The Art of Frank Norris, Storyteller* (Columbia: University of Missouri Press, 1988), 6, 12; Dillingham, *Frank Norris*, 74, 106, 116, 127; Walker, *Frank Norris*, 220–222, 232; McElrath, *Frank Norris Revisited*, 18.

73. Don Graham, *The Fiction of Frank Norris: The Aesthetic Content* (Columbia: University of Missouri Press, 1978), 13; Lawlor, *Recalling the Wild*, 91–92; Robert A. Morace, "The Writer and His Middle Class Audience: Frank Norris, A Case in Point," in Don Graham, ed., *Critical Essays on Frank Norris* (Boston: G. K. Hall,

1980), 59; Dillingham, *Frank Norris*, 52; Marchand, *Frank Norris*, 23; Walcutt, *American Literary Naturalism*, 135; Walker, *Frank Norris*, 53.

74. John Perry, *Jack London: An American Myth* (Chicago: Nelson-Hall, 1981), 139, 151; Sinclair, *Jack*, xv-xvi, 23–25, 32–37; Francis Shor, "Power, Gender, and Ideological Discourse in *The Iron Heel*," in Leonard Cassuto and Jeanne Campbell Reesman, eds., *Rereading Jack London* (Stanford, CA: Stanford University Press, 1996), 91; Earle Labor, *Jack London* (New York: Twayne, 1974), 95.

75. Jack London, *Martin Eden* (1908; reprint, New York: Penguin, 1946), 223–224; Labor, *Jack London*, 47; Perry, *Jack London*, 84, 89, 156; Sinclair, *Jack*, 35–36, 55, 57, 67; Wilson, *Labor of Words*, 95, 97–98, 100–101.

76. Sinclair, *Jack*, 58, 95, 126, 134, 227; Labor, *Jack London*, 83, 87; Perry, *Jack London*, 90.

77. Walcutt, *American Literary Naturalism*, 255; Charles Carrington, *Rudyard Kipling: His Life and Work* (1955; reprint, New York: Penguin, 1986), 304–305; Jackson J. Benson, *John Steinbeck, Writer: A Biography* (1984; reprint, New York: Penguin, 1990), 648–649.

78. Wilson, *Labor of Words*, 194, 197–199, 201.

CHAPTER 3 REPORTERS AS NOVELISTS, 1890–TODAY

1. Walker, *Richard Wright*, 122–125.

2. Ibid., 125; Swanberg, *Dreiser*, 83–85, 146, 164, 172–173, 294–297.

3. Again, it should be noted that the "new" journalism of the 1960s and 1970s wasn't "new", at least by the nomenclature of historical periods when original styles of journalism had been called "new" as well. See Michael Schudson, *Discovering the News: A Social History of American Newspapers* (New York: Basic, 1978), 186–188; Frus, *Politics and Poetics of Journalistic Narrative*, 134–136; Wolfe, "Stalking the Billion-Footed Beast," 45–56.

4. West, *Daniel Defoe*, 4–5, 237–238.

5. William Dean Howells, *A Modern Instance* (1882; reprint, New York: Penguin, 1984), 213, 450–451; William Dean Howells, *The Rise of Silas Lapham* (1885; reprint, New York: Penguin, 1986), 3–23; Robertson, *Stephen Crane*, 18–20, 22–27; Cady, *Road to Realism*, 208.

6. Robertson, *Stephen Crane*, 132–135; Frus, *Politics and Poetics of Journalistic Narrative* 15–28, 35–41, 50–52.

7. Fenton, *Apprenticeship of Ernest Hemingway*, 103; Ronald Weber, *Hemingway's Art of Non-Fiction* (London: Macmillan, 1990), 26; Moreau, *Restless Journey of James Agee*, 278; Laurence Bergreen, *James Agee: A Life* (1984; reprint, New York: Penguin, 1985), 307–309; Harvena Richter, *Writing to Survive: The Private Notebooks of Conrad Richter* (Albuquerque: University of New Mexico Press, 1988), 191.

8. Benson, *John Steinbeck*, 3–4, 38, 41, 46–47.

9. Robert O. Stephens, *Hemingway's Nonfiction: The Public Voice* (Chapel Hill: The University of North Carolina Press, 1968), 6; Carlos Baker, *Hemingway: The Writer as Artist* (1952; reprint, Princeton, NJ: Princeton University Press, 1972), 58–69.

10. Carlos Baker, *Ernest Hemingway: A Life Story* (New York: Scribner's, 1969), 147–155; Bertram D. Sarason, *Hemingway and The Sun Set* (Washington, DC: National Cash Register Company, 1972), 8–18, 33–38, 47–56; Baker, *Writer as Artist*, 63.

11. Melvin Mencher, *News Reporting and Writing: Second Edition* (1977; reprint, Dubuque, IA: William C. Brown, 1982), 162; J. F. Kobler, *Ernest Hemingway: Journalist and Artist* (1968; reprint, Ann Arbor, MI: UMI Research Press, 1985), 18; Lee, *Willa Cather*, 157, 187; www.annabelle.net.

12. Vasant A. Shahane, *Rudyard Kipling: Activist and Artist* (Carbondale: Southern Illinois University Press, 1973), 14–15, 17, 71, 74, 84, 132; Cornell, *Kipling in India*, 108, 115, 127, 145–150; Lord Birkenhead, *Rudyard Kipling* (London: Weidenfeld and Nicolson, 1978), 63, 145, 163–164; Martin Seymour-Smith, *Kipling* (London: Macdonald, 1989), 55, 69; W. L. Renwick, "Re-reading Kipling," in Andrew Rutherford, ed., *Kipling's Mind and Art: Selected Critical Essays* (Stanford, CA: Stanford University Press, 1964), 7, 10, 13; Lionel Trilling, "Kipling," in Ibid., 87; Noel Annan, "Kipling's Place in the History of Ideas," in Ibid., 109; James Harrison, *Rudyard Kipling* (Boston: Twayne, 1982), 66; Philip Mason, *Kipling: The Glass, the Shadow and the Fire* (New York: Harper and Row, 1975), 119–122; Harry Ricketts, *Rudyard Kipling: A Life* (New York: Carroll and Graf, 1999), 219; Carrington, *Rudyard Kipling*, 284–285; Bonamy Dobree, *Rudyard Kipling: Realist and Fabulist* (London: Oxford University Press, 1967), 4; J. I. M. Stewart, *Rudyard Kipling* (New York: Dodd, Mead, 1966), 116.

13. Richard Lingeman, *Sinclair Lewis: Rebel from Main Street* (New York: Random House, 2002), 23, 86, 91, 553; Schorer, *Sinclair Lewis*, 141, 143, 153–154, 156–157, 338, 361–369, 448–450.

14. Lee, *Willa Cather*, 259–288; Woodress, *Willa Cather*, 399–411; Downs, *Becoming Modern*, 14, 83–85, 94–96, 101–10?, 123–125, 131–132, 136.

15. Robertson, *Stephen Crane*, 197, 199, 202–206, 240; Fishkin, *From Fact to Fiction*, 150–151; Fenton, *Apprenticeship of Ernest Hemingway*, 229–236, 259; Frus, *Politics and Poetics of Journalistic Narrative*, 60–63; Scott Donaldson, *By Force of Will: The Life and Art of Ernest Hemingway* (New York: Viking, 1977), 10–11, 24, 38, 245; Matthew J. Bruccoli, *Ernest Hemingway, Cub Reporter* (Pittsburgh, PA: University of Pittsburgh Press, 1970). Robertson notes that these passages also have been analyzed by Keith Carabine, J. F. Kobler, Jeffrey Meyers, and Elizabeth Dewberry Vaughn (Robertson, *Stephen Crane*, 240).

16. Ernest Hemingway, "Pamplona in July," in *By-Line: Ernest Hemingway*, ed. William White (1967; reprint, New York: Penguin, 1980), 105–114; Weber, *Hemingway's Art*, 26.

17. Hemingway, "Pamplona in July," 113; Ernest Hemingway, *The Sun Also Rises* (1926; reprint, New York: Scribner, 2003), 220–221.

18. Benson, *John Steinbeck*, 182, 198, 233, 332–333, 341–348, 439–440, 609, 612, 682.

19. Ludington, *John Dos Passos*, 256, 260, 295–296, 301, 308–309, 317, 351, 404; Strychacz, *Modernism, Mass Culture, and Professionalism*, 149; Fishkin, *From Fact to Fiction*, 168–169, 183–184.

20. Miller, *Erskine Caldwell*, 72, 94, 116, 118, 121, 123–124, 127, 129–130, 132, 134, 150, 166, 201–202, 259, 263–269, 357.

21. Walker, *Richard Wright*, 124, 237–238.
22. Moreau, *Journey of James Agee*, 198–199, 262, 277–278; Bergreen, *James Agee*, 169–177, 179, 243–245, 253, 257, 260–261.
23. Richter, *Writing to Survive*, 90, 95–97, 130–132, 173, 189, 191–193, 195; David R. Johnson, *Conrad Richter: A Writer's Life* (University Park: The Pennsylvania State University Press, 2001), 135–136, 154.
24. Frus, *Politics and Poetics of Journalistic Narrative*, 92–95; For Hersey's concerns about "New Journalism," go on-line and type in key words: "john hersey" and "new journalism." Click on item entitled "Chapter III/Shades of Journalism" and go to his quotes. John Hersey, "The Legend on the License," *Yale Review* 70 (1980): 1–25.
25. Shelden, *Graham Greene*, 322–327, 334–335, 364–369, 372, 393.
26. Branch, *James T. Farrell*, 31–33, 163, 168–170.
27. Clarke, *Capote*, 290–295, 298–304, 317–324, 342–349, 357–360, 363, 397–399, 401–402; Frus, *Politics and Poetics of Journalistic Narrative*, 255.
28. Mary V. Dearborn, *Mailer: A Biography* (Boston: Houghton Mifflin, 1999), 40, 235, 244, 246, 259, 348–351.
29. Joan Didion, *Slouching Toward Bethlehem* (1961; reprint, New York: Washington Square, 1981), 19.

CHAPTER 4 THE TAINT OF JOURNALISTIC LITERATURE

1. West, *Daniel Defoe*, 218.
2. Morris, *Ambrose Bierce*, 151, 212–213, 222; O'Connor, *Ambrose Bierce*, 177–180.
3. Morris, *Ambrose Bierce*, 187, 206–207, 227, 236.
4. Brome, *J. B. Priestley*, 106; Robertson, *Stephen Crane*, 30; Harrison, *Rudyard Kipling*, 20; Carrington, *Rudyard Kipling*, 368; Arthur W. Brown, *Margaret Fuller* (New York: Twayne, 1964), 82, 121–122.
5. Louis Filler, *Voice of Democracy: A Critical Biography of David Graham Phillips: Journalist, Novelist, Progressive* (University Park: The Pennsylvania State University Press, 1978), 75.
6. Beauman, *E. M. Forster*, 192, 245, 309–310, 330, 333–334, 354–355, 370.
7. Shelden, *Orwell*, 424–426.
8. Filler, *Voice of Democracy*, 138; Brome, *J. B. Priestley*, 133; Downs, *Becoming Modern*, 23; Lutes, *Front-Page Girls*, 135, 139, 146, 148, 150; Scott Elledge, *E. B. White: A Biography* (1984; reprint, New York: Norton, 1986), 219, 223.
9. Pearson, *W. M. Thackeray*, 153; Silverman, *Edgar A. Poe*, 132; Jonathan Yardley, *Ring: A Biography of Ring Lardner* (New York: Random House, 1977), 393; Hermione Lee, "'Crimes of Criticism': Virginia Woolf and Literary Journalism," in Treglown and Bennett, *Grub Street*, 118, 121, 129.
10. Filler, *Voice of Democracy*, 69; Benson, *John Steinbeck*, 984; Charles P. Frank, *Edmund Wilson* (New York: Twayne, 1970), 154–155; Cary Tennis, "Tom Wolfe," *Salon.com* (Feb. 1, 2000): 3.
11. Ellen Wright and Michel Fabre, eds., *Richard Wright Reader* (New York: Harper and Row, 1978), 34.

12. Faith Berry, *Langston Hughes: Before and Beyond Harlem* (Westport, CT: Lawrence Hill, 1983), 309–311, 326; R. Bruce Bickley, Jr., *Joel Chandler Harris* (Boston: Twayne, 1978), 95–130.

13. Ann Waldron, *Eudora: A Writer's Life* (1998; reprint, New York: Anchor, 1999), 66; Joan Givner, *Katherine Anne Porter: A Life* (1981; reprint, New York: Touchstone, 1982), 130.

14. Norman Mailer, *The Armies of the Night: History as a Novel/The Novel as History* (New York: New American Library, 1968), 21–22; Dearborn, *Mailer*, 119, 237.

15. Dearborn, *Mailer*, 152–153.

16. Howe, *Sherwood Anderson*, 124, 206–207, 228–229, 249–250; Sherwood Anderson, "In Washington," in Horace Gregory, ed., *The Portable Sherwood Anderson* (1972; reprint, New York: Viking, 1949), 447–454.

17. Miller, *Erskine Caldwell*, 213, 216–217, 219–221, 319–320.

18. Benson, *John Steinbeck*, 913, 922, 973; Moreau, *Restless Journey of James Agee*, 276–277; Doug Underwood, "Depression, Drink, and Dissipation: The Troubled Inner World of Famous Journalist-Literary Figures and Art as the Ultimate Stimulant," *Journalism History* 32 (Winter, 2007): 186–200.

19. Holton, *Cylinder of Vision*, 149; Colvert, *Stephen Crane*, 146; LaFrance, *Reading of Stephen Crane*, 176; Beer, *Stephen Crane*, 222.

20. Dearborn, *Mailer*, 177.

21. Kaplan, *Mr. Clemens and Mark Twain*, 209–211; Howe, *Sherwood Anderson*, 30, 45.

22. Fenton, *Apprenticeship of Ernest Hemingway*, 1; Meade, *Dorothy Parker*, 19, 25–27, 30, 113–114; Anne Edwards, *Road to Tara: The Life of Margaret Mitchell* (New Haven, CT: Ticknor and Fields, 1983), 75; Clarke, *Capote*, 4, 15–25, 57–59.

23. Yardley, *Ring*, 58–59.

24. Morris, *Ambrose Bierce*, 12–14; Walker, *Richard Wright*, 25–26, 31–38; Clarke, *Capote*, 326–327; Billy Altman, *Laughter's Gentle Soul: The Life of Robert Benchley* (New York: Norton, 1997), 24–27.

25. Carrington, *Rudyard Kipling*, 401–402.

26. Ambrose Bierce, "The Short Story," in *Tales of Soldiers and Civilians and Other Stories* (1897; reprint, New York: Penguin, 2000), 253–259; McWilliams, *Ambrose Bierce*, 234–235; Meade, *Dorothy Parker*, 210; H. L. Mencken, "Dreiser," in *A Mencken Chrestomathy* (1949; reprint, New York: Vintage, 1982), 504.

27. Miller, *Erskine Caldwell*, 340–341; Benson, *John Steinbeck*, 91–92, 95.

28. Morris, *Ambrose Bierce*, 172–174; Finis Farr, *O'Hara: A Biography* (Boston: Little, Brown, 1973), 243–244, 253.

29. Burton Bernstein, *Thurber: A Biography* (1975; reprint, New York: Ballantine, 1976), 590, 620–622; Altman, *Laughter's Gentle Soul*, 333–334.

30. Shelden, *Graham Greene*, 143–144, 175, 189–192, 346, 352.

31. Selina Hastings, *Evelyn Waugh: A Biography* (Boston: Houghton Mifflin, 1994), 157, 183, 212, 288–289.

32. Farr, *O'Hara*, 151, 193–194, 222.

33. Shelden, *Orwell*, 131–132, 181–184, 202, 397.

EPILOGUE. THE FUTURE OF JOURNALISTIC FICTION

1. Robertson, *Stephen Crane*, 14–16; Roggenkamp, *Narrating the News*, 126–128.
2. Someone such as James, Thomas Strychacz said, has become central to academic scholarship because his discourse of complexity (or what one critic has called James' "cultivated obscurity" and his "stylistic barrier against the mob") helps to reinforce the power of the literary specialist. Robertson, *Stephen Crane*, 45; Strychacz, *Modernism, Mass Culture, and Professionalism*, 1, 20–21, 24, 27–28, 32, 37; Bernstein, *Thurber*, 74, 140, 144, 226, 512; Lutes, *Front-Page Girls*, 94–118; Wikipedia attributes the quote to Henry Adams, while others attribute it to his wife. http://en.wikiquote.org/wiki/Henry_Adams; http://attrition.org/quotes/chiamus.html. Wells quote, http://en.wikipedia.org/wiki/Henry_James#Style_ and SS_themes.
3. Towers, "Flap Over Tom Wolfe," 15; Wolfe, "Stalking the Billion-Footed Beast," 55–56.
4. Towers, "Flap Over Tom Wolfe," 15–16.
5. Biographical searches in Literature Resource Center, Suzzallo Library, University of Washington.
6. Frank Norris, "Dying Fires," in *The Best Short Stories of Frank Norris* (Forest Hills, NY: Ironweed, 1998), 130, 132–133, 136.
7. David Lodge argues that in the twentieth century, there was a split between cutting-edge literary fiction and middle-brow entertainment fiction. Henry James, James Joyce, and Virginia Woolf are some of the names on the "cutting edge" side of the divide, while many of the other journalist-literary figures could presumably be considered to be on the other. Lodge believes that toward the end of the twentieth century, the divide grew less and "literary best-sellers" have become possible. See Lodge's review of Jane Smiley's biography on Charles Dickens, *Atlantic*, October 22, 2002, www.theatlantic.com. Jane Smiley, *Charles Dickens* (New York: Viking, 2002). For Mailer quote, see Tennis, "Tom Wolfe," 3.
8. Ghiglione, "The American Journalist," 9.
9. Robert Solotaroff, "Robert Stone," *Dictionary of Literary Biography, Volume 152: American Novelists Since World War II, Fourth Series* (Gale Group, 1995), 216–231.
10. Norman Mailer, *The Naked and the Dead* (1948; reprint, New York: Henry Holt, 1998), xi–xii.
11. McCrea, *Addison and Steele Are Dead*, 27, 41, 69, 91, 93, 141–142, 146–147, 167–168, 196, 199, 210.
12. Strychacz, *Modernism, Mass Culture, and Professionalism*, 3–4, 15, 23, 203. For a discussion of the development of the professionalization of literary studies at British universities – including Oxford and Cambridge – see Gross, *Rise and Fall of the Man of Letters*, 167–189.
13. Acocella, *Willa Cather*, 24–27, 32, 34–35, 37–65, 73–75; George Weigel, "God, Man, and H. L. Mencken," *First Things* 53 (May, 1995): 50–59.
14. Jane Smiley, "Say it Ain't So, Huck: Second Thoughts on Mark Twain's 'Masterpiece,'" *Harper's* (Jan., 1996): 61–67.

15. Reynolds, *Walt Whitman's America*, 373.
16. Smiley, *Moo* (New York: Knopf, 1995).
17. In fact, one can argue that the future of literary journalism is in good shape with practitioners supporting and promoting each others' careers and scholars who study the field hoping to create a new "canon" of non-fictional literary classics. And yet, this development only mirrors the growing emphasis upon specialization in contemporary life and may make it more challenging for writers to succeed across genres and to be recognized and celebrated for that.
18. David Kirby, "Cowboys learn their lit – from the French," *Christian Science Monitor* (Mar. 6, 2003): 16. Also see "Who Were the Most Popular Authors Last Year (2004)," Santa Fe Public Library Home Page. Click on "About Books and Literature."

Index

LaVergne, TN USA
16 March 2010

176096LV00001B/9/P

DATE DUE	RETURNED